WHO WROTE THE DEAD SEA SCROLLS?

The Search for the Secret of Qumran

NORMAN GOLB

SCRIBNER

New York   London   Toronto   Sydney   Tokyo   Singapore

SCRIBNER
1230 Avenue of the Americas
New York, NY 10020

Copyright © 1995 by Norman Golb

Manufactured in the United States of America

DESIGNED BY ERICH HOBBING

1   3   5   7   9   10   8   6   4   2

Library of Congress Cataloging-in-Publication Data

Golb, Norman.
Who wrote the Dead Sea scrolls?: the search for the secret of
Qumran/Norman Golb
p.   cm.
Includes bibliographic references and index.
1. Dead Sea scrolls—Criticism, interpretation, etc. 2. Judaism—History—Postexilic
period, 586 B.C.–210 A.D.—Sources.
I. Title
BM487.G65   1995
296.1'55—dc20   94-23295
CIP

ISBN 0-02-544395-X

FOR MY CHILDREN

Contents

Contents

List of Illustrations

(Maps drawn by Kathryn Thorne, Thorne Data Graphics)

Foreword

The study of old manuscripts is not a popular subject at universities, and until the discovery of the Dead Sea Scrolls it was not one that the public followed closely. Starting in 1947 there has been a notable change in the cultural atmosphere. Reading about the discoveries taking place in the Judaean Wilderness and later perusing some of the texts, a wide audience began to perceive how much of the history of two great religions, and of those times in general, was shrouded in silence. By piecing together fragments of long-lost writings, magnifying bits of words and letters, and slowly building new vocabularies of meaning and connotation, students of ancient languages and civilizations were laying the foundation for a better understanding of the past and casting new light on it. It was apparent that such understanding was the result of a dynamic process, achieved through discovery and the fundamental investigation of ancient sources.

This public awareness of the value of ancient manuscripts probably would not have occurred except for the particular circumstance that those texts were what they were, and were found where they were found. The Greek papyri of Egypt discovered in such relative abundance during the past two centuries, the fifteen hundred Greek and Latin scrolls brought out from under the lava of Herculanaeum, the remarkable Coptic gnostic manuscripts revealed virtually at the same time as the first Qumran scrolls, the multitude of medieval Hebrew treasures extracted from the Cairo Genizah—all these together never moved the Western world as did the treasures from the caves near the Dead Sea. The wisdom of the Greeks and Romans, their literary treasures, formed a cultural monument powerfully shaping European consciousness— and yet in our own century, prevailing at the heart of this consciousness, were the values articulated by writers of the ancient Hebrew books forming the Bible of the Jews. Lying behind the social and intellectual vigor of the Jewish people in antiquity, those books and values had acted as a mesmerizing force upon the Hellenistic world when it conquered Palestine and then in turn was conquered by the faiths of its inhabitants, as first Judaism and then a nascent Christianity placed their indelible stamp on the Roman empire. The West will not tire of seeking to solve what remains the profound puzzle of its own metamorphosis into its Jewish and Christian self, and no other discoveries of modern times have approached the scrolls in their potential for casting light on that remarkable phenomenon.

My preoccupation with this theme and others related to it began well over forty years ago, when I worked on the scrolls as a graduate student. In my own case, these ancient texts, representing several centuries of Jewish history, initially served not as an end in themselves, but as an introduction to the study of Hebrew manuscripts written over a far longer period. While I eventually drew the conclusion that the discipline of scroll studies could not properly be divorced from other Hebrew manuscript investigations, the scrolls still came to form one of my primary fields of teaching and research at the University of Chicago over more than three decades. This book began as an effort, based on that experience, to clarify my views on the question of the scrolls' origin and meaning, always in relation to wider historical themes.

For reasons described in the first several chapters that follow, by the late sixties I had become disenchanted with the traditional belief that the scrolls derived from a small, extremist Jewish sect living in the desert near where they were found. In the specialized studies and more general articles that followed, I explained why the increasing burden of evidence made the traditional theory untenable. While expressing my admiration for the work of pioneers in Qumran studies, I also expressed the hope that my critique, and the new interpretation of Qumran origins that I offered in place of the old, would be useful in the overall elucidation of the remarkable contents of these texts. I increasingly urged free and open debate on that basic question in the course of the 1980s and into the early nineties—and thereby met face-to-face with the reality of Qumran scholarship as it had come to be practiced. It became starkly clear to me that traditional scholarship on the scrolls had become a highly politicized endeavor whose purpose was to protect the old sectarian theory at all costs, rather than a collegial effort welcoming new ideas. What had begun as a scholarly enterprise, in other words, had transformed itself—despite all appeals for open debate—into an ideological agenda. I have found myself obliged to deal with that agenda in the following pages, in the hope of contributing to a greater awareness of what is at stake in the controversy. My criticisms are offered in a spirit of constructive fellowship, and in the hope that it will encourage a higher quality of discourse.

In view of the fact that the scholarship and politics of Qumran studies have become so deeply interwoven, and in view of the way my own scholarly labors were affected by this process, it cannot be said that this was an easy book to write. I was aided, however, by many friends, colleagues, and students, as well as by my immediate family. I primarily owe the idea of developing a critique of Qumranology into book form to my son Joel, an editor and scholar, who took the crucial first steps in encouraging my discussions with the publishers and in helping us reach our mutual decision to publish this work. He thereafter served as the editor of the manuscript, offering a searching critique of all drafts of the work; and his insights and overall sense of logic and balance proved indispensable. Over more than a decade, my son Raphael uncovered precious information with an unerring eye for detail; in addition to his careful editorial reading, he played a vital role in furthering the publication of several of my studies on the scrolls. Elements of these studies appear, usually in changed and developed form, at several junctures in this book.

While not directly engaged in the process of writing this book, my daughter Judy was ever a source of deepest love and inspiration as the project unfolded. And my wife Ruth, through her grace and sense of beauty, turned whatever periods of difficulty might otherwise have accompanied the work into days of warmth and friendship. I am deeply thankful to her for the steadfast encouragement she gave me, particularly in the face of her own work and responsibilities.

During my abundant years at the University of Chicago, I have benefited from association with many versatile and erudite colleagues in the Department of Near Eastern Languages and Civilizations and at the Oriental Institute. I have learned much about the goals and values of scholarship from them, as well as from many outstanding students, both graduate and undergraduate. I am particularly grateful to the director of the Oriental Institute, Prof. William Sumner, for his aid and encouragement. Under his leadership the Institute sponsored, with the New York

Academy of Sciences, the 1992 International Conference on the scrolls—held just one year after the texts were made accessible to the world of scholarship; and he was instrumental in establishing the Institute's Dead Sea Scrolls Research Project.

My colleague and former student Professor Michael Wise offered countless important insights on the scrolls and their cultural and historical background. I am grateful to him for his incisive comments on many passages in this work, which were of much help to me in the course of development of the manuscript. Over a two-year period, our student and research assistant Anthony Tomasino unstintingly offered his time and knowledge; his grasp of ancient Christianity and the intertestamental history of the Jews is reflected in several of the chapters that follow.

My colleague in historical studies, Michael Maas of Rice University, offered many helpful comments on parts of the manuscript, as did Matthias Klinghardt, a friend and New Testament scholar at Augsburg University. I would also like to express a special word of thanks to Katharine Washburn, a superb editor and belletrist in the best sense of that term, for her incisive comments on the manuscript in its last stages.

I am also indebted to Kathryn Cochran, an advanced graduate student in the University's Department of English, for her devoted and unusually careful labors in word processing and proofreading the manuscript.

Over the years, I was greatly aided in my research on the scrolls and other historical topics by two fellowships granted me by the John Simon Guggenheim Memorial Foundation, and by additional research aid from the Lucius Littauer Foundation, the American Philosophical Society, and the National Endowment for the Humanities. My heartfelt thanks also go to the administration of the University of Chicago for granting me an extended research leave during the 1992–93 academic year, which enabled me to bring the manuscript of this work to completion without the interference of other academic responsibilities. Part of my research on the Qumran texts was carried out at Cambridge University, where over many years I have benefited from the collegial hospitality made possible by a life membership in Clare Hall granted to me by its Fellows and President.

I owe a debt of gratitude as well to Mark Chimsky, formerly editor-in-chief of Collier Books and my editor at Macmillan, for his goodwill, unceasing encouragement, and most perceptive advice regarding the style and flow of the following chapters. His assistant, Rob Henderson, was of aid in countless ways during all stages of preparation of the manuscript. I am also grateful to my editor at Scribner, William Goldstein, for his important help in the final stages of the book's preparation.

Yet it would be absurd to think that I could have written this book without constant return to Israel for both shorter and longer periods of study. The many friends and colleagues there who have encouraged my investigations include, first and foremost, Menahem Banitt, Yehoshua Blau, Israel Eph'al, Michael Klein, Joel Kraemer, Shelomo Morag and Ya'acov Shavit. I particularly wish to salute my fellow members of the Society for Judaeo-Arabic Studies—themselves for the most part living and working in Israel—whose incisive scholarship and collegial goodwill continue to be a source of pride and sustenance of spirit.

Intended both as a treatment of the scrolls in their relation to Jewish history and as a chronicle of the rise and fall of a notable idea of modern scholarship, this work differs from studies in literature, languages, and other disciplines in an important respect. While also involving the investigation of texts and sources, the immediate challenge of historical study is not only to decipher, translate, and interpret pertinent records but, beyond this, to construct the narrative necessarily lying behind the words of the texts. The words are not, of course, the history itself, but rather provide the means to write it. Yet once this is accomplished, a fundamental contrary element is brought into play, particularly as one proceeds further and further back through the centuries and discovers the increasing sparseness of historical testimony. Whatever historical witnesses we possess for these older periods, they remain islands in a sea of muteness. Compared to what we might have known had the records of the human past not mostly perished, we can learn little from ten existing documents of one vanished king, from fifty of another, or yet a thousand of another. We do not, in effect, possess the wholeness of history, but only some of its pages—and a historian faces his severest challenges when he attempts to grasp the silences that lie between them. For this goal, philology and analysis of texts are only preliminary tools aiding another process. This consists not in whimsy or fantasy, nor in the imagination of the painter or poet, but rather in the synthesis of new ideas regarding the historical unknown, made from separately experienced elements: the faculty, that is, by

which we attempt to reconstruct what is absent. Except for those
narrow historical works that only recite the barest known facts,
there are none that do not require this mental synthesis—and no
process is more difficult for the historian to master or use judi-
ciously. Aware that this book will inevitably contain shortcomings,
I take comfort in Master Tarphon's observation two millennia ago
that "It is not your duty to complete the work, but neither are you
at liberty to desist from it."

Chicago
Spring 1994

PART I

A NEW THEORY OF SCROLL ORIGINS

CHAPTER 1

The Qumran Plateau

S pread out below the escarpment where the Dead Sea Scrolls
were discovered, Khirbet Qumran dominates the sea's
northwestern shore. Apparently unmentioned in ancient
written sources, it had already drawn the attention of explorers
even in the nineteenth and early twentieth centuries. Gustav
Dalman, one of the most famous of these earlier visitors,
described it aptly in 1914 as a place of mystery, sitting atop a
promontory that jutted out toward the shore from the cliff's face
and seeming "exceptionally well suited for a fortress." In 1940,
the eminent historian and archaeologist Michael Avi-Yonah likewise perceived it as a fortress, situating it among a large number
of known military sites in the Judaean Wilderness whose main
purpose during biblical and intertestamental times was the
defense of Jerusalem against incursions from beyond the Jordan
River and the Dead Sea.[1]

Then, late in 1947, only several years after publication of Avi-
Yonah's map containing this designation, bedouin tribesmen
made their famous discovery of the first seven scrolls on the
escarpment, in a cave situated just over a kilometer north of
Khirbet Qumran. Muffled at first by the outbreak of hostilities
between Jews and Arabs following the partition of mandatory
Palestine, news of their discovery caused great excitement upon
reaching the Jewish side of Jerusalem and the outside world; the
scrolls clearly stemmed from antiquity, had been hidden away as
much as two thousand years ago, and thus appeared to be of great
value for the history of Judaism and early Christianity. One of the
first texts discovered—later named the *Manual of Discipline*—
contained a description of a sectarian group whose beliefs and
practices resembled those of the ancient pacifist sect known as
the Essenes, a fact duly noted in 1948 by Eliezer Sukenik of the
Hebrew University. When in 1949 archaeologists based in East
Jerusalem managed to locate and explore the cave, they found

3

fragments of many more Hebrew scrolls, including what seemed to be an appendage to that same Essene-like work.

Now it was only natural for scholars to recall that, late in the first century A.D., Pliny the Elder in his *Natural History* had actually located a group of Essenes on the western shore of the Dead Sea, somewhere above the town of En Gedi. Might not the *Manual*, and thus, it would seem, all the scrolls found with it, be the lost writings of this group, hidden away in a time of distress? Pliny wrote that these Essenes did not marry and lived in isolation, "with only the palm trees for company." Might not the isolated Khirbet Qumran site, close to where the scrolls were discovered, be the long-lost home of this radically ascetic group?

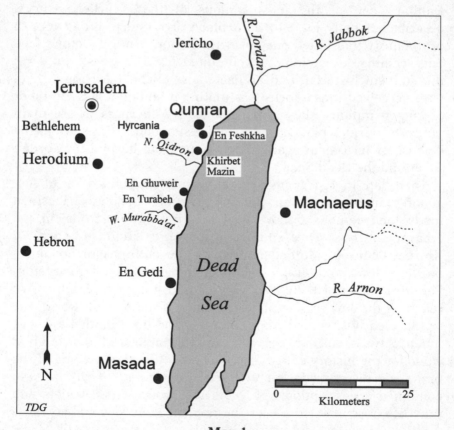

Map 1

Sites of discoveries in the Judaean Wilderness during and after 1947, with related cities, towns, and fortresses.

According to Josephus, the Essenes were one of the three main
sects (or, as he calls them, "philosophies") of the Jews of Second
Temple Palestine, the others being the Pharisees and the Sadducees. They were more ascetic and more esoteric than the
Pharisees or Sadducees, characteristics that made them particularly interesting to the ancient Hellenistic audiences for whom
Josephus and Philo wrote. Thus, even though the group was
smaller than either of the others—about four thousand in number,
according to both writers[2]—they devoted more space to describing them than to either of the other main sects.

One of the most striking characteristics of this group was their communal life.[3] Even though Josephus says that the Essenes were not concentrated in a single settlement, but rather that they were found in
every city of the Jews of Palestine, the settlements within the cities
formed cohesive, closed communities. Those who aspired to join the
group were first put through a probationary membership. After
proving themselves for three years, they were allowed to become full
participants in the group upon taking strict vows of piety and
secrecy. Group members all pooled their money and resources,
and each was given an allowance from the community fund.
Members of the sect would worship and dine together, and place
themselves under the discipline of the democratically elected officers
of the group.

The group's way of life was simple and stern. The principle
occupation of the Essenes, according to both Josephus and Philo,
was agriculture.[4] Philo explicitly states that the Essenes avoided
every form of commerce, particularly commerce in weapons.[5]
Furthermore, Josephus and Philo agree that the Essenes owned
no slaves, believing that the practice of slave ownership was a
great injustice.[6] They were stricter than any other sect in Sabbath
observance, in avoidance of oaths, and in maintenance of ritual
purity.

Josephus describes their religious beliefs in his *Antiquities*.[7]
Unlike the Sadducees, who believed in complete human freedom,
or the Pharisees, who believed that only some things were preordained, the Essenes believed that God was completely in control
of all earthly affairs. Nonetheless, they also believed that the soul
was immortal, and would be either rewarded or punished in the
afterlife for deeds done in this world. Neither Josephus nor Philo
says anything about the Essenes believing in the resurrection of
the dead into new physical bodies. In fact, Josephus claims that

the Essenes believed the body to be a prison house where the soul was temporarily confined until death.[8]

There are several discrepancies between Josephus's account and that of Philo on some of the more unusual practices of the group. Both Josephus and Philo claim that Essenes did not marry, Josephus ascribing their celibacy to their aversion for "the wantonness of women, believing that none of the sex keeps her plighted troth to one man,"[9] while Philo writes that they deem marriage to be incompatible with their communal life, "since wives are naturally selfish creatures."[10] Josephus does allow, however, that one group of Essenes existed who did not shun marriage, but took wives simply to propagate.[11] Another point of disagreement concerned the sacrificial rites of the Essenes. According to Josephus, because they practiced a different form of ritual purification, they could not perform their sacrifices with the other Jews. Rather, they held their own ceremonies, officiated at by their own priests.[12] Philo, on the other hand, claims that the Essenes performed no sacrifices at all, and instead demonstrated their piety by sanctifying their minds.[13] Finally, Josephus seems to imply that the Essenes engaged in some form of sun worship, a practice that Philo apparently knows nothing about.[14] On most matters, however, Josephus and Philo are in agreement about the Essenes—particularly in their unbridled admiration for the group, which they both hold up as a paragon of self-discipline and charity.

Although only Pliny the Elder states that a group of Essenes lived near the Dead Sea, the possibility that they actually occupied Khirbet Qumran and hid manuscripts in nearby caves became more tantalizing to archaeologists as the contents of the first Qumran cave were subjected to study—and as the bedouin began bringing more manuscript finds to Jerusalem from repeated forays in the Judaean Wilderness. A group under the direction of Père (Father) Roland de Vaux of East Jerusalem's famous Ecole Biblique et Archéologique finally made soundings at the site in December of 1951, clearing five rooms within the largest of the buildings that were eventually to be uncovered. The excavators noticed an aqueduct and a system of pools and cisterns. One described a "main outer wall . . . constructed of large, undressed stones" and stated that the "quality of the work is very poor, and in no way resembles that of a Roman fort which we first took it to be."[15] This, of course, contradicted the earlier explorers' impression of a fortress; the further assertion—later dropped—that the "inner walls are of equally poor workmanship, being mostly of rubble and mud" added to a growing intimation that the site could, in fact, have been the home of the Essenes. The discovery of a jar and some cooking pots and lamps identical in shape to similar objects discovered in the first manuscript cave led to the seemingly appropriate assertion that "it would appear . . . that the people who lived at Khirbet Qumran deposited the scrolls in the cave" and that the situation fit in well "with Pliny the Elder's account of the Essenes."[16]

A wave of enthusiasm for this idea thereafter engulfed scholars and the lay public alike, especially as new manuscript-filled caves near Khirbet Qumran came to light. These included a total of five caves in 1952, among them the famous Cave 4, holding thousands of fragments from at least five hundred different scrolls, the larger part of which were previously unknown nonbiblical writings. The new manuscript discoveries made in the additional caves were quickly absorbed into the increasingly popular hypothesis: The Essenes had had a large library at Khirbet Qumran, they had written and copied many works there—and it was they who had hidden them away in time of danger.

Exploring the Khirbet Qumran site in greater detail thus became a necessity, and the archaeological team working in the Judaean Wilderness proceeded to do so in 1953 and the following three years. These were periods of far more intensive investigation than the first soundings, and the results, as described by the chief investigator, Père de Vaux, were quite startling.

In his report, published subsequently, De Vaux stated that "the buildings were reduced to ruins by a military action," signs of which included "collapsed walls, traces of a fire (and) iron arrows."[17] Relying on archaeological indications of the battle, he stated that it was characterized "by a violent destruction. . . . The tower, fortified by its ramp of stone, offered the greatest resistance. . . ."[18] Evidence was found of the burning of roofs and the collapse of ceilings and superstructures, and the presence of iron arrowheads of Roman type showed that it was a troop of Roman soldiers who attacked and eventually took the settlement. For reasons not understood today, de Vaux failed to add a crucial point later furnished by Frank M. Cross, who participated in the excavations and later published a book on the site and on the

Figure 1
Aerial view of Khirbet Qumran after the excavations.

manuscripts found in the caves: The walls, he stated, were "mined through [and] the building ruins . . . sealed in layers of ash from a great conflagration."[19] The undermining of walls by tunneling beneath them was, of course, a classic technique of ancient military strategists in besieging enemy fortifications that could otherwise not be breached. Such tunnels were supported by wooden beams that, after the work of the burrowing troops was completed, would be set on fire, resulting in the collapse of the walls protecting the besieged troops.

The team uncovered a highly developed system for channeling and storing a large supply of water. From Wadi Qumran, an aqueduct had carried the winter rainwaters into the settlement, where they fed into six huge reservoirs, as well as a deep cistern of a much earlier date than the reservoirs. In the northwestern portion of the settlement was another cistern, square-shaped, that had been used for bathing or for collecting still more water. So impressed were the excavators by this water system that Père de Vaux was moved to say that the "number and importance of the cisterns" constituted the settlement's "most striking feature."[20]

Later measurements of these cisterns showed that they could hold as much as 1,127 cubic meters,[21] enough to serve the basic needs of over seven hundred and fifty people during eight months—that is, throughout the dry season following the winter and spring rains, and until the first rains of the following season had begun to replenish the reservoirs.*

Although de Vaux made no inferences of his own about the matter, this finding fit in well with the indications of a battle fought at the site (which de Vaux inferred had taken place in A.D. 68). Any of its defenders would have needed just such a supply of water, for Qumran was isolated from other sources: The closest spring was a few kilometers to the south, at a site on the shore of the Dead Sea known as En Feshkha—"the Feshkha Spring"—inaccessible to Qumran's inhabitants during a siege.

The excavators unearthed other ruins as well: among them, remnants of surrounding walls and, most notably, substantial remains of a heavily fortified tower that had once dominated the site. The "massive tower" (in the words of de Vaux) had walls that were between 1.2 and 1.5 meters thick, and included three interior rooms on two levels that originally could be reached by a circular staircase. A second-story portal had once opened onto a gallery facing southwest into the settlement's interior. The outside of the tower formed the northeastern perimeter of the building complex, with the main gate of the settlement lying at its base. Père de Vaux stated that the "defensive concern was further emphasized by the isolation of this tower, which was separated from the other buildings by two open spaces." A road had led from the north to this tower, along the plain bordering the Dead Sea.[22]

Qumran itself, according to de Vaux and his colleagues, had originally been built as an Israelite fortress in the seventh or eighth century B.C. Apparently, the site had afterward been abandoned until around the start of the second century B.C., when the ancient Israelite foundations were used to construct a relatively

---

*This calculation is based on the need by an individual adult male of no more than six litres of water per day under desert conditions. 1,127 cubic meters = 1,127,000 liters. This divided by 6 (i.e., liters per person per day) = 187,666 liters. This divided by 240 (i.e., 8 [months] x 30 [days]) = 782—the number of individuals who can be sustained by 1,127 cubic meters of water over an eight-month period. (I wish to thank Professor Israel Eph'al of the Hebrew University for the basic elements of this calculation.)

modest group of buildings. This group, however, was soon replaced by a more elaborate complex erected toward the middle of the second century B.C., and it was then that the tower was first installed. Two of the tower's stories, made of stone, were still intact when it was uncovered in 1951; brick remnants of a third story were found in the rubble.[23] In any case, Père de Vaux, like Dalman and Avi-Yonah before him, perceived the strategic nature of the site even without reference to the tower, observing later that "from the plateau of Qumran the view extends over the whole of the western shore from the mouth of the Jordan to Ras Feshkha and over the entire northern half of the [Dead] Sea."[24]

In the course of their investigations, the archaeologists discovered that the Qumran buildings had been damaged, perhaps by an earthquake and fire. There has always been some debate about the precise time of this event, but de Vaux may be justified in suggesting that it took place in 31 B.C., the time of an earthquake in Palestine we know of through Josephus. On the other hand, some or all of the damage could have been caused by an undocumented military attack on the site, possibly during the Parthian invasion of Palestine (40 B.C.).[25]

Whatever the precise date of the damage to Qumran, archaeological evidence described by de Vaux makes clear that the destruction was followed by abandonment of the site and its eventual repair and reoccupation. Most of the rooms were cleaned of debris, secondary structures were added, and buildings weakened by the earthquake or another cause were reinforced, some walls being doubled in thickness and others strengthened by buttresses.[26] The greatest attention, however, was paid to the tower: Various measures were introduced to protect it, the most significant being the construction of a solid ramp of unfinished stone on all four sides, proceeding from its base upward at a 45° angle to the second story of the building (see Fig. 2). This ramp, de Vaux pointed out, was highest on the northern and eastern sides—those sides, that is, which faced outward and formed the salient defensive point of the settlement.[27] Standing at the top of the tower, one would have had a still clearer view of the plain to the north and south, and over the sea. The buttressing of the tower showed that it was important to the group of Jews who rebuilt the settlement and inhabited it until the battle that took place close to A.D. 70. Since no coins of the reign of Herod the Great (40–4 B.C.) were found in the excavation, it is possible that the site was abandoned entirely

a

b

Figure 2
The Khirbet Qumran tower:
(a) the tower as it appears
today; (b) the stone ramp
as it abuts the original
vertical wall.

during that period and not repaired or reinhabited until even as late as the sixties of the first century A.D., with the outbreak of the First Revolt of the Palestinian Jews against Rome (A.D. 66).

From coins found in the ruins and a statement made by Josephus, de Vaux inferred that the Roman siege and capture of the site had taken place in the summer of A.D. 68—that is, during the First Revolt, approximately twenty months before the siege of Jerusalem tightened early in the spring of A.D. 70.[28] The attack's actual dating is obviously important, but was by no means satisfactorily solved by de Vaux. The latest Jewish coins found at the site were from Year III of the revolt (A.D. spring 68/spring 69). The earliest Roman coins, on the other hand, were minted in and near Caesaria in A.D. 67–68. The Tenth Roman Legion, Josephus writes, captured Jericho in the summer of 68, after which Vespasian had some men thrown into the Dead Sea with their hands tied to see if they could stay afloat.[29] De Vaux expressed the belief that, as the last Jewish coins could have been minted as early as spring of 68, and the earliest Roman ones at virtually the same time, the summer of 68 provided an optimal time for the taking of Khirbet Qumran, particularly in view of the fact that Vespasian's troops had by then approached a point not many miles away to the north.[30]

This scheme breaks down, however, once it is recognized that, during a revolt of such serious proportions, it would be rather unlikely that fresh Jewish coins would turn up so quickly in a wilderness settlement at considerable distance from the revolt's centers; the Roman coins simply indicate that the legionnaires had some dated to A.D. 67–68 in their possession. The hidden premise in de Vaux's argument is that both the Jews and the Romans possessed newly minted coins when they fought each other at Qumran, but one need only examine the coins in one's own pockets to see how unlikely this interpretation is. In fact, de Vaux himself elsewhere in his work on Khirbet Qumran emphasized that "silver coins remained in circulation for a long time and are of little use in dating an archaeological level except as a vague *terminus post quem*."[31]

The coins only show that the attack on Qumran could not have taken place *before* A.D. 68. As there is no evidence whatever suggesting that Roman legionnaires penetrated into any part of the Judaean Wilderness until A.D. 70, it is somewhat more likely that the attack on Qumran took place as a part of the general offensive against the Judaean Jews following the capture of Jerusalem in A.D. 70. It was only after the fall of the capital that the Romans captured several known fortresses of the region, i.e., Herodium, Machaerus, and Masada. Had they stormed the Qumran site two years earlier, they would have more likely moved promptly southwest and taken the Herodium fortress soon thereafter—not after the fall of Jerusalem as actually happened. Such a move would have allowed them to surround Jerusalem entirely, rather than from three sides only as they actually did.[32] In fact, Josephus explains that at the beginning of the siege of the capital, the Roman Tenth Legion arrived at the Mount of Olives "having come *by way of Jericho* where a party of soldiers had been posted to guard the pass formerly taken by Vespasian."[33] This strongly implies that there were no Roman troops stationed farther to the south. It would thus have been preferable on both numismatic and historical grounds to place the capture of Qumran in the period after the fall of Jerusalem, when the Roman troops under Lucilius Bassus began their entrance into the Judaean Wilderness, the last remaining area of Jewish resistance.

Accompanying de Vaux's faulty reasoning on the date of the attack on Qumran was an apparent reluctance, on both his part and that of his colleagues, to draw certain compelling inferences about the nature of Khirbet Qumran—for example, that Jerusalem and the events transpiring there might have had something to do with the site. This reticence heavily affected their treatment of the site's nature, as is clear in their discussion of other findings made during the excavations. De Vaux uncovered evidence that the site was not simply abandoned when the Roman force overcame the defenders. Rather, a new period in its history began, one which he designated Period III, extending to at least A.D. 73. Roman soldiers, quite likely the same ones who had conquered Qumran, now used the tower and part of the ruins for military purposes, since the site offered a superior view and was excellently situated. Until at least the end of the war with Rome in A.D. 73, explained de Vaux, the Romans had to police the sea and adjacent shore.[34]

From such archaeological evidence, it in fact becomes clear that the site's military function extended over a very long range of time. Qumran had been a fortress in Israelite times. Then, when it was rebuilt centuries later, and while it continued to maintain its dominant geographic position, the rebuilders gave most careful attention to features of a military nature. Thereafter, in approximately A.D. 70, Roman forces fought a pitched battle there, clearly against an armed force inhabiting the site. Finally, after taking it from them, the Romans used it as a fort of their own, albeit on a smaller scale than earlier.

Nevertheless, those associated with the dig at Khirbet Qumran in the 1950s were unwilling to state that the site had been a fortress during the crucial period when Essene sectarians were supposed to be inhabiting it—i.e., in the first century B.C. and the first century A.D., until its capture by the Romans circa A.D. 70. This reluctance was noticeable throughout de Vaux's writings on Khirbet Qumran and is also manifest in the work of his colleagues. The most telling statement was that of F. M. Cross, who wrote that it was impossible to determine whether "the Essenes in whole or in part fled their settlement with the approach of the Romans, or were trapped in Qumran and slaughtered"—and then added that "there is some likelihood that the Essenes, at least in part, put up resistance. Certainly someone resisted the Romans, using Qumran as a bastion."[35]

While admitting that Qumran served as a bastion, Cross as well as de Vaux and all other writers subscribing early on to the Essenic hypothesis were thus unwilling to state candidly that the site was in fact a fortress at the time of the Roman attack. De Vaux came close to admitting as much in 1954. Stating that "the building was destroyed by a war," he raised the remarkable possibility that "the entire community departed [before the battle] and that other people retrenched at Khirbet Qumran: in the same year of [A.D.] 68, the *sicarii* were active at Masada and En-Gedi."[36] In suggesting that these zealous Jewish warriors, who played such an important role in the revolt against the Romans, had *taken the place* of the Essenes at the time of the battle—an explanation for which there is no archaeological evidence whatsoever—de Vaux betrayed a grave concern about his findings. For how indeed could the Essene sect have occupied what the excavations proved was a military site? Ancient writers on the Essenes agree that they were the most peaceful of men, not at all given to waging war. Philo Judaeus was the earliest of these writers (ca. A.D. 20) and a contemporary witness. He resolutely states that: "You cannot find among them any maker of arrows, spears, swords, helmets, corselets, or shields, any maker of arms or war-machines, any one busied in the slightest with military avocations or even with those which, during peace, slip easily into mischief."[37] Josephus, who wrote his *Jewish War* over a half century later (that is, after the revolt had ended in defeat for the Jews), does mention a certain John the Essene—clearly a singular exception—who had served as a general of the rebel force in Timna (some twenty miles due west of Jerusalem and far from the Judaean Wilderness). But he nowhere suggests that actual Essene groups defended strongholds or fought in battles. What he does say about them is that while traveling they bore only defensive weapons.[38] Pliny the Elder, writing about the same time as Josephus (the date of the preface to his *Natural History* is A.D. 74), reinforces this impression of the peaceful ways of the Essenes living above En Gedi:

> On the west side of the Dead Sea, but out of range of the noxious exhalations of the coast, is the solitary tribe of the Essenes, which is remarkable beyond all other tribes in the whole world, as it has no women and has renounced all sexual desire, has no money, and has only palm-trees for company. Day by day the throng of refugees is recruited to an equal number by numerous accessions of persons tired of life and driven thither by the wave of fortune to adopt their manners. Thus through thousands of ages . . . a race in which no one is born lives on forever: so prolific for their advantage is other men's weariness of life.[39]

Nothing in Pliny's account either would lead one to believe that the Essenes included a warrior group inhabiting a fortress.

In some way, the archaeological team had to resolve this troubling contradiction, and it was quite clearly for this reason that de Vaux first suggested that another group, perhaps the militant *sicarii*, had somehow taken over the site from the Essenes before the battle began. The same contradiction evidently led Cross to suggest that some Essenes had defended the site while simultaneously implying that another group may have actually done the fighting. But when in 1958 other writers began raising the possibility that yet another ancient militant group, the so-called Zealots of Josephus's history, had occupied the site from well before—and up through the time of—the battle, de Vaux rejected this interpretation out of hand, without referring to his own earlier view of possible occupation of the site by the extremist *sicarii*. Defending the integrity of Khirbet Qumran's original identification as the home of Pliny's Essenes of the Dead Sea shore was clearly important to the archaeological team.

In any event, other disturbing evidence was being unearthed by the archaeologists, calling their identification of the Qumran site into still further question. On the same plateau occupied by Khirbet Qumran, less than fifty meters east of the buildings, was a large cemetery first explored in the 1870s.[40] At that time only a few of the twelve-hundred-odd tombs had been opened, and de Vaux and his colleagues now applied themselves to exploring others. They opened a total of forty-three, finding the bodies of thirty men, seven women, and four children,* yielding a ratio for the excavated graves of approximately one woman to four men (it may be that there were no skeletons, or else only unidentifiable remains, in two of the graves).[41] Pliny states, however, that the Essenes of the Dead Sea shore "had no women, had renounced all sexual desire," and that "no one is born" into their "race."

Declaring that the cemetery was divided into a main section, with graves oriented in a north–south direction, and other sections—an extension of the main section as well as two "secondary" ones, where the skeletons of the women and children were discovered—de Vaux confronted the awkward conflict as best he could, building on the by then cherished hypothesis of Essenic origins: The cemetery's layout might "indicate that the women were not members of the community, or at any rate not in the same sense as the men buried in the main cemetery. It may also signify that a development had taken place in the discipline of the community. The rule of celibacy may have been relaxed, and marriage may have become lawful. This would explain why the tombs of women are located in what seem to be extensions of the main cemetery."

Now the heavily conditional nature of this passage reflects,

---

*This is the figure given by de Vaux, but he does not state precisely how the identifications were made. Until today, anthropologists and others differ as to how the sexual identification of ancient skeletons can best be achieved. It remains an obvious desideratum to examine all of the skeletons in the Qumran graves under rigorous scientific circumstances. Dr. Nicu Haas, together with other researchers, in 1968 engaged in an anthropological study of eleven skeletons that had been excavated by S. H. Steckoll at the Qumran cemetery. The findings showed that these were the remains of six men, four women, and a child of two, tending to confirm de Vaux's earlier report on the ratio of male to female skeletons. (De Vaux himself does not state who performed the study of the skeletons excavated by his own team.) See further N. Haas and H. Nathan, *Revue de Qumran* 6 (1968), pp. 323–344.

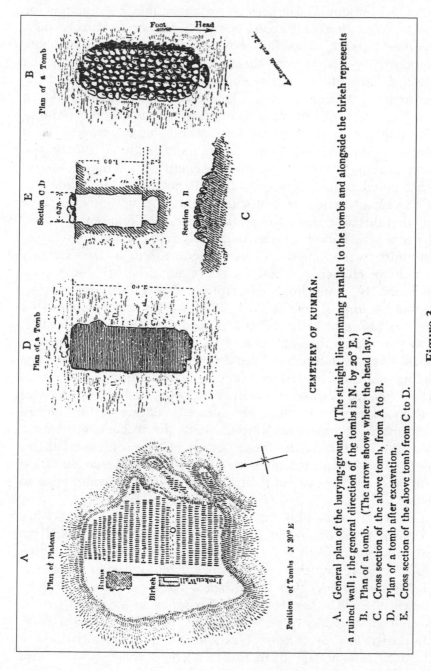

Figure 3

The Khirbet Qumran cemetery, as depicted in the 1870s.

among other things, distinct uncertainty as to whether the cemetery area containing women's skeletons might legitimately be
called an "extension" of the main cemetery. In fact, de Vaux found it
altogether difficult to explain how Pliny's report of a celibate
Essenic order—recorded by that author circa A.D. 75—could be
made to fit in with the archaeological findings. He hazarded the
suggestion, in the end, that the skeletons of women and children
might "signify that there were different groups within the community, a main group which would have renounced marriage . . . and
one or several groups which would have allowed it. . . . Clearly, the
women's tombs do not strengthen the argument that the community was related to the Essenes, but they do not rule it out either."[42]

With the advantage of historical hindsight, we may perceive
today that this assertion appears rather strained and even evasive.
To be sure, the finding did not completely rule out a claim that the
community was related to the Essenes; but it considerably
reduced the chances, insofar as the claim had originally been
built precisely upon Pliny's description of a celibate community.
Josephus, writing about the same time as Pliny, indeed states that
there was also a noncelibate Essenic order, but does not locate it
in any specific or singular area of Palestine.[43] Pliny alone placed
celibate Essenes in a defined region of Judaea, the archaeologists
insisting that Qumran was the place he was alluding to.

The evidence both of the women's graves and the battle with
the Romans, along with the highly strategic nature of the Qumran
site, should have been enough to dissuade the archaeologists from
continuing to espouse the theory of an Essene settlement there.
But they had committed themselves deeply to this interpretation
almost at the very outset of their investigation, and would cling to
it tenaciously.

And then at some time during the process of discovery, either
de Vaux himself or one of his associates must have raised yet
another question about Pliny's description: the date of its writing.
Following his reference to the Essenes dwelling by the Dead Sea
shore, Pliny remarks that *"lying below the Essenes was formerly
the town of Engedi, second only to Jerusalem in the fertility of its
land and in its groves of palm trees, but now like the other place
[= Jerusalem] a heap of ashes.* Next comes Masada, a fortress on a
rock, itself also not far from the Dead Sea. This is the limit of
Judaea."[44]

This statement could only have been written *after* Jerusalem had been destroyed by the Romans in the wake of its capture in the summer of A.D. 70. By this token the Essenes living above En Gedi could not have been identical with the group of people then living at Qumran, who in and after A.D. 70, according to the archaeological team's own findings, were Roman soldiers, not Jewish sectarians. Pliny's Essenes would have had to be another group, living elsewhere—and apparently closer to En Gedi. In addition, what pertinence could Pliny's statement possibly have had for the problem of identifying those living at Khirbet Qumran *before* A.D. 70, when conditions in Judaea were strikingly different? The Essenes living above En Gedi when Jerusalem lay in ruins could have arrived as refugees fleeing the war with Rome from virtually any area of Palestine. Jerusalem itself was known to have had a "gate of the Essenes,"[45] implying a relatively large number of these sectarians within the city before the revolt, and it may well be that they themselves fled to Pliny's location above En Gedi during or after the siege. But how could this "throng of refugees," as Pliny describes them, have ended up at *Qumran* if, as the excavation proved, Roman troops occupied this very site by approximately A.D. 70?

The question may not have been formulated quite this way but, however put, it was obviously posed and had to be answered. The response de Vaux offered was that Pliny's text was not the original one, but rather had been *altered*. The thirty-seven books of Pliny's *Natural History* had been written over many years; according to de Vaux, Pliny himself may never have visited the Essenes' home but only heard of it from an eyewitness; the words referring to En Gedi, "now like . . . [Jerusalem] an ash-heap," were only a remark inserted when the text was being edited in approximately A.D. 75. Thus, de Vaux explained, the original words on which Pliny later built could have been written or otherwise conveyed to him *before* the Khirbet Qumran site was captured by the Romans.[46]

All this, of course, is pure speculation, reminding us of the occasional tendency of scholars to emend texts so as to make them more consonant with their own interpretations. The likelihood that the crucial statement was a mere editorial addition is reduced virtually to zero by the fact that numerous passages in Pliny's description of Palestine reflect post–A.D. 70 conditions. Only a few paragraphs earlier, for example, he indicates that Machaerus—the great fortress of the Jews east of the Dead Sea— was also reduced by the Romans, and that Vespasian, who was emperor from A.D. 70 to 79, founded the colony Prima Flavia at Caesarea.[47] Thus Pliny clearly wrote his description from a post–70 A.D. perspective.

The only way to harmonize de Vaux's various hypotheses (e.g., that Pliny's text was altered; that the Qumranites "relaxed" their rule of celibacy; that celibate and noncelibate groups inhabited the site simultaneously)—hypotheses adopted with enthusiasm by many writers while being not at all reflected in Pliny's description—is to assume that the rudiments of the description were somehow recorded *many* years before the attack on the site. At that time, according to one of de Vaux's hypotheses, Khirbet Qumran might still have been inhabited only by celibate Essenes. But this was obviously a yet more remote likelihood. There was no archaeological evidence whatever indicating that Khirbet Qumran was at any time inhabited by Pliny's Essenes or indeed any other celibate community; moreover, by the 1960s still no indications had emerged of an endorsement of celibacy in any of the scrolls discovered in the caves near the site.

As the excavations continued, quite a few scholars began backing away from the hard-and-fast Qumran-Essene equation. But while perceiving that, minus tortuous exegesis, Pliny's statement could not literally refer to the Khirbet Qumran site, many writers nevertheless remained intent on espousing the idea that the site had been inhabited by a sect. For they reasoned that Qumran was located near caves where manuscripts were found and that many of these texts contained ideas and expressions that seemed notably sectarian as compared with those appearing in earlier known texts of intertestamental and rabbinic Judaism, so that the concept of a sect living at Qumran had a certain inherent verisimilitude. The main focus of attention continued to be the *Manual of Discipline*, whose columns revealed a mode of heterodox thinking sharing much with Essenism as both Philo and Josephus describe it.

Seeking further evidence of sectarians, some researchers pointed to the water reservoirs, most of which had steps leading down them, and asked whether at least a few of them could not in reality have been ritual baths rather than simply reservoirs. In doing so, they emphasized that ancient writers were struck by the Essenes' practice of frequent ritual bathing, neglecting to note that as far as we know *all* practicing Jews of the Roman period bathed ritually in consonance with biblical laws. In any case, de Vaux and his team rejected the possibility of the reservoirs serving as baths, since the steps were a characteristic feature of reservoirs of the period located elsewhere in Judaea. The steps were designed simply to facilitate the collection of water as the level decreased during the dry months. Two water basins were also discovered at the site; de Vaux agreed they were used for baths, while explaining that "archaeology was powerless to say whether those baths . . . had a ritual character."[48] When in use, the reservoirs would of course have been covered over during the dry season to prevent evaporation. The figure of approximately seven hundred and fifty men whose water needs could be provided by the reservoir system of Qumran was reminiscent of the number of troops—eight hundred men—deployed by Herod at Masada on his march to Arabia.[49] At Herodium, a yet more imposing bastion than Qumran, the two largest water cisterns had a capacity of 2,725 cubic meters, theoretically allowing for the supply of a stationary force of approximately 1,800 men over a period of eight dry months.[50] As Ehud Netzer, the excavator of Herodium, has indicated, however, these large cisterns, unlike those at Qumran, were not easily accessible to the defenders of this site.[51] Practically speaking, it does not appear likely that during a state of siege many more than a thousand troops could have been adequately provisioned at Herodium by these supplies of water. It would seem that for the defense of the Judaean Wilderness fortresses the rebels of the First Revolt could count on approximately nine hundred or a thousand troops at each site, but not more. The twelve hundred graves of the Qumran cemetery fit quite well into that round figure. During the siege of Qumran leading up to its seizure by the Roman force, considerably more of the rebels and their families were probably within its walls than could have been adequately provided for by the cisterns over a full eight-month period.

As indicated above, however, during the Khirbet Qumran dig pottery was found—some in a potter's workshop, some elsewhere. The styles of the jars matched those of pottery discovered in Cave 1 and in other manuscript-bearing caves nearby (see below, Chapter 2), providing what was thought to be an organic, physical bond between the caves and the site.[52] Even if no statement espousing the idea of celibacy could be found in the *Manual* or the other scrolls, even if there were other differences between the doctrines of the *Manual* and of the classical Essenes—so the reasoning went—there was surely an intrinsic bond between Khirbet Qumran and the cave manuscripts, the texts obviously having been written by people who inhabited the site, and who thus

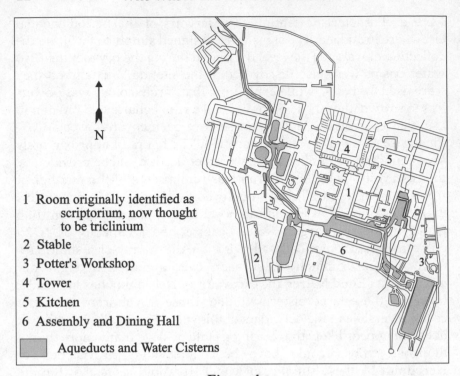

Figure 4
Plan of the Khirbet Qumran site, showing principal structures and
the water storage system.

might legitimately be considered to form an Essenic type of order,
or at all events a sect of some kind. And proof for this view, it was
believed, might even be extracted from evidence at the site.

That evidence has since been much debated, but remains a cor-
nerstone of all variants of the Qumran-sectarian hypothesis. It
concerns the shape and appearance of certain rooms and other
constructions on the site. Including the reservoirs but not the
cemetery, the archaeologists counted over one hundred and forty
locations—rooms, vestibules, chambers, courtyards, and so
forth—spread over an area of approximately 4,800 square
meters.* The function of many of the locations was unclear;
among those the archaeologists claimed to be able to identify

*See the detailed plan of the site in R. de Vaux, *Archaeology and the Dead
Sea Scrolls* (Oxford, 1972), plate 39.

Figure 5
Aerial view of Khirbet Qumran water cisterns and walls.

were rooms they designated, respectively, as a stable, a kitchen, a mill, an oven, a pottery workshop, and a forge, as well as food storage areas. Clearly, a significant group or community was living here in the first century B.C. and first century A.D., but was it in fact an Essenic or other Jewish sect—or rather a military force? For at a desert outpost, the latter would actually have needed all the services suggested by such rooms, doubtless at least as much as any communal group of Jewish sectarians.

De Vaux and his archaeological team nevertheless believed that other locations within the site indeed offered evidence of sectarian use. One hall he described as a "refectory," a term usually reserved for dining rooms of monasteries or convents; another as a "council hall," in allusion to the requirement laid down in the *Manual of Discipline* for regular meetings of the "Council of the Unity" (a kind of governing body of the sectarian group described in that text). Nevertheless, the entirely arbitrary nature of these identifications becomes clear with any careful examination of the two halls. While one of them may well have been used for dining purposes, the circular paved area at its western end that de Vaux claimed "apparently marks the place where the president of the assembly held forth"⁵³ may equally well have been the place where the commandant of a military camp or his officers sat during meals. Based on the actual evidence, the only compelling designation of this room is that of a dining hall, not a refectory.

The other site, the so-called council hall, was given that designation because of a low, built-in bench running along the walls of this relatively small chamber. De Vaux observed that on one wall there were indentations indicating cupboards, while on another a basin had been hollowed out that could be filled with water from the outside. These hints, together with the encircling bench, stimulated de Vaux to state that the room "appears to have been destined for restrained sessions, at which the members did not wish to be disturbed—[i.e., it was] a sort of council hall."⁵⁴

A viewer not committed, however, to the vision of Khirbet Qumran as the home of Essenes or another sect could say nothing about the function of this room other than that it was a place where people met for one reason or another. It could just as well have been a room for prayer and the recitation of the Pentateuch—that is, a rudimentary synagogue, similar in character to the chamber with built-in benches clearly used for that purpose at Masada, albeit somewhat simpler in character (see Fig. 6). There is no archaeological evidence that those occupying the site were anything other than God-fearing Jews, and all such believers, sectarian or not, would have needed precisely a communal room of this kind.⁵⁵

It is thus apparent that neither the one room nor the other offered compelling evidence of sectarian use. In any case, de Vaux suggested that a considerably larger adjacent hall with an imposing entrance bay "could have served for larger assemblies of people."⁵⁶ The bay of which de Vaux spoke, we may observe in passing, is but one of many carefully constructed elements in elegant Herodian architectural style adorning this and other areas of Khirbet Qumran, vitiating entirely the early impression of the archaeologists that it was of poor construction (see Fig. 7). Khirbet Qumran was designed as an important site. The room in question may well have served as a gathering place for larger assemblies of people, but these people may as easily have been Jewish military troops as sectarians.

a

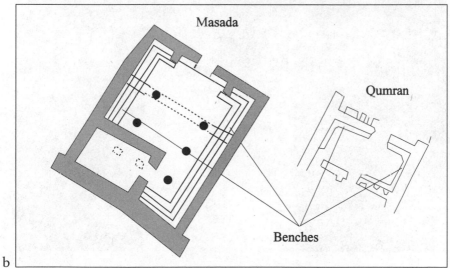

b

Figure 6
Khirbet Qumran rooms: (a) dining hall; (b) room with built-in
benches, as compared with similar one at Masada.

Figure 7
Aspects of architecture of Khirbet Qumran: (a) remnants of columns
(arrow); (b) entranceway to hall south of tower.

What de Vaux appeared to consider more compelling evidence of sectarian activity at Qumran were the interesting elements left in the pile of debris that the excavators encountered near this hall. The debris was the result of the collapse of the building's second story, including the floor and whatever furnishings were there, at the time the Romans breached the walls and took the site. It included portions of what were taken to be three plaster tables and two inkwells (a third inkwell was also found elsewhere in Qumran), from which de Vaux inferred that the second story contained a kind of *"scriptorium"*—a term used beforehand only for writing rooms of medieval monasteries. According to de Vaux, the Essenic monks of Qumran undoubtedly engaged there in making copies of the works they composed.[57] (See Fig. 4, locus 1.)

This news of a scriptorium at Qumran was eagerly welcomed in many parts of the world[58] where the discoveries had garnered the rapt attention of scholars. The most free-flowing expression of assent came from André Dupont-Sommer, who wrote that

> The remains of a *scriptorium* have been discovered, and of a very long narrow table . . . and pieces of one or two shorter tables. These were doubtless writing tables, since two inkpots were found in the same place. . . . It seems therefore that this was the place in which the scrolls from the caves were copied. The copyists who bent over these tables and dipped their pens in these inkpots were not . . . just ordinary secular scribes. . . . No, the copying of Essene books, which were holy and secret, required scribes recruited from among the members of the sect themselves.[59]

Such conclusions, based upon the finding of three "tables" and a few inkwells, today seem astounding in their lack of caution. Already by the late fifties, a fundamental question had been raised regarding the use of such tables for the purpose of copying scrolls. Not only did ancient depictions of scribes not show them copying by sitting at tables, but the very height and pitch of the tables seemed unsuitable for the purpose of copying scrolls.[60] The most obvious objection, unfortunately not discussed until long after the dust of the earlier debate had settled, was that the hall's rubble contained not the slightest hint of most of the materials that bona fide scribes used constantly in their work, such as parchment and the tools for smoothing it, needles and thread with which to bind the parchment together, line markers to indent into the parchment for straight rows of script, and pens and styluses.

So shaky was the evidence for the room in question being a scriptorium that one scholar would later write that:

> The arguments against this being a writing table were ably marshalled by . . . Metzger and have been found convincing by many better qualified to judge than this reviewer. An examination of the supposed table in the Palestine Archaeological Museum strengthens this negative attitude; yet de Vaux refused to give an inch on his previous theory. . . . The whole question of a *scriptorium* is far from decided. . . . If there is no *scriptorium*, there is no copying, or better, the wholesale copying that some writers envision does not exist. . . .[61]

The idea of a scriptorium at Qumran, based upon drastically insufficient evidence, had only resulted from a need that the dig's archaeologists felt to find a substantive connection between the manuscripts lying in the caves and the Khirbet Qumran site. From the evidence of a few slabs that then appeared to be tables, and of the inkwells, the most that could really be inferred about the room was that it served as an office or headquarters, and the straightforward evidence of military activity at the site ought to have suggested its use by whatever commanders were charged with directing such activity. To be sure (as we shall see in Chapter 11), it has since been determined that the slabs are not from tables but from *benches*, lined along the walls of the so-called scriptorium as in a Roman-style *triclinium* or parlor (Hebrew *traqlin*), with obvious consequences for the room's identification. On the other hand, given the evidence that shows Khirbet Qumran to have been occupied by a military force, it is clear that those of the troops who could write—as in the case of Roman soldiers who occupied Vindolanda in Britain,[62] and members of the Bar Kokhba forces during the Second Revolt in Palestine—would have had need for basic writing materials to compose letters. The inkwells indicate only that some writing was done by inhabitants of the site, not that a contingent of pious scribes lived there.

What is more, no manuscript fragments written on parchment or papyrus were found at Khirbet Qumran, not even in the supposed scriptorium—an obvious embarrassment for those who theorized that scribes copied manuscripts there and then hid them later in nearby caves. Showing some sensitivity to this problem, de Vaux dismissed it with the following formula: "The conclusion cannot be resisted that the source of these manuscripts was the community installed in the Qumran area. It is natural that in the ruins of Khirbet Qumran, exposed as they were to the weather, texts written on skin or papyrus should have failed to survive."

De Vaux issued this statement in the French version of his book (1961), several years before the results of the discoveries at Masada—the great fortress lying near the southern end of the Dead Sea—were known. Possessing ruins similar to those at Qumran, Masada shared virtually the same climate—and yet archaeologists did find parchments and papyri in the ruins in the expeditions of 1963–65. This discovery made it all the more remarkable that no parchments or scribal tools were found beneath the rubble of a Qumran room claimed to have been the very one where the scrolls were copied. Nonetheless, just as remarkably, de Vaux's statement remained unrevised, unlike so much else, in the English translation of his book (1972), which appeared long after reports of the Masada discoveries had been widely published.[63]

De Vaux furnished two additional arguments for an organic connection between Khirbet Qumran and the caves, the first being that "in the ruins of Qumran themselves inscriptions have been found written on ostraca or pots" whose *writing is the same as that of the documents.*"[64] This remains perhaps the most enigmatic of the claims offered throughout the years by Qumranologists opting for such a connection. These ostraca,* or potsherds bearing names, are indeed inscribed in Hebrew, but no more can be inferred from their appearance than that the handwritings are characteristic of those used in Judaea between the first century B.C. and the first century A.D. A large number of scroll handwritings had become known by 1960, showing very many styles of writing—none of which was ever shown to be specifically comparable with the handwritings of the ostraca. As we shall see in Chapter 5, the Qumran scroll handwritings share the basic characteristics of scripts in the scroll fragments found in the ruins of Masada, but the Qumran ostraca resemble neither the former nor the latter so much as they resemble those ostraca found at Masada. What the ostraca of Qumran and Masada have in common are documentary characteristics, as opposed to the nondocumentary, scribal characteristics of the parchment and papyrus texts of those two sites.[65] The ostraca of Qumran prove nothing except that those inhabiting

*For this and other technical terms, see Glossary.

the site when they were inscribed circa 50 B.C. to A.D. 70 were Palestinian Jews rather than Romans.

At the same time—in an argument since supported by virtually all traditional Qumranologists—de Vaux pointed to an affinity between the type of pottery found in the caves and that found at the settlement as proving such an organic connection.[66] De Vaux had himself first asserted that the cave pottery was Hellenistic, and on this basis had originally dated the hiding of the scrolls in the caves as somewhere toward the end of the second or the beginning of the first century B.C. Later on he realized his error, acknowledging that the jars were not Hellenistic but Roman, and of the second half of the first century A.D.[67] Meanwhile, he had found jars of the same type during the excavations at Khirbet Qumran, and also two rooms at the site that could be reasonably identified as a potter's workshop and as a storage room for pottery.[68] The inhabitants, so de Vaux explained, had filled jars made for the purpose with their precious manuscripts, then hid them in the caves; the fact that the manuscripts stored in the jars included sectarian texts showed that the inhabitants of Qumran were a sect.

In making these claims, however, de Vaux in effect generated an unwarranted turning point in the use of pottery for historical deductions. For it is an axiom of archaeological investigation that if jars of the same or similar styles are found in different locations, this does not necessarily indicate an organic connection between them, but only simultaneous habitation of the locations during the particular period to which the pottery may be dated. By employing a modicum of historical imagination tempered by common sense, one might more properly have inferred that those who wished to hide the scrolls in the caves asked the inhabitants of nearby sites, including Khirbet Qumran, for jars to aid them in doing so. That was in no sense tantamount, however, to claiming that the Qumran inhabitants themselves hid or possessed literary scrolls. The storing away of manuscripts in jars was, of course, not a phenomenon unique to Qumran, but customarily practiced in the ancient Near East. (Jeremiah speaks of writs of evidence, both sealed and unsealed, that the Lord commanded him to place "in an earthen vessel, that they might continue [i.e., to be preserved] many days" [Jer. **33**.14], while manuscripts stored in jars have been discovered at archaeological sites of both Pharaonic and Roman Egypt.)[69]

The rashness of de Vaux's interpretation became yet more evident with the discovery of pottery of the same type as that found at Qumran, in caves of Wadi Murabba'at and at En Ghuweir, both sites approximately fifteen kilometers south of Qumran, during other excavations.[70] (See Map 1.) These findings forced de Vaux subsequently to acknowledge that "The pottery of Qumran now appears less 'autonomous' or 'original' than I stated it to be at an earlier state." Indeed, pottery of the same type as the cylindrical Qumran pieces with wide necks thought to contain scrolls is known from at least two other sites, Quailba (ancient Abila, in upper Transjordania) and Jericho.[71]

De Vaux had at first argued eloquently that "there is only one site which corresponds to Pliny's description, and that is the plateau of Qumran . . . situated some way back from the shore and at a higher level, and healthier than the shore itself. . . . Furthermore, there is only one important group of buildings contemporary with Pliny between En Gedi and the northernmost point of the Dead Sea, that is the buildings of Khirbet Qumran and Feshkha."[72] In an added remark in the English edition of his work on the archaeology of Qumran, de Vaux qualified this by allowing for "the possibility that the small buildings of Khirbet Mazin and 'Ain el-Ghuweir [= En Ghuweir] could have belonged to the same community as Qumran. In any case they would have been no more than annexes of very minor importance."[73] De Vaux thus posited, despite Pliny's focus on the Essenes' poverty and asceticism, a serious complex of important Essenic buildings—hence those located at Qumran.

Elsewhere in the English work, de Vaux added the observation that "We should bear in mind that particularly during the second Iron age and the Roman period the west bank of the Dead Sea was more thickly populated than we have been accustomed to imagine."[74] Indeed, in the late 1960s, explorations of the area between Khirbet Qumran and En Gedi by the archaeologist Pesah Bar-Adon had revealed many Second Iron Age settlements supported by agriculture, thus destroying de Vaux's original idea that the Khirbet Qumran site alone was capable of being compared with the one described by Pliny. The effort at identifying these sites, however, only illustrates how much the world of scholarship and archaeology had succumbed to the Qumran-sectarian hypothesis. Trusting fully in it, and finding that the sites included one—at the En Ghuweir locality—with an area of graves similar in shape, style, and orientation to the graves in the Khirbet Qumran cemetery, Bar-Adon earnestly proposed in several articles that the one at En Ghuweir was *another* settlement of what he called the "Judaean Desert Sect."[75] (See Map 1.)

Bar-Adon offered his proposal after opening twenty of the En Ghuweir graves and discovering skeletons of seven women and one child (approximately seven years old), as well as those of twelve men. This was of course a higher percentage of women's skeletons than had been found at Qumran. In the absence, here as well, of any evidence of celibacy, Pliny's description of the celibate Essenes of the Dead Sea shore, rather than being acknowledged as having a bearing on the findings, was tacitly set aside in favor of an idea that had already come into play with respect to Qumran itself.

The growth of this idea can be summarized quite briefly: During the 1950s and early 1960s, a number of scholars, perceiving certain emerging conflicts between the archaeological findings and the Qumran-Essene theory, had become particularly concerned with the discovery of the graves there. Committed in principle to the theory, they nevertheless suggested altering it a bit, now speaking not of the Essenes but rather—without being more specific—of the "sect of Qumran." This idea, considered at least slightly more neutral than the original one, was expressed after 1967 in the signs erected at the site as well as in the Shrine of the Book in Jerusalem, referring consistently to "the sect that wrote the scrolls" and to its "home" at Qumran. In turn (as we shall see in ensuing chapters), the idea became entangled with a growing confusion regarding the beliefs and practices of the people thought by the Qumranologists to be living at the site.

Thereupon, with the discovery of graves at En Ghuweir identical in style and orientation to those of the Khirbet Qumran cemetery, the same logic was simply extended. While Père de Vaux had insisted that Khirbet Qumran was the very site described by Pliny, no indication of celibacy at Qumran emerged, and so the relevant portion of Pliny's statement was simply removed as a decisive criterion for identifying the Qumran inhabitants. Now having discovered graves at En Ghuweir identical to those at Qumran and likewise containing the skeletons of women, Bar-Adon took the liberty of extending the new theory a little further: Pliny's celibate "Essenes" were perhaps not really Essenes and perhaps not really celibate, and they lived not in a single habitation but in two places separated from each other by a distance of fifteen kilometers. This judgment marked the first archaeological step toward development of what may be termed the dogma of pan-Qumranism.

De Vaux himself, although continuing his strong support of the Essene theory, later addressed this proposal by saying that "it may perhaps be . . . rash to apply the designation 'Essene' to the building excavated near 'Ain el-Ghuweir or to the cemetery which may have been attached to it."[76] Bar-Adon's interpretation in effect showed to what awkward lengths the Qumran-Essene theory could carry archaeologists in their quest to recover the lost history they believed they were pursuing. Yet despite the cautionary words from de Vaux—who himself had acknowledged a lack of caution in his own earlier use of the pottery evidence—Bar-Adon's ideas on the interrelationship of these sites would continue to make a career of themselves. As late as the mid-eighties, support for them was still being sought, this time through the use of neutron-activation tests on the pottery of Qumran and En Ghuweir, conducted under the direction of Professor Joseph Yellin of the archaeometry unit of the Hebrew University and of curator Magen Broshi of Jerusalem's Shrine of the Book. The results achieved not surprisingly indicated that the pottery of the two sites did *not* in fact have the same origin. Yet the negative finding did not prevent Broshi from stating that "this test does not negate the possibility of an ideational or even organizational closeness between the inhabitants of the two sites" and then somewhat paradoxically adding that "if there was a connection between them, it has to be demonstrated by other proofs."[77] Bar-Adon's confusing views on this matter were thus persistently carried on despite the lack of any factual evidence to support them.*

Even today there are scholars who insist that the twelve hun-

---

*In 1993, H. Eshel and Z. Greenhut described twenty more such graves at still a third site, located between En Ghuweir and En Turabeh (see Map 1), and referred to fifty-two others located both to the north and south of Khirbet Qumran. The authors then pointed out that "graves of the same kind have been found in Jericho and in the East Talpiyot neighborhood of southern Jerusalem." (See H. Eshel and Z. Greenhut, "Hiam el-Sagha, a Cemetery of the Qumran Type, Judaean Desert," *Revue Biblique*, **100-2** [1993], pp. 252–259.) The authors concluded by suggesting that the "size of the Qumran cemetery . . . , when compared to the size of similar cemeteries in the Judean desert, demonstrates the importance of Qumran and reinforces the assumption that Qumran was the site that Pliny and Dio Chrysostom referred to in their description of the Essenes." The naive circularity of the authors' argumentation and their willingness to bend the new archaeological findings to suit the purposes of the old theory are, given the facts now known about Khirbet Qumran, somewhat astonishing.

dred graves lining the plateau next to the site are those of several generations of Essenes or related sectarians. Yet no stratification whatsoever characterizes these graves; they are all on the same horizontal level, laid out in regular, quite even rows, and with a uniform style of stone overlay—all factors showing that they were dug at one time.[78] They are obviously better interpreted as the graves of the warriors who fought at Qumran. The graves of the same type found elsewhere in the Judaean wilderness may well trace the Roman army's steady advance toward Masada.

According to an anthropological survey of skeletal remains taken from some of the graves, they included those of individuals who had been massacred. Z. J. Kapera has reported that H. Steckoll, another excavator of Qumran graves, in a paper published obscurely in Italy, indicated that burnt bones were among the skeletal remains.[79] Approximately 10 percent of the skeletons, in addition, had broken bones. These were further indications of a post-battle, military cemetery, installed—because of the practical necessity of quick burial—close to the site that had been defended.

The entire debate on the possible sectarian origin of the site is at all events rendered moot by further study of the cemetery, which had originally been conceived of as being that of the so-called sect members over several generations. The graves nearest the walls of the settlement were only thirty-five meters away from them. For reasons of ritual purity, rabbinic law later on ordained, for normative Judaism, a distance of at least fifty cubits between a Jewish settlement and cemetery (*Mishnah*, Bab. Bathra **2**.9),* and the thirty-five meters at Qumran just barely satisfied such a requirement. It is impossible to believe, however, that the purity-obsessed brethren described in the *Manual of Discipline*, who were governed by priests, would have allowed themselves to build a communal cemetery so close to their settlement, particularly when more abundant space was available farther away. The Pentateuchal legislation regarding impurity of dead bodies, and the special susceptibility of priests to that legislation (see, e.g., Leviticus, chapters **8–21**) would have resulted in a quite impossible situation at Khirbet Qumran, had the rules of the *Manual* ever been in force there. The close proximity of the graves to the settlement by itself proves that the people who wrote the *Manual of*

---

*"Carcasses, graves and tanneries must be kept beyond a distance of fifty cubits from the city."

Discipline—or indeed any other such purity-brotherhood—could have had nothing whatever to do with Khirbet Qumran. (See Map 2, p. 37.)

At the same time, precisely who the Jews were who garrisoned Khirbet Qumran itself at the time of the First Revolt is a question that still cannot be answered with complete assurance. Josephus characterizes the Jewish War as a complex effort involving the participation of many parties and factions among the Jews. Some he calls "Zealots," others *"sicarii,"* others factions that followed one or another leader; he describes still others simply as troops fighting on different fronts against the Romans, led by one or another commander. According to him, after the *sicarii* captured Masada from a Roman garrison, Eliezer ben Yair governed it for approximately seven years while they conducted raids in the neighborhood. Other Jews joined the *sicarii* at Masada before and during the course of the siege. The team under Yigael Yadin's direction that excavated Masada between 1963 and 1965 found manuscript fragments there, obviously from scrolls belonging to the inhabitants (see Chapter 5). It was tempting to think that these were scrolls reflecting beliefs of the *sicarii*, but this could not be proved from the preponderance of ideas contained in the texts as they had become known by 1970.

Already in 1958 Cecil Roth presented the view that the Qumran site was inhabited by Zealots, and that the scrolls found in the caves and at Masada belonged to them. This view was developed later by G. R. Driver.[80] Both Roth and Driver relied particularly on the fact that some of the scrolls known by then, particularly the *War Scroll*, expressed a remarkably militant apocalypticism.

Because of the great variety of often conflicting ideas that were being discovered in the scrolls (discussed in several chapters below)—and in the absence of firm evidence linking the cave manuscripts with the Khirbet Qumran site in an organic way—the arguments presented by Roth and Driver could not be considered entirely satisfactory. They did, however, possess the merit of attempting to connect the contents of the scrolls with salient events of Jewish history in the period of the First Revolt. As of today, forty years after the excavations, further archaeological investigation of the site is urgently needed to shed light on the identity of the Khirbet Qumran defenders. After de Vaux's team had finished their basic work in 1956, little additional investigation was carried out at the site, nor had a complete scientific report on the dig been published by the early nineties.[81] Signs faithfully reflecting the identifications of de Vaux and his team were put up at the site by the Israel Department of Antiquities after 1967, and they have remained in place.

The impact the Khirbet Qumran site made on me when I studied it for the first time in 1969 was powerful. Examining the tower, the rooms, the fine architecture whose remnants could still be seen, the strategic view across the Dead Sea, I could not avoid perceiving that the site, once divorced from the statement of Pliny the Elder, was quintessentially an ancient military fort, erected, according to the hints of architecture, at the time of stabilization of the Hasmonaean state, circa 140–130 B.C.. The First Book of Maccabees—the most important of the Maccabee histories—states that Jonathan the Hasmonaean charged his most trustworthy men with "the building of fortresses in Judaea" (1 Macc. **12**.35; ca. 144 B.C.). Josephus writes that Simon the Maccabee

> went through all Judaea and Palestine as far as Ascalon, making their fortresses secure and strengthening them with works and guards. [Jonathan] further advised them [= the people] to make the fortresses throughout the country far stronger than they were in their present state of security. And so, when this plan was approved by the people, Jonathan himself began the building in the city, and sent out Simon to make the fortresses in the country secure. . . . [82]

Current historic maps of Israel, following the cue of several scholars, identify the so-called fortress of the Hassidim mentioned in one of the Bar Kokhba manuscripts of the second century A.D. with Khirbet Qumran itself. The Hassidim, or "Pietists", were that very group of "mighty men of Israel" (1 Macc. **2**.42) who came to the aid of the Maccabees in their struggle against the Syrians, and the site already may well have been named after them in the second century B.C. But a strategic bastion of this kind could hardly have been handed over to a peace-loving sect such as the Essenes during Herodian times, and surely not during the period of the First Revolt of A.D. 66–73. A strong military force was stationed there during the war with Rome, as the archaeological evidence acknowledged by Père de Vaux himself has indicated.

There was thus nothing whatever at Khirbet Qumran to attest to its being a monastery, a place where monks or other notable sectarians lived, or a center where scholarship, intense writing activity, or the

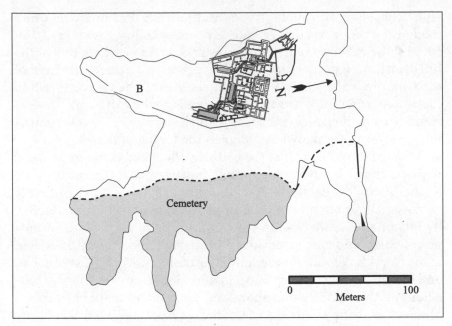

Map 2
Khirbet Qumran and the adjacent cemetery.

copying of books was pursued. The evidence showed that identification of the site as the home of Pliny's Essenes was untenable. It was
in the same category of archaeological blunders as Heinrich
Schliemann's original attribution of treasures discovered by him at
Troy to the renowned King Priam; the description of the skull
found at Piltdown in Sussex as that of a pre-Neanderthal species of
man; or the claim that bricks inscribed with alphabetic signs, discovered in the hamlet of Glozel, France, dated back to Neolithic times.
What clearly emerged from an examination of the site untrammeled by *a priori* judgments based on literary texts found in the caves
was that Khirbet Qumran was an important archaeological monument of the First Revolt, symbolically attesting to events in the
greater history of the Jews of intertestamental times.

The specific importance of the site could be best determined by
observing both its position and the characteristics of its architecture. Surrounding Qumran was a defensive wall—the one mined
through by the Romans in order to capture the site. Today only
remnants of this wall are preserved—actually only some of the

"fill," consisting of rubble, stone, and mortar, that in ancient and medieval times served to give body and stability to walls of finished stone in monumental structures. Only a few fragments of the finished limestone that formed the inside and outside facings of the Qumran walls have survived; the best example can be found in the tower, where it was fortunately preserved by the surrounding ramp of stone boulders (see Fig. 2). Thick slabs of limestone such as this one must originally have formed the facing of the entire tower and the surrounding walls; the walls in effect could not have stood without them. In the course of time, however, when Qumran came to be abandoned, the good limestone facing was evidently removed, as so often happened in the case of ancient monuments, by inhabitants of the region who utilized them for their own purposes. Such edifices, faced in well-finished stone, were of course characteristic of the monumental architecture of Hasmonaean and Herodian times. Both Masada and Herodium are of this character. Another fortress that shows the same monumental features is Machaerus, lying southeast of Qumran across the Dead Sea at the strikingly short distance of approximately twenty kilometers. Khirbet Qumran is situated almost halfway, as the crow flies, between Jerusalem and Machaerus. (See Map 1.)

Before 90 B.C., the Hasmonaean Alexander Jannaeus had subjugated the inhabitants of Moab, east of the Dead Sea, and built Machaerus as a bulwark to ward off attacks by the Aramaic-speaking Nabataeans who occupied Petra and other areas to the south.[83] Destroyed by Gabinius, the governor of Syria, circa 60 B.C., Machaerus was rebuilt by Herod the Great, and his son Antipas murdered John the Baptist there. During the First Revolt, it was one of the two principal fortresses (the other being Masada) to which the *sicarii*, Zealots, and other Jews fled during the Roman siege and capture of Jerusalem. As with Masada, Machaerus was besieged by the Romans. Its strategic location and massive construction were such that it could not be taken by storm, but as the Romans set to work building a siege-ramp, the refugees holding out there finally surrendered and much of the garrison was slaughtered.[84] The site, being in Jordan, has never been examined by Israeli archaeologists nor seriously integrated into studies of the Second Jewish Commonwealth, and yet it marks the limit of expansion of the Jewish state under the Hasmonaeans. (See Fig. 8.) Land areas to the north of the fortress were settled by Jews during and after the time of Jannaeus, and it would appear that the Romans only nominally controlled this expanded ter-

Figure 8
Machaerus, fortress of the Jews east of the Dead Sea
in Hasmonaean and Herodian times, built circa 90–80 B.C.

ritory after their conquest of Palestine under Pompey in 63 B.C. South of Machaerus, on the other hand, lay the Nabataean regions, and the fortress served as the main bulwark against possible land attacks by them upon the expanded Jewish region east of the Jordan and the Dead Sea. Khirbet Qumran, for its part, was not only a bulwark against possible Nabataean incursions into Judaea by sea, but also provided the most direct means of communication between Machaerus and the capital.

The two fortresses on either side of the Dead Sea, within direct sight of each other, could mutually communicate by either fire signals or carrier pigeon,[85] and in this way correspondence with Jerusalem could be readily maintained. In time of need troops could be sent straight across the sea to Machaerus by boat from landings situated near Khirbet Qumran. The boats employed for this purpose were perhaps of the type used in the Dead Sea as depicted in the Madaba map (sixth century A.D.), which had both oars and sails and could generate considerable speed on the highly buoyant waters of the sea.[86] Khirbet Qumran was thus an integral part of the defense system of encircling fortifications designed to ward off attacks against the capital and the heartland of Judaea;* and it also served as a stronghold, in times of both peace and war, to guard the route carrying salt, balsam, asphalt, and sugar from the Dead Sea region to the capital.[87] As the geographer Menashe Harel has pointed out,

> In ancient times two good roads were built from the shores of the Dead Sea to the hills of Hebron and Jerusalem . . . both ascend the hills to the watershed by several steps. One road climbs from Nahal Zohar at the southern end of the Dead Sea . . . and the other *runs north of the Qumran ruins* via Wadi el Dabr, whose continuation is known as Wadi Mukallik (Nahal Og). The latter route . . . was built from the shore of the Dead Sea via Tel el Muhalhal, which overlooks the sea from an altitude of –80 metres. From here the road continues via Darb er Rajab and Nabi Musa to Ras el Mashad, 'Aqabat es Sukkar, Khirbet el Khan el Ahmar, Qasr el Khan and Wadi el Hod, where it joins up with a section of the modern road from Jericho to Ma'ale Adummim, and thence to 'Ein Hod, El 'Eizariya to the south of the Mount of Olives, and finally to Jerusalem.[88]

As Harel has convincingly shown, the boats that plied the Dead Sea—such as those vessels whose sailors, according to Josephus, would gather "black masses of bitumen" from the surface of the sea—could carry their cargoes of asphalt, salt, and other products from the southernmost tip of the sea northward to the mouth of the Wadi Mukallik, located just to the north of Khirbet Qumran.[89] (See Map 4, page 106.) From here the cargoes could be transferred to camelback for the rest of the journey to Jerusalem. This sea route was clearly of commercial importance, particularly since no road ran along the western coast between the southern end of the sea and the boat landings near Qumran. Khirbet Qumran was thus strategically located to protect this route.

The purposes of Khirbet Qumran and Machaerus obviously changed with the outbreak of the First Revolt in A.D. 66, but

---

*The fortresses surrounding Jerusalem were arranged in concentric circles, Khirbet Qumran being a stronghold of the fifth and outermost circle. See the map designating the various fortresses surrounding the capital in *Biblical Archaeologist* **44**, no. 1 (Winter, 1981), and the accompanying article by M. Harel, "Jerusalem and Judaea: Roads and Fortifications," pp. 8–20. As for the Dead Sea, its total length from south to north is approximately forty-seven miles.

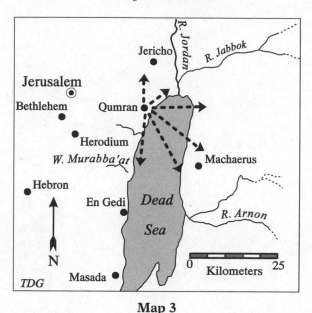

Map 3
The view from the tower of Khirbet Qumran.

remained primarily military nevertheless: i.e., to serve as rallying points for the rebel forces in the eastern part of Judaea, and prevent a quick Roman penetration southward toward En Gedi and Masada. This policy temporarily paid dividends, but by A.D. 72 both Qumran and Machaerus had fallen, Herodium also had been taken, and the Romans were well on their way to completing their final suppression of the revolt with their capture of Masada and the mass suicide of its diehard resisters.

Given the strategic position of Khirbet Qumran, its massive defense tower, the highly developed water system, the clear proofs of a siege and pitched battle between Romans and Jews in approximately A.D. 70, and the many other elements discussed above that had come to light by the 1960s, it was clear to me by the end of that decade that the entire question of the large number of manuscripts discovered in the caves to the west of the site had to be urgently reopened. Without heavily forced exegesis, it was no longer possible to believe that such a large collection of texts could have been in the hands of the military troop inhabiting Qumran at the time the scrolls were hidden away.

CHAPTER 2

The Manuscripts
of the Jews

*I*began to understand the problem posed by the scrolls only
after studying other Hebrew manuscripts from various periods and places. This research, of long duration, furnished me
with the tools for a solution to the riddle of the scrolls' origin
entirely at odds with the one urged on the reading public by
Edmund Wilson and other writers in the 1950s and 1960s. The
solution, pursued through a maze of facts and down many investigative dead ends, eventually generated heated debate. My examination of the Khirbet Qumran site did no more than confirm what
I had earlier begun to suspect through the study of the manuscripts.

As a graduate student in the early fifties, I had left the reassur-
ing confines of the University of Chicago's Oriental Institute in
order to study the first of the newly found scrolls under W. F.
Albright's tutelage at Johns Hopkins University. A world-famous
Hebraist and Semitics scholar, he was the doyen of biblical
archaeologists in his day. He was also president of the American
Schools of Oriental Research, and in direct contact with the team
of scholars exploring the Judaean Wilderness for new manuscripts in the wake of the discovery of the first seven scrolls in
1947. By that token our group at Hopkins was among the first to
be informed of the latest discoveries as they were being made.
Already a gray eminence, Albright was deeply respected by his
students for his immense knowledge and his fairness, and when
we pored together over the newly discovered *Manual of Discipline*
and other early scroll editions, we felt the special bond of kinship
that forms when discoveries begin to spark new ideas through the
give-and-take of debate.

Albright epitomized the dignity of learning, and when he
expressed agreement with the developing theory that the scrolls

had all been written by a sect of Essenes living near the caves where they were discovered, none of us had reason to question his endorsement or the theory itself. In our dissertations we generally referred to the writers of the texts as the "Essenic covenanters of Qumran."

By this time Israel's War of Independence had been fought, and Jerusalem was a divided city. The team of Catholic and Protestant scholars working in the Judaean Wilderness and in Arab East Jerusalem was composed in large part of priests and their students—surely not, at that time, of Israeli scholars on the other side of the fence. At the height of the hostilities, Professor Eliezer Sukenik of the Hebrew University, an esteemed archaeologist, had managed to see most or all of the seven newly discovered texts, and to purchase three of them. Several years later (1954), the other four were purchased in the United States for the Israel Museum, which now shelters all seven of the original scrolls in its Shrine of the Book.*

At that time the scrolls included two texts of the biblical Book of Isaiah, as well as works that were then completely unknown. One of them was a collection of religious hymns, or *Hodayot*, in a style similar to that of the biblical Psalms, of which eighteen columns and various fragments had been preserved. In addition, there was a short commentary (*pesher*) on the Book of Habakkuk, now known as the *Pesher Habakkuk* or *Habakkuk Commentary*, in which the anonymous commentator attempts to relate the prophet's words to events of his own time and the impending future. Included in the finds was an embellished Aramaic retelling of early stories of Genesis, which has come to be known as the *Genesis Apocryphon*. There was an imaginative description of a war to take place in an apocalyptic era between the good and evil troops of mankind, known at first as the "War of the Sons of Light against the Sons of Darkness," and then simply as the *War Scroll*. Also found was a work of eleven surviving columns, some of its paragraphs describing a gigantic initiation ceremony to be undergone by individuals endowed with the power to choose and follow a life of virtue.

*The scrolls purchased originally by Sukenik were the *Hodayot*, the *War Scroll*, and one of the two manuscripts of the Book of Isaiah. The other four were purchased by Sukenik's son, Yigael Yadin, in New York City from the Syrian Metropolitan of Jerusalem, Mar Athanasius Samuel.

It is this last work (which we shall examine more closely in Chapter 3) that soon became known as the *Manual of Discipline*, for instructions in several columns following the description of the ceremony of initiation set out procedures for gaining admission to the group, as well as a mode of disciplined behavior for its full-fledged members. This included eschewing personal wealth, leading a communal life of radical spirituality and physical purity in which ceremonial meals would be taken together, and participating in study sessions given over to expounding "secrets" of the Pentateuch and in meetings meant for discussing the group's laws and behavior.

Exploration of the Judaean Wilderness for new manuscripts in the area of Qumran had in the meanwhile come under the jurisdiction of the Jordanian government, which at the time of the truce in 1949 found itself in control of that part of former mandatory Palestine. The Jordanian authorities would let neither scholars holding Israeli passports or visas, nor in fact Jews in general, cross the line to join in exploring the northern region of the Dead Sea coast.

By the end of 1954, the year I and several colleagues had completed our Hopkins dissertations, extensive exploration was going on in the Judaean Wilderness, while in Jewish Jerusalem scholars were scrutinizing the seven scrolls already in their hands, all of which, with the exception of the *Genesis Apocryphon*, had by then been rudimentarily published. Later, while living in Jerusalem as a postdoctoral researcher in the mid-1950s, I was able from certain vantage points to see over the walls and fences into East Jerusalem and the Old City, but could do no more than speculate about new discoveries emerging from the investigation of the thousands of manuscript fragments that kept arriving at the Rockefeller Museum from the desert caves near Khirbet Qumran. News of such discoveries would reach us after long delays, usually through reports appearing in the *Revue Biblique*, published by the Dominican Ecole Biblique in East Jerusalem; it was this school that dominated the explorations under Père Roland de Vaux's charismatic leadership. De Vaux and his group were joined by those members of the American Schools of Oriental Research in residence at its East Jerusalem headquarters, by G. Lankester Harding of the Jordanian Department of Antiquities, and by a few other scholars who became part of the international team engaged in exploring and deciphering the texts. Those who happened to be on the other side of the Jerusalem fence did not begin to enter into the picture, and some of us were not long in perceiving that we might never have a firsthand part in the investigation of the scrolls.

I then undertook the study of other manuscripts under the direction of S. D. Goitein, one of Jerusalem's most remarkable scholars. These were the documentary manuscripts of the Cairo Genizah—the huge collection of medieval Jewish writings that, during the latter half of the nineteenth century, had been conveyed by Solomon Schechter and other travelers and scholars to libraries in Europe from the attic storeroom of an ancient Cairene synagogue. By the mid-1950s, Goitein was already immersed in a prodigious labor on these multifaceted Hebrew and Arabic texts; I began to learn how to exploit them for historical reconstruction. I observed that, unlike the scrolls being discovered in the Qumran caves, the Genizah manuscripts included many genuine historical *autographs*, consisting of actual records penned long ago by people of all walks of life, rather than only copies of literary texts made by scribes long after their authors had composed them.

Goitein was a patient and reserved man; in our sessions he led me word by word, letter by letter, through many of the autographs: court proceedings, personal and business letters, contracts of marriage and divorce, bills of sale, lists of books bought and sold, and virtually every other kind of record characteristically used in literate societies. Handwritten eyewitness accounts of this nature constitute the building blocks of historical investigation, and in this respect differ from cultural products such as imaginative literature (whether poetry or prose), which can offer no more than indirect insight into the dynamic forces shaping past societies or the events that made them what they were.

By 1957 still other remarkable discoveries of scrolls and scroll fragments had taken place in the Judaean Wilderness, but only the small official team under Père de Vaux's guidance was authorized to study and publish them. Returning to the States late that year, I resolved to put aside further research on the scrolls, at least until the new discoveries were published, and began concentrating instead on the autograph documents of the Cairo Genizah. Scholars of these manuscripts had open and friendly access to them at Cambridge University Library as well as other academic institutions;* in the following few decades I spent much time at Cambridge with these texts, preparing some of the most valuable ones for publication. The two salient questions I asked, of necessity, regarding each of the leaves I examined, were (a) whether the leaf was *documentary* or *literary* in character, and (b) whether it was an *autograph original* or a *copy* made by a scribe of an original record written earlier on. This was the same basic and time-honored method followed by papyrologists responsible for publishing the manifold Greek papyri of Roman and Byzantine Egypt.

Scholars trained in the study of the Genizah texts can determine their salient characteristics quite readily. Pure documentary autographs, for example, are written on individual sheets of parchment or paper in a relatively bold and often rough script, contain personal and geographic names and, not infrequently, precise dates. They are as a rule written on only one side of the sheet, but personal and business correspondence sometimes spills over onto the reverse side as well as into the margins. If the document contains original correspondence, there will often be several creases showing where the letter was folded before being entrusted to its courier. *Legal* documentary originals will have the signatures of witnesses and also, like letters, precise dates and statements indicating where they were written. Many other types of documentary autographs—such as book lists, inventories, and accounts of purchases and sales—do not necessarily have such features, but the characteristically rough handwriting styles and the larger spaces between the lines on the individual pages usually indicate their autographic character. If a particular text has the requisite autographic features, the researcher may move ahead with some confidence in evaluating its historical quality and import.

Autographs of this sort, possessing the solidity and immediacy of eyewitness description, were particularly sought out by historians of the Cairo Genizah, such as Goitein, E. Ashtor, and, before them, Jacob Mann—the true pioneer of research on these texts during the first several decades following their arrival in England in the 1890s. Without the aid of published chronicles or modern

---

*The major collections of Genizah documents are, beside the leading one at Cambridge, those of Oxford, the British Museum, the State Public Library in St. Petersburg, and the Jewish Theological Seminary of America in New York City.

synthetic histories, and using mainly autograph texts, Mann constructed a narrative record, where earlier there had been only a large blank space, of the Jews of mediaeval Egypt from the tenth through the twelfth centuries. Other researchers carried his work forward with greater philological and linguistic skill—Ashtor, for example, produced a history of Egyptian Jewry in the two centuries following the period explored by Mann, and Goitein published a multivolume study of mediaeval Mediterranean Jewish society, based on thousands of Genizah autographs.[1] (I note in passing the several hundred articles by Goitein on individual fragments, as well as the many important articles by Mann, Ashtor, D. H. Baneth, and others.) As my own work on the autographs proceeded, I moved in a somewhat new direction, having observed that beyond their value in forming pictures of past societies, some of the Genizah texts could be used as historical touchstones to evaluate and possibly change long-standing assumptions of conventional written history.

The manuscript that first suggested this possibility to me was an autograph letter on parchment, written by Jews somewhere in the south of France over nine hundred years ago, and included in the mass of Cairo Genizah manuscripts brought to Cambridge University in 1896. Written in a bold, semicursive (i.e., rounded rather than square) documentary script and in rich idiomatic Hebrew, it contained a number of intriguing elements, including four consonants rising from a hole above its central portion. This word, as the letter's context made clear, identified the name of the place where it had been written. By magnifying the consonants, a word whose transcription was MNYW clearly emerged. The letter described the plight of a proselyte who had previously fled, probably from the north of France, to the southern French city of Narbonne, where she married the scion of a prominent Jewish family, fleeing afterward to the enigmatic MNYW upon learning that emissaries from her noble Christian parents were seeking her return home.

Some time after the couple had settled down in MNYW, the Jewish community there was attacked, the proselyte's husband was murdered in the synagogue, and two of their three children were kidnapped by the attackers. Unable to support the widow, the surviving Jews sent her and her remaining infant son to other shores; we know that she eventually arrived in Cairo from the discovery in the Genizah of the letter describing her travail. The variety of circumstances described in the letter were characteristic of events surrounding the First Crusade. The letter proved to be a unique document of the Jews of Monieux (formerly *Moniou*)—a town of the high Provence going back to Roman times, whose now partly ruined watchtower looms over the shortest route between Avignon and the Mont Genèvre pass across the Alps. This was the route taken in 1096 by the Provençal crusaders, the largest crusading force ever assembled; strikingly, the Hebrew text of Monieux remains the only one specifying a stop on that route, and the only eyewitness document describing an attack on Jews by French rather than German crusaders. Since, after World War II, Crusade historians—perhaps in an unconscious effort to restore French honor in the wake of Vichy—had begun attributing such attacks solely to German crusaders, the full import of the Monieux autograph as a corrective to the contemporizing tendencies often at work in historical writing soon became apparent.

The main thrust of my work on this document, which took place in the 1960s, was toward showing how a significant aspect of mediaeval history could be illuminated by the initial decipherment of four Hebrew consonants constituting the crucial place-name of a Genizah autograph.[2] I had by then studied many other such texts. My basic signposts were those valued by all students of history who center their work on ancient manuscripts: indications of original authorship and other eyewitness characteristics, personal and place-names, dates, and signatures.

While this research was under way, developments in the study of the Dead Sea Scrolls continued. The manuscript team had published its first volume of texts in 1955, and, starting in the 1960s, I conducted a yearly seminar at Chicago on all the available texts. The excavation of the Khirbet Qumran site had been completed by 1956, and de Vaux's Schweich Lectures dealing with it saw print in 1961.

During this period, the theory first formulated by Eliezer Sukenik in 1948—i.e., that the writings found originally in Cave 1 were those of Essenes, and reflected their very own thinking—had been further developed by de Vaux and members of the manuscript team, and had been taken up by a powerful exponent in Paris, André Dupont-Sommer. By 1953 the latter had already published two books and a dozen articles supporting the theory; in

1959 he elaborated on his views in a work of great erudition and eloquent rhetoric, whose publication in an English translation by Geza Vermes brought the great majority of scholars decisively over to the side of the Qumran-Essene theory.[3] For several years after its publication, I continued to support his views firmly, teaching them regularly to my students in the course of our seminar.

The ideas expressed by Dupont-Sommer included the opinion that scholars had been unable to trace many early Christian ideas back to Judaism because they were previously "familiar mainly with Pharisaic . . . or Rabbinic Judaism: of Essene Judaism they had but imperfect, and more often than not, indirect knowledge. From now on," Dupont-Sommer declared, "the Qumran documents take us into the heart of the Essene sect and lift the veil from its mysteries, rites and customs. They are, of course, only a remnant of an immense corpus of literature, now largely lost. . . ."[4]

In this way Dupont-Sommer helped lay the groundwork for the idea that the classical descriptions of the Essenes—those of Philo, Pliny the Elder, and Josephus recorded in the first century A.D.— were not necessarily accurate, but could be both supplemented and *corrected* by recourse to the texts discovered in the Qumran caves. He believed these scrolls represented the Essenes' views from within. By 1960 members of the scrolls manuscript team had already determined that fragments of over six hundred non-biblical texts had survived in the caves; their partial publication and evaluation was accompanied by a growing recognition that the ideas in them were not always consistent with one another. Confronting this fact, Dupont-Sommer stated that "these documents are not all of the same age and can betray, from one document to the next, a certain evolution in institutions and beliefs. Traces of a similar evolution may be seen in one and the same document, between one passage and the next."[5]

In this approach, internal contradictions in the scrolls simply reflected phases in the development of Essenism, any apparent inconsistencies with the Essenic ideas described in the first century being understood as arising from insufficient knowledge on the part of the ancient writers, who would not have been adequately initiated into the mysteries of Essenism to have described this movement accurately. Amalgamating this view with Père de Vaux's picture of the Khirbet Qumran inhabitants, Dupont-Sommer suggested that

"in the solemn quietness of the bare and torrid desert it is possible
to imagine the people . . . who led such a hard and exceedingly austere life there. . . . It is now time to read the books which nourished
their spirit, books to which they committed their mystic beliefs . . .
These books were secret, but . . . they are now in our hands, in their
authentic text . . . just as they were written and copied about two
thousand years ago.[6]

In some measure, others had expressed Dupont-Sommer's
views beforehand, but never so eloquently and persuasively.
Combined with his immense prestige in the world of Semitic
scholarship, this was enough to convince all but a few scholars of
the truth of the Qumran-Essene hypothesis. His election in 1968
as Perpetual Secretary of the Académie des Inscriptions et Belles
Lettres would endow that hypothesis with crowning authority, as
it came to be championed at leading American and European universities and in all Israeli institutions of higher learning.

In 1961—the same year as the publication of de Vaux's lectures, and almost simultaneous with circulation of the English
version of Dupont-Sommer's work—a second volume of texts in
the team's publication series appeared, brilliantly deciphered by
Joseph Milik, a Polish priest who was the most industrious member of the original scrolls team.[7] Surprisingly, these were not texts
found in the Qumran caves, nor, for the most part, were they
whole or fragmentary scroll texts written on leather. Rather, they
were mostly single, hastily scrawled sheets of papyrus, discovered
during the explorations of the early 1950s in caves of the rugged
Wadi Murabba'at, approximately twenty kilometers south of
Khirbet Qumran. These fragmentary texts, many of them in a
highly cursive script and difficult to read, were of the period of
the Bar Kokhba Revolt (A.D. 132–135), and included letters written by its leader Simeon bar Koziba (Bar Kokhba) to his military
commanders, as well as a number of legal documents relating to
landownership during and before the revolt—over fifty documents
in all. They contained signatures of witnesses and dates, and
names of various individuals figured in both the letters and the
deeds. There were place-names as well: not only previously
known ones (Masada, En Gedi, Herodium) but also unknown
localities such as Beth Mashko, 'Ir Nahash, and Mesad Hasidin.
The importance of the documents was made manifest in several
references, within two deeds, to Jerusalem as the site of a Jewish

landholding, indicating that in A.D. 134 (a date whose vernacular equivalent was found in one of the two deeds) Jerusalem was indeed in the hands of rebels under Bar Kokhba, contrary to the prevailing historical opinion.

Publication of these texts more or less coincided with the announcement that two expeditions by Yigael Yadin in 1960 and 1961, to wadis located inland from En Gedi, had resulted in further manuscript discoveries related to the Bar Kokhba period. They would not be published until many years later (as of this writing, they are still not fully published), but I and others interested in the history of the period were able to study the Murabba'at discoveries knowing they were part of a larger cache of documents hidden away in various places by participants in the Second Revolt.[8]

I began to read these texts seriously in the mid-1960s, and became increasingly struck by the fact that they were genuine eyewitness autographs—of the same historical quality, that is to say, as the Cairo Genizah documents I had been working on. Soon afterward, my students read the Bar Kokhba texts with me in a seminar, obliging me for the first time to compare these manuscripts with the Qumran scrolls, which had been so much more familiar to us. I felt it was particularly important to study these papyrus texts in view of the fact that their discovery had not been treated with the same widespread enthusiasm as that accorded the Qumran scrolls, written a mere century or two before them: unlike the earlier scrolls, they were being studied hardly anywhere, despite their value as eyewitness originals.

I found myself forced to confront certain realities regarding the nature of the Qumran texts and the widespread approach to their study. The universal enthusiasm over the Dead Sea Scrolls had its source not so much in new information they might provide on an ancient sect or the Jews of the intertestamental period, but in the light they might cast on the origins of Christianity—a subject of very wide appeal indeed. By contrast, while the Bar Kokhba texts might prove especially valuable for understanding the Second Jewish Revolt and the mores and customs of the Jews in the first third of the second century A.D., it was thought they could apparently add little to the knowledge of early Christianity, and thus, whether they were autograph documents or not, their study was of less pressing importance to many scholars.

Yet the very excitement regarding the Qumran scrolls seemed

Figure 9
Two examples of Bar Kokhba documentary scripts.

based, at least in part, on a fundamental misconception of their nature, now remediable through their comparison with the Bar Kokhba texts. I was obliged to tell my students that—despite Dupont-Sommer's insistence on calling them "documents"—the Dead Sea Scrolls did not share the *documentary* characteristics of the Bar Kokhba texts. They in fact did not show any evidence of being historical autographs. They carried no signatures, no dates, no colophons or other indications of original authorship. They included no personal or official autograph letters, no lists of names of sectarians, no deeds of ownership or sale, no court records. (As we will see below, photographs of a small number of documentary scraps have since been published; but these contain no indication of their provenance, thus exposing the crucial role such indications can have in establishing an organic link between a cache of texts and the site of their discovery.)

Where historical personages were alluded to in the scrolls, it was only in the setting of biblical commentaries or other literary writings, generally in explanation of what the authors considered to be hidden or secret meanings of cherished spiritual writings. Just as significantly, while the scrolls consisted of works of literature, none of them seemed to show signs of an original author in the act of writing down his thoughts; none, that is, could be considered what is properly called a *literary* autograph. While such autographs—or *holographs*—also could not be found among the Bar Kokhba texts, a considerable number had been discovered in the Cairo Genizah, and they were characterized, as might be expected, by rough, cursive, and irregular writing as well as by numerous erasures and marginal additions. The scrolls, by contrast, were apparently all smoothly written copies of literary works, made by scribes, and—judging by the nature of the scribal errors—sometimes two or more steps removed from the original authors' texts, now vanished, upon which they were based. I reminded my students of the paleographers' cardinal distinction between scribal copy and author's original, and of the corollary requirement that a text be considered a copy unless its autograph status were demonstrated beyond reasonable doubt.

I expressed these observations reluctantly: The implications were serious and I had no particular desire to exile myself from the community of believers in the Qumran–Essene hypothesis. Yet if the origins of the scrolls were ever to be fully grasped, the facts as they emerged had to be stated. No eyewitness letters, legal documents, or inscriptions attested to a sect of Essenes—or any other sect—living at Qumran; and none of the scrolls apparently referred to either Qumran or nearby places such as En Gedi or Masada. What scholars of the scrolls had in fact been doing, in the absence of bona fide historical data, was to treat these writings as if they *were* documents, attesting to a particular, integral history.

Already by 1952, convinced that the manuscripts being discovered in the Qumran caves had actually been composed, in whole or in part, at Qumran, Père de Vaux and his team sought quite naturally to answer the inevitable question, Where might the texts of this Essene settlement have been produced? They discovered their "scriptorium," and an officially sanctioned sign containing the word *Scriptorium* was eventually staked at the site. Tellingly, in later describing this room and what he believed was accomplished there, Père de Vaux stated: "Certainly manuscripts were copied in the *scriptorium* of Qumran, and in the case of several manuscripts it is possible to discern the hand of the same scribe. We may also suppose, *even before studying their content*, that certain works were composed at Qumran."[9] This was the view that Dupont-Sommer would so heartily embrace and develop, and that would then be taken up by hosts of scholars everywhere. Qumran was conceived, in the words of these authors, as an Essenic "laura" or "motherhouse," where members of the sect both composed religious writings and made copies of them in scroll form. Since the scripts represented in the scrolls varied in age from about 200 B.C. to as late as A.D. 60 or 65, it could be inferred that this process of writing and copying had continued for perhaps two hundred and fifty years or more. In this vein, James Muilenberg asserted in 1954 that "We are now beginning to get a general impression of the scribal activity of the community inhabiting Khirbet Qumran. . . . The size of the scriptorium . . . suggests that the transcription of sacred and other writings constituted no small part of the religious activity of the group."[10]

Dupont-Sommer and his colleagues were thus using the term "document" to reflect their faith in the scrolls' status as prime testimony of Essenic belief. The Bar Kokhba texts, however, made clear that original Hebrew autographs of a documentary character, such as administrative letters or deeds and contracts, could indeed survive from antiquity in the Judaean Wilderness. As applied to Qumran, what of course particularly mattered was the complete absence of documentary autographs attesting to any activities of Essenic sectarians. The *Manual of Discipline*, for instance, mandated a written record of the spiritual rank and position of each member of the order which that text describes, but no such list was found among the scrolls.[11] If they were indeed from Qumran, having been gathered in haste from chambers at the site and from its "scriptorium"—which would doubtless have been the production center for the sect's official letters and other documents as well—how could such documents have been so carefully excluded from the hiding process when word supposedly came that Roman troops were approaching? It strained credulity to argue that those leading a motherhouse of Essenes would have let deeds and records representing a period of between one and two hundred years perish in the ruins, while taking care to hide away hundreds of literary writings.

This constituted, at the time, a grave challenge to the Qumran-Essene theory. (The eventual surfacing of nonliterary, documentary fragments, discussed on pages 60–61, while rendering the Qumranologists' "perishability" explanation defunct, has not in any sense diminished the challenge insofar as the necessary sectarian, Qumranic markers are completely lacking.) It was just as remarkable that no documents of a *personal* nature had ever turned up in the caves. Did not the Essenes write letters to each other, and would they not have wanted to preserve them, as urgently as the Jews of the Bar Kokhba period apparently did? It seemed odd that none of the Qumranologists had pointed out this difficulty after publication of the Bar Kokhba volume in 1961.

The lack of literary autographs (that is, literary works in the original author's own handwriting) was a still more serious problem. This fact pointed to the utter absence of hard evidence that authors actively worked at Khirbet Qumran or the surrounding area—the very proposition de Vaux and Dupont-Sommer had been so ardently urging. While arguments from silence are never absolutely conclusive, common sense indicated a jarring clash between this absence and the notion that an important group of sectarians, supposedly living very close to where the texts were found, had actually authored them in a monastic setting, and then passed them on to scribes to copy in a scriptorium. The logical question was: What happened to the original autographs claimed to have been produced and used at Khirbet Qumran?

Neither Père de Vaux nor Dupont-Sommer, nor the vast majority of scholars who followed their interpretation of the discoveries, had ever raised this question directly. Perhaps the one who came closest was Frank M. Cross of Harvard, who had spent considerable time studying the palaeography of the Qumran texts. In his early book on the scrolls, he explained that a few copies of the *Manual of Discipline* stemmed from the first quarter of the first century A.D., one on papyrus being still earlier, but that "it is unlikely that even the oldest of them is an autograph."[12] Cross thus recognized the need to distinguish between an author's autograph and scribal copies; while Yigael Yadin—Eliezer Sukenik's son, and himself deeply involved in Qumran studies—similarly acknowledged a difference between the actual date of authorship of the scrolls and "the date of the copies now in our possession."[13] Neither they nor anyone else, however, had proceeded to confront the implications that a glaring lack of autograph scrolls possessed for the notion (however elaborately dilated) of a spiritually and intellectually active movement centered at a desert site over several generations.

The more I considered this dead silence, the clearer it became that the question of the scrolls' origin represented a problem for scholarship that had not really been solved. The Qumran-Essene theory had been posited in the first few years of the scrolls' discovery, but the ensuing manuscript finds did not confirm it; instead, the very nature of those finds had confounded the theory with latent anomalies. Although superficially of a historical nature, the theory had not been developed by manuscript specialists or historical researchers, but by archaeologists and biblical scholars. They had quite naturally devoted most of their attention to Khirbet Qumran's archaeology, intertwining it with the use of imaginative religious writings found in the caves to construct their vision of a creative and highly spiritual Qumran-Essene sect. Neither their past training nor subsequent scholarly labor had prepared them to pose substantially different kinds of questions that must necessarily inform sober historical judgment.

Thus, under the impact of a methodologically flawed vision, a generation of scholars had enthusiastically endorsed the notion that virtually all the Palestinian Jewish manuscripts from intertestamental times ever recovered—in the form of fragments of over eight hundred scrolls—were the spiritual product not of the wider community of Palestinian Jews, but rather of a radical sect that in the first century had numbered, according to both Philo and

Josephus, only about four thousand members scattered through-out Palestine.[14] At first the theory had been simply that the seven scrolls discovered in 1947 belonged to those members of the sect who, according to Pliny, lived in a settlement near the Dead Sea above En Gedi. Then, as new scroll discoveries ensued during the early fifties, scholars working on them enriched the theory: Not only had the original seven scrolls been written by the Essenes, but all (or virtually all) those discovered after 1947 belonged to the same sect. In the words of Dupont-Sommer, the Essene sect was "representative of one of the most lofty and fruitful mystical movements of the ancient world, . . . one of the glories of ancient Judaism . . . [whose members,] more than any other Jewish move-ment, were privileged to prepare the way for the institution of Christianity."[15] What is more, he declared, the discovered Essenic scrolls were themselves "only a remnant of an immense corpus of literature, now largely lost." And similarly, Frank Cross asserted that the Essenes "prove to be the bearers, and in no small part the producers, of the apocalyptic tradition of Judaism."[16]

Through much similar scholarly speculation, the Essenes became the heroes of Jewish antiquity, extolled by 1960 in scores of books and hundreds of articles for pristine virtues that were said to have directly influenced the earliest Christians. And in this scheme, virtually all Palestinian Jews of intertestamental times were relegated for practical purposes to a position beyond the horizon of historical discourse. The necessary implication of the Qumran-Essene theory was that while several hundred works of the four-thousand-strong Essene movement had escaped destruc-tion, virtually no shred of manuscript stemming from the first-century A.D. population of Judaea as a whole—numbering at least two million individuals at the beginning of the First Revolt—had been spared.

To be sure, some examples of the chance survival of special manuscript collections are known. However, both their nature and the conclusions scholars have drawn about them simply underscore the quandary in which Qumranologists wrapped themselves by continuing to champion the idea of an organic interconnection between the scrolls and the Qumran site.

The private collection, for example, of over eighteen hundred Greek and Latin Epicuraean literary works in the possession of a wealthy Herculanaeum family was fortuitously saved from destruction when Vesuvius erupted in A.D. 79; in the eighteenth century, it was discovered under volcanic ash in the very library room in which it had been kept. Since the library collection was found within a room of a private villa, it was reasonably inferred that the inhabitants of the villa possessed it. (The conjecture has been hazarded that the family of Julius Caesar's father-in-law, Lucius Calpernius Piso Caesonius, owned the villa, but since no inscriptional or other documentary material has ever confirmed this suggestion, it remains no more than speculation.)[17] A collection of thirteen gnostic Christian Coptic books in codex form was discovered in a jar near Nag Hammadi (Chenoboskia) in upper Egypt late in 1945, but only the chance finding of some documentary fragments in the binding of one of these codices proved that the texts had once belonged to one or more inhabitants of Chenoboskia or of the surrounding region.[18] On the island of Elephantine, also in upper Egypt, Aramaic records of the Judaean military colony established there in the sixth and fifth centuries B.C. came to light in 1906; as these were largely autograph texts, including letters and legal documents containing precise geographic information, the fact that they were written on Elephantine was demonstrable, allowing a relatively secure historical reconstruction based on their contents.[19]

Lacking special circumstances of discovery or identification, however, such specific findings are not possible; the many thousands of Greek papyrus fragments discovered in Egypt, for instance, could not be related with certainty to specific places in that country (those documentary texts containing place-names excepted). Of the literary papyri, it could only be stated that they had apparently once been read in the general region where they were found, not that they had necessarily, or even most likely, been composed there. The Cairo Genizah texts represented still another type of manuscript history: thousands of literary and documentary texts from many lands, crammed into the attic of the Palestinian synagogue of Fustat (Old Cairo) because they were considered worn out or otherwise no longer valid or useful.* Only where there were specific documentary indications in the texts, or

---

*Many Qumranologists, revealing an unfortunate lack of familiarity with the subject, erroneously speak of this synagogue as a *Karaite* one. The Karaites and Babylonian Jews also had synagogues in mediaeval Fustat, but the Genizah manuscripts derive from the attic of the synagogue of the Palestinians.

where the handwritings were traceable to particular residents of the city, could it be said with any degree of assurance that the manuscripts had originated in Fustat itself. Their having been found in the attic of a Fustat synagogue provided no presumptive warrant of that sort, and of course (as in the case of the proselyte bearing a letter from France) it could be determined by documentary evidence that many of the texts came from elsewhere.

In any case, scholars who had participated in formulating the Qumran-Essene hypothesis were opting for still another paradigm, claiming—despite the absence of any manuscripts, documentary or otherwise, in the ruins of Khirbet Qumran itself—that its inhabitants had written, copied, and possessed scrolls, which, in addition, they later hid at a time of danger. My own somewhat painful awakening to the hollowness of this paradigm came at a time when my investigation of the Genizah papers had given me an increasing appreciation of the role of manuscripts in the reconstruction of the history of the Jews. I had come to perceive the complexity and vast dimensions of that history as it was preserved, in however tattered a state, not in printed books but in handwritten sources. *Published* histories were based only on a small fraction of the texts that had become available with the discovery of the Cairo Genizah. These records were in effect opening up new horizons for research—whereas the more than eight hundred Qumran scrolls known to exist in the mid-1960s had, by contrast, been kept separate from the broad parameters of Jewish history. Instead, they were being interpreted in such a way as to contribute only to the narrow construction of an Essene narrative.

Having no early access to photographs of the unpublished scrolls, my original assessment of the Qumran manuscript configuration was necessarily based on descriptions of the finds by members of the official team of editors. In 1982, however, tiny fragments of what appear to be four or five documentary texts from the caves were published. Thereafter, small portions of fifteen documents were included among the photographs of the unpublished texts that appeared in 1991 (see Chapter 7). These latter texts, as well as they could be understood by 1994, appear to consist of accounts of grain sales, lists of witnesses, and deeds of purchase; there may also be an acknowledgment of debt from the reign of Herod (ruled 37–4 B.C.) and an act of ownership dating to the reign of Tiberius Caesar (ruled 14–37 A.D.). They reflect the private ownership of goods and property, a fact basically inconsistent with the principles of communal ownership laid down in the *Manual of Discipline*.* Thus, as of this book's writing, no evidence of communal, Essenic records, nor any genre of literary autographs such as might support the idea of creative writing activity at Khirbet Qumran, has come to light. Moreover, no geographic terminology has been found in any of the extant parchment and papyrus texts that might indicate a connection with places of habitation in the Judaean Wilderness.

In the 1960s, however, it was still possible to believe—despite the problems revealed by a consideration of the manuscripts—that the weight of the evidence required continued support of the Qumran-Essene hypothesis. Participants in the team under de Vaux's direction were familiar with the contents of many of the scrolls, still unpublished in the mid-sixties; they might have discovered material within those texts to support their favored hypothesis in significant ways. They and others had often been privileged to visit Khirbet Qumran and study at close hand the archaeological and architectural remains that had so moved Père de Vaux. Perhaps they had found decisive inscriptional or pottery evidence, for example, that in some way demonstrated a unique organic connection between the site and the nearby caves. The bedouin might have furnished them with still other evidence, unknown to outsiders, that had somehow resolved the manuscript anomalies and proved the correctness of their interpretation. At all events, despite the acclaim and consensus that had emerged in its support, a careful probe of the fundamental reasons for its endorsement was clearly called for and had to be undertaken, without reliance on conclusions reached under color of the theory itself.

I resolved to do this independently of any team or group effort, and, as a first step, in spring of 1968 urged Robert Adams, then the director of the Oriental Institute, to invite Père de Vaux to give a lecture on his findings. He accepted, and on the day of his arrival I went to the airport to meet him and bring him to the university. He of course was easily recognizable from photographs of

*For the likely source of these documentary fragments, see below, pages 147–148 For the minuscule published fragments that may be documentary, see M. Baillet, *Qumran Grotte 4, III (4Q482–4Q520)*, Discoveries in the Judaean Desert VII (Oxford, 1982), nos. 515–520, pp. 299–312.

the Jerusalem team and Edmund Wilson's piquant description published earlier. Wilson, to be sure, had described not only de Vaux's striking physical features,* but also traits of his personality and character, speaking of his "intellect, expertness, fortitude, tenacity, an element of daring and—what now seems so rare in France—effectiveness."[20] Wilson had become entirely won over to de Vaux's interpretation of Qumran origins, writing with unquestioning certitude of the Khirbet Qumran complex as a "monastery," of the room we have mentioned as a "scriptorium," and of the scrolls as Essenic documents produced there. His view of de Vaux as a brilliant and somewhat dashing figure was by then shared by most scholars, who were fully convinced of the truth of his arguments. C. T. Fritsch, a professor at Princeton Theological Seminary, had believingly written in 1956:

> It was my privilege to visit Qumran several times during this period [of excavations in 1953 and 1954] and to be conducted around the excavations by Père de Vaux himself. So vivid was his description that I could almost see the members of the community eating together in the large dining room, or copying manuscripts in the scriptorium, or scurrying to the caves with their precious library as the Roman Tenth Legion marched down from Jericho to destroy the community.[21]

By the time of de Vaux's visit to Chicago, the 1967 war between Israel and the surrounding Arab countries had taken place, and the barriers between the two parts of Jerusalem had fallen. In the weeks that followed, Jews surged *en masse* into the market streets of the Old City, and Arabs from East Jerusalem gained a first-hand view of the other side: a period of euphoria for some, but for the custodians of the Rockefeller Museum and others a difficult time. De Vaux, Pierre Benoit, and other Dominicans of the Ecole Biblique found themselves facing a new reality: the museum and

---

*"He has brown eyes of the high powered headlight kind that seem magnified by his glasses' thick lenses, and long white regular teeth that are always displayed in talking. His sharp nose is of a salience and aquilinity that strongly suggests the Old Testament, as does his coarse bristling brown beard. With his belted white-flannel Dominican robe, the hood of which falls back on his shoulders, and at the belt of which hang his beads, he wears a beret, heavy shoes and what look like substantial blue golf stockings. He tells stories extremely well, continuously smokes cigarettes and altogether has style, even dash." (E. Wilson, *The Dead Sea Scrolls*, pp. 46–47.)

the scroll treasures in its vaults were now under control of the Israel Department of Antiquities rather than the old cadre of Jerusalem Arab officials with whom they had cultivated such a close relationship in the past.

Just before or during the hostilities, the scrolls had been packed in crates for shipment to Amman, but in the heat of battle the trucks sent to haul them off had failed to arrive at the muse-um in advance of its being entered and secured by Israeli troops. The Israeli authorities nevertheless implemented a *modus vivendi*, leaving de Vaux's authority intact and the original team's jurisdiction over publication of the scrolls unaffected. Yet de Vaux was bitter over the reunification of the city and the obliga-tion now thrust upon him to deal with the Israeli officials, and he expressed his feelings about the matter with little restraint on the way from the airport to the institute. A considerable crowd had gathered at Breasted Hall for his lecture, in which he reviewed the Qumran discoveries along the lines set forth in his published reports, emphasizing as well—always in remarkably cultured English—the broad scholarly consensus that they had generated. During the ensuing discussion, I expressed some tentative reser-vations about aspects of the prevailing hypothesis, pointing out the lack of documentary support for it and other problems that had emerged.

One was the fact that, by 1968, published Qumran texts includ-ed many that were non-Essenic, and some that could even be termed anti-Essenic. One editor, for example, in describing a scroll that contained apocryphal psalms, explained that its author "was adept at writing classical Hebrew. But through that medium he reflected Hellenistic ideas. . . . We must manifestly acquaint ourselves with a hellenized Jew of the Palestine area. *It is highly doubtful, however, that the Qumran community, in its fight against the hellenism of the Jerusalem priesthood, would have knowingly permitted distinctively Hellenistic ideas to shape its essential theol-ogy. . . .*" The acknowledgment of Hellenistic elements in these texts was, of course, in direct conflict with the standard theory of Qumran origins, provoking hesitation on the text editor's part in his attempt to resolve the problem: *"no suggestion should be made on the basis of the supposed imagery . . . , that any facet of Orphism was consciously subscribed to by the writer of the poem or by his readers: discussions of live and dead symbolism are not provoked."*[22] From this wording, however enigmatic, it was clear that the author acknowledged that this scroll contained ideas not in harmony with Essenism.

I mentioned this and a few other problems in my remarks, suggesting that it might perhaps be better, in view of what seemed to be certain emerging anomalies, to reexamine the entire theory, taking account of the growing number of texts and other recent evidence. Père de Vaux was quite visibly upset by my remarks. He said a few words about the problems I had raised but then, turning to the audience, stated with vigorous conviction, "If you go to the Dead Sea, stand looking at that plateau, and then study the excavation structure by structure, *you will know* that this is the very site of the Essenes described by Pliny nineteen hundred years ago."

De Vaux's pronouncement—"you will know . . ."—struck me as more a declaration of faith than a statement of science. At that point I determined to make a study of Khirbet Qumran as soon as possible. As we have seen, the site offered no support whatever for de Vaux's theory, but rather numerous counterindications to it. A very well built group of structures was once situated there, directly contradicting the original claim of de Vaux, Lankester Harding, Edmund Wilson, and others that the buildings were crudely made.[23] The site, firmly planted in the desert and dominating the coast, was strategically located on a promontory whose military value was obvious. If one examined the archaeological and topographical evidence without making efforts to harmonize it with the contents of the cave manuscripts, it could be seen to conflict directly with de Vaux's overall interpretation. While the authority of Sukenik, de Vaux, Dupont-Sommer, Yadin, and all their many colleagues loomed large, there was in fact no proof of a "scriptorium" at Khirbet Qumran, nor the slightest indication that literary manuscripts had ever been composed, copied, or kept there. De Vaux's theory appeared to be nothing more than the product of its time, when Essenic fever swept through the ranks of scholars.

CHAPTER 3

1947: The First
Scroll Discoveries

By 1970 I could encounter virtually no scholar who did not firmly believe that a Jewish sect had inhabited Khirbet Qumran in antiquity. The belief was held almost universally.

One of the exceptions to this rule consisted in the claim of a few writers that the scrolls had been written not in the period of Hasmonaean rule and Roman domination but in the Middle Ages*—a view in direct conflict with the scribal characteristics of the scrolls. The scroll handwritings often resembled those known from Palestinian Jewish inscriptions of intertestamental times, while ancient Greek biblical fragments, as well as a significant number written in the old, so-called Canaanite or palaeo-Hebrew script, had also been found in the caves along with the other scrolls (see Fig. 10). The jars found in some of the caves at the same stratigraphic level as the scrolls were themselves from the period of Roman domination. These facts proved quite effectively that the scrolls had to be ancient rather than medieval texts.

Another significant factor that played a role in showing this to be the case was the scrolls' literary character, revealing many features known from the Apocrypha and Pseudepigrapha. These were writings of Jewish authors, composed approximately between 150 B.C. and A.D. 100, that are included in manuscripts of the Septuagint (i.e., the Greek translation of scripture promulgated by the Jews of Alexandria)—but which were never recog-

---

*See especially the articles of Solomon Zeitlin of the Dropsie College relating to this subject that appeared in the *Jewish Quarterly Review* during the 1950s. This view was notably supported by Sidney Hoenig of Yeshiva University in published articles, and by Ellis Rivkin of the Hebrew Union College in his lectures to the rabbinical students there. On those few writers who recognized the antiquity of the scrolls but did not assent to the Qumran-sectarian theory, see the discussion in ensuing chapters.

nized as canonical, or holy, by rabbinical Judaism.* The Hebrew and Greek originals of these writings are mostly lost; their content, however, shows a fascination with apocalyptic speculation and mystery and with imaginative reworking of biblical narrative—features highly characteristic as well of the Qumran scrolls. These characteristics of the scrolls, so untypical of the literature of the mediaeval Jews, became known during the 1950s and 1960s, and the theory of mediaeval origin was eventually seen to be unfounded.

As is the case with all literature remote from our own time, the seven scrolls discovered in 1947 bristle with interpretational difficulties, compounded by the far less than perfect state of their preservation. Among them,[1] and holding pride of place in the configuration of discoveries almost from the day of its inspection by Eliezer Sukenik, was the *Manual of Discipline*. Containing descriptions of a considerable number of practices and beliefs otherwise associated with the Essenes, it was the chief cause for the scholarly embrace of nearby Khirbet Qumran as a motherhouse of the sect: The *Manual*, it seemed, proved the authenticity of Pliny's statement, and that he had been alluding to Khirbet Qumran when composing his description.

Even before the war between Jews and Arabs in 1948, Sukenik had managed to study a few of the scrolls that had made their way to the Syrian Metropolitan in Jerusalem, and to purchase three others that had been in the hands of an antiquities dealer. These three—one of the two Isaiah scrolls, the *Hodayot*, and the *War Scroll*—offered no definite clues to authorship. However, when Sukenik examined one of the four scrolls in the Metropolitan's possession, he felt that he had discovered just such evidence. "I found in one [of the scrolls]," he later wrote, "a kind of book of regulations for the conduct of members of a brotherhood or sect. I incline to hypothesize," he continued, "that this cache of manuscripts belonged originally to the sect of the Essenes, for, as is known from different literary sources, the place of settlement of this sectarian group was on the western side of

---

    *"Apocrypha" (from Greek *apokryphos*, "hidden") is the general term for this class of writings, while "Pseudepigrapha" refers to those works of the Apocrypha that were characteristically written under a false name or attributed to biblical figures. "Apocalyptic" writings of the Apocrypha are those that mainly feature afterlife or otherworldly speculation. See Glossary.

the Dead Sea, in the vicinity of En Gedi." By the "book of regulations," Sukenik was clearly referring to the work later designated
as the *Manual of Discipline*, which has since then dominated all
discussion on the origins of the scrolls.[2]

There is good reason why this should have been so at the beginning, for it is a most unusual composition—with one exception
completely unlike any other example of Jewish intertestamental
literature known before 1948. Only in 1970—that is, after I had
begun reconsidering the evidence used to construct the Qumran-
Essene hypothesis—did it become clear to me that the central role
accorded the *Manual* was due to a flawed linkage of facts and
conjectures stemming from the accidental discovery of this text
considerably in advance of most of the other scrolls.

With publication of the eleven columns of the *Manual* in 1951,
readers found themselves immersed in a strange sea of initiation
rites, curses, blessings, and regulations. The scroll could be analyzed as having three main sections. In the first, the initiants into
the described fellowship, known in Hebrew as the *Serekh hayahad*
("Order of the Unity"), were to enter voluntarily, bringing all their
"knowledge, strength, and wealth" into the "Unity of the Lord,"
and agreeing not to veer from observance of any of the Lord's
decreed laws.* All who entered this Unity were to "pass before
God," and promise not to forsake Him, even under the most dire
circumstances "during the reign of Belial" (i.e., the satanic per-
sonification of evil). The Aaronic priests who gathered together
under these conditions for the ceremony of initiation were to
recite the Lord's righteous and merciful deeds, the Levites were to
render account of the Israelites' past sins, and thereupon the initiants were to confess their own sins as well. The priests were
then to bless all those in the Lord's "lot," the Levites to curse
those in the "lot" of Belial, both groups then joining to curse those
initiants who were insincere, always using explicit formulas
spelled out in the text. This procedure was to be followed yearly
during the reign of Belial: The priests were to "pass first in order"
(or "into the order") according to their spiritual excellence, then
the Levites, and finally "all the people" by "thousands, hundreds,
and tens."

This last statement in particular (column **2**, lines 21–22) shows

---

*In this and all following passages from the *Manual* and the other scrolls,
the translations are mine.

the visionary nature of the first section of the *Manual*. The author
had in mind a well-ordered ritual of initiation into a new kind of
Israelite society that would take the place of the old, with its
acquiescence in royal privilege and the supremacy of the priestly
sacrificial cult. Not merely some individuals, but the entire nation
in its thousands would participate, with the priests and Levites—
newly reformed through their solemn undertaking to perform the
Lord's will—taking leading roles in ceremonies meant in effect to
inaugurate a new covenant, based on spiritual and moral principles. In this utopian society, each person would have his rank and
"know his place" everlastingly; all would live in a "unity of truth
and humility of goodness," with constant "fondness for lovingkindness and thinking upon righteousness."

In such a society, there would be no room for anyone refusing
to go along with the new principles of moral and spiritual conduct. Such recalcitrants would not benefit from mere outward
acts of atonement or baptismal purification: Only through sincere
inner acts, through a spirit of "holiness for uniting in His truth"
and of "righteousness and humility" toward the Lord's statutes,
could they cleanse themselves of sin, to then "be accepted through
sweet-smelling atonements before the Lord" and become part of
the eternal "covenant of unity."

The author thus concludes his vision of a new society, and we
may perceive in his words an overriding dissatisfaction with the
actual Jewish order of his time, and a bitterness toward it. No one
who has studied Josephus's account of the convolutions of the
Hasmonaean state, with its eventual factionalism, intrigues, mur-
ders, spiritual debasement, and corruption of the priesthood—
evils that continued unabated into the period of Roman
domination after Pompey's capture of Jerusalem in 63 B.C.—can
doubt the sincerity of whoever penned these lines. He and his followers were here laying down the broad outlines of what they
hoped would be a new kind of Jewish society, where wealth might
be shared for the common good and deep moral and spiritual
meanings imposed upon the ancient Pentateuchal statutes.

But the treatise is then abruptly interrupted by a new section,
characterized by severe ethical predestinarianism. We are introduced at the outset (column **3**, line 13) to the figure of an "instructor" (Hebrew *maskil*) whose task is to teach all "sons of light"
about the true natures of men. The "all-knowing Lord," we learn,
is responsible for everything that is and was: He has preordained

the destinies of all living creatures, and their ultimate actions and fate cannot be changed. But in creating mankind, he put two spirits—one of truth and the other of perversion—in its charge: Truth has its source in a "dwelling place of light," while wickedness derives from a "source of darkness"; the "chieftain of lights" has dominion over all the sons of righteousness, while the "angel of darkness" rules over the "sons of perversion," each group walking, respectively, in the paths of light and darkness.

Any fault or sin committed by sons of righteousness, the author explains, is attributable to the angel of darkness, for reasons that are secret except to the Lord until the age of His own complete dominion dawns. If in the author's own time the righteous suffer, it is due to this same influence of the angel of darkness. Nonetheless, although having Himself created these two opposing angelic spirits, "the Lord of Israel and the angel of His truth aid all sons of light"—the Lord loving the one spirit and hating the other. Those of humble mien, we are told, thereby possess all desirable moral and spiritual virtues—slowness to anger, mercifulness, understanding, supportive belief in the Lord's deeds and His benevolence, zeal for righteous laws, acts of lovingkindness toward all the "sons of truth," and revulsion at all ritual impurity. The reward of these righteous ones will be not apocalyptic battles, but "peace throughout length of days, and fruitfulness of progeny [Hebrew zera', literally "seed"] as well as eternal blessings and everlasting bliss in life eternal and a diadem of glory together with (full) measure of glory in never-ending light."

The wicked, of course, possess starkly opposing qualities and in the end will suffer torture and damnation, the unremitting enmity between truth and perversion continuing until that "final season" when the Lord, in the mystery of His ways, will put a stop to all perverse wickedness. At that time, by means of "His truth," He will purify men of their perverse ways, sprinkling upon each person a "spirit of holiness" as one sprinkles water on those who are impure, "so that righteous ones might be made to learn the knowledge of the upper reaches, and those perfect in their ways be instructed in the wisdom of the sons of heaven."

What the author clearly intended with this description was to account for the existence of evil in a world claimed to be dominated by a benevolent and righteous Lord—such as the Pentateuch and prophetic writings described. The effort is manifest in the postulation of two angelic beings divinely created for respective dominion over mankind's good and evil actions, their rule an ironclad one, rendering it impossible for individuals to change their moral ways for better or worse—except insofar as such changes are preordained by the two angelic forces. At the same time, while the reason for the presence of an evil-producing angel of darkness remains an ineffable mystery of God's ways, the dominion of the two heavenly deputies will only continue until a final age of bliss, when the Lord will emerge supreme and banish all evil. Only He grasps the reason for this order of things, and it is fruitless for man to inquire into the reasons for his fate. Mankind's condition is at all events temporary, and those under dominion of the angel of light will ultimately secure eternal life. A profound gap in thinking thus emerges between this and the earlier portion of the text, which encouraged the voluntary commitment of Israel to a new order in time to come, without ever referring to angels of light and darkness ruling over mankind.

In a third section of the *Manual* (beginning with column 5, line 1), yet another concept is at play, bearing no relation to the preceding one and only a tenuous connection with the first. The author now describes an "order" to be followed by the "men of the unity who volunteer to turn back from all evil and grasp everything that he has commanded": They are meant to separate themselves from their perverse counterparts and enter into "a unity of Torah and wealth"—to walk humbly, and "circumcise in unity the foreskin of evil inclination and stubbornness."

Whoever comes into the Council of the Unity, we learn, has to enter the Lord's covenant in the presence of all the volunteers, promising to return to the Torah of Moses wholeheartedly. The latter are not, however, to touch "the purity of the men of holiness," since they can "only become pure if they first turn back from their wickedness." These volunteers can have nothing to do with evildoers: They are not to discuss matters of Torah with them, nor eat or drink anything of theirs, and must not accept gifts from them but only acquire their goods by purchase. After being examined for their moral and intellectual virtues, the volunteers are to be enrolled and ranked according to degrees of excellence, each one then being obliged to obey his superiors in rank; his "spirit and deeds" are to be examined year by year, appropriate changes then being made in the ranking.

The volunteers are to eat and offer blessings together. In every place where at least ten members of the council are found, "a man who expounds Torah day and night" is to be constantly present, along with a priest—the members sitting before him in proper order; it is he who should "initially send forth his hand to be blessed by the first of the bread or new wine." And one third of the nights of the year, the "masters" (in Hebrew, *rabbim*) are diligently and in unity to "read in the book, expound judgment, and utter blessings."*

The author then expounds on a special procedure for periodic meetings of these *rabbim*. The priests are to sit in the first position, "elders" second, and all others in their designated places, in this way seeking judgment and counsel. No one may speak out of turn or interrupt a colleague, or say anything not desired by the masters. At their head is an officer (*paqid*) whose chief duty is to look after the intellect and deeds of "everyone from Israel volunteering to join the Council of the Unity." The promising candidate is first brought into the covenant and instructed in all the laws of the Unity. Afterward he is ushered in to stand before the masters, who test him. If deemed successful, however, he does not have immediate access to either the "purity" of the masters or their funds, but rather is tested for another complete year.† If again deemed successful, he now hands over his personal funds to the foreman (*mebaqqer*) of the *rabbim*, but is still not allowed to associate with them or share their drink for another year. Finally, fully accepted among his brethren on the Council "for Torah, judgment and purity," his personal funds are joined to those of the collective.

This portion of the text then turns to punishments for infractions of the rules: measures such as being separated from the "purity" or "drink" of the masters for certain periods, being denied portions of allotted bread, or expulsion. Among the wrongful acts listed are lying about one's personal funds or misusing the

---

*Until today, there is no absolute certainty about the meaning of the term *rabbim*, which may also be translated "[the] many." (The latter rendering is preferred by most translators of this text.) Similarly, the words that I have translated "*to be blessed* with the first of the bread or the new wine" are often translated "*to bless* the first of the bread, etc." (The underlying Hebrew expression is, however, distinctly in the passive voice.) The requirement to read "in unity" (*yahad*) may here connote reading in unison.

†The Hebrew term underlying "purity" is *tohorah*, which indicates not only "purity" in its abstract sense (= pureness) but also in the concrete sense of food and drink having the requisite *ritual* purity that renders them edible for those strictly following the priestly and Levitical laws laid down in the Pentateuch. Ritual purity of clothing is probably also implied, cf. below, pages 77–78.

community's, responding sullenly to requests or inquiries, using foul language while studying or praying, acting deceitfully, interrupting a fellow member's discourse, spitting or sleeping during sessions of the *rabbim*, exposing oneself in public, guffawing, drawing out the left hand to gesticulate, and gossiping. Even after ten years, we read, the members are to be accountable for their actions and can be expelled.

This third portion of the *Manual*, with its detailed rules, would thus appear to be an actual working document governing the daily life of a sectarian group; and indeed the fact that one of the described infractions is followed by a stipulation of a six-month penalty, with an *alternative* penance of one year written above it, appears to strengthen this view. However, the rules are followed by a concluding passage (column **9**, lines 3–6) that puts a different slant on the author's intentions: "*When these things happen in Israel*," he states, "according to all these regulations . . . *at that time* will the men of the Unity set aside a house of holiness for Aaron to be united [as] a holy of holies, and a house of Unity for [all] Israelites who walk in perfection." These lines, like the first treatise's portrayal of mass induction into the Unity, express a grand vision for future days. They show that the author's detailed plan, while aimed in his own time at a few men with spiritual stamina sufficient for lives of purity and Torah interpretation, was in effect meant to offer a paradigm of virtue for future Israelite society in its totality. That new society would have two main groups—the house of Aaron, forming a metaphorical "Holy of Holies" (after the secret tabernacle and Temple precinct of that name), and the house of Israel, constituting the main part of a morally and religiously perfect ecumene.

Throughout the first and third treatises, the use of spiritualizing metaphor is striking. The author (column **2**, lines 2–4) is uncomfortable with the literal sense of the famous Priestly Blessing (Num. **6**.24–26), which expresses the hope that the Lord might "shine His *face*" upon those being blessed; he thus changes the anthropomorphic passage to "may He *light up your heart with intellect of life*." The original blessing's ensuing words, "May the Lord *lift up his face* unto you," are changed to yield an entirely different meaning: "May the Lord lift up *the face of His lovingkindness* unto you," the face now being treated, in other words, as a metaphor defining an aspect of the Lord's perfect goodness in His capacity as supreme spiritual Being.

Notable metaphoric strategies are particularly prevalent in sections of the *Manual* mentioning animal sacrifice. In the future-looking epilogue of column **9**, for example, Israel's eventual acceptance *in toto* of the rules of the order is described as an "atonement for wickedness and wrongdoing . . . a voluntary (offering) . . . better than the flesh of (animal-) offerings and the fat-portions of sacrifices, (as) an offering [*terumah*] of lips for judgment, as the sweet-smelling incense of righteousness, (as) perfection of the (righteous) way akin to free-will afternoon (animal) sacrifice." The underlying idea is that the biblical descriptions of animal sacrifice in fact stand for something else—that is, for human "offerings" consisting of positive spiritual and moral actions—and this addresses a practice obviously troubling to many Jews of intertestamental times; it reflects a growing sentiment against animal sacrifice that harks back to Amos, Hosea, and Isaiah and can subsequently be traced quite widely throughout the Hellenistic world, among such figures as Zoroaster and the authors of the Testament of Levi and the gnostic *Poimandres*.

The *Manual* is a text of a highly spiritualizing quality, its emphasis centered on the deeper meaning of the Torah to be reached through study sessions held one night in three each year, in which the spiritual sense of holy writings was to be intensified. The author of this text believed that, as earlier ordained to Joshua (**1.8**), the words of the Law were never to be expunged from the mouths of the true Israel, who rather had to ponder them "day and night"—and to this end the *Manual* stipulates that an expounder perform his task constantly, wherever ten members of the Unity are available. Any locality is suitable for this spiritual act of Torah study to take place constantly, as long as the ten are present. Even the words of Isaiah (**40.3**), "A voice calls out in the wilderness, clear ye the way of the Lord," have, in consonance with this idea, a special meaning: "When all these become a Unity in Israel, they will be separated through these rules from the settlement of the men of wickedness, going to the wilderness to clear there the way of the Lord, as is written 'In the desert clear ye the way [of the Lord], make ye straight in the wilderness a path for our God'—*this is the expounding of the Torah* that [the Lord] commanded through Moses to do according to every revealed thing, season by season. . . ."

In this manner, the author of the *Manual* suggests that the deeper meaning of Isaiah's words about going into the wilderness has nothing to do with a literal intrusion into desert territories. Undoubtedly, some charismatic expounders of the prophetic truth had construed these words of Isaiah literally—as did John the Baptist several decades later. Here, however, they are treated as a veiled allusion to Torah study, the words of holy writ appearing as a wilderness of seemingly impenetrable ideas and command- ments, needing to be cleared of their outward, superficial mean- ing by deep and intensive study, so that, wherever a group of ten members of the Unity are living, the true way to the Lord can be discovered.

What kind of group, then, were the Unity-brethren described in these columns? It is clear that they held communal meals and meetings, engaged in Torah expounding, maintained a high degree of ritual purity, considered private wealth spiritually defil- ing, and looked forward to a time when their acts and views would be adopted by many more of their fellow Jews. They also had various overseers to handle decorum, infractions of rules, and the collective treasury, and priests played a specific part in the structure of their organization. They sat by rank at their com- munal gatherings, with the priests first, the "elders" next, and then ordinary members according to the degree of esteem each had achieved.

This is a basic description of the beliefs at play primarily in the third prose section of the manuscript. A fourth section of poetry follows, but casts no new light on these beliefs, or on the Unity group's organization. The first section of the *Manual* possibly was meant, originally, as an addition to the third, describing the elabo- rate initiation rituals to take effect eventually, as the Unity- brethren achieved their hope of becoming predominant in Jewish society. The third section—lacking reference to blessings of priests, curses of Levites, or thousands of initiants—on the other hand describes the actual forms of initiation and acceptance into the order as a much simpler process.

This brief description is not one that I would have offered in the early years of scroll discoveries, accepting as I did the dominant view on the "sect of Qumran" offered by the first researchers. The most influential single idea promulgated then was that the *Manual of Discipline* described the beliefs and practices of a sect actually living at Khirbet Qumran; and this in turn generated a conviction that all the other scrolls discovered in the caves of the Judaean Wilderness had belonged to the same sect. The archaeological conclusions were then directed, as it were physically, toward protecting this basic claim. The hollowness of three of the central arguments regarding the nature of the *Manual* was nevertheless quite apparent upon critical analysis:

1. There was, first of all, the claim that the *Manual* encouraged prospective and actual adherents to the Unity, or *Yahad*, to head for the wilderness—this migration in effect explaining the group's location on the Khirbet Qumran plateau: The presumed inhabitants had literally followed the injunction implicit in Isaiah's words (**40**.3) about a voice crying out in the wilderness to clear the "way of the Lord." "The retreat into the desert is no doubt meant to be taken here in its literal sense," asserted Dupont-Sommer; "it is the retreat of the Essenes to Qumran"—concluding, in line with this exegesis, that "in the solemn quietness of the bare and torrid desert it is possible to imagine the people . . . who led such a hard and exceedingly austere life there, the grave mature men depicted by Philo. . . ." Yet, though all leading Qumran scholars of Dupont-Sommer's time were convinced by this argument, there is nothing whatever in the words of the *Manual* to support it; while the author does indeed refer to the verse from Isaiah, he promptly, as noted above, explains it as a metaphor referring to the expounding (*midrash*) of the Torah. Neither in the *Manual* nor anywhere else in the Qumran texts is it proposed that sectarians literally leave their habitations in order to go to the desert, either to study or for any other purpose.

2. The early scroll scholars further suggested—especially in view of the abundant reservoirs and the isolation of the site—that the Qumran plateau was an ideal place to practice the special laws of purity that, so the *Manual* indicates, applied to all the priests and other full-fledged members of the Unity.* And yet this rather central notion, as we have seen in Chapter 1, was quite thoroughly vitiated by the discovery that the Qumran cemetery, claimed to belong to the selfsame sect, was located only thirty-five meters from the settlement's surrounding wall.

3. The most remarkable of the claims, harking back to Pliny, was that the *Manual* advocated, either directly or by implication, a state of celibacy on the part of its members. Yigael Yadin proposed this, for example, in 1962. Explaining that "the sect does

---

*Elsewhere in this book, the Hebrew term *Yahad* is often used to designate the Unity-brethren.

not oppose the marriage of its members," he added, without benefit of any text citations, that the *Manual* "indicates that within the
sect itself there were groups of members who refrained from marrying." In a similar fashion Frank M. Cross had earlier asserted
the existence of data suggesting that the Qumran "community" "at
least was largely celibate"—the only data cited being the adjacent
cemetery with its larger number of male than female skeletons.[3]

Now in addition to the fact that "fruitfulness of seed"—that is,
of semen and thus offspring—is specifically mentioned in the
Manual as a blessing of the virtuous believer (column **4**, line 7),
other passages in the work reinforce a sense of general nonceliba-
cy on the part of those adhering to its rules. The author, for example, looks forward to a time when all of Israelite society will be
dominated by the beliefs and practices of the Unity (column **9**)—a
destructive wish indeed if celibacy were one of its principles.
Somewhat more significantly, the text says nothing of members of
the Unity sharing sleeping quarters or spending all their time
together: They are to unite for Torah study one of every three
nights of the year, wherever a group of ten members can be
found, and hold group purity meals and consultative sessions
together—such self-imposed responsibilities mandating no exile to
a desert wilderness. In this light, it is crucial to note that while
the Unity-brethren of the *Manual* are reminiscent in many
respects of the Essenes as described by Philo and Josephus—
particularly of marrying Essenes—many of the two groups' common features are shared, in turn, with the Haburah (or "friendship") groups of early rabbinic times, described in texts of the
second century A.D.

These passages of early rabbinic literature reveal the continued
existence well beyond the destruction of the Second Temple of
groups of purity-loving brethren.* By the time of the rise of the
scholar-class to juridical hegemony toward the end of the first century A.D., they apparently no longer possessed the same broad
social ideals characterizing the authors of the *Manual*, but rather

---

*See *Mishnah*, Demai **2**.2, and particularly *Tosephta*, Demai **2**.2–22.
S. Lieberman was the first to call attention to some of the features of the
Haburah purity discipline, but he did not explicate most of them, nor show
their significance for the question of the claimed celibacy of the *Manual*. See
S. Lieberman, "The Discipline in the So-Called Dead Sea Manual of
Discipline," *Journal of Biblical Literature* **71** (1952), pp. 199–206.

maintained essential features of the older purity mystique in attenuated form. The members no longer called themselves "men of the Unity," but "Friends," *Haberim*, and the group to which observers in any one place belonged was not termed a *Yahad* or "Unity" but a *Haburah* group. They were concerned principally with observance of the purity ordinances, but also with the complex laws of tithing, which in itself shows an earlier priestly influence within the order. The described categories of purity in which they were interested were those of bread, wine, and clothing. The "purity" of these items consisted in a certifiable lack of contact with any impure thing or source of impurity as described in the Pentateuch—with the additional qualification that the food-purities contain no untithed products. Induction of new members took place in the presence of the entire *Haburah*, but the inductee could then personally induct any of his offspring or slaves who wished to join the order. As in the *Manual*, there were periods of probation before induction: one of thirty days each for "drink" (i.e., wine) and clothing according to the school of Hillel, and of thirty days for wine and twelve months for clothing according to the school of Shammai. But while one thus had to be taught appropriate behavior, immediate acceptance was nonetheless offered to those candidates known for "humble observance" of the Law.

The probation period, according to these early rabbinic texts, was evidently used both for members of the *Haburah* to instruct the candidates and for observation of their conduct, the focus being on whether they were capable of maintaining the ritual purity of the items in question. Great effort and skill were needed to do so, since, according to the laws of the Torah, impurity was acquired by one's merely touching what was ritually impure—e.g., a dead body, or one who was impure himself for having touched a corpse or through sexual contact—or being found in a dwelling that sheltered a corpse. There were different categories of membership in the early rabbinic purity-order: first of all, the category of the Friend per se and, below him, of the *Ne'eman*, or Trustee, whose discipline was not quite as severe; but also—apparently emerging in the course of a long development whose origins are lost—two groups among the Friends: the fully observant, and those who observed the mysterious category known as "Wings" but did not agree to fully observe the category of "Purities" itself (see Glossary). The various categories were apparently a necessary response, in the course of time, to the rigorous

and complex nature of the scriptural purity laws, whose observance could be mastered only with the greatest difficulty. Indeed,
even most scholars of the Law had to go through the process of
probation and induction; the only exception was that of a "sage
who presided over a house of study [*yeshibah*]," who not only did
not have to go through the induction ceremony but could himself
privately induct others. In explicating some of the surviving rules
of conduct of the Friends, the description of these purity-brethren
in the *Mishnah* and *Tosephta* not only mentions their children but
also *marriages*, which could be either to the daughters of com-
moners unrehearsed in the subtleties of the laws of purities, or
else to daughters of other Friends. One may particularly note that
the strict observances of the Friends did not in any way preclude
their living in their own homes, or taking wives and begetting
children.

Returning now to the case of the prerabbinic *Manual of
Discipline*, we may indeed appreciate why it was that, in 1948
and the years immediately thereafter, scholars enthusiastically
assented to the developing proposal that celibate Essenes living
nearby had written it. The judgments were formed and issued in
the first few years after its discovery. Critical analysis of Pliny's
statement regarding the Essenes had not yet been attempted, and
the theory that Khirbet Qumran was inhabited by Essenes was
posited after only one brief session of excavation there, before its
military features emerged with clarity and evidence was uncovered that showed a Roman garrison had occupied the site approximately in and after A.D. 70. The *Manual* itself, clearly the most
remarkable of the first seven scrolls discovered, bore palpable
similarities to practices and beliefs of the Essenes described by
the classical writers. The scholars engaged during 1950 in preparing the *Manual* for publication under the auspices of the
American Schools of Oriental Research were apparently not yet
keenly aware of the purity-groups described in early rabbinic literature and instead focused narrowly, always with the description
of Pliny in the background, on the points of connection between
the views in the *Manual* and those of the Essenes. The larger picture was not yet grasped, and, disregarding the ancient author's
description of the blessing of progeny to be attained by the virtuous initiants, they imagined the *Manual* to be composed by a
brotherhood that excluded women and that thus could be understood as conforming to the exigencies of Pliny's description.

Nothing in the *Manual*, however, actually implied a situation of celibacy on the part of those who followed its rule.

In retrospect, the early interpretation of the *Manual* represented an error of judgment made virtually before critical thinking about the problem had even a chance of occurring. If by superior hindsight the reasoning process of the first scholars engaged in formulation of the hypothesis is to be faulted, this is not only by dint of the singular identification of the *Manual* they proposed, but yet more because of what followed in the course of their investigations.

Six other scrolls had been brought by the bedouin out of the first Qumran cave. Two of these were the above-mentioned scrolls of the Book of Isaiah; the other four were previously unknown writings, like the *Manual*. One of the latter texts was the Aramaic romance popularly known as the *Genesis Apocryphon*, containing imaginative tales based on the lives of early figures in Genesis, particularly Lamech, Noah, and Abraham, who relate details of their lives in first-person narratives. This work has demonstrable affinities with elements of two famous intertestamental writings, Jubilees and Enoch, but there is nothing in its contents to suggest any relation to the *Manual*.

To varying degrees, however, the three other nonbiblical texts were perceived as having links (either direct or indirect) with the *Manual of Discipline*. Such links came to form the basis of an increasingly imaginative portrayal of the "Essenes of Qumran." One of these three texts, the *War Scroll*, depicts a giant battle to take place in an age to come, its apocalyptic tenor emerging at its very start. This warfare ritual is about

> the attack of the sons of light against the lot of the sons of darkness, the army of Belial, the troop of Edom, Moab and the Ammonites, the army of Philistia, the troops of the Kittim of Assur, and those allied with them who perpetrate wickedness against the covenant. The sons of Levi, Judah and Benjamin, the diaspora of the desert, shall fight against them, troop by troop, when the diaspora of the sons of light return from the desert of the nations to encamp in the desert of Jerusalem. (Column **1**, lines 1–7.)

The work portrays the weapons, banners, and garments of the warriors, and the words to be inscribed on much of the paraphernalia of war, in virtually endless variety and detail, along with intricate battle formations on the part of the thousands of warriors. The work's main purpose is to depict the mighty power of the Lord in granting ultimate victory to the sons of light in the course of highly mannered arrays and ceremonies, conducted while the priests and Levites in Jerusalem offer full-fledged animal sacrifices. The *War Scroll*, like the *Manual*, is not consistent in perspective: It appears to be made up of two or three sections containing more than one author's vision of the apocalyptic battle ceremonies. It is suggested in the main section of the text that warfare will take place over forty years, and encompass battles with most of the countries of the known world. Yet the battle formations seem always to stream out from the gates of Jerusalem, to where the warriors return after their forays. The *War Scroll* is one of the strangest apocalyptic texts yet discovered, remarkable both for its highly imaginative descriptions of the preparation, formation, and equipment of battle and for its superficial, indeed almost mechanical, religiosity. In these basic respects, its spirit is the very opposite of that of the *Manual of Discipline*.

And yet scholars studying this text in the 1950s did not hesitate to associate it with the very group whose practices and beliefs are reflected in the *Manual*. André Dupont-Sommer, for example, quickly identified the "sons of light" of this text with "the Essenes themselves," describing the work as "essentially a collection of military regulations" they would employ "at the end of time." He and many others felt free to make this connection because the expressions "sons of light" and "sons of darkness" appear in both the *Manual* and the *War Scroll*, along with such other terms as "Belial" and "the Lord's secrets" (an expression used to cope with events apparently revealing the absence of divine omnipotence). Neither the description by Philo and Josephus of the Essenes as entirely peaceful in their habits and beliefs, nor the *War Scroll*'s emphasis, directly contrary to that in the *Manual*, on the literal application of the sacrificial precepts, nor the failure of its authors to mention the virtue of Torah study, appear to have generated reflection as the Qumran-Essene identification of this text became ever more popular.

There are, to be sure, a few other parallels in usage and expression between the *War Scroll* and other literature found in the caves that must be mentioned. The "Prince of the entire Congregation"—upon whose shield is to be written his name, those of the twelve tribes and that of Aaron (*War Scroll*, column 5, lines 1–2)—reminds one of the "Prince of the entire Congregation" referred to in an interpolated passage of the *Damascus Covenant* (see below) as one who "when he arises will destroy all the sons of Seth" (folio **7**, 21–22). The "desert of the nations" is also mentioned in a fragment of a *pesher*, or commentary, to Isaiah, interestingly enough in the same breath as the "Prince of the Congregation."[4] How determinative can these few parallels be, however, with respect to the question of the intrinsic relationship of the War Scroll with these other texts? We do not know the extent of use of the expression "Prince of the entire Congregation" to designate a heroic or even messianic figure in apocalyptic Jewish thinking of the intertestamental period, or how popular was the conception of a future "desert of the nations"; nor do we yet clearly understand the methods and means by which authors in intertestamental Palestine borrowed from or were influenced by one another.

It is true that scholars often adduce literary parallels as a way of showing close organic affinities between different texts, but more frequently than not the affinities turn out to reflect nothing more than currents of thought and expressions that were widespread in a particular culture. The appealing Zoroastrian doctrine that light stood for goodness and darkness for evil had apparently already spread to Palestine before the age of the Qumran texts, and there is no reason to believe that it became the property there of any single sect, any more than such expressions as "Belial" and "the Lord's secrets" necessarily denote sectarian ideas. The large difference between the spiritual orientation of the *Manual* and that of the *War Scroll* constitutes a central stumbling block to the idea that their authors belonged to precisely the same religious movement.

However, the two remaining original scrolls—the *Hodayot* ("Thanksgiving Hymns") and the *Pesher Habakkuk* ("Exposition of the Book of Habakkuk")—contain elements that reminded scholars of the *Manual of Discipline* in ways that appeared more urgent and convincing. To understand why this is so, we must recall that, almost a half century before the scrolls were discovered, another manuscript had been found in the Cairo Genizah collection at Cambridge University Library that also stemmed from an ancient sectarian or separatist community of Palestinian Jews—a manuscript seen, after 1951, as having certain affinities with the *Manual*. First called *Fragments of a Zadokite Work* by its discoverer, Solomon Schechter, it has since become known as the

Damascus Covenant. The work—fragments of which would also be discovered in the early 1950s in Qumran Cave 4—contains references to unrecorded events in the history of the Palestinian Jews, and espouses, among its doctrines and religious practices, a considerable number that were quite unknown from other Jewish writings at the time of its discovery.

The Cambridge fragment begins with an exhortation to its readers to "hearken . . . and consider well the deeds of the Lord"; the author describes how the Lord had "saved a remnant of Israel" from destruction, and how, three hundred and ninety years after the start of the Babylonian Captivity, He began to work His redemptive powers upon these survivors. They were without a leader for twenty years, until the Lord finally sent them a "Teacher of Righteousness" to "lead them in the way of His heart." The writer interprets the prophetic reference to the "Star of thy Lord" (Amos 5.26) as signifying the "Expounder of the Law who came to Damascus," citing the promise given in the Torah that a *"star shall come forth out of Jacob"* (Num. 24.17). This "Expounder" —undoubtedly a historical personage—is clearly the Teacher of Righteousness himself, whose actual name is never given in the text, his sobriquet being taken from another prophetic verse: "It is time to *seek the Lord, until he come* and *teach righteousness* to you" (Hosea 10.12).*

Other passages in the manuscript make it evident that the separatist group described there had suffered greatly at the hands of its opponents, finally migrating with its leader northward from Palestine to "the land of Damascus." Here it established a "new covenant," evolving a code of law appropriate to its changed surroundings and sectarian orientation. The group allowed no form of polygamy nor marriage between uncle and niece, and no carrying of utensils even within one's home on the Sabbath—practices later recorded in the early rabbinic law as allowable. Their society was strict and Torah-centered, but many of the regulations appearing in the legal section of the manuscript (folios 9 ff.) parallel those of

---

*The underlying Hebrew word for "seek" is *darash*, which also means "to expound." The author evidently interpreted the words of Hosea as follows: "It is time to seek the meaning of the Lord's messages to His prophets until that person will arise who can truly teach righteousness in accordance with His ways." The actual subject of the clause from Hosea italicized above is unknown, but is construed by ancient Jewish and Christian exegetes as being the Messiah.

the rabbinic Jews, as described in early Tannaitic sources (i.e., the earliest corpus of rabbinic law, second century A.D.).[5]

Within a hierarchical framework of priests, judges, and communal officers, the Damascene Covenanters gave special prominence to the descendants of the high priest Zadok (tenth [?] century B.C.). Because mediaeval writers had described an ancient sect of "Zadokites" whose beliefs were in a few instances identical with those of the Covenanters, Schechter inferred that the Genizah text was a last surviving remnant of the writings of this sect. By the term "Zadokites," the mediaeval writers apparently meant the Sadducees; but, strangely enough, the "Zadokite" doctrines they described did not tally in most respects with those of the Sadducees as given in the ancient Hebrew and Greek sources. For this reason, Schechter did not feel justified in calling his newly found text a genuine remnant of the literature of the original Sadducees. Rather, he thought it might perhaps be the product of an offshoot of the sect—possibly the Dosithean schism mentioned by a variety of early authors; it might be classified as a "Zadokite" work, its origins lying in that turbulent period when both rabbinic Judaism and earliest Christianity had their births. Among the notable statements in the manuscript are several referring to overseers, and others to a writing of the group, termed the "Book of HGW" (pronounced *hagu* or *hago*: *Damascus Covenant*, folios **8**.2;**10**.6), which both those priests responsible for groups of ten members as well as all judges (whether priests, Levites, or Israelites) had to know well, along with the "Foundations of the Covenant" (Hebrew, *berith*). The legal section of the *Damascus Covenant* makes clear that members could possess their own property, and two alternative modes of living are sanctioned—those in cities and those in "encampments."

With the discovery and publication of the *Manual*, scholars perceived that certain lines of connection could be drawn between it and the *Damascus Covenant*: The figure of an overseer appears in both writings, and at several junctures the *Covenant* describes modes of group conduct and regulation resembling those stipulated in the *Manual*. The presumed linkage of the *Manual*'s system of discipline with the isolated Khirbet Qumran site was enough to encourage many writers to view the alternate "encampment" existence described in the *Covenant* as pointing precisely to such a settlement as Qumran. The roles of the priests also seemed similar in the two texts.

And then, as the *Pesher Habakkuk* and the liturgical *Hodayot* came to be scrutinized, parallels emerged between them and words or ideas in the *Damascus Covenant*. These connections, once made, had the effect of convincing scholars even further that all the manuscripts being discovered were doctrinally interconnected.

The *Pesher* on Habakkuk is more curious and historically more important than the *Hodayot*. It represents the attempt by an ancient writer to relate statements made in that prophetic work (one of the shortest in the Bible) to various events—either those that had transpired by the interpreter's own time, or others that he believed would soon, or some day, occur. The interpretations virtually never flow naturally from the words of Habakkuk themselves. Rather, they are forced from the wording of that dense biblical text by dint of the interpreter's own overriding concerns. In certain comments, he alludes somewhat darkly to specific past events and personalities: to those who were "traitorous against the new [covenant], who did not believe in the covenant of the Lord," who "disbelieved when they heard what would happen to the final generation from the mouth of the priest whom the Lord [appointed] to explain all the words of his servants the prophets." Yet in dealing with numerous adjacent verses, the commentator skips to the future, asserting, for example, that Habakkuk's words concerning the "bitter and swift Chaldaeans" (Hab. 1.6) are but a metaphor for the merciless *Kittim*.* The way he uses this expression throughout the commentary makes it quite likely that the allusion is to the Romans. These "Kittim" will conquer many nations and bring fear upon them.

As the interpretation unfolds, it becomes clear how, in the course of explaining the prophetic writing, the author's agenda in fact required shifting back and forth in time. For in ensuing historical passages, his focus is increasingly on a "Teacher of Righteousness" who once suffered at the hands of his enemies—and whose message consisted at least in part in the very interpretation of Habakkuk championed by the commentator.

Thus, explaining the words of the prophet, "Why do you look on, you traitors, and remain silent while a wicked man devours

---

*The term *Kittim* refers in the Hebrew Bible to a sea people (cf., e.g., Jeremiah 2.10), but their precise historical identification is disputed and remains unknown.

one who is more righteous than he?" (Hab. **1**.13), the interpreter indicates that

> this refers to the House of Absalom, and the people of their group who were silent regarding the rebuke against the Teacher of Righteousness, not aiding him against the Man of the Lie who despised the Torah in the midst of their entire congregation.

The events and personalities are not specifically identifiable, but clearly relate to the period of the Teacher's mission. The Man of the Lie is probably identical with the Wicked Priest, who is described in the *Pesher* (column **8**.8 ff.) as having gradually changed from an honest into a corrupt "ruler" over the Jews, one who illicitly enriched himself and rebelled against the Lord's statutes. Because this priest acted wickedly against the Lord's "chosen one," i.e., the Teacher, he was once entrapped and wounded by his enemies (*Pesher* **1**.9). On another occasion he pursued the Teacher "to the house of his exile" (**11**.4) on the Day of Atonement.

Because we have no independent knowledge or understanding today of the events related, the commentary at times seems like an effort to explain the obscure by the yet more obscure; but there can be little doubt that the author's meaning was clearly understood, through hints and allusions, by members of the circle to whom his message was addressed. In the time of the interpreter, the Wicked Priest was apparently still alive; because of the latter's perfidy, we read, he would someday be swallowed up by the "cup of the (Lord's) wrath" (**11**.12 ff.) and paid back in full for his wickedness against the "Poor" (Hebrew, *ebyonim*). The partly untranslatable passage, Habakkuk **2**.17, includes the phrases "The violence of Lebanon," the "spoil of beasts," the "blood of men," and "the violence of the land, of the city, and of all that dwell therein." The interpreter explains that the word "Lebanon" stands for the Council of the Unity—an expression identical with the one used several times in the *Manual*—and that the "beasts" of the same verse of Habakkuk stand for the "simple ones of Judah who perform the Torah" (column **12**, lines 1 ff.). "The Lord," asserts the interpreter, "will render destructive judgment (on that Wicked Priest) just as he plotted to destroy the Poor." The "city" stands, according to the interpreter, for Jerusalem, "where the Wicked Priest performed his abominations, defiling the sanctuary of the Lord," and the phrase "the violence of the land" refers to "the cities of Judah (where) he stole the wealth of the Poor." The doers of the Torah, we are informed, will ultimately be saved "by virtue of their toil and their belief in the Teacher of Righteousness" (**8**.1). While the final-generation priests of Jerusalem will gather lucre "from the booty of the nations," in the "end of days it will be given over to the Kittim" (**9**.4)—and "on the day of judgment the Lord will destroy all worshippers of graven images and the wicked from the earth" (**13**.2). The theme of righteousness of the poor and wickedness of those amassing lucre has resonances, as we have seen, with the *Manual of Discipline*.

So unusual are the commentator's interpretations that he feels obliged to justify them all by a startling theological gloss on the words of Habakkuk **2**.1, "The Lord said, 'Record (the) vision fully explained upon the tablets so that the reader can quickly run through it.'" He remarks (column **7**, top) that the Lord commanded Habakkuk "to write the coming events concerning the last generation, but did not inform him of the final end of that time." He then adds that the words "so that the reader can quickly run through it" refer to the "Teacher of Righteousness *to whom the Lord divulged all the secrets of the words of his servants the prophets*"— hence all the prognostications in the commentary concerning the future and the end of days, as well as the prophetic hints to past events.

In offering this rather forced explanation of Habakkuk's words, the commentator is obviously suggesting that he was either a disciple of the Teacher, a recipient of the latter's own writing on Habakkuk, or else the Teacher himself. It must be called to mind that many of the biblical prophets recount their revelatory experiences in the third person, just as Josephus, for example, later wrote about himself in that manner. The intermingling of two categories of spiritual testimony—one related to the past and the other to the future—within a single interpretational framework reads more cogently as the personal anguished experience of a charismatic leader rather than the work of a disciple, but it remains impossible to determine with finality who wrote this commentary.

Nevertheless, the *Pesher* is clearly concerned with the career and ideas of a historical personality known as the Teacher of Righteousness. Since such a Teacher likewise appears in the *Damascus Covenant* as a revered charismatic leader—whose role, to judge by various tenets expressed in that text, was also to oppose what was apparently a corrupt Jerusalem establishment and leadership—the inference was properly drawn that the two works reflect aspects of the same religious movement and refer to the identical founder and leader.

In addition, the *Pesher* and the *Covenant* share several similarities in wording and ideas with the *Manual of Discipline*, while both the *Pesher* and the *Manual* refer to a "Council of the Unity." Thus the inference was properly drawn that these three texts were in some way interrelated.

Nevertheless the description in the *Covenant* of the Teacher's migration with his followers to the "land of Damascus" was troubling: It clashed notably with the developing view that a single group was responsible for all of the writings being discovered in the caves and that this group, under the leadership of the Teacher described in the *Pesher Habakkuk*, had its home at Khirbet Qumran. According to this interpretation, Qumran was itself the Teacher's "house of exile," where he was attacked by the Wicked Priest, as described in column 11 of the *Pesher*.

Because of the mesmerizing power of the Qumran-Essene hypothesis, a solution had to be found that would incorporate the *Covenant*'s account of the Teacher's migration to Damascus. André Dupont-Sommer thus came forward with the suggestion that—despite the wording of the *Covenant* to the contrary (7.18–19)—the Teacher was put to death *before* the Covenanters' migration to Damascus, and that the Covenanters then returned to Judaea "and to Qumran in the desert of Judah in particular, the site of their original settlement."* The complexity of this explanation, as well as the lack of any textual support for it, motivated scholars to seek other explanations. Père de Vaux, continuously fixated upon the centrality of Qumran, proposed as a possibility that "only one part of the community" left Judaea for Damascus, and that this "schism would have arisen right at the origin of the community, even before it settled at Qumran"—another theory unwarranted by any statement in the *Covenant* or the related writ-

---

*See A. Dupont-Sommer, *Essene Writings from Qumran*, p. 119; the view is not supported by any passage in the *Covenant* and is contradicted by the author himself in his translation of the passage concerning the Teacher's migration to Damascus (p. 134).

ings. Others had been wrestling with the problem, and, unable to find a reasonable solution based upon the express wording of the manuscripts, proposed that the expression "Land of Damascus" in the *Covenant* did not literally mean what it said. Rather, this phrase was to be construed as a *metaphor* for Khirbet Qumran itself. The Covenanters had really migrated to Khirbet Qumran, not to Damascus. This explanation, it was felt, would leave intact the interpretation of Qumran as the motherhouse of the "sect of Qumran."

Thoroughly convinced of the Qumran origins of both the sect and the scrolls, scholars were generally relieved by this explanation, and accepted it gratefully while yet slightly hedging their assent. Referring to the originators of the theory, Père de Vaux stated that "one is tempted to agree with those authors...." Millar Burrows commented that he was "attracted to the view that what is meant by the migration to the land of Damascus is the movement of the group to Qumran itself." Frank Cross was yet more positive in his reaction, for straightforward reasons: he was

> increasingly inclined to those views which hold that the "land of Damascus" is the "revealed" name for the desert settlement of the Essenes. . . . The problems raised are formidable under any principle of interpretation, but they are insurmountable, I think, if "Damascus" is not taken as the desert retreat in the wilderness of Qumran.[6]

A singular impediment to this view of "Damascus" as a metaphor for Qumran is provided by the fact that the writer responsible for explanatory additions in the *Covenant* nowhere hinted that the term is to be understood metaphorically. On the contrary, he makes use of it precisely in those sentences serving as explanatory additions to passages that he believes require metaphorical explanations themselves. In the *Covenant* we read, for example, the following passage (**6**.2–5):

> The Lord remembered the covenant of the ancients, and raised from Aaron men of understanding, and from Israel men of wisdom. He made His law known to them, and they dug the well. "The well that princes dug, that the nobles of the people delved with the staff" (Num. **21**.18).— The "well" is the Torah, its "diggers" are the repen-

tant ones of Israel who left the Land of Judah and dwelt in the Land of Damascus.

Attempting to explain the metaphorical sense of the biblical expression "the well that princes dug," the interpreter who added the explanatory glosses to the Covenant here expounds the view that the "princes" stood for those devout followers of the Teacher of Righteousness who accompanied him from the land of Judaea to the land of Damascus, where they continued the true interpretation of the Torah under his tutelage. The writer gives no indication that the "Land of Damascus" is itself a metaphor for anything else, and the fact that he writes coordinately of the "Land of Judah" and the "Land of Damascus" as the two places of migration makes that possibility even more remote.

The gratuitous elements in Cross's formulation would eventually lead him to urge the abandonment of circumspection altogether in dealing with the problem of Qumran origins. In 1971 he proposed that

> The scholar who would "exercise caution" in identifying the sect of Qumran with the Essenes places himself in an astonishing position: He must suggest seriously that two major parties formed communalistic religious communities *in the same district of the Dead Sea* and lived together in effect for two centuries, holding similar bizarre views, performing similar or rather identical lustrations, ritual meals and ceremonies. He must suppose that one (the Essenes), carefully described by classical authors, disappeared without leaving building remains or even potsherds behind; the other (the inhabitants of Qumran), systematically ignored by the classical sources, left extensive ruins, and indeed a great library. *I prefer to be reckless* and flatly identify the men of Qumran with their perennial houseguests, the Essenes.[7]

Cross's basic error was in assuming that a communalistic religious community actually lived at Khirbet Qumran and that Pliny's Essenes had their home in the selfsame district of the Judaean Wilderness. As we have already seen, there is no warrant for either of these assumptions. We are thus obliged to ask whether, if we do not assent to them and the ensuing necessity of interpreting "Damascus" as a metaphor, and if we do not forsake prudence and adopt what Cross himself recognized as a reckless course of interpretation, the problem of mutual liaisons between these texts is indeed as insurmountable as he insisted.*

To this question one must respond quite firmly that whatever insurmountable difficulty was posited arose uniquely out of the Qumranologists' overriding belief in the theory of a sect inhabiting Qumran—not at all out of statements made in the texts themselves. Even in the 1960s or earlier, by analyzing the first texts found without recourse to the Qumran-sectarian hypothesis—and without seeking refuge in metaphorical explanations—readers could have had an entirely satisfactory understanding of the basic course of events they describe. The key to this understanding lay in resolutely putting out of mind any overriding notion of the scrolls' interrelationships and origins in favor of inductive analysis of their contents.

Thus it was appropriate to posit, on the basis of their wording—and not because they were found in the same cave or the same jar—that the *Pesher Habakkuk* and the *Manual of Discipline* were interrelated, for both mentioned a "Council of the Unity" as a basic institution. The *Damascus Covenant* and the *Pesher*, on the other hand, have in common a "Teacher of Righteousness" whom the writers of both texts adulate, and "a Man of the Lie" whom they hate. Both of these texts, as well as the *Manual*, are oppositional in nature: The *Pesher* speaks of the Jerusalem priesthood as defiled by graft and enticed by lucre, and this theme is echoed in the *Covenant*'s abhorrence of the "lucre of wickedness, defiled by the vow, the ban and lucre of the [Temple] sanctuary" (**6**.15). Both of these texts speak with compassion of the poor: The *Covenant* requires its followers to protect them (**6**.20), while the *Pesher* accuses the Wicked Priest of exploiting them and stealing their

---

*We observe that, in later years, Cross's student James VanderKam, now of Notre Dame University, would take up the banner raised by Cross, approvingly citing the above-quoted statement as a way to deal with the question of who occupied Khirbet Qumran in antiquity. See his article "The People of the Dead Sea Scrolls: Essenes or Sadducees?," in H. Shanks (ed.), *Understanding the Dead Sea Scrolls* (New York, 1992), pp. 50–62, cf. pp. 57–58. VanderKam makes the same error as does Cross in dogmatically postulating the presence of a sect at Qumran and thereupon setting up a choice as to which sect it may have been, an Essenic one or another. The preponderance of evidence shows that the espousal of such a choice of alternatives is itself due to the absence of caution, as in so many cases in humanistic and scientific learning where signals deeply believed to constitute true and valid evidence have proven in the end to be misleading.

earnings in "the cities of Judah" (column **12**). The *Manual* trans-
mutes these passionate views into a general abhorrence of wealth
as spiritually defiling.

These three texts thus effectively reflect stages in the development of an important protest movement in intertestamental
Judaism whose specific historical circumstances are still unclear.
The movement had, at all events, no demonstrable connection
with the Khirbet Qumran site, nor with any particular theater or
locus of military operations. The members may have lived
throughout Jewish Palestine (as did the Essenes, according to
Josephus), and a group, if not all, of them had at one time migrated to Damascus under the leadership of their revered Teacher.

We seem to be closest to the Teacher's own ideas in the *Pesher*'s
interpretations of the prophecies of Habakkuk, but elements of
the *Covenant* speak with the same voice: "Now listen, all those (of
you) who know righteousness, and understand the deeds of the
Lord." The "congregation of traitors . . . rendered the wicked just
and the righteous wicked." "The Lord who loves knowledge, wisdom and understanding has set cunning and knowledge at His
disposal—they serve Him well; slowness to anger is His, and
abundance of forgiveness so as to grant atonement to those turning back from wickedness" (**1**.19; **2**.3 ff.). These are the words we
would expect of a Teacher who preached "righteousness"—but the
words, if they were once his, are now imbedded in a work over-
laid with accretions and explanatory glosses, so that the text is
often not fully intelligible.

The clearest and most demonstrable set of interpretive breaks in
the *Covenant* is made up of those very passages attempting to
explain how certain scriptural verses foretold the migration to
Damascus; these do not belong to the Teacher himself but to one or
more of his followers. From pertinent hints and suggestions in
both the *Pesher* and the *Covenant*, it appears that the Teacher
began his oppositional career by preaching against the Jerusalem
establishment, whom he accused of deceit, graft, exploitation of
the poor, and failure to understand the true meaning of the
prophetic writings. As the *Pesher* indicates, he was eventually banished from the capital; in the end, as we learn from the *Covenant*,
he made his way to the Damascus region in the company of some
or all of his followers, who—either there or upon returning to
Judaea—gathered the Teacher's literary remains and enlarged
exegetically upon them. These followers, along with others, would

carry on the salient features of his teachings—abhorrence of priestly corruption, protection of the poor, and emphasis on the search for the true meaning of the Torah and prophets. These ideas were transformed into spiritual ideals within the framework of the concept of purity-holiness. The new conceptual structure was then developed and given literary life by a group of relatively sophisticated religious thinkers who eventually recorded their doctrines and practices in works such as the *Manual of Discipline*.

To judge by the few pertinent texts that have survived, the followers must have eventually branched off into several groups. One text that we have not yet looked at is the so-called *Rule of the Community*, or *Messianic Rule*, which archaeologists found in Cave 1 with many other Hebrew fragmentary works less than two years after the first discovery. Only two columns of this writing are extant—enough, however, to show the different direction taken by one such group. The scribe's handwriting seems to be the same as that of the copyist who transcribed the Cave 1 text of the *Manual*, and writers have theorized that the two extra columns once stood, physically speaking, as the opening part of that work. It begins with the avowal that "This is the rule for all the community of Israel at the end of days." Here the initiants specifically include women and children. From his youth each "member in Israel" is to study the "Book of HGW"—as also ordained in the *Covenant*—and to be increasingly inducted into the "statutes of the covenant" as he matures, for a period of ten years (**1**.7–8). The initiant is to have no sexual intercourse, nor to involve himself in legal matters, before the age of twenty. At twenty-five he may take his place "in the foundations of the community of holiness," fully participating in the community's responsibilities; and at thirty, he may become a full-fledged warrior, among those who will "stand at the heads of the thousands of Israel, as chieftains of hundreds, fifties, and tens, (as) judges and overseers for their tribes."

Prohibited from engaging in most of these activities are simpletons and anyone who is lame or blind, or with other physical impediments. So eschatological is the author's treatment that he provides for the birth and the presence of the "Messiah of Israel" in the midst of the envisioned community; the order of mealtime ceremonies is in fact to be held in his presence. As in the *Manual* and *Covenant*, the priests and Levites play a prominent role in the community, but no mention is made of purity practices, the collection of communal funds, or the spiritually defiling nature of wealth; and the role of study that figured so prominently in the third part of the *Manual* is reduced in the *Messianic Rule* to a relatively formal period of ten years.

The work represents, in sum, another evolving branch of the same movement—a branch whose leader had developed principles and ideals at variance with those in the other writings we have considered. The *War Scroll*, as we have seen earlier in this chapter, is yet more contingently related to the core *Yahad* texts than is the *Messianic Rule*. All of these writings together form significant elements in what was clearly a widespread pattern of religious and social thinking during the intertestamental period. Yet their actual contents have never warranted their relegation to any one locality in Jewish Palestine of that age. Without an overarching sectarian hypothesis to rescue them from critical analysis, and minus satisfactory internal evidence—i.e., probative statements within the texts themselves—indicating a connection, it could not be demonstrated that these scrolls were ever organically related to the Khirbet Qumran site. At the most they only encouraged scholars to *assume* a connection of this kind, but later discoveries would, in combination with the archaeological evidence, demonstrate that this assumption was untenable.

Despite latent interpretive problems, it remains the case that the seven Dead Sea Scrolls discovered in 1947 constituted a compact and manageable unit: There were enough affinities among these texts to permit seemingly reasonable generalizations about the corpus. The many new texts discovered in the following decades, however, offered solid ground for questioning this unitarian vision. As we have seen and shall observe below, Qumranologists failed to cope coherently with the problem posed by the new material, in the process neglecting a fundamentally different but potentially far stronger explanation of the scrolls' historical meaning. In the following two chapters, we will look at both the contents of more texts and at the nature of their traditional interpretation, before exploring the specific historical circumstances that surrounded the burial of the scrolls two thousand years ago in the Judaean Desert caves. Only afterward will the full implications of their discovery become apparent.*

*As this book was going to press, I received from Dr. G. Brooke of Manchester University the published form of a lecture given by him at a meeting of traditional Qumranologists in Paris in 1992. In this lecture, so I now learn, Brooke sought to contravene the understanding of the *Manual of Discipline*'s two "wilderness" passages as metaphors for the expounding of the Torah's deeper meaning (above, pp. 73–74). Instead, the author, through minute and even tortured analysis of the syntactical structures and interrelationships of those passages and others that contain metaphors, arrives not unexpectedly at the view that, at least in a certain sense, the passages were meant to be construed literally: Under certain conditions "it could be that the so-called 'Manifesto' in an early form did not envisage a move to the wilderness. In a second and subsequent stage such a move became part of the community strategy. . . . it may be possible to argue in relation to the actual move to the wilderness that it was not universally carried out within the group responsible for these texts." Brooke indicates that his analysis has been conducted "with more subtlety than Golb's overall appreciation allows," and concludes that the "community which redacted and passed on these texts had a literal and actual experience in the wilderness before which and during which the way was prepared metaphorically through the study of the law." (G. J. Brooke, "Isaiah 40:3 and the Wilderness Community," in G. J. Brooke with F. Garcia Martinez [eds.], *New Qumran Texts and Studies* [Leiden, 1994], pp. 117–131.)

This artful blending of two mutually opposing interpretations of the "wilderness" passages cannot, however, obscure the grave difficulty of Brooke's position. Although he "unashamedly" proposes that "the [*Manual of Discipline*] community . . . actually went to the wilderness" (ibid., p. 126), he carefully adds that this "of course [was] *not necessarily to Qumran*" (my italics). This puts an entirely new slant on Brooke's interpretation, opposing as it does the standard view of Qumranologists—including the very ones he heavily relies upon in his article for support of his literalist interpretation of the "wilderness" passages—to the effect that the imputed desert migration was to Qumran itself and nowhere else. The writers whom Brooke cites offer, as a corollary to their belief in a sectarian migration to Khirbet Qumran, unusually forced explanations to account for the absence, anywhere in the substantive disciplinary sections of the *Manual*, of a requirement to migrate to the desert. As we have seen (pp. 70–71), constant Torah-expounding was required "in every place" holding ten council members. While paying assiduously close attention to the syntax of the two "wilderness" passages, Brooke has overlooked almost entirely the social context of the *Manual*'s third (and main) section. Although there were groups and individuals in intertestamental Palestine who did literally exile themselves to the desert, those who adhered to the discipline of the *Manual of Discipline* may not, by the ordinary rules of evidence relating to historical phenomena, legitimately be included among them.

CHAPTER 4

The Qumran-Essene Theory: A Paradigm Reconsidered

The *Messianic Rule* was one of over seventy fragmentary manuscripts taken from Cave 1 alone. In late January 1949 an expedition discovered this cave after only a few days of searching on the escarpment lying just west of Khirbet Qumran, approximately one kilometer north of the site (designated 1Q on Map 4, page 106). Once explored and excavated, it was found to contain remnants of a large variety of Hebrew literary texts. Twelve of these were scriptural writings, including fragments of a scroll of Leviticus written in the Old Canaanite or palaeo-Hebrew script (see Fig. 10), attesting to their great age. Among the nonbiblical texts were fragments of commentaries on the biblical Micah, Zephaniah, and Psalms, in general similar to the *Pesher Habakkuk* found earlier. Fragments of writings of the Apocrypha were identified, including two of Jubilees and one of the Testament of Levi, along with pieces of previously unknown pseudepigraphical writings. Among the discoveries were new fragments of the *War Scroll* and the *Manual of Discipline*. There was a considerable variety of liturgical poetry lacking all evidence of sectarian orientation.[1]

The commentary fragments drew particular attention, because they seemed to stem from the same movement that included the author of the *Pesher Habakkuk*: a *pesher* on Micah preserved portions of words that could be taken to mean "Preacher of the Lie," "Teacher of Righteousness," and "Council of the Unity" (in a declining order of certainty), and contained the Divine Name YHWH (the so-called Tetragrammaton) in its palaeo-Hebrew form, as did the *Pesher Habakkuk*. The several words preserved from a *pesher* on Zephaniah, although containing no such key expressions, at all events did preserve the Tetragrammaton in its archaic form as well. Only a few words were left from a *pesher* on Psalms, appearing to offer no hint of its provenance. Other texts were rather more enigmatic in a collection the editors felt free to describe as being from "the library of the Essene Community."[2] For example, the previously unknown pseudepigraphs, only retrieved in small fragments, were furnished with titles by the editors such as *Book of Noah* or *Sayings of Moses*. What they had in common were imaginative expansions on biblical themes, such as the author of the *Genesis Apocryphon* had accomplished—but they contained no appeals to a "Unity" brotherhood or "Teacher of Righteousness," and no notable ideas resembling those of the *Manual* or the *Damascus Covenant*.

One work did make use of an unusual expression found in certain other Qumran texts: *"the secret of what will be."* This is in fact an entirely suitable expression for describing the unknown future of humankind, bearing no necessarily sectarian overtones. Although only a few columns of the work were (partially) preserved, enough could be deciphered to clearly indicate the growing diversity of the texts. The most trenchant lines were these:

> When the wellsprings of wickedness are closed off, when evil is banished by righteousness as darkness is banished before light, and as smoke ceases to be—then will evil forever end and righteousness be revealed as is the sun that holds fast the world. Then will all those who believe in the secrets of . . .* be no more. Knowledge shall fill the earth and perversion will cease. . . . The utterance is soon to come to be, truthful is the vision, and in this way you will know that it goes not back upon itself. Do not all nations hate wickedness—while yet it lurks among them all? Do not all peoples praise truth—yet is there a language or tongue that grasps onto it? What nation desires that another stronger than she oppress her? Who desires that an evil man should steal his money? —Yet what nation exists which has not oppressed another, and where is the people that has not stolen another's wealth?

Two themes intertwine in this remarkable passage: the eventual triumph of righteousness and knowledge (*de'ah*), and the present hypocrisy of nations. The author declares that evil will someday be banished by righteousness, just as light banishes darkness—but he shows no awareness of the *Manual's* theology of light and darkness. Once righteousness triumphs, the soothsayers who have spoken of the Lord's mysterious ways will no longer have a cause

*The word following "secrets of" is illegible.

to champion. Although the nations proclaim their pursuit of truth and righteousness in mock assent, this is only a shield hiding a lust for gain—no nation is truly virtuous. In the author's vision, no apocalyptic battles take place, and no charismatic prophets of truth appear to bring about a triumph of virtue. It is highly likely that in carrying forward this sober and expressive rumination, the author is urging an inner turnaround in the hearts of men to achieve the devoutly sought age of goodness.[3]

The text's message, expressed with great simplicity, is unlike any other preserved in the manuscripts of Cave 1; when read with the other anomalous texts then being discovered, its signaling of their doctrinal variety could have helped set the stage for reevaluating the problem of Qumran origins. However, when one scholar attempted to relate this work to the time of the Hasmonaean rulers, explaining it as a sermon addressed to them, his interpretation was summarily rejected by the official editor on the grounds that "it does not appear likely that the founders of the Hasmonaean dynasty were remembered very favorably by the Essenes."[4] From this response and others like it, we see that the Qumran-Essene hypothesis had become a fact in the minds of the editors, serving as a touchstone for the interpretation of the manuscripts—a procedure in disharmony with normal scholarly method and common sense.

In addition, virtually each new fragment brought out of Cave 1 yielded words or lines in a Hebrew script different from all the others, enabling scholars to count a *growing number of scribes* responsible for copying down the texts. Over fifty different handwritings were represented in this first Qumran cave alone—where, according to the notion of a sect living at Qumran and the corresponding identification of one building there as a scriptorium, one would have rather expected to find several *groups* of texts, each written by a much smaller number of scribes, and with a relatively large number of texts done by a single scribe. Such was the situation on the island of Elephantine, in upper Egypt, where, as we have already noted, Aramaic manuscripts of the fifth century B.C. were discovered many years ago. Michael Wise of the University of Chicago, an incisive interpreter of the Qumran texts and their cultural milieu, has pointed out that, by any reasonable estimate, the number of inhabitants at Elephantine was perhaps fifty times the estimated number of "sectarians" who have been claimed to live at Khirbet Qumran, and that nevertheless the

Elephantine inhabitants "relied upon only a dozen or so scribes. And this total served over a period of three or four generations." As Wise points out, only three or four scribes at the most could have been active there in a given generation.[5] Thus, the large variety of handwritings exhibited by the Qumran scrolls should alone have marked an opportunity for pause—at all events with the publication of these Cave 1 texts in 1955—to reconsider the wide acceptance of the dominant hypothesis. But scholars did not respond to this evidence either, and an opportunity was again missed to break the grasp of an increasingly tenacious idea.

With the exploration of the first Qumran cave completed, scientific exploration in the Judaean Wilderness temporarily stopped. The Ta'amireh bedouin, however, continued their clandestine digging, eventually finding the autograph manuscript fragments from the Bar Kokhba period in the Wadi Murabba'at gorge—as we have observed, a discovery whose bearing on the question of the actual physical nature of the Qumran texts was never publicly discussed, and which apparently made no impact on investigators bent on seeking the lost history of the Essenes of the Dead Sea shore. The subsequent period of archaeological activity was characterized by startling new manuscript finds in other caves not far from the Cave 1 site. In 1952, the bedouin returned to the Qumran area, and in February they found additional Hebrew manuscript fragments in a cave (subsequently named Cave 2) located less than two hundred meters to the south of the first cave. (See Map 4, site 2Q.) This second cave yielded some thirty small fragments, divided evenly between writings that are now considered part of the Hebrew Bible and very fragmentary non-biblical writings. Among the latter were bits of the apocryphal Jubilees and Ecclesiasticus (Ben Sira), three unidentifiable pseudepigraphs and a liturgical fragment, and a scrap of an Aramaic description of a future-day Jerusalem.

This last fragment opened up what would become a new genre of Qumran manuscripts: namely, imaginative compositions that, in the closest detail, describe various buildings conceived of as being part of the Temple complex, along with their dimensions, all envisioned as part of a cultic capital in a future age. But the scrolls editors, ever true to their faith in a uniform Essenic sectarianism at Qumran, simply asserted that "the presence of such a document at Qumran confirms the sacerdotal attachments of the sect and its interest in the (sacrificial) cult."[6]

In any case, with the above discoveries to consider, it dawned on the East Jerusalem scholars that the Qumran area might contain many more manuscript-laden caves, and in March 1952 they quickly organized and set to work on an expedition with several teams; that month they explored over two hundred caves in the vicinity of Qumran, discovering pottery in a score of them. On 14 March, they entered the cave now known as 3Q, and brought to light fifteen parchment pieces. These included a few biblical fragments, and also some small scraps which the editors described as being, respectively, from a commentary on Isaiah, a hymn of praise, angelic descriptions, an apocryphal prophetic text, a "writing of the sect,"[7] and several unidentifiable fragments. Of the six or seven legible words in the so-called sectarian writing, not one proved that the fragment stemmed from any particular sect. The words included, for example, the Hebrew for "you have sinned," "in a spirit of"(?), and "to turn back wickedness"—all biblical expressions that could have been used by any Jewish writer of the intertestamental period interested in the topic of sinfulness. Again, the small remainders of scrolls were each in the handwriting of a separate scribe.

Considerably more intriguing than these parchment finds was the discovery farther back in the same cave of two sections of a scroll made of *copper*. When partially deciphered, the scroll's contents seemed to consist of descriptions of hidden artifacts and treasures, with geographical indications of various hiding places. Later on it would become evident that the described items also included manuscripts. This document constitutes what is undoubtedly the most important single text discovery ever made in the Qumran caves, and we will closely consider it, and how the official scroll editors dealt with it, in Chapter 5.

The archaeological teams found no further manuscript caves in the area they were investigating, and so terminated the expedition in the spring of 1952, thus offering the skilled Ta'amireh bedouin an opportunity to return to the vicinity of Qumran. They began to explore the marl caves south of the settlement, and in the summer penetrated into what later became known as Qumran Cave 4 (4Q). Here they made a sensational discovery: Approximately one meter beneath the surface was a huge number of fragments from what had been several hundred manuscripts. When word reached the researchers in East Jerusalem, another expedition was mounted (September 1952) and the archaeologists succeeded in finding fragments of at least a hundred additional manuscripts in that cave.

The finds of Cave 4 remain the high-water mark of manuscript discovery in the Judaean Wilderness. Once in Jerusalem, the fragments in their thousands were first sorted and classified, primarily by Josef Milik, and then, in 1954, they were assigned to an expanded team of scholars for eventual publication. Starting already in the mid-fifties, the journals *Revue biblique* and *Biblical Archaeologist* published descriptions and partial text editions. Accounts by team members made it possible to gain an impression of the variety of texts coming from this cave: commentaries and paraphrases on many books of the Bible, apocalyptic visions, liturgical works and psalms, apocryphal writings both known and previously unknown, "wisdom" texts in the style of the Book of Proverbs, interpretations of Pentateuchal laws, messianic speculations, and even horoscopes and puzzles. All of these and much more highlighted the Cave 4 discoveries.[8]

Who had written and read this dizzying variety of literary types and genres? Were all these texts only written by and destined for the members of a small sect living on a plateau in the desert—or was the entire phenomenon in reality a much broader one, reflecting various elements in the Jewish society of intertestamental times? The answer was crucial and remains so, because at issue is our very understanding of Jewish life and thought in its latest prerabbinic manifestation and in the period of the earliest Christianity. This is of course the central scholarly issue today, in which virtually everyone working on the scrolls has a stake.

Archaeologists occupied at the 4Q site in September 1952 soon found two other manuscript caves close by: 5Q and 6Q, the latter explored some time earlier by the bedouin, who had emptied it of manuscript remains. In addition to a total of fifteen biblical fragments, the texts found in these caves included various new apocryphal and apocalyptic fragments, as well as a few writings of sectarian character, notably fragments of the *Damascus Covenant*. Three years later, in the spring of 1955, archaeologists discovered four more caves in the area of Qumran (7Q–10Q), but they contained only a small number of minuscule fragments. Cave 7 contained text fragments written *only in Greek*, and on papyrus. Most of these were unidentifiable, but one proved to be a fragment of Exodus, and another possibly the apocryphal Letter of Jeremiah.

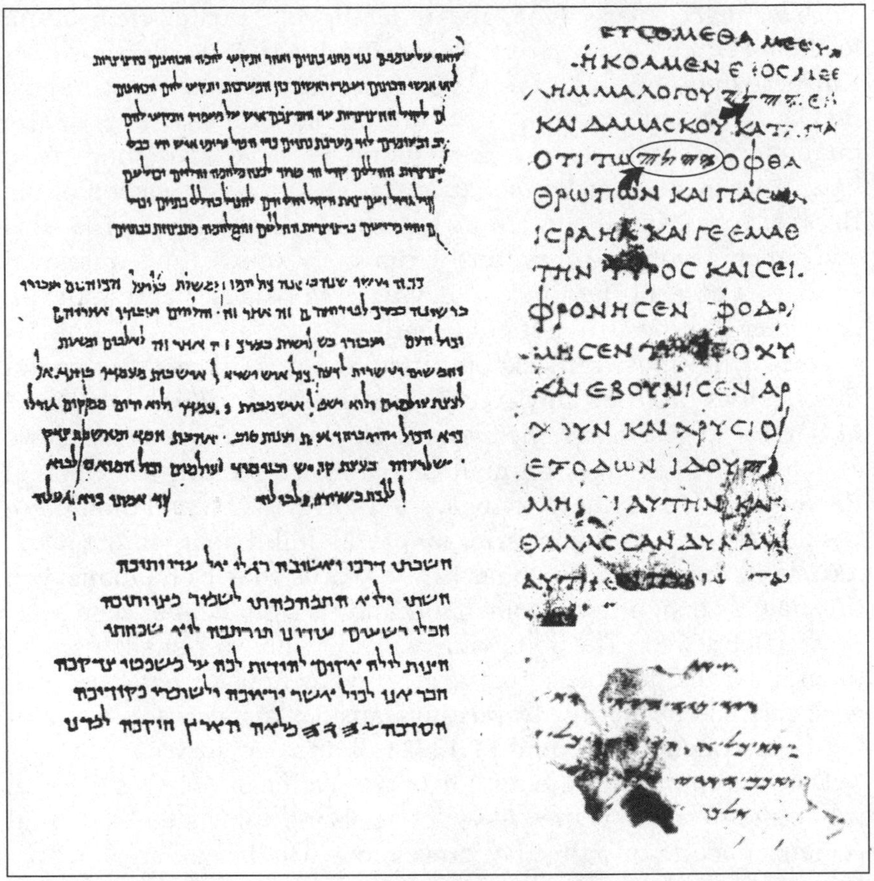

Figure 10
Examples of scribal handwritings found among the scrolls:
(a–c) samples of Hebrew/Aramaic square script; (d) Greek uncial
script, with Tetragrammaton (circled) written in palaeo-Hebrew
script; (e) palaeo-Hebrew scribal script.

Then, in February 1956, the indefatigable Ta'amireh bedouin located another manuscript cave near Cave 3, to the north of Khirbet Qumran. This cave (11Q) held some of the most important treasures discovered at Qumran, including a few nearly intact scrolls such as had been found in Cave 1. Among these finds were an ancient Aramaic translation of a large portion of the Book of Job, a scroll containing extracts from the Book of Psalms and other devotional literature from both known and unknown sources, a copy of the Book of Leviticus in palaeo-Hebrew script, and other writings still not published.

One of the most remarkable finds to result from these explorations was that of phylacteries (Hebrew, *tefillin*) discovered in several caves. Until the present day, strictly observant Jews attach leather thongs to small capsules, containing the text of Exodus **13**.1–16, Deuteronomy **6**.4–9 and **11**.13–21, and bind these casules to forehead and arm in literal fulfillment of the Deuteronomic injunction to "bind [these words that I command you this day] as a sign upon your hand and as frontlets between your eyes" (Deut. **6**.8). The following words, "And you shall inscribe them upon the doorposts [*mezuzot*] of your house" (**6**.9), are likewise carried out literally by posting capsules (or *mezuzot*) containing Deuteronomy **6**.4–9 and **11**.13–21 on the doorway.[9]

Both Josephus and the author of the Letter of Aristeas refer to the custom among the Jews of wearing phylacteries. What remains uncertain to this day, however, is whether all ancient parties and/or sects among the Jews literally and uniformly applied the injunction to bind the words commanded by the Lord "as a sign upon your hand . . . and as frontlets between your eyes." The author of the Letter of Aristeas states that the Lord "has put the [divine] oracles upon our gates and doors . . . and upon our hands, too, he expressly orders the symbol to be fastened . . . " —but he says nothing about the fastening of phylacteries to the forehead.[10] Josephus in his own description of the laws of Moses describes the latter practice as well, but does not tell us what specific verses were embedded in the boxes.[11] The Samaritans for their part did not have the custom of wearing phylacteries at all. The New Testament refers once to the wearing of phylacteries by Jews, but without indicating whether they were worn on the arm, hand, or both (Matt. **23**.5).

Now a considerable number of phylacteries were found in Caves 1, 4, 8, and perhaps elsewhere—approximately thirty in all.[12] The authors of the *Manual of Discipline*, insofar as they evince the very opposite tendency to interpret the literal injunctions of the Pentateuch as metaphors, were not good candidates for carrying out such an injunction literally. But whether the members of the Unity, or *Yahad*, group we encountered in Chapter 3 did or did not actually wear phylacteries, it was already obvious by 1970 that those phylacteries discovered in the caves could not have belonged to the individuals of any single Jewish group, whether encamped upon the desert plateau of Qumran or living elsewhere. For the texts of most of the phylacteries found in the caves—published by several scholars in the 1950s, 1960s, and 1970s—*showed no consistency with one another*.

This unusual feature of the Qumran phylacteries would be quite accurately described by Josef Milik in his 1977 edition of many of those from Cave 4.[13] Some texts are much lengthier than others, taking in relatively long passages of the Pentateuch, including Exodus **12**.43–**13**.16 and Deuteronomy **5**.1–**6**.9 and **10**.12–**11**.21; and to these lengthy sections the Song of Moses (Deut. **23**) was also once added. Four additional texts are much shorter, approximately equaling the passages used eventually by the rabbinical Jews.[14] In four cases the admonition contained in the sixth chapter of Deuteronomy beginning with the familiar words "Hear O Israel, the Lord is your God"—universally considered to be at the very core of the content of phylacteries—is itself excluded. The distribution of the various passages is, in Milik's words, "most capricious."[15]

Milik himself tried to retain the integrity of the Qumran-Essene hypothesis by claiming that these great variations among the texts showed only that the practice remained essentially, "if one might say so, private and semi-sacred."[16] It defies logic, however, to believe that a small and radical sect, whether of Essenes or others, who were according to the standard theory highly restrictive and formal in their religious legislation and practice, would have allowed their members to be so inconsistent with one another in carrying out a religious law that has been considered sacrosanct among practicing Jews for well over two millennia. This would be all the more the case if—as the old theory held—this sect was actually localized, as a *Yahad* or "Unity," in and around the Khirbet Qumran site. The great variations in the contents of the phylacteries can, on the other hand, be reasonably explained in consonance with the abundant variety of the scrolls, tending to show that they derived from various currents in ancient Judaism, not just one.

Yet even with this crucial new evidence, the multifarious contents of the various caves did not shake scholarly faith in the theory of Essene origins. The first conclusions had been based on only seven texts. Now, however, there were fragments from approximately eight hundred scrolls—and the response was to claim that Essenism had been a much more comprehensive movement than had been supposed until just after the discovery of the first cave. This was perhaps a legitimate approach in the sense of being theoretically possible, but one also threatening to broaden the sense of "Essenism" until this group was defined out of existence. No scholar of the time even concerned himself with offering a cogent explanation for the wide variety of phylactery versions found in the caves.

Thus we see that as more manuscript-bearing caves came to be discovered, the Qumran-Essene theory was expanded in like measure. Having started out with the hypothesis that the Essenes had produced the seven texts found originally in Cave 1, scholars were now vigorously defining these sectarians as the producers of hundreds of literary texts on an increasing variety of subjects—this despite the estimate shared by Philo and Josephus of only four thousand Essenes in all of first-century Palestine. As we have seen earlier, tacitly implicit in this idea was the assumption that all of the literature of first-century Palestinian Jews *other* than the Essenes had simply disappeared—and the belief that at the same time this one small sect had, as it were miraculously, saved many of its own literary treasures from destruction.

In fact, the great variety of discovered texts clearly undermined such a belief, and at the same time raised a new question: Would not other Jews of Palestine, to whom abundant caves were readily accessible, have acted similarly during the war with Rome, when their lives, culture, and religion were no less threatened than were those of the Essenes? By this token, could there be any certainty, given the totality of facts known even by 1955, that the Essenes alone were the ones responsible for the hiding of all these manuscripts?

In the very heyday of the finds, moreover, scholars not only began to observe the telltale ruins of a military site, and growing varieties of manuscript texts and handwritings, but were also starting to encounter historical testimony that in itself should

have forced them to weigh far more carefully the standard proposals being championed. Only one year after the first discoveries, Eliezer Sukenik had pointed out that, toward the middle of
the third century A.D., the learned and prolific church father
Origen had made use of a Greek translation of the Bible that, so
he stated, had been found "together with other Hebrew and Greek
books in a jar near Jericho."[17] Origen wrote that this find had
been made during the reign of Antoninus Severus (i.e., Caracalla)
who ruled from A.D. 211 to 217.

Among his numerous literary activities in the service of
Christianity, Origen devoted over two decades of his life to a study
of the Greek versions of the Hebrew Bible and their relationship
to the original text. In the process he learned Hebrew and spent
several years in Palestine, including sojourns in A.D. 216, 230, and
231–233, when he established a school of Christian learning at
Caesarea. In this way, and in the course of other periods of study
and travel, he produced his renowned work known as the
Hexapla, in which he arranged, side by side, columns containing
several versions of the biblical text.* Origen was meticulous in the
execution of this work, among other things marking off in the
Septuagint all passages not found in the original Hebrew, and in
the Hebrew those passages not found in the Septuagint. He states
that he himself found the text he used for the "fifth edition"—
which version he meant is uncertain—"in Nicopolis, near Actium"
(i.e., in northwestern Greece), and in the same breath indicates
that the "sixth edition" was found together with the other writings
in the jar near Jericho.

We do not know if it was Origen himself who found these writings, nor precisely which text of the Hexapla was contained in the
jar; but since he states that the discovery took place in Caracalla's
reign—i.e., between 211 and 217—it is not unlikely that it was
made either during Origen's first Palestinian sojourn in 216, or
else shortly before his arrival. He was already then a well-known
church figure, and delivered lectures, sponsored by the
Palestinian bishops, both in Jerusalem and Caesarea during that
visit. Gaining considerable fame in this way, and at the same time

*The first column consisted of the Hebrew original, the second of the
Hebrew transcribed into Greek, while four columns consisted of the Greek
versions of Aquila, Symmachus, the Septuagint, and Theodotion. (The text of
Psalms apparently had three additional columns.)

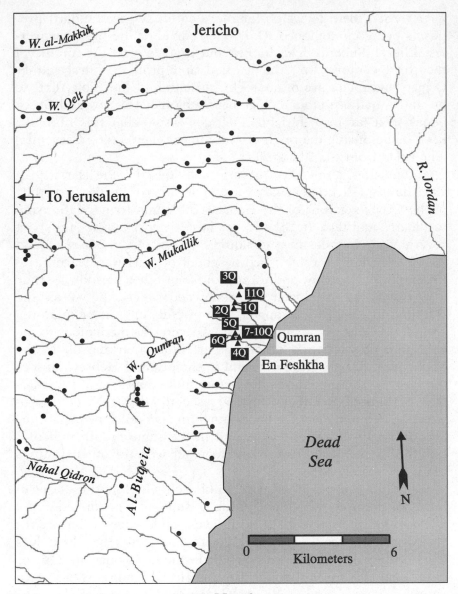

Map 4
Some wadis and caves of the Judaean Wilderness, including caves
where scrolls were discovered.

deeply immersed in his research, he would have been quick to benefit from discoveries made in the region where he was so active, and there can be no serious doubt concerning the historical reliability of his statement. Approximately seventy years after Origen's death in A.D. 254, his biographer, Eusebius, slightly paraphrased his account, saying that "in the Hexapla of the Psalms, after the four well-known editions, he placed beside them not only a fifth but also a sixth and seventh translation; and in the case of one of these he has indicated that it was found at Jericho in the time of Antoninus. . . ."[18]

Whether the discovery occurred "near" or "at" Jericho, and regardless of the precise identification of the translation discovered, it is quite clear that both Origen and his biographer connected it with the vicinity of Jericho—not with the area of the Judaean Wilderness bordering on the Dead Sea and containing the Qumran caves. Yet this did not prevent Père de Vaux from suggesting, as early as 1949, that Origen had actually visited the cave where the first Qumran manuscripts were found.[19] Although this suggestion was taken up by many writers afterward,[20] it did not reappear in de Vaux's books on the archaeology of Qumran (1961 and 1972). And almost as soon as the idea had been broached, it was partially eclipsed by the fact, pointed out by Otto Eissfeldt of Germany, that a yet more important discovery of Hebrew manuscripts had taken place near Jericho several centuries after the manuscript-laden jar was discovered in Origen's time.

Eissfeldt observed that in a letter written in approximately A.D. 800—and actually published at the beginning of this century—the Nestorian Patriarch Timotheus I of Seleucia, officiating in Baghdad, himself made reference to the discovery of Hebrew manuscripts ten years previously in a cave "near Jericho."[21] Timotheus wrote to Sergius, the Metropolitan of Elam, that he had learned this fact from "trustworthy Jews" who had converted, and who told him that

> the dog of a hunting Arab . . . entered a cave and did not come out. His master followed him and found a dwelling within the rocks, in which were many books. The hunter went to Jerusalem and informed the Jews. They came in throngs and found books of the Old Testament and others in Hebrew script. . . .

The continuation of Timotheus's letter leaves no room for doubt about the historical value of the information. He writes that since there was a well-read scholar among the group of converts, he asked him about various passages quoted in the New Testament as coming from the Hebrew Bible, but which had never been found there. The convert's response was that there were in fact such passages among the discovered books, and also that "we have found more than two hundred psalms of David among our books." In pursuit of further information, Timotheus then wrote to two other church associates (at least one of whom lived in Damascus) asking them to investigate the discovered writings with the aim of determining whether they contained particular passages of the kind that interested him. (Such curiosity is, of course, fully understandable in the case of a pious church figure.) The patriarch added in his letter to Sergius that he had received no response to his inquiry, and had "no suitable person" whom he could send to investigate on his behalf. "This is as fire in my heart," he continued, "burning and blazing in my bones."[22]

Not only are the circumstances under which Timotheus wrote his letter to Sergius entirely above suspicion, but the description of the discovery also has striking points in common with the twentieth-century revelations of the Qumran caves. In both cases, many books were found, not just a few; they were written in Hebrew script, included both biblical and extrabiblical writings— even to the detail of preserving noncanonical psalms—and were all discovered in caves. There is, to be sure, no indication that the earlier writings described by Origen were retrieved from a cave, but in that case the manuscripts were discovered in a jar and, like those found in several Qumran caves in the twentieth century, included texts written in both Hebrew and Greek.

Thus two old sources, one from the third century and the other from the end of the eighth, had called attention to the discovery of caches of Hebrew manuscripts near Jericho, of which the larger was found in a cave—and this raised the possibility of a more widespread phenomenon of manuscript concealment in intertestamental Judaea than had been anticipated by the original proponents of the Qumran-Essene hypothesis.

After the letter of Timotheus became known to Qumranologists, a number of them, clearly seeking to protect the original theory, proposed that Timotheus too was referring to discoveries made only in the Qumran caves themselves: Timotheus, as well as Origen, had simply spoken *imprecisely* of the discoveries having taken place "near Jericho." Again it was Père de Vaux who, as early as 1950, took a leading role in making this proposal, but others followed during the 1950s and 1960s.[23] Although de Vaux discusses neither Timotheus's words nor Origen's in his later writings, the idea continues to be held by some scholars even today. According to this explanation, the underlying reason for the discovery in the twentieth century of hundreds of scrolls ostensibly in the *same area* as similar finds made over a millennium earlier would have to be that the Jerusalem Jews visiting the cave site in Timotheus's time had simply not discovered all the manuscripts hidden in various surrounding caves. By this implicit premise, the discovery of manuscripts near Khirbet Qumran in the twentieth century was held to show that the early writers had really been alluding to exactly the same location, even though the two ancient discoveries were both described as having taken place in the vicinity of Jericho.

We thus observe the continuous effort by Qumranologists to assimilate anomalous pieces of evidence into the structure of their favored paradigm.

I began to perceive the gravely tendentious nature of this line of reasoning after my 1969–70 visits to Khirbet Qumran and its surroundings. According to Timotheus's informants, news of the find had moved "throngs" to come to the site, and these were not bedouin but believing Jews. The idea that they would have overlooked the possibility of finding other ancient and potentially sacred Hebrew scrolls in the nearby caves was in reality difficult to credit. What is more, neither Origen nor Timotheus actually states that the finds were made near the shore of the Dead Sea, which is much closer to Qumran than Jericho. Ancient writers would have been more likely to refer to the Qumran plateau as being not "near Jericho" but "near the Dead Sea" (see Map 1). Origen in particular, who lived for some years in Palestine and was intimately acquainted with its geography, would never have spoken so vaguely. There are, on the other hand, many caves much nearer to Jericho than those at Qumran.

In subjecting the words of Origen and Timotheus to a special exegesis, the Qumranologists failed to acknowledge their far more likely implication: that over the past seventeen centuries Hebrew manuscripts had been discovered not only in the single area of Qumran, but in *at least* two hiding places in the neighborhood of Jericho as well. This, of course, all the more adversely affected the claim of a unique, organic connection between the Qumran settlement and the manuscripts of the nearby caves; it pointed, rather, to another cause for the hiding of manuscripts in the Judaean desert in antiquity—something perhaps implicitly acknowledged in the studied insistence by professional Qumranologists that all the discoveries, new and old, had taken place in the Qumran caves, not anywhere else.

Although by 1960 enthusiasm for this latter idea in its full-blown state had begun to cool slightly, Père de Vaux did not yet show any willingness in his books on the archaeology of Qumran to grapple with the significance of this geographical configuration of Hebrew manuscript discoveries in the Judaean Wilderness. And in 1962, Yigael Yadin wrote that "Timotheus' letter . . . shows that even at the end of the eighth century many manuscripts of the kind found in 1947 and later were discovered near the Dead Sea, perhaps even in the same caves. . . ."[24] As indicated, however, while not stating the *precise* distance between Jericho and the site where the manuscripts discovered in his time were found, Timotheus had spoken of Jericho—not the Dead Sea.

Thus, whether by purposeful muteness, misstatement, or ostensible lack of concern, scholars working on the Qumran scrolls continued to disparage the powerful historical testimony they were steadily uncovering. The discovery of the Qumran scrolls and other manuscripts in the Judaean Wilderness set in play an investigative methodology and accompanying series of assumptions leading early on to the development of the Qumran-sectarian hypothesis. Afterward, following the classic pattern of theory building and defense described by Thomas Kuhn and other writers,[25] the artisans of the hypothesis not only disregarded certain emerging anomalies, but also attempted to eliminate others by innovative exegesis, including imputations of textual falsification, the treating of arbitrary characterizations as facts, and the use of unproven subtheories as premises in arguments that seemed to have the ring of authority. Although the procedure seemed reasonable at first, it owed much to the striking mass appeal of archaeological discovery: Few people believed that archaeologists could actually be wrong in explaining the significance of artifacts and structures from the Holy Land, revealed to the world after two thousand years by their own hands and the sweat of their brows. The masterly rhetoric of Dupont-Sommer and Edmund Wilson, and attractive presentations of the theory in popular journals of archaeology, only encouraged the benevolent sentiment of readers.

No general public can easily resist the appeal created by the picture of dedicated scholars, many of them of great piety, hunching laboriously over the precious manuscript fragments culled fortuitously from desert caves, earnestly seeking to explain their enigmatic meaning. Nevertheless, it was clear to me by 1970 that the Qumran-sectarian hypothesis constituted a notable leap of faith stemming from misapplication of the archaeological discoveries. A comparison, moreover, with the scholarly treatment of other archaeological and manuscript finds would have revealed how traditional Qumranologists, in the course of formulating their views, had grossly deviated from principles of investigation normally adhered to in relevant disciplines. We can see this most readily by turning back to the case of the thirteen Nag Hammadi Gnostic writings, which offers instructive parallels with that of the Qumran discoveries, while illustrating how documentary texts may be used both to formulate and to assess hypotheses.

After these Gnostic-Christian manuscripts were discovered and studied, it was suggested that the books had been buried in a jar in a pagan cemetery as an outcome of the promulgation of St. Athanasius's edict suppressing heretical writings. The monk Theodorus had translated this decree into Coptic and then circulated it among the various monasteries of coenobites (i.e., monks who lived together in a community rather than solitarily), founded by the Egyptian St. Pachomius in the fourth century. Two of these monasteries had been located very near the discovery, one being at Pabau (5½ miles) and the other at Chenoboskia (3½ miles).[26] In time it was discovered that the bindings of more than eight of the codices contained discarded letters, accounts, and other documentary items, some of them precisely dated (e.g., to A.D. 345 and 348). The scholar who first studied this "cartonnage" in a preliminary way, J. W. B. Barns, maintained that the codices came from one of the two monasteries and had been hidden away either immediately after the decree or "at a later date, when the heresies which produced these books were no longer a living issue, and their study had become unnecessary."[27] Barns, pointing out that the volumes were found near Chenoboskia while the documentary fragments seemed to contain no trace of heterodox or heretical ideas, reasoned that since "it is hardly conceivable that there would have been more than one orthodox monastic organization simultaneously operating in the same place, *we should be justified in concluding, even without further evidence*, that the Nag Hammadi material came from a Pachomian monastery."[28] Remarkably, this assertion appeared only a few years after publication of the English version of Père de Vaux's study of the Khirbet Qumran site, where he wrote that "Certainly manuscripts were copied in the *scriptorium*. . . . We may also suppose, *even before studying their content*, that certain works were composed at Qumran."[29]

Yet when the documentary papyri from the covers on the codices were studied in greater depth and finally published in 1981, the editor responsible for the introduction, J. C. Shelton, could no longer agree with the assessment of the origins of the texts contained in Barns's preliminary report of 1975. Instead, he demonstrated that evidence for monasticism in the documentary texts was limited to only some of the correspondence in a single codex, while there were no documents "in which a specifically Pachomian background comes plainly to the fore." While Barns had assumed a monastic origin of the codices, and asserted that the binding of the manuscripts must have been the work of the same establishment that produced them (and that the waste papyrus used in the bindings necessarily had an intrinsic connection with the binders), Shelton could perceive "no prima facie connection between scribes and bookbinders, nor between those two parties and the owners of the codices." Given the large number of subjects covered in the documents, he concluded that it was "hard to think of a satisfactory single source for such a variety of documents except a town rubbish heap—which may indeed have been the direct source of all the papyri the bookbinders used." He also pointed out that the "few [documentary] texts which give some indication as to the way of life of the persons concerned are difficult or impossible to reconcile with Pachomianism."[30] The autograph documents discovered in the bindings of these texts could thus serve as an invaluable touchstone in determining the strength of a hypothesis based, to begin with, upon literary texts. In fact, close analysis of the autographs in juxtaposition with revealing statements in the literary texts tended to disprove the then dominant hypothesis that the latter derived from a specific religious site.

The scholar most active in research on the Nag Hammadi papyri in the years immediately following their discovery had been Jean Doresse, a French Egyptologist and specialist in Coptic texts. He was the first to recognize the general nature of the discoveries, and among a very few who had direct access to the texts during the first several years after they were found. Although the discovery had occurred as early as 1945, it was not announced until 1948 (at first only in Egypt) and then in a more detailed way by Doresse himself in 1949. By that time, however, the earliest Dead Sea Scroll discoveries had been broadcast to the world, and for a long time the Judaean Wilderness finds almost totally eclipsed those of upper Egypt. Doresse was both chagrined and fascinated by this unexpected twist of fate. "Am I perhaps a little inclined to underrate the interest of those much-admired manuscripts discovered near the Dead Sea?" he asked. But later, as though unconsciously influenced by the approach being taken to the Dead Sea Scrolls, he went on to inquire, "What was the sect that owned these [Gnostic-Coptic] manuscripts?"

This followed Doresse's own acknowledgment of the apparent doctrinal variety in the Nag Hammadi texts. While first stating that the "interest of the new manuscripts is enhanced by the homogeneity of the writings they contain, their undoubted unity," he could yet perceive, at a relatively early stage of research on the manuscripts, that the interest of the texts was "further heightened by their diversity," for they depicted "the same Gnostic myth under the most varied form." The writings were, as he acknowledged, "even accompanied by some works from alien groups— Valentinian or Hermetist, in whom our sectaries were interested." The sect of Gnostics whom Doresse chose as the likeliest ones to have been responsible for these writings were a group known to Epiphanius and other early heresiographers (ancient chroniclers of the Christian heretics) as the Sethians. Doresse pointed out certain features in some of the writings that reminded him of that sect. Yet even while insisting on that identification, he suggested still others: "One might, no doubt, think also of the Ophites or of the Naassenes. . . . One might also wonder whether one had to do with Archontici or Barbelognostics. . . . But it would be useless to try to be more precise; we know from the heresiologists that the sects borrowed from one another without the slightest compunction. . . ." In short, even though Doresse could perceive that the Nag Hammadi literature was complex and often self-contradictory, he insisted on trying to trace it all to a single sect, and, once expressed in 1958, his view gained some adherents.[31]

Eventually, however, as knowledge of the contents of the texts continued to grow, the "Sethian" bubble was punctured. At a colloquium on the origins of Gnosticism held in 1966, T. Säve-Söderberg posed the questions whether "one dogmatic system can explain all the different texts," or whether the texts could even have been "acceptable to one and the same congregation of Gnostic believers."[32] Säve-Söderberg showed that, according to the very contents of the texts, the necessary answer to both these questions was a negative one. As he put it: "Even a superficial analysis of the dogmas of the different texts reveals the impossibility to bring them under a single denominator, and a detailed study of e.g. the attitude towards the Old Testament of central notions and ideas bears out the conclusion that the library cannot reflect the dogmas of one sect, however broadminded and syncretistic. It is hard to believe that all these texts were even acceptable in all details to one and the same congregation or single Gnostic believer." Säve-Söderberg instead suggested the possibility that the library was collected by one or more heresiographers intent on combating the views of the Gnostics, rather than by the Gnostics themselves. He pointed out that in one manuscript (no. VI), the copyist, writing to his client, had stated: "This is the first discourse that I have copied for you. But there are many others that have come into my hands: I have not transcribed them, thinking that they have already reached you. For I hesitate to copy them for you, thinking that if they had already reached you, they would weary you. Indeed the discourses of Hermes that have come into my hands are very numerous."[33]

Thus, not only did the variety of contradictory ideas militate against the idea of the writings having emanated from a single Gnostic sect, but the above documentary note preserved by chance in one of the texts itself pointed in another direction. Emphasizing that a final judgment could only be arrived at when the entire library was published, Säve-Söderberg cautioned that, until then, "each text should be judged and analysed more or less as an isolated phenomenon, not as part of a unity, which the Chenoboskion library does not at all represent." His view was subsequently supported by other scholars, and the eventual publication of the full Nag Hammadi corpus finally put an end to the controversy.[34]

It is not difficult to see why the history of interpretation of the two discoveries took such different turns. Jean Doresse, early pioneer of Nag Hammadi studies, was relatively young and had no prestigious or influential position when he undertook his work on these texts. He did not possess the aura of scholarly authority that surrounded Eliezer Sukenik as well as Père de Vaux, André Dupont-Sommer, and others who either developed or else gave their strong endorsement to the Qumran-sectarian theory in the early stages of discovery. To use an expression all too common in modern scholarly parlance, they "accepted" the theory, and this act turned the world of learning decisively in its favor—whereas Doresse's view of the origins of the Nag Hammadi writings, unenhanced by the politics of intellectual charisma, simply entered the normal channels of debate and investigation and, by critical judgment, was eventually found to be wanting. Throughout the volumes of publications of the Nag Hammadi texts, one would look in vain for an endorsement of any particular theory of origin of these Gnostic manuscripts, or for comments that might tend to lead the reader in a particular direction. They were instead published in a straightforward manner, with accompanying English translations. And this treatment of the discovery was diametrically opposed to that practiced by the editors of the Qumran scrolls who, in the course of publication of the Oxford text editions, introduced numerous comments reflecting a persistent effort to bolster a Qumran-sectarian myth of origins, protect it, and give readers the impression that the myth was in fact truthful and unassailable—despite the logical contradictions that have continued to assail it in increasing numbers.

CHAPTER 5

The *Copper Scroll,*
the Masada Manuscripts,
and the Siege of Jerusalem

The discovery in Cave 3 of the *Copper Scroll* in March 1955 marked a great advance in scroll research, although not initially portrayed as such. The results of its unrolling and decipherment would eventually demonstrate the great importance of the statements of Origen and Timotheus for solving the riddle of the scrolls. The contents of the text, found in a recess behind other manuscripts, would provide key elements in a new understanding of the scrolls' origins. In addition, the story of the gradual revelation of its contents, and particularly of the subsequent attempts to cast doubt on its authenticity, would turn out to form a highly instructive lesson on the emerging politics of Qumran studies. The discovery placed an indelible stamp on all subsequent debates relating to the scrolls and the Khirbet Qumran site.

The scroll was found in two sections, and could not immediately be unrolled because of its age-induced brittleness and inflexibility. Since it was inscribed into the copper with a stylus, however, some of the words of each section were discernible, backwards and in relief, on the reverse side of the outermost layer. A good number of these words were made out by the Heidelberg scholar K. G. Kuhn during a visit to Jerusalem in the autumn of 1953, and the next year he published an article suggesting that the scrolls contained descriptions of hidden Essene treasures.[1]

This view was supported by a number of scholars, but met with skepticism by members of the Jerusalem team. In 1955, however, Dr. John Allegro of Manchester University, who had by then become a member of the editorial team, interested the Manchester Institute of Technology in opening up the two scroll sections, one of which was then brought to the college from Jerusalem by G. Lankester

Figure 11
Qumran Cave 3, site of the discovery of the *Copper Scroll*
and other texts.

Harding. Beginning on 30 September, Professor H. Wright-Baker of the college, using a sawing machine of his own invention, proceeded to cut up the scroll into thin, concave vertical strips. (The sections could not be flattened out for fear of splintering.) Accumulated dirt was gradually cleared away from the lines of script. The strips were then photographed, inventoried, and placed next to one another in proper order, thus yielding a consecutive text.

Allegro later wrote that he participated in the cleaning, deciphered the first column "and another column or two," and then "rushed air letters to Harding with the news." In November, Allegro sent Harding "[the] complete transcription of the first part, together with a provisional translation and notes." The second part of the scroll arrived in Manchester at the beginning of January 1956, and was cut open in the same manner between the eleventh and the sixteenth of January. Describing the process, Allegro subsequently stated: "My readings followed by air," adding that the entire scroll was sent back to its custodians in April.[2]

By these efforts, which showed every sign of scholarly industry and collegial goodwill, Allegro had quite unwittingly set into motion a train of events that would culminate in a way no one could have anticipated—with the castigation of him by his colleagues in Jerusalem, the withering of his academic career, his self-exile to the Isle of Wight, his attacks on the Jews, Judaism, and Christianity in subsequent writings, and ultimately a somewhat premature and lonely death in 1988.[3]

In Allegro's 1956 book on the scrolls, in which he devotes only a few pages to the *Copper Scroll*, he sketchily describes the early events, at the end stating that Kuhn's hypothesis of an inventory of hidden treasures "has been proved marvelously accurate. It is indeed an inventory of the sect's most treasured possessions, buried in various locations." He then goes on to emphasize that additional information must "wait on the release and publication of the whole text, a task entrusted . . . to Father Josef Milik of the French School in Jerusalem."[4] He thus appeared, at the time, to be perfectly willing to await Milik's publication.

The text that Allegro first transcribed and translated did indeed turn out to contain inventories of hidden treasures, as Kuhn had surmised. According to the scroll's explicit wording, those treasures were stored away in various hiding places, mostly in the Judaean Wilderness. The text contains a total of twelve columns, about five inventories to each, written in a nonliterary Hebrew idiom datable to the first century A.D. The fact that it is written on copper, a valuable metal, suggests that its authors attached importance to it. It bears all the hallmarks of a genuine documentary autograph: The writing does not exhibit the elegance and consistency of professional scribes, and the inventories are given without embellishment. As in the Bar Kokhba texts, genuine toponymns of the Judaean Wilderness are found in the *Copper Scroll*. They include such familiar places as Jericho, the Valley of Achor, and the Wadi Qidron, as well as localities that are for the most part unidentifiable, such as Sekhakha, Harobah, Duq, Kohlat, Milham, and Beth Hakerem.* The hiding places of the treasures include

---

*In Palestine, as in other parts of the world, many ancient place-names—including a large number found in the Hebrew Bible—can no longer be identified. Many of the ancient localities have been destroyed or otherwise disappeared, while others have undergone name changes that make their original identification difficult or impossible.

caves, tombs, and aqueducts. There are a great many treasures, deviating significantly in size and character from one another. So authentic is the *Copper Scroll* that the foremost Continental proponent of the Qumran-Essene hypothesis, Dupont-Sommer, described it as "a document drafted with all the baldness of book-keeping," and suggested that "the reason for its having been engraved on resistant material, and kept in two copies, is that it is an important archive, not of invented riches, but of very real ones."[5]

Allegro's colleagues in Jerusalem must have avidly studied the tentative transcriptions and translations of the two parts of the text he dispatched to them, but do not appear in the end to have been pleased by the results gained from the opening of the scroll. This did not happen at once, for their reaction to the transcriptions of the several columns Allegro sent earlier on had been positive, and they had dispatched the other portion of the scroll apparently without hesitation to Manchester for opening.

We may thus reasonably infer that it only slowly dawned upon de Vaux, Milik, and others in Jerusalem that the contents of the *Copper Scroll*, if taken at face value, represented a danger for the Qumran-Essene hypothesis. The four thousand wealth-eschewing Essenes of first-century A.D. Palestine could not have had anything like the quantities of silver and other precious metals described in the text—nor could any other small sect. If the text was indeed an authentic autograph, its treasures could only have come from the Temple, whose custodians in intertestamental times amassed great sums of wealth from the Temple dues and donations provided by a large, widespread population of Jews both in and outside of Palestine. And since this scroll had been found in one of the caves along with literary manuscripts written on parchment, the possibility must have become suddenly apparent that the scrolls as a whole could be conceived of as having derived not from Qumran, but from Jerusalem itself. Convinced, however, that they must be right in their view that the Essenes had written the scrolls, and that this had been accomplished at Khirbet Qumran, the principal scroll team members decided to declare the text before them a work of *fiction*.

Following this group decision, apparently reached some time in May 1956, Lankester Harding wrote to Allegro and to Wright-Baker suggesting as much. This was followed by an official statement by Père de Vaux and Lankester Harding, which was dispatched from Jerusalem to the British Academy in London, the Académie des Inscriptions et Belles Lettres in Paris, and elsewhere. It was read at the Académie on 1 June. Dupont-Sommer was a witness to the event in Paris, and thereafter wrote that

> the extracts from the scroll certainly give the impression that we are faced with real deposits, carefully described and scrupulously indicated. But the report of June 1st expressly dismisses this interpretation: the inscription, it says, is nothing but a collection of traditions relating to places where ancient treasure was supposed to have been hidden. It continues as follows: "It is difficult to understand why the Essenes of Qumran were so much concerned with these stories of hidden treasure, and especially why they saw fit to engrave them on copper, which at that time was a costly metal. . . . At all events, this guide to hidden treasure is the most ancient document of its kind to have been found, and is of interest to the historian of folklore."

Dupont-Sommer also quotes de Vaux as having stated that the *Copper Scroll* was the "whimsical product of a deranged mind."[6] The report was circulated widely in the world press.[7]

The actions and statements described above reveal a concerted effort, even prior to publication of the *Copper Scroll*, to convince the public that its existence cast no doubt upon the sectarian origin of the texts and the singularity of the finds in the Qumran caves. It marks the first notable attempt in Qumran studies to shore up the standard hypothesis by announcing a highly dubious interpretation of a scroll long before its actual publication. (Other such efforts are discussed in ensuing chapters.)

Allegro, as his correspondence of this period reveals,[8] was entirely puzzled at first by these efforts, but eventually understood their true nature. While he himself had originally believed that the treasures were those of the Essenes, he pondered the matter further after observing the reaction of his Jerusalem colleagues, concluding in the end that the treasures were connected not with Qumran but with the Temple treasury—and that the *Copper Scroll* was the work of Zealots rather than Essenes. Only a few weeks after de Vaux's announcement, Chaim Rabin (then of Oxford) published an article proposing that the scroll described Temple treasures and had nothing to do with the Essenes; and this view was expressed at about the same time by K. G. Kuhn, who in this way renounced his earlier explanation that the text dealt with

Essene treasures.[9] Considerable tension thereafter developed between the editorial group in Jerusalem, all supporting Père de Vaux's contention of an imaginative product, and Allegro, who from the first rightly found their claims ludicrous.[10] A later remark of Frank Cross epitomized the editorial team's stance: "I should prefer to propose, tentatively to be sure," he stated, "that we have to do with traditional, i.e. fabulous treasures, perhaps of the Temple of Solomon . . . it is just possible to imagine a priestly hermit of Qumran taking such folkloristic traditions seriously enough to preserve them in copper."[11]

The tension was clearly of concern to Dupont-Sommer, for he felt obliged to state, in the late 1950s, that

> It may be that in going into the problems raised by the still enigmatic inscription Allegro will have been led to modify his first position [that the scroll describes Essene treasures] to a certain extent. While awaiting the publication of his book, he has kindly let me know that he resolutely maintains, against Milik, the theory of a genuine inventory, and also that the particular interpretation which he suggests concerning the Copper Scroll *is in no way opposed to the general thesis of an Essene origin of the . . . writings from Qumran.*[12]

This statement reveals that, while Allegro finally perceived the *Copper Scroll* as in some way connected with the treasures of the Temple, he did not at first fully recognize the danger this view posed for the standard theory of the origin of the scrolls. It also indicates that Dupont-Sommer himself understood what the danger was.

Even before the scroll was actually opened, Dupont-Sommer had expressed the belief that it enumerated the treasures of the Essenes.[13] He reaffirmed this view after the appearance of Milik's tentative translation of the text.[14] However, when Allegro published his own full transcription in the form of line drawings in 1960, Dupont-Sommer stated that the publication revealed "the complexity and difficulty of the manifold problems involved in the study" of this manuscript, indicating he would await Milik's publication of the complete work before himself "attempting a thorough study of this still highly enigmatic document."[15]

In the end, he could do nothing but repeat his view that the treasures had to be those of the Essenes. His reason for rejecting a linkage of the *Copper Scroll* to the Temple was Josephus's assertion that the Romans found treasures of the Temple within its precincts after Jerusalem was taken.[16] Josephus, however, was not in Jerusalem at the time of the siege, and his account does not pretend to have the status of eyewitness reporting of each and every event that transpired within the walls of the capital before and during the siege. As Dupont-Sommer himself mentions, Josephus also explains that the Romans found "many precious things" in trenches under the city; but Josephus does not describe the inhabitants in the process of hiding them.[17] The *Copper Scroll* thus simply supplements his account, by hinting that, in addition to treasures left in the Temple and hidden underground within the city, others were buried in caches deposited primarily in the Judaean Wilderness.

The problem was an acute one for the Qumranologists, some of whom were now developing a new view: that the scroll could indeed be genuine, but in that case its hiding away had nothing to do with the storage of the other scrolls found in the caves—it was rather caused by the intrusion into Cave 3 of people who were not Essenes, either operating at the same time or later. Father de Vaux would later attempt to doubly distance the *Copper Scroll* from the other Qumran texts by denying its genuineness while *also* suggesting that it should be entirely separated from the other texts physically and with respect to time:

> The only point we would make here is that this exception [= the *Copper Scroll*], if it were indeed shown to be such, would serve to prove the rule: it would be easier to explain the unique character of this document, so foreign to the outlook and preoccupation of the community, if it emanated from some other source and had been deposited at a later stage. This would confirm our conclusion: none of the manuscripts belonging to the community is later than the ruin of Khirbet Qumran in A.D. 68.[18]

The manuscript was obviously a vexation for de Vaux.

Milik's tentative translations had appeared by 1959 in the form of articles. Allegro realized that the Jerusalem group was intent on pushing ahead with the portrayal of the text as a fiction, and so he published his own transcription and translation, describing the scroll as utterly genuine. Later he would actually lead an archaeological expedition in a vain search for the treasures themselves.

All this brought cries of protest from the team in Jerusalem. These actions were followed by Milik's elaborate publication of the text (1962) in the Oxford series of scroll publications, in which he reiterated the by then "official" position that the scroll was an imaginative product or a forgery.[19]

In the meanwhile, however, the damage to the Qumran-Essene hypothesis caused by growing knowledge of the contents of this text had made itself felt. Already in 1958 Cecil Roth, the Oxford historian, having become familiar with the earlier discussions relating to the *Copper Scroll*, expressed the view that the Qumran scrolls had belonged not to the Essenes but to the Zealots, and that it was the latter group that had hidden away its treasures in the Judaean Wilderness (see further below, Chapter 10). Allegro's support of this view was followed by his 1960 publication of the scroll. The Jerusalem editorial group and all those taking their cue from them treated this interpretation with derision and eventually silence, while continuing to nurture their own vision by whatever evidence could be adduced to make it seem plausible and authentic. Long after Milik's publication of the *Copper Scroll* in 1962, however, his own effort to have it labeled a fiction would fail.[20]

One of the most telling episodes in the official team's efforts to discredit Allegro's claim of authenticity for the document was the publication by Père de Vaux of a review of Allegro's book that appeared in 1961. There he wrote that the "book opens with the history of the discovery [of the *Copper Scroll*] which is presented with regrettable imprecision"—this "imprecision" turning out, in fact, to be Allegro's failure to list the actual names of the three institutions that participated in the hunt for the manuscripts in 1952. (In Allegro's book we find only brief mention of one of the "searching teams" of "archaeologists" who found the *Copper Scroll*.) Taking Allegro to task for stating that three successive directors of the Jordanian Service of Antiquities had invited him to publish this scroll, de Vaux declared that if they had told Allegro as much, they did so with no mandate, since publication rights "belonged to those who discovered it." This was a most dubious assertion, implying that archaeologists who find written texts have prior rights to their publication, even though palaeographers and manuscript scholars may generally be more expert in deciphering and interpreting them.

In this spirit, de Vaux also asserted that Allegro had merely been given the task of making "provisional transcriptions" of the text in Dr. Wright-Baker's laboratory, while the scroll had been officially assigned to Milik for publication. Allegro, however, had loyally done what he had been asked to do, and had sent his transcriptions on to Jerusalem—only to learn afterward that, without any consultation with him as the first decipherer of the text, de Vaux and his group had decided to condemn it internationally, by public announcement, as a merely imaginative work. De Vaux's attempt here and elsewhere in his review to discredit Allegro is obvious.

De Vaux accused Allegro of acting "contrary to simple honesty" in publishing without permission two photographs that were the property of the Palestine Archaeological Museum: actions of this kind "disqualify an author," he stated. Yet Milik, in the provisional translations of the *Copper Scroll* he published prior to Allegro, had assented to de Vaux's claim that the document was a figment of the imagination while making no mention of the fact that Allegro had been the first to transcribe the document—a far more questionable act that did not, however, appear to bother de Vaux at all. When Milik later published his own full edition of the text, a substantial number of the errors of transcription made by Allegro turned up in his own work; yet he failed to recognize any contribution on Allegro's part. He wrote that he would not refer in any way to his colleague's work, "for the reasons that one may divine by reading the observations of R. de Vaux [against Allegro's book in the *Revue Biblique*]."[21]

Since Allegro, however, had read through the entire text and recognized that it could be nothing other than a historic document, his general behavior was entirely appropriate. De Vaux attacked his scholarship, but the criticism contained hardly anything of scientific value. Allegro had dared to publish an independent edition of the *Copper Scroll*, but, far more importantly, he had displayed sufficient courage and integrity to oppose de Vaux on the question of the authenticity of the one Qumran manuscript bearing hallmarks of a genuine historic autograph. The leader of the Jerusalem team was sufficiently anxious about the matter to issue his most unusual international announcement, six years in advance of the text's official publication and after the opened scroll and Allegro's transcription had been in his care a mere two months.* It was only with the passage of time that a majority of those scholars engaged in the study of the *Copper Scroll*[22] would begin to acknowledge the genuineness of this precious manuscript—a turning point first achieved by the late David Wilmot in a dissertation prepared at the University of Chicago in the 1970s but never submitted due to his untimely death. As of today, the text continues to undergo careful scrutiny by, among others, Al Wolters of Redeemer College (Ontario) and, following him, P. Kyle McCarter of the Johns Hopkins University, both of whom affirm the authenticity and historic quality of this text. McCarter's conclusion represents a *volte-face* from the position espoused by his own teacher, Frank M. Cross, and this willingness to express so notable a difference indicates how important he must consider the issue to be.

At the end of the *Copper Scroll*, we read that "in a pit . . . to the north of Kohlat . . . is hidden a copy of this writing together with its explanation."[23] This shows clearly that the *Copper Scroll* was a genuine autograph text, whose contents had been themselves copied down, apparently with augmentations, into another scroll, apparently also hidden away for safekeeping. The nonliterary nature of this scroll, the dry cataloging of the deposits, the rough handwriting, and the fact that it was found in one of the Qumran caves and in the same first-century A.D. context as the other scrolls, make any effort to distance the scroll from the particular history of the Qumran texts extremely difficult to countenance. Moreover, of decisive importance to the question of the authenticity of this scroll is the fact that, in at least eight passages, *writings* are mentioned as being buried adjacent to the treasures.

One of the most notable such passages is the statement (first seven lines in column **7**) that one is to dig at the northern opening of the "Cave of the Pillar," three cubits downward, where an

---

*There can be little doubt that not only scholarly differences, but deep personal and even religious antagonisms as well, not infrequently revealed in Allegro's correspondence with other members of the Jerusalem team, lay at the heart of the treatment meted out to him by de Vaux and Milik. He eventually would respond by leaving his academic calling and, in the longer term, publishing an attack on Christianity in the guise of the thesis that the earliest Christians had achieved religiosity by consuming hallucinatory mushrooms. (See also note 3 to this chapter.) Nevertheless, Allegro did go on with his work on the scrolls into the 1960s.

amphora containing a *scroll* (Hebrew, *sefer*) is to be found, and, underneath it, forty-two silver talents. Strikingly, this passage follows another to the effect that thirty-two talents have been hidden in a tomb located at the "Brook of the Dome . . . as (one) comes from Jericho to Sekhakha." The Cave of the Pillar was thus also situated between Jericho and Sekhakha—the latter an otherwise unknown place, albeit one that, in view of the fact that no intervening place is mentioned in the directions, could hardly have been more than a few kilometers from Jericho.* (Were there intervening places, such as abounded in the wider area around Jericho, between that city and Sekhakha, the author would have reasonably named the most appropriate nearby place to clarify his directions, rather than resorting to the use of Jericho for this purpose.) The passage clearly refers to the hiding of a book in a cave near the latter city: not, however, one of the caves above Qumran, as such a site was too far from Jericho—a full seven miles away—to be identifiable with Sekhakha. Yet more notable is the statement at the beginning of column 8 that *scrolls* (*sefarin*, plural), have been hidden along with ritual vessels at an aqueduct, also apparently located near Jericho.[24] Other "writings" (Hebrew, *ketab*; plural, *ketabin*) are mentioned as being placed near hidden treasures in at least five other passages of the scroll.[25] These may have been documentary records specifying the various treasures placed near them, just as the *Copper Scroll* itself is designated as a *ketab*—not a *sefer*—at the end of the final column.

These various statements, of course, offer a striking parallel to those of Origen and Timotheus regarding the discovery of Hebrew manuscripts near the same city. However, because the places mentioned in the *Copper Scroll* had to be much closer to Jericho than is Qumran, they render more doubtful still the interpretation of the finds reported by Origen and Timotheus as simply earlier discoveries of manuscripts at Qumran. What necessarily emerges from the combination of evidence, considered without dark hints of forgery, is that ancient Hebrew manuscripts were hidden away

---

Copper Scroll, column 5, line 12; ed. Milik, p. 289. This place has been identified by Cross and Milik with Khirbet Samrah, an important ruin of the Buqeiah region (cf. the study of Milik, "Rouleau de Cuivre," p. 236, no. 7), but the identification has been rejected by B. Z. Lurie (*Megillat hanehoshet*, p. 84) for the cogent reason that Sekhakha is mentioned elsewhere in the *Copper Scroll* in connection with a nearby dam, whereas the area surrounding Khirbet Samrah is entirely unsuitable for the construction of a dam.

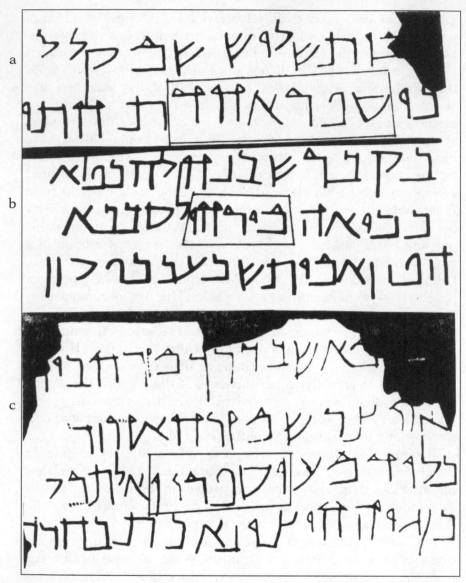

Figure 12

Three passages from the *Copper Scroll* describing (a) the hiding of a
scroll along with treasures, (b) the hiding of items near Jericho, and
(c) the hiding of scrolls near precious vessels.

not only in the Qumran caves, but in various places in the Judaean Wilderness and the plain of Jericho, with the burial of artifacts of great material value occurring simultaneously—and that events in Jerusalem, the obvious place of origin of the *Copper Scroll*, had something to do with this hiding activity.

Let us now focus on the actual places of hiding of the Qumran scrolls, and what they might indicate about the direction from which the hiders came. According to the traditional theory, the Qumran-sectarians decided to conceal their precious texts upon learning that the Roman force encamped at Jericho was, or would soon be, on its way south to capture the settlement. By this very token it is difficult to understand why the hiders would have traveled northward—i.e., in the direction of Jericho—to conceal so many of the scrolls. Common sense would dictate that they should rather have hurried to the south and west (where various hiding places could equally well be found), thus distancing themselves as much as possible from the threatening force, and putting themselves on their way to Masada in line with the standard theory. What is more, the most northerly situated manuscript caves— Caves 2, 1, 11, and 3 in that order moving northward (see Map 4, page 106)—are between as much as one and one and three-quarters of a kilometer north of Khirbet Qumran; but many caves lying on the same escarpment closer in to Khirbet Qumran were found to be entirely *devoid* of manuscripts. This implies hiding activities of a more complex character than that urged by champions of the traditional theory. Moreover, unlike the manuscripts found in all the other caves, those of 7Q consisted, as mentioned earlier, only of fragments written in Greek, indicating that they possibly derived from a different source than other scrolls.

These facts are difficult to understand in terms of the Qumran-sectarian theory, but readily explainable on the basis of movements of the hiders from the capital eastward to several areas of the Judaean Wilderness: first, to locations near Jericho; then, as the Roman buildup there proceeded in the months prior to the onset of the siege on the capital, to caves south of the Wadi Mukallik (Caves 3, 11, 1, and 2); and eventually, those near Wadi Qumran, lying yet farther to the south, i.e., Caves 4 through 10. (See Maps 4 and 7.)

To understand the full impact of the activity thus revealed, we may now turn to a different, somewhat later manuscript discovery that brilliantly illuminates the significance of the *Copper Scroll* and the discovery of manuscripts near Jericho in earlier centuries.

Spurred on by their various cave discoveries, scroll investigators had begun searching elsewhere in the Judaean Wilderness for more evidence of salient events in the history of first-century Palestine, and for what they hoped might be further traces of the ancient Essene sect. As we have seen, autograph documents relating to the Bar Kokhba revolt of A.D. 132–135 and reflecting other events of the early second century had been discovered in Wadi Murabba'at, to the south of Qumran, and, later on, in wadis lying inland from the region of En Gedi, yet farther to the south.

Subsequently, Israeli archaeologists turned their attention to Masada, the great rock fortress in the desert south of En Gedi, about fifty kilometers from Qumran. This was one of two known bastions overlooking the Dead Sea that figured prominently in the First Revolt, the other being Machaerus, lying east of the sea—both fortresses dating at least to the time of Alexander Jannaeus, who continued the policy of consolidation and expansion of the Hasmonaean state begun by the Maccabees in the prior century.

Masada lay within the confines of the state of Israel from its inception, and Israeli archaeologists conducted a survey there in 1955–56.[26] They did the basic work toward uncovering the main structures of the site, producing many important plans of it. The results convinced the participants that the entire site could eventually be uncovered, and once the wadis near En Gedi had been explored, this remarkable effort was carried out over two seasons (beginning in October 1963 and ending in April 1965).

Masada had been succinctly described in the previous century:

> Seen from the north it is an immense rock, half a mile long by an eighth broad, hewn out of the range that runs down the coast, and twisted round so as to point boldly north-east along the sea. It is isolated, precipitous on every side and inaccessible except in two places where winding paths, half goat tracks half ladders, may be followed by men in single file. On the west this stronghold falls only some 400 feet upon a promontory that connects it with the range behind. Everywhere else it shows, at least, 1,300 feet of cliff, but seaward as much as 1,700. The fortresses are very few that match this one in strength.[27]

There was good reason to explore it. Either Jonathan the Maccabee or Alexander Jannaeus had begun its construction, and eventually it was built upon, elaborately, by Herod, who enclosed it with a huge tower-studded wall. The *sicarii* seized it from a Roman garrison in A.D. 66, long before the siege of Jerusalem had begun, and conducted raids from it on neighboring territories, which Josephus carefully describes.[28] Various participants in the rebellion, including Menahem ben Judah, his nephew Eliezer ben Yair and others, and a band under Simon ben Giora, repaired there from Jerusalem before or during the siege. When the capital fell to the Romans, great numbers of the Jews fled, three thousand of whom were slain in the otherwise unknown forest of Jardes, evidently as they tried to make their way to Masada. The Roman siege (begun late in A.D. 73) and the eventual capture of this fortress followed several key events in the wake of the capture of Jerusalem: A Roman force under Bassus seized the important fortress of Herodium, approximately twelve kilometers south of the capital; Machaerus was besieged and surrendered; and the massacre of the three thousand refugees in the Jardes forest ensued.[29] While it is not known how many refugees actually fled to and reached Masada, Josephus states that, at the end of the Roman siege of this stronghold, only two women and five children survived, while in the final hour 960 Jews committed suicide there.

The capture of Masada was the last major event in the First Revolt.[30] Afterward, the Romans established a garrison there, some habitation of the site occurred during the Byzantine period, and gradually the site was abandoned. Falling into ruins, it was covered by the dust and debris of accumulated centuries.

In the ruins, however, much could still be made out. At the end of the last century, G. A. Smith discerned on the plateau not only the remnants of the surrounding wall but "cisterns and tombs, the remains of a castle and of a great palace, a [Byzantine] chapel with the apse still standing . . .";[31] and, as indicated, the Israeli archaeologists uncovered many basic features of the complex during their survey in the 1950s.

Some time afterward, in two seasons of digging—October 1963 to May 1964 and November 1964 to April 1965—archaeologists under the direction of Yigael Yadin uncovered the entire area of Masada, including Herod's palace and the portion of the site used by the *sicarii* and refugees from Jerusalem during the period of resistance to the Romans. In the ruins were found, beside many artifacts of the period, inscribed coins, jars with names of their owners, ostraca, and most importantly, fragments of at least fifteen Hebrew texts. Two of these—fragments of scrolls of Deuteronomy and Ezekiel—were found in the building identified as a synagogue, located adjacent to a portion of the northwestern section of the surrounding wall. One fragment of Leviticus was discovered near a wall of a terrace at the palatial villa covering the northern end of the plateau. Other texts were found in rooms in or near the great wall—several in one particular casemate (i.e., a room or chamber of a rampart)—in the areas of Masada that had been mostly occupied by the Zealots and the refugees from Jerusalem. They included a fragment of Leviticus, fragments of two copies of Psalms, portions (twenty-six fragments) of the original Hebrew text of the Wisdom of Ben Sira (= Ecclesiasticus), fragments of two copies of Jubilees, fragments of several otherwise unknown literary texts, some documentary papyri fragments in Hebrew, Latin, and Greek, and, most remarkably, a part of the so-called *Songs of the Sabbath Sacrifice* (known also as the "Angelic Liturgy"). Manuscript fragments of this latter work, but in other handwritings, had also been found, *mirabile dictu*, in Qumran Caves 4 and 11 more than a decade earlier.

The literary texts were, generally speaking, of the same character as those found at Qumran—i.e., canonical writings, apocryphal and pseudepigraphic compositions, and texts otherwise unknown. In addition, the handwritings in the fragments were all different from one another just as they almost constantly were in the Qumran scrolls. They had, however, been discovered at Masada, quite far away from Qumran and a fortress never imagined to have been a place where Essenes lived. Yadin and his colleagues were in fact now looking at the decisive evidence pointing to the actual home of the manuscript finds of the Judaean Wilderness.

When, in 1960, some of the Qumran fragments of the *Songs of the Sabbath Sacrifice* had been published, the editor inferred that the work implied a special calendar dividing the year into twelve months of thirty days.[32] Previous writers had held that such a calendar was peculiar to the "Qumran Essenes"[33]—an explanation that might have been strongly shaken had they known the very same work was hidden at Masada, many of whose defenders came from Jerusalem before and following the capture of the city in A.D. 70. The discovery of this and other Qumran-like fragments at Masada obviously ought to have led to a questioning of the notion that the Dead Sea Scrolls could only have been written by a particular sect living at Qumran.

Instead, a special explanation was once again introduced into the debate on scroll origins, this time by Yadin himself: This particular scroll, and perhaps others found at Masada, had a peculiar history—either alone or with others, it was brought there by the Qumran Essenes themselves, who, he claimed, joined up with the defenders in the last few years of the revolt. When offering this explanation, Yadin refrained from as much as mentioning Jerusalem in connection with the Masada scroll finds.

There is, however, no evidence in Josephus or elsewhere that Essenes in small or large numbers had joined the Masada defenders. In support of his position, Yadin resorted to Josephus's reference to John, the Essene warrior of Timna.[34] (Other Qumranologists had earlier adduced the same figure when confronted by the signs of battle at Khirbet Qumran and by the contents of the *War Scroll*, attempting thereby to give an entirely new, warlike image to the reputed "Essenes of Qumran.") Posing the question whether other Essenes might not have joined the revolt, Yadin answered affirmatively by reference to the *Songs* found at Masada.

We need to consider more closely the reasoning behind Yadin's decision to treat the *Songs* text in the way he did. In his first report on the Masada excavations, he asserted that Josephus had stated that "many sects of Jewry took part in [the revolt against Rome], either as a whole or in part or at a certain stage of its developments,"[35] but the only references here to the Essenes were the two passages mentioning John the Essene. Josephus himself does not allude to military activity by groups of Essenes anywhere in his writings.

Yadin formulated his views in a slightly different fashion for his popular volume on Masada. Insisting that there was "in fact direct evidence in the writings of Josephus of Essene participation in the war," he wrote:

> It will be recalled that Josephus, at the beginning of the revolt, was one of the Jewish commanders responsible for the Galilee region, and he certainly was acquainted with other commanders of the revolt. When he lists the names of the commanders of the revolt and their sectors, he relates that the commander of the important central sector . . . was someone named John the Essene.

Yadin then switched from description to direct conclusion:

> Is it likely that only one Essene joined the revolt and became an outstanding commander? I think not. It is more likely that a considerable number of Essenes also joined the rebellion. And after the country had been destroyed and Masada remained the sole stronghold and outpost in the war against the Romans, it is likely that all who had fought together and survived found shelter there, among them Essene participants. It would have been natural for all such groups to have brought with them their holy writings. This, it seems to me, explains the presence of the Qumranic sectarian scroll at Masada. . . .[36]

That Yadin believed the "Qumranic sectarian scroll" to have been brought to Masada not by Essenes in general but in fact by the Essenes of Qumran is clear from other statements he hazarded:

> Most scholars believe that the sect which had the scrolls of Qumran was the Essenes. . . . These say that the Essenes lived on the western shore of the Dead Sea in an area which very much suggests the location of Khirbet Qumran. . . . I believe that the evidence in the hands of the majority who identify the Qumran sect with the Essenes is so strong that one needs to find another explanation for the presence of a Qumranic scroll in the Masada stronghold of the Zealots. It seems to me that the discovery of this scroll serves as proof indeed that the Essenes also participated in the great revolt against the Romans. . . .[37]

Now since Yadin held the view that those surviving the fight against the Romans would naturally have brought their writings with them in seeking shelter at Masada, he might quite reasonably have raised the possibility that at least some of the Masada scrolls came from Jerusalem, the main center of Jewish resistance against the Romans prior to its capture. It was moreover evident that the contents and the handwritings of the literary texts found at Masada as a whole showed the same general character as those found at Qumran—and thus for this reason alone Yadin should have offered at least some explanation of the origin of the *other* Masada texts, not only the *Songs of the Sabbath Sacrifice*. He was, however, entirely silent on this important matter.

No subsequent treatment of the Masada literary finds by other traditional Qumranologists has since raised this problem, despite its self-evident nature, and it seems fair to conclude that, to this day, supporters of Yadin's interpretation are not anxious to grant the likelihood that any of the nonbiblical scrolls were brought to Masada from the capital. At all events, they refrain in their writings from as much as discussing this fundamental problem.

Yadin's handling of the question of origin of the Masada texts came into play in the views of Cecil Roth and G. R. Driver, who postulated that the Qumran scrolls were products of the Zealot movement and that Khirbet Qumran was itself one of their strongholds. Josephus had indicated that the *sicarii* as early as A.D. 66 took Masada from the Romans then occupying it,[38] and Roth, among other scholars, held that the *sicarii* were in essence a subgroup of the Zealots. He was thus quick to point out that the discovery of a "Qumranic" text at Masada—i.e., the *Songs of the Sabbath Sacrifice*—supported his own view of scroll origins. Yadin's case, he stated,

> is that the highly significant manuscript in question is an intrusion. This suggestion is contrary to the accepted canons of scholarship. Unless there is a very strong argument against it, archaeological evidence must be interpreted within the context of the place where it was discovered: if this rule is not observed, a scholar will always be at liberty to disregard as extraneous any object or ancient record which runs contrary to his preconception. . . . The only argument for its being an intrusion is that it does not square with preconceived notions, themselves susceptible to weighty, and in some opinions overwhelming, objections. . . .

Roth also pointed out that the conception of Essenes living together with Zealots—their very opposites in belief and temperament—was somewhat ludicrous.[39]

Yet, despite the lack of a reasonable basis for Yadin's assertion, Edmund Wilson strongly seconded it, stating that the Masada copy of the *Songs*

> must have been brought there by someone from the Sect, who . . . wanted to keep his [sectarian] schedule. . . . Josephus, as Yadin points out, speaks twice of John the Essene as one of the generals. . . . And is it not possible that some of the Essenes, still clinging to the schedule of their dissident calendar, had come up from the vulnerable Qumran on the shore to the formidable heights of Masada?[40]

Thus the renowned man of letters had come to the aid of a second charismatic archaeologist, once again supporting a highly questionable interpretation of the manuscript finds in the Judaean Wilderness.

Yadin later collaborated with John Strugnell's student Carol Newsom in a joint study of the Masada fragment of the *Songs* (1984). In this study, published in the year of Yadin's death, they reiterated his view of the origin of this text, explaining that "Historically, the discovery of this fragment of a Qumran work is significant because it implies the participation of members of the Qumran community, almost certainly to be identified with the Essenes, in the revolt against Rome." By this time, all nonbiblical writings found in the Qumran caves and themselves not part of the official Apocrypha and Pseudepigrapha of the Old Testament were being called "Qumran works"—with the refinement that those particular texts obviously composed before the assumed sect was thought to have established itself were to be considered as "pre-Qumranic." So intent were the authors on convincing readers that Essenes had written the *Songs* that they deemed it necessary to repeat that the "participation of the Essenes in the revolt is attested by Josephus"—although they could cite no more than the same two passages dealing with the military activities of John the Essene general. Josephus does write that the Essenes suffered great torture and humiliation at the hands of the Romans during the revolt, but never states that the Essenes fought back. On the basis of the example of a single known Essene military person, one is hardly justified in speaking of "Essene participation" in the First Revolt.[41]

Moreover, in the passages of the *Songs* that the editors published one could detect no ideas reminiscent either of the Essenes as portrayed by Philo, Josephus, and Pliny, or of the authors of the *Manual of Discipline*. This became even more apparent when Newsom published the full text of the *Songs* the following year.[42] These poetic fragments were totally unlike any of the Qumran scrolls previously attributed to sectarians on the basis of their content. Although after two thousand years the poet's imaginative ideas are as fragmentary as the shreds of parchment on which they are preserved, they can be at least partially restored and translated. The poet conceives of the Temple sacrifices as the merely mundane counterpart to the cantillation of angels in heaven. While each earthly sacrifice conducted day by day is proceeding, the angels have their own repertoire of chant. Here are three examples of the songs attributed to them:

(a) [A son]g for the sixth Sabbath offering, on the ninth of the [second] month. [Praise the Lord] of those lords, who dwell in the uppermost heights . . . holy of holies; and raise paeans to His majesty . . . the [kn]owledge of the eternal [angelic] lords, those called up to the highest heights. . . . [43]

(b) Chant mightily to the Lord of Holiness by the seven chants of His wonders; chant unto the King of holiness, seven by seven times, the words of the chants of wondrousness—the seven paeans of His blessings, the paeans of the greatness of His . . . , the seven paeans of the exaltation of His kingdom, the seven paeans of [. . .], the seven paeans of thanks for His wonders, the seven paeans of jubilation for His might, the seven paeans of chant for His holiness. . . . [44]

(c) . . . The mighty murmur of song [surges] on the heights of their wings, the sound of the lords; they bless the edifice of the Chariot's throne, (there) above the cherubs' firmament, [near] the Firmament of Light they sing, beneath the seat of His Glory. But when the wheels revolve, the Angels of holiness return. From amidst those wheels of His Glory there is as if the glimpse of fire of the spirits of the Holy of Holies, round about, the glimpse of stalks of fire, as the image of lightning. . . . [45]

Such lines, sensitively written, often in alliterative patterns, and with rich use of exaltative vocabulary, are characteristic of the *Songs* as a whole. There is nothing "sectarian" about them. They reflect the thinking of a Palestinian Jewish poet who sought by creative imagination to spiritualize the ancient cult-ritual of animal sacrifice—objectively speaking, a cruel and bloody act perpetrated on innocent beasts—without declaring the act itself to be meaningless or wrong. The poet sublimates its meaning by use of beatific idiom; ultimately the sacrifice itself becomes a mere earthly shadow of the angelic adoration of the Deity.

In her edition of this work, however, Newsom posed a revealing question: "One must ask of every manuscript found at Qumran," she stated, "whether it is a composition of the Qumran community itself or a pre-Qumran composition copied and preserved in the Qumran library." This, of course, reflected the thinking of Yadin and of innumerable fellow Qumranologists, leaving no middle ground for works that might be neither "Qumranic" nor "pre-Qumranic."

In this manner, Newsom was able to refrain from considering

the possibility that the scrolls, in whole or in part, may have originated in Jerusalem. At the same time, she avoided dealing with
the objections raised earlier by Cecil Roth. The important question provoked by the discovery of fragments of the *Songs* at
Masada was—perhaps not surprisingly—relegated to a single footnote where, referring to the view of Yadin, she stated that the
"presence of a copy of the [*Songs*] at Masada is perhaps best
explained by assuming that it was taken there by a member of the
Qumran community who participated in the revolt against
Rome. . . ."[46] Thus, suppression of the critical considerations was
accompanied by a rather unenthusiastic endorsement of the
explanation offered by Yadin. My criticism of this treatment[47] was
preceded by that of a traditional Qumranologist, F. Garcia-
Martinez, who, observing Newsom's failure to deal with other
possible explanations of the presence of this fragment at Masada,
questioned the adequacy of her handling of the basic problem.[48]

In 1990, Newsom retracted her earlier position.[49] Frankly
acknowledging that no substantive grounds prevailed for treating
this work as a sectarian text, she stated that "If one examines the
Sabbath Songs with respect to content and rhetorical purpose,
there is nothing clearly sectarian about them. . . . Previously I had
expressed my agreement with Yadin's suggestion that the text
might have been carried there by a member of the Qumran community after the destruction of Khirbet Qumran. . . . I admit,
though, that the suggestion has something of the flavor of the theory of epicycles introduced to save the ptolemaic cosmology from
erosion by apparently contradictory empirical observations. . . ."

There were, in effect, never any valid grounds for Yadin's original claim, and Yadin himself had adduced none. In his first discussion of Masada, he had divided up the scroll finds into three
groups: those which he called "Biblical" texts, "Apocryphal and
Sectarian Writings," and "Papyri" (i.e., the documentary papyri
mentioned above).[50] He left no room in his classification for other
writings of the Jews—those that might be nonsectarian, or nonpseudepigraphic, merely reflecting the literature of Palestinian
Judaism as a whole, even though never classified in Christian
Bibles as "Apocrypha" or otherwise known about previously. He
made no statement, in fact, that might indicate he even conceived
of the Jews of intertestamental times as writing and possessing
such literature—thus failing to look beyond the texts to the vital
issues at the heart of his own work.

Yadin's declaration that we "can state with certainty that [the *Songs of the Sabbath Sacrifice*] is one of the writings of the Dead Sea sect,"[51] while protecting the old Qumran-sectarian theory, clearly moved against the known fact of capture of Masada by Judaean *sicarii* and the augmentation of the force there by refugees—e.g., Zealots but perhaps also others—from the siege of Jerusalem. Roth's criticism of Yadin for misappropriating the *Songs* in an attempt to bolster the Qumran-Essene hypothesis was entirely justified. But Edmund Wilson, as we have seen, was quick to come to the aid of Yadin, dismissing Roth and his Oxford colleague G. A. Driver as "too old and inflexible, it seems, to assimilate new material."[52]

Yadin's explanation was not only in itself unwarranted, but had the effect of promoting pan-Qumranism to new heights: those manuscripts near Jericho mentioned by Origen were said to be earlier discoveries that originated at Qumran; the many manuscripts referred to by Timotheus were also really Qumran manuscripts; the fragments of over eight hundred scrolls found at Qumran originated there too; and now the *Songs* fragment and perhaps still other Masada texts were likewise being claimed to come from Qumran. By Yadin's view, the Hebrew literature of first-century Palestinian Jews other than Essenes had disappeared, while that of the claimed Qumran-Essenes was represented through the centuries by at least four discoveries that could not possibly have consisted, at the beginning, of less than a thousand manuscripts.

To accept such proposals conjointly was, on careful reflection, extremely difficult. The one cogent inference that could be drawn from the presence of first-century Hebrew manuscripts at Masada was that the Jewish *sicarii* who inhabited that site possessed scrolls they had brought there after taking the fortress in A.D. 66, while other Jews took scrolls with them, in addition to basic possessions, when they withdrew from Jerusalem to that site. (Roth himself erred in not considering that part of the story, out of his own enthusiastic efforts to bolster the Zealot theory.) In the Masada excavations, surviving remnants of these possessions were discovered, including such texts as the *Songs of the Sabbath Sacrifice*—a work which, before the Masada discoveries, was erroneously believed to have had a unique connection with sectarians thought to be living at Khirbet Qumran.

Thus, without recourse to the artificial proposal of a bond

between Masada and the theorized Qumran-Essenes, the Masada discoveries powerfully suggested—as the *Copper Scroll* had done—that manuscripts were removed from Jerusalem during the revolt; that literary texts of the Palestinian Jews, in other words, were deemed precious enough by them to warrant rescue during times of danger. It is not difficult to see why this obvious explanation for the discovery of manuscripts at Masada and elsewhere in the Judaean Wilderness was not adopted when the finds were first made: The potent force of the Qumran-Essene hypothesis essentially derived from the order in which the discoveries came about.

Let us remind ourselves of the unfolding sequence traced in the preceding chapters. The seed of the original paradigm was planted in the very first months of discovery, immediately after some columns of the *Manual of Discipline* had been read, and was thereupon cultivated by eminent scholars. The Khirbet Qumran site, once cleared away, was thereupon inserted as a tangible element within the nascent paradigm. Subsequent finds in the wilderness were then used to buttress the same paradigm, which by the 1960s had taken on the characteristics of a deeply rooted tree with many flowering branches. Only by removing oneself from the excitement and sweep of events prevailing during the years of discovery, and by considering the totality of finds without respect to their accidental chronological sequence, could one fully appreciate the problems inherent in the traditional approach or begin to resolve them by a more satisfactory explanation of the evidence.

One of the gravest difficulties encountered in the early years of discovery had to do with identification of Khirbet Qumran as the main settlement of Essenes in Palestine. This identification, as we have observed, was first made primarily on the basis of rules contained in but one of the seven original scrolls, the *Manual of Discipline*. Laws of this scroll having an Essenic flavor were then connected with Pliny's statement that the solitary and celibate Essenes lived west of the Dead Sea with only the palm trees for company, and that lying below them was En Gedi. At first it seemed logical to infer that the Khirbet Qumran settlement, located near the caves, was just this site, and that Essenes living there had hastily hidden the *Manual*, along with other writings of theirs, before the arrival of Roman troops at the settlement. When Khirbet Qumran was excavated, however, the various elements of a fortresslike complex were revealed, and the archaeologists working at the site uncovered evidence proving that it had been stormed by Roman soldiers after a hard-fought battle.

As we have seen, the fact that the resisters were obviously members of an armed troop—precisely unlike the Essenes as they are described in the classical sources—did not deter the archaeologists from identifying the site as an Essene settlement. Hence they rejected a basic feature of the classical description of the Essenes—namely, their peace-loving and nonmilitary nature. Josephus, after all, had described the by now familiar John the Essene as having served in the war against Rome. As an explanation of the nature of the Masada finds, the memory of John would then be evoked anew. (In any event, he may simply have been called "the Essene" because of an original Essenic background subsequently forsaken in favor of the rebels' cause, just as converts from Judaism to Christianity in mediaeval times would occasionally have the term *Judaeus*, "the Jew," attached to their newly assumed names.)

In retrospect, this process illustrates how texts can be bent to the needs of a rampant hypothesis. At the time, the urge to find the traces of the long-lost Essenic sect, whose mystique and religious appeal had been enhanced by a tradition of learned and semilearned writing stretching back several centuries,[53] was what mattered most. In seeking such traces, in voicing enthusiastic assent to the sectarian theory, scholars largely disregarded the blatant contradictions assailing the theory already by the mid-1960s. Among these contradictions were the following:

- The peace-loving Essenes guarded a military site and fought as warriors there.
- Celibate Essenes lived at or near Khirbet Qumran even though no general endorsement of celibacy was to be found anywhere in the Qumran manuscripts.
- The members of the "sect," living all together in their isolated desert location, wore phylacteries while not yet sharing a consensus as to the actual wording of the Pentateuchal texts contained in them—even though the *Manual of Discipline* provided for authoritative and decisive leadership of the claimed sect by priests.
- Even though skeletons of women and children were found in the Khirbet Qumran cemetery, the site was nevertheless that of the Essenes of Pliny, who describes them as celibate.

- Two types of Essenes, marrying and nonmarrying, both inhabited areas in or near the Khirbet Qumran site at the same time, and Pliny simply mentioned only the celibate ones.
- The four thousand Essenes described by Josephus and Philo were in reality a much more important sect, being the authors of at least most of the apocalyptic literature of the Jews.
- In the Qumran fortress, there was a manuscript-writing room where Essene monks composed and copied texts, although no autograph manuscripts that might attest to this literary creativity have ever been found, and although (in contrast with the findings at Masada) neither the so-called scriptorium nor any other Khirbet Qumran *locus* contained a single scrap of parchment when excavated.
- Although a great many scribes copied just those manuscript fragments that survived in the caves, the manuscripts, as a product of the "sect of Qumran," were written or copied at least mainly, if not entirely, at Khirbet Qumran.
- The Qumran settlement was surely a "laura" or "motherhouse" of the Essene movement, even though no legal deeds, letters, or other bona fide documentary evidence attesting to this claim have ever been discovered.
- The purity-loving "sectarians of Qumran," with priests at their head, established a cemetery within the short distance of thirty-five yards of the settlement even though there was much more available space for a cemetery at considerably greater distances from the place of habitation.
- The mention of "Damascus" in a manuscript describing the migration of an ancient sect to that city was really an allusion to Khirbet Qumran, and descriptions of the discovery of manuscripts near Jericho during the first millennium A.D. were likewise allusions to such discoveries in earlier times precisely in the caves near Khirbet Qumran.
- The single Qumran scroll inscribed on copper and describing, in straightforward bookkeeping fashion, the burial of great treasures and scrolls in the Judaean Wilderness, was either a mendacious or an irrelevant document and did not originate in Jerusalem; or else it was an authentic document that showed the Essenes were far wealthier than classical sources portrayed them as being.
- Although Pliny speaks of a single settlement of Essenes above En Gedi, there were really many such settlements in the area, since graves resembling those in the Khirbet Qumran cemetery have been found in widely scattered parts of that region.

- One or more key scrolls found at Masada did not come from Jerusalem, but rather originated at Qumran itself, having been brought there by those very "Essenes of Qumran" who were seeking refuge from the Roman onslaught.

Taken collectively, these claims—even any three or four of them—constitute an impossible combination of ideas. When they are juxtaposed, they show in an obvious way that another interpretation of the scroll discoveries is needed. Once seen in the light of the descriptions in the *Copper Scroll*, the statements of Origen and Timotheus, and the great variety and number of scrolls found in the Qumran caves, the Masada discoveries render both unnecessary and obsolete the mental gymnastics required to sustain a mythology of Qumran origins. The finds point firmly to the Jerusalem origin of all of the scrolls.

The Qumran manuscripts were, by the evidence, part of yet larger collections of scrolls, hidden away at some time during the first century A.D. in *various* places throughout the Judaean Wilderness, including Masada, the caves near Khirbet Qumran, and areas near Jericho. Artifacts of great material value quite obviously from Jerusalem had been buried in the same general area and at the same time, and the concealment of both scrolls and treasures was owing to an important historic cause—one clearly revealed by the Masada discoveries, and which we may now explore.

Let us first recall Josephus's description of the circumstances surrounding the Roman siege of Jerusalem: "Galilee was now wholly subdued," he writes, "after affording the Romans a strenuous training for the impending Jerusalem campaign."[54] He then tells of the entrance of the fugitives from Galilee, led by John of Gischala, into the capital:

> . . . The whole population poured forth and each of the fugitives was surrounded by a vast crowd, eagerly asking what had befallen outside. . . . They casually mentioned the fall of Gischala. . . . When, however, the story of the prisoners came out, profound consternation took possession of the people, who drew thereupon plain indications of their own impending capture. But John . . . went round the several groups, instigating them to war by the hopes he raised, making out the Romans to be weak, extolling their own power, and ridiculing the ignorance of the inexperienced; even had they wings, he remarked, the Romans would never surmount the walls of Jerusalem. . . . By these harangues most of

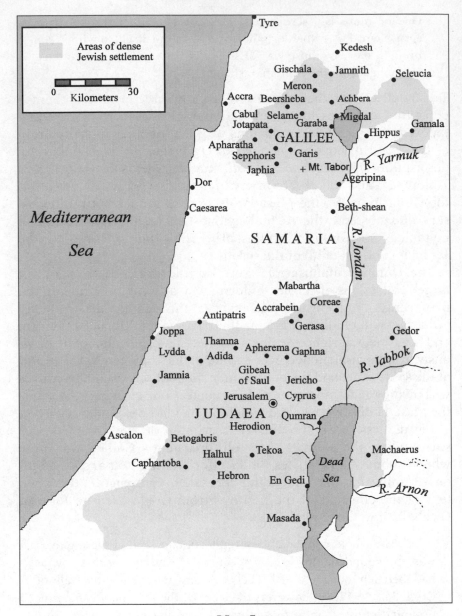

Map 5
The Jews of Palestine at the time of the First Revolt (A.D. 66–73).

the youth were seduced into his service and incited to war; but of the sober and elder men there was not one who did not foresee the future and mourn for the city as if it had already met its doom.[55]

Under these circumstances the more thoughtful inhabitants of Jerusalem would have behaved no differently than other people facing a siege. They had little choice but to hide away their wealth, their books, even the phylacteries that eventually turned up in such relative abundance in the Qumran caves.

This process may have started shortly after the fall of Galilee and the entrance of the refugees into the city; it perhaps continued for a few months after the siege on Jerusalem had begun, close to A.D. 70. Some of the objects were hidden, as Josephus tells us, beneath the city itself. But between the fall of Galilee (November A.D. 67) and the opening stages of the siege, inhabitants of the capital were free to come and go as they wished. During later stages of the siege, particularly before Titus built a siege wall entirely surrounding the city late in the spring of A.D. 70, they continued to have access to territories outside the walls; even as conditions in the city worsened, many outside deposits were evidently made. Those charged with hiding artifacts of importance would clearly have sought to do so in areas the Romans did not yet control; but already by the summer of A.D. 68 the only such territory was that portion of Judaea lying to the east and south of the city—that area, in other words, where Hebrew scrolls were discovered in the third, ninth, and twentieth centuries.

Not being within the city, Josephus did not know of this activity, but nevertheless he described how during the siege Judah son of Ari, commander of a company at the siege, had "secretly escaped through some of the underground passages" (*War* 7.215),[56] fleeing then to the Jardes forest. The Jerusalemites were particularly able to utilize points of egress in the southern part of the city, where Roman troops would not concentrate until the capture of the second wall of the capital had been completed (end of May, A.D. 70).[57] In this regard, we may note that as Josephus describes the war council called by Titus, he furnishes the reason for constructing a new siege wall in June of A.D. 70: "Titus pointed out the extreme difficulty of throwing up earthworks, owing to lack of materials, and the even greater difficulty of guarding against sallies; for to encompass the city with troops would, owing to its extent and the

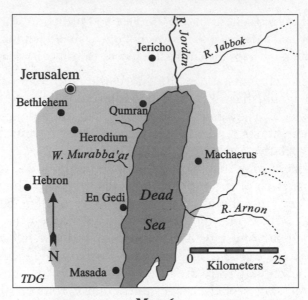

Map 6
Approximate area of Judaea still under
control of the Jews at the time of the Roman
capture of Jerusalem.

obstacles presented by the ground, be no easy matter, and would, moreover, expose them to enemy attacks. They might guard the obvious outlets, *but the Jews, from necessity and their knowledge of the locality, would contrive secret routes*; and, should supplies be furtively smuggled in, the siege would still be further protracted. . . . " (*War* **5**.496–497).[58]

Thus we see that the siege itself, as well as the prior impending threat of it, in fact provided the compelling and decisive reason for the hiding away of scrolls and precious treasures of the capital—an effort carried out with considerable success, despite the obvious obstacles that hindered it.

Prosaically understood as an authentic record of treasures hidden away by the Jews of Jerusalem during the first century A.D., and seen in light of the events Josephus describes, the *Copper Scroll's* particular importance dramatically emerges. Several wadi systems led out eastward from Jerusalem's environs. (See Map 4.) To the northeast were the great wadis Farah and Qelt; almost due east were the gorges leading into the Wadi Mukallik, which eventually emptied into the Dead Sea near its northwestern tip; and to the southeast was the Brook Qidron (known later as the Nahal Qidron and the Wadi al-Nar), which had its inception at the Pool of Siloam—within the boundaries of Jerusalem—and the Spring of Gihon. The Qidron then headed with its tributaries into the Judaean Wilderness and finally to the Dead Sea, south of Qumran. Between Mukallik and Qidron additional wadis began converging in the so-called Buqeiah region, coming together in the Wadi Qumran gorge adjacent to Khirbet Qumran, which received such a great abundance of that system's water in the several rainy months of the year. Crucially, the *Copper Scroll* not only specifically mentions a deposit of four talents of silver hidden by "the dam at the mouth of the gorge of the Qidron," but also describes numerous hiding places near aqueducts, water channels, and other installations. (Typical vestiges of such hydraulic systems may still be observed, for example, in the Wadi Qelt; they were characteristic of wadis in Judaea situated near and between places of habitation.)

Two passages in the scroll make mention of hiding places for treasures in the Valley of Achor: a wadi that in modern times has been identified with the Wadi Qelt, Mukallik, or Nu'eimah—but which may also be identified with the Wadi Makkuk, the main east–west riverbed about four kilometers north of Wadi Qelt. This ended in the gorge below Quruntul and near the Tell el-Sultan, and its identity with Achor would place the Achor treasures close to the majority of other deposits described in the *Copper Scroll*. The listing of riverbeds, water systems, and gorges described in this scroll as hiding places forms a word map of the complex system of wadis leading out from Jerusalem through the Judaean Wilderness and toward the Dead Sea. The great treasures described as hidden there, and the scrolls and "writings" associated with them in several columns of the text, are thus geographically traceable directly back to Jerusalem. The complex of wadis and gorges leading away from the city was attainable to its inhabitants through the various routes and passages Josephus describes, some of which remained unknown to the Romans at the time of the city's siege.

We see, then, that the very phenomena constituting grave anomalies in the Qumran-Essene hypothesis emphatically underscore the scrolls' Jerusalem origin. The reason no substantive large numbers of original letters and legal documents and no autographs of literary works but only scribal copies have been found at Qumran is that the writings came from *libraries*, with some personal items of their owners—e.g., phylacteries and a few documentary records—hurriedly thrown in. What the Jewish inhabitants of Khirbet Qumran and its surroundings quite likely did was to contribute to the storage of bundles or sacks of texts in large jars that were then hidden in desert caves, while many other scrolls were stored in some of the caves in greater haste, minus such protection. In Cave 4, for example, the scrolls were evidently *buried*, without being stored in jars. The great number of scroll remnants, exhibiting a variety of disparate doctrines, many without tangible sectarian bias, indicates their place of origin was a large cultural center in Hellenistic and Roman Judaea, such as only Jerusalem was before A.D. 70. The abundance of hidden treasures, the geographical configuration of the discoveries, and the *Copper Scroll* word map point unmistakably in the same direction. Timotheus's ninth-century description—"a dwelling within the rocks in which were many books"—likewise hints that the scrolls found near Jericho were from a place of cultural importance.

It is important to note that the official archives of Jerusalem were destroyed in a fire set by the Jewish insurgents in A.D. 66

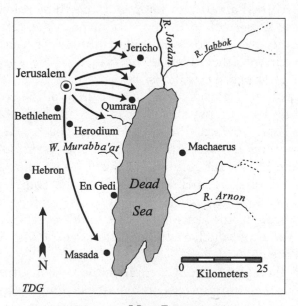

Map 7
Geographical representation of the
hypothesis of Jerusalem origin of
the scrolls.

during the interfactional strife raging there at that time, described by Josephus in vivid detail.[59] Because of the loss of these archival records, virtually no documentary texts of the years immediately before A.D. 70 survived, with the exception of the several scraps that have turned up in the finds of Cave 4. Only remnants of the libraries and collections of books that evidently abounded in the city have been found in any number in the Judaean Wilderness; these texts show, conversely, that in antiquity, libraries existed among the Palestinian Jews in the same way as among inhabitants of other parts of the Mediterranean world. It is reasonable to infer that these and other conclusions reached above would have been arrived at by scholars both naturally and inevitably, if only the actual order of discoveries had been *reversed*.

In this hypothetical series of events, the first manuscript finds would have occurred at Masada, a site long known to have been the last stronghold of the Jewish revolutionaries, many of whom had fled the capital after its fall. The interesting literary fragments discovered there would quite obviously have been attributed to those Jews, and before long scholars would have justifiably claimed that the new fragments, however meager, cast new light on Jewish thought and literary creativity in Jerusalem in the years before the First Revolt. If the Masada discoveries had come before the others, there would have been no reason then to say anything at all about the Essenes.[60]

In this reverse order, the next discovery would have been of nonliterary, documentary texts in the wadis near En Gedi and then at Murabba'at. From these texts, interpreters would have perceived that genuine, substantive Hebrew autograph letters and legal deeds of the period of the Second Revolt had astonishingly survived and could help to elucidate significant aspects of this period of history. Some scholars would then very likely have asked whether autographs of the First Revolt as well were hidden away somewhere in the Judaean Wilderness.

A search of the caves to the north of Wadi Murabba'at might then have resulted in the revelation of Qumran Cave 4, with its thousands of literary fragments. Scholars would obviously have called to mind the testimony of ancient writers regarding the discovery of still other Hebrew manuscripts in caves near Jericho during the third and eighth centuries. They would have begun to see that a large-scale phenomenon of sequestration of hundreds and perhaps thousands of Hebrew scrolls had taken place at approximately the time of the First Revolt. Moving northward, those exploring the area would have found other manuscript-bearing caves that in effect contributed to the same recognition; and any disappointment in finding only a few shreds of letters or other autographs among the literary texts would have been assuaged by Josephus's words about the burning of the archives of Jerusalem in A.D. 66. The scholars would have concluded that the literary texts revealed many new aspects of thought, including heterodox ideas, that could be attributed, along with views already known from the apocryphal and apocalyptic literature, to the Palestinian Jews of that time. They would have inferred that the quasi-biblical idiom of most of the texts was that in use among the Jews for literary purposes during intertestamental times.

The subsequent discovery of the *Copper Scroll*, with its references to the burial of precious metals and artifacts as well as texts, and its strong geographical hints, would have at once supplied investigators with the final clue needed to solve the mystery of the massive concealment of Hebrew scrolls.

Finally, arriving at what is now called Qumran Cave 1, those continuing the search would have discovered a number of additional scrolls—a few biblical texts, others showing affinities with the apocryphal literature, and at least one virtually intact scroll that appeared to contain ideas similar to certain ones held by the Essenes. These would have confirmed the earlier finding, based on the Cave 4 discoveries, that a wide spectrum of doctrines and ideas, incorporated at least partly in several religious movements, were represented by the discoveries of the Judaean Wilderness. The *Yahad*, or Unity group, would have been clearly recognizable as one religious movement of the time—but would not have been perceived as the owner of all the manuscripts discovered, or as a group whose ideas could be read into all or most of the scrolls.

It is only because the discoveries did not occur in this hypothetical order that a theory of entirely different character was formulated and then developed, within countless articles, books, and theses, into the colossal structure that, by the late sixties, imprisoned its builders.

CHAPTER 6

Scroll Origins: Rengstorf's Theory and Edmund Wilson's Response

In the autumn of 1969, soon after personally examining the Khirbet Qumran site—and having by then been forced to conclude that not a single published Qumran text except the *Copper Scroll* showed signs of being an original literary autograph—I undertook a review of all the texts that had become available. Noticing that virtually each new one was in a handwriting different than all the others, I began to see that the growing number of scripts was starting to pose still another problem for the sectarian hypothesis: How many scribes, after all, could have lived together at Khirbet Qumran at any one time, or even over three or four generations? With its specimens of at least fifty additional handwritings, the first volume (1955) of the Oxford series of scroll publications—dealing only with the manuscripts of Cave 1—contrasted strongly with the mere seven scribal handwritings present in the scrolls discovered in 1947. The second volume, containing as it did texts from a later period (early second century A.D.), was not relevant to the developing picture; but the third, published in 1962, revealed specimens of over eighty additional scripts dating from before A.D. 70. Later, in 1965, a single scroll among those found in Cave 11—the so-called *Psalms Scroll* containing both canonical and noncanonical psalms—was published as well, and this too turned out to be in still another scribe's handwriting. Afterward, in 1968, John Allegro's edition of the first Oxford volume of texts from Qumran Cave 4, consisting of commentaries on prophetic scriptures and on portions of the Book of Psalms along with other works of interest, revealed at least twenty more scripts.[1]

With a total of over one hundred and fifty scribal handwritings already identifiable by the mid-1960s, it was evident that virtually each new text being published was in a different hand than that of its predecessors. Meanwhile, by that time, several popular books by scholars who were part of Père de Vaux's team—J. T. Milik, J. Allegro, and F. M. Cross—had appeared, all describing the fact that fragments of at least *four hundred* different compositions had been discovered in Cave 4. Assuming roughly the same ratio of handwritings to texts in the unpublished scrolls as in those published, this would imply that there were as many as three to four hundred more scribal handwritings preserved among the Cave 4 manuscripts alone. If so, this would be a fact of the deepest significance. For by no stretch of the imagination could it be thought that, even over two centuries, as many as four or five hundred scribes had worked in the room that de Vaux had so confidently labeled a "scriptorium," or that groups of twenty or thirty such scribes would be gathered at any one time in such a harsh desert location, removed from the very city whose inhabitants would have been the main readers of the scrolls they were ostensibly producing. If verified, this very large number of scribes would in itself require a different explanation of the hiding of the Judaean Wilderness manuscripts than the one being so ardently championed by the official team.

Being attached at the time as a visiting associate to the American School of Oriental Research in Jerusalem (by then renamed the Albright Institute), I was able to report on some of my tentative conclusions regarding the manuscripts at a seminar convened by the acting director in the winter of 1970. A heated debate followed my talk, characterized particularly by a categorical rejection, on the part of those Qumranologists who were present, of each of the several problems I treated. According to them, the *Copper Scroll* had to be a forgery. The "Damascus" of the *Damascus Covenant* had to refer to Qumran since nothing else made sense. If no manuscript had been found in the "scriptorium," it was because weather and climate had destroyed every last shred. No other site but Khirbet Qumran could have been the place where Pliny's Essenes lived. They argued that since everyone agreed that a sect had lived at Qumran, what right did I have to challenge such a broad consensus?

Such was the tone of the debate, and that evening I became acutely aware of the feeling of ideological kinship that had developed among traditional Qumranologists as they pursued their fiercely held view of the scrolls' origins. I perceived how, with the heretic who had championed the authenticity of the *Copper Scroll* now extirpated from their midst, their belief in the sectarian interpretation had solidified; I saw how they were now laboring, in a spirit of privileged cooperation, toward the elaboration of what to them seemed a fundamental truth. Sitting at the big oak seminar table in the school's library, I felt an intense coldness developing toward me among the traditional Qumranologists as, gathered about, they heard my responses to their objections. As they made their way back to their rooms and apartments in the Albright Institute and the Ecole Biblique, I began to understand that their thinking about the scrolls could only change through reasoned discourse based strictly upon the growing evidence; and that this had to be sought without any deference whatever either to opinions about the scrolls held by dominating figures of the academy and their disciples or, in general, to the large body of conventional wisdom that had accumulated about the scrolls since 1948. New facts had emerged in the wake of the successive discoveries, and the members of the original team, with some additions and subtractions, were patiently perusing the several hundred texts of Cave 4 that still remained unpublished in 1970. If the past experience of papyrologists and other manuscript scholars was any indication, these texts were bound to cast fresh light on the fundamental question of Qumran origins.

Reviewing the results of the seminar, I decided that the time had come to seek permission to examine the unpublished scrolls that rested under glass in the drawers of the Rockefeller Museum. I felt that a palaeographic investigation of the original fragments, one by one, would reveal the number of scribal handwritings preserved in the scrolls, and this would form an important element in the developing debate. Had the scrolls been written by fewer than two hundred scribes—a number that one might perhaps live with in defending the notion of a sectarian scriptorium at Qumran—or by a much greater number of copyists as I had begun to suspect? The matter was obviously of crucial importance.

While in Jerusalem, I therefore wrote to Père de Vaux (23 March 1970), who was still in overall charge of the Qumran project, asking him for permission to examine the unpublished fragments. I told him I needed to do this "in order to complete a study on certain aspects of the texts found at Qumran and Masada," and added that

I wish to stipulate that I do not intend to *copy* any of the texts either for publication or other purposes, but only to examine various readings in the manuscripts proposed by other scholars and to study at close hand certain of the exterior phenomena associated with them.

De Vaux wrote back to me on 26 March, saying that

as far as I am concerned as chief-editor of the manuscripts deposited at the Palestine Archaeological Museum [the technically correct name of the Rockefeller], I will be glad to give you access to the original fragments of the *published* texts. I am sorry to say that I cannot let you study the unpublished fragments, unless you have the explicit permission of the scholar who is in charge of their edition.

By then it was well known that the official editors were loath to allow rank outsiders such permission. In addition, since I had already openly expressed the heretical view that the scrolls could only have come from libraries in Jerusalem, I decided there would be no sense in making requests of the various editors, who had mostly returned to their countries of residence. My year in Jerusalem was by then running out, and I knew there could be no way in the remaining time that I would gain access to the unpublished texts so as to count the handwritings. I did not know that two more decades would elapse before facsimiles of all the Cave 4 manuscripts would be published in the wake of an acute controversy, and that they would confirm that at least five hundred scribes had copied the scrolls.

With only a few more months remaining before I had to leave Jerusalem, I made efforts to discuss the problem of the scrolls' origins with as many colleagues as I could. Some even attempted to arrange a forum at the Hebrew University on the possible Jerusalem origin of the scrolls, but these efforts were always in the end blocked. Yigael Yadin was overseas that year. In response to a letter I sent him detailing some of the problems I had observed in the traditional hypothesis, he suggested that the fact no legal documents were found in Qumran was "easily explained by the different nature of the occupants; i.e., people who had no privately owned property as against those of the Bar-Kokhba period." Some of the texts found at Qumran, he suggested (letter of 10 April 1970), could have been brought in from other Essene communities, including the one known to have existed in Jerusalem; and it was important "to emphasize the fact that only in Qumran and the neighboring caves were the typically cylindrical jars found which clearly demonstrate the connection between the caves and the occupants of Qumran." (For what would appear to be a more likely explanation of the jars, however, see above, pages 30 and 148.)

Although by then advanced in years, my Johns Hopkins mentor, W. F. Albright, also corresponded with me about the issue (6 July 1970). "As you know," he wrote,

> I have been very flexible with regard to the attribution of original compositions from Qumran and the vicinity to a given sect. Most of them I consider as definitely Essene, but many of them . . . are pre-Essene. . . . I really cannot see non-Essene natives of Jerusalem bringing their books down to be stored in caves near the Dead Sea. How on earth could they be sure of their safety? . . . As for the absence of personal letters and memoranda, I have little doubt that they existed only under the direct control and constant supervision of the elders of the community, and that individual Essenes—who owned no property—were not supposed to have personal documents of this sort with them. Where the official archives were stored, is another question; it is perfectly possible that they may someday be discovered in a still unknown cave under or near Qumran. I agree that they would hide them rather than carry them along if they fled somewhere else—though that is possible, since the Essenes must have had very important community documents, such as deeds, leases, wills and official letters to other leaders of the Essene world.

Albright's view on the lost documents of the Essenes was thus at variance with Yadin's—though both continued to hold the Essene hypothesis as a virtual article of faith, firmly conceiving of the manuscripts as the property of a single sect. André Dupont-Sommer and Père de Vaux were likewise steadfastly loyal to the idea they had been so instrumental in creating. They were supported by Cross, Barthélemy, Milik, Baillet, Benoit, and the others who had become a part of the dominant circle of scroll scholars—plus all of their students. By the spring of 1970 I recognized that were I to keep on pressing the basic issues, I would face increasing antagonism from a large number of scholars in many countries. Throughout April and May, word continued to spread about my ideas on the origins of the scrolls, and on 9 June the *Jerusalem Post* ran a story on the subject based on an interview with me. It carried the headline "Dead Sea Scrolls Come from Jerusalem, U.S. Professor Says." The story was promptly labeled outrageous by a group of scholars who first planned a letter of protest to the *Post* but in the end opted for silence.

By this time a second edition of Edmund Wilson's book on the scrolls, wholeheartedly championing the Qumranologists' theory, had appeared worldwide, convincing still more members of the cultivated reading public in America, Israel, and elsewhere that the scrolls had been written in antiquity by an Essenic sectarian group residing on the Khirbet Qumran plateau. The Israel Museum's Shrine of the Book had been completed in 1965, and, year by year, thousands of Israelis and foreign tourists came streaming to it to gain some inspiration from a personal viewing of several of the most complete and important scrolls. I observed that the tour guides at the museum had begun adopting the traditional hypothesis in their presentations, and also that a number of the explanatory signs accompanying the scrolls asserted they were all the products of a single "sect."

In conversation with the curator, Magen Broshi, I urged that the practice be changed. Afterward I addressed a note to him to the same effect. In an answer which reached me shortly after I had completed my year in Jerusalem, he wrote that "in no place in the Shrine is it stated that manuscripts were composed or transcribed at Qumran, and hence there is no need to make any change [in the wording of the description of the manuscripts]" (16 June 1970; my translation). I responded the following month from Cambridge: I had been referring, I emphasized, "not to the Essene hypothesis or to the view the texts were actually written at Qumran—ideas I know are not adopted in your description—but rather to the statement which does indeed appear within the museum referring to *'the sect which produced the scrolls.'*" Would it not be better, I suggested, "to change the phrase in question to *'the group or groups which produced the scrolls'*?"

That change would, of course, have resulted in avoiding the transformation of an interpretation into an assumed fact. The curator, however, did not respond to my second inquiry. I waited another year and then wrote again, asking what had happened to my proposal. Again I received no reply.

As if to make amends in advance for the silence, Broshi's letter to me of 16 June 1970 actually contained a valuable piece of information: "Did you know," he wrote, "that Professor [K. H.] Rengstorf [of the University of Münster] had suggested the theory that the [scroll] manuscripts were written in Jerusalem?"

Broshi's letter had been forwarded to me in Cambridge, and on 1 July—the day of its arrival—I replied, expressing my regret at having been unaware of Rengstorf's idea. I recall having been somewhat chagrined by the letter, not only for my own laxity in missing this article, but equally for the fact that no scholar participating at the seminar held the previous winter had volunteered this information. I had never as much as heard a view of this kind broached in the States before my departure for Jerusalem, and no specialist with whom I spoke after presenting my paper at the American School had mentioned Rengstorf. As of 1970, his theory was simply not being discussed. "The library here [at Cambridge University] is closed today for inventory," I wrote back to Broshi, "but I shall look Rengstorf's article up tomorrow and see to what extent we actually agree in the matter, and also what particular line of reasoning led him to his own conclusion" (1 July 1970).

I found an English article on the subject by Rengstorf in the stacks of the library the following morning—a lecture of sixteen pages delivered at Leeds University in the autumn of 1959 and published (not in a journal but as a separate item) in 1963. A fuller German counterpart had appeared in 1960 and was also on the shelf.[2] As I studied Rengstorf's argument, I began to see why the Qumranologists had taken so little notice of it in print: The learned German professor, well trained in both Hebrew and Greek studies, had totally disdained the traditional approach, opting for an entirely new explanation of the scrolls' origins.

Writing in the late fifties, he had not yet read the still unpublished *Copper Scroll*, but he had seen the soundness of K. G. Kuhn's 1956 view that the scroll described treasures of the Temple. Adopting this explanation, and without yet knowing that the *Copper Scroll* actually described scrolls as having been hidden away along with the treasures, Rengstorf inferred that the Qumran scrolls were all together *from the library of the Jerusalem Temple*. Rejecting as "quite absurd" the claim that the Essenes wrote or copied so many hundreds of books by themselves in the "scriptorium," Rengstorf suggested that the library had been hidden away "in view of some serious danger threatening it." The concealment may very well have taken place in the year 68, [and] would cast a most instructive light upon the attitude of the high-priestly families responsible for the Temple towards the revolt against Rome. They regarded the revolt as having no prospect of success. Since they could not protect the Temple itself from destruction, they at least tried to save anything that could be saved: . . . a great treasure of gold and silver and a library with archives in which the tradition and the spiritual life of Judaism since the time of Nehemiah were preserved. If an attempt was made to save precisely the library from destruction, this gives us a glimpse of the good sense of the much-maligned High Priests: they sensed what was about to happen and they were clear in their minds that it was by no means the worship of the Temple which now assured the continuance of Judaism, but the One Book and in association with it all the other books as the repository of its spiritual and intellectual life. Hence they tried to save the Temple library as well.[3]

For the late 1950s, this theory was a perfectly plausible one. Even though the ancient descriptions of Origen and Timotheus about the discovery of manuscripts near Jericho were already known and being discussed, Masada had not yet been excavated, and Rengstorf could not possibly have guessed that scrolls were buried there as well. That discovery and other evidence would show the need for a more nuanced explanation of the scrolls' origin than the one he had proposed; but, all the same, Rengstorf had come close to batting a very big home run.

To abet his interpretation, however, Rengstorf had offered another proposal that would prove to be its Achilles' heel. For him, Khirbet Qumran was anything but a site of Essenic settlement: "There are a number of good reasons," he stated, "for assuming that up to the destruction of the Temple there was an outlying station of the Temple administration at Qumran." He expanded on this theme in his German study, attempting to show that the nearby En Feshkha site, with its own special features, was part of an agricultural station attributable, in view of the finding of the scrolls in the caves, to the Temple priesthood.

Rengstorf did not indicate that he himself had ever visited Qumran, and, writing in Germany on the topic in the late fifties, even before the first edition of de Vaux's book on the archaeology of the site saw print, he apparently had no ready access to the hints de Vaux provided to the site's military nature. He clearly thought that the notion of priests living in an outlying area near the Dead Sea was at least as plausible as that of a peace-loving sect living there, and since he was in fact able to adduce textual evidence showing that families or groups of priests possessed such outlying landholdings, he expressed his view on Khirbet Qumran without much trepidation. He was attacked for it, particularly in 1962 by H. Bardtke, another German scholar—to whom he responded vigorously in 1968, only to be attacked again by Bardtke.[4] It was de Vaux, however, who in the second edition of his work on the archaeology of Qumran (1972) would have what then appeared to be the final say on the matter. "It is doubtful," he stated,

> whether the temple priesthood had or retained such estates in so abandoned an area as Qumran, and this doubt changes into absolute disbelief when we remember that from about 600 to 150 B.C. the site remained deserted. On the other hand the proportions of communal buildings at Qumran, the number of the caves made use of, and the great cemetery of more than a thousand tombs are out of proportion with the needs of the personnel attached to an estate of a few square kilometers. On the contrary, all these factors imply the existence of an organized community which made use of the buildings and caves and which was forced, at some point of time, to abandon the site but to leave its library behind there.[5]

We can perceive today that de Vaux's judgment on the identification of Khirbet Qumran was no less fallible than Rengstorf's. However, by attacking Rengstorf's view on precisely the detail representing its weakest element, de Vaux, cloaked with an aura of authority he had gained from his leadership of the Qumran excavations and earlier writings, succeeded in conveying the impression that Rengstorf's interpretation of the scrolls' origins was entirely without merit; and it ceased to attract any further interest.

Studying Rengstorf's arguments in the summer of 1970, I saw that he had nevertheless correctly perceived the basic significance of the accumulated literary treasures found in the caves. It made no overwhelming difference, in effect, if he had too narrowly construed the historical circumstances—he could hardly have done better at the time he wrote. Concentrating only on the Temple itself, without yet being able to conceive of other libraries in Jerusalem whose owners could equally well have hidden away their contents, he had adduced considerable evidence for literary activities within the Temple precincts. For example, he pointed out that in the ancient Near East, temples were characteristically used "for housing archives and libraries" and that Josiah's reforms (2 Kings **22**.8 ff.) presupposed them. He reminded readers of an important statement in a letter of the Jews of Judaea to Aristobulus and other coreligionists in Egypt transmitted in the Second Book of Maccabees (**2**.13–15), to the effect that certain events were narrated "in the archives or memoirs of Nehemiah," who had "founded a library and collected the books about the kings and the prophets, and the books of David, and letters of kings about sacred gifts." Judah the Maccabee, according to the same passage, "collected for us all the writings which had been scattered owing to the outbreak of war." Rengstorf pointed out that the authors of the letter* had stated that these writings "are still with us," and they offered to lend them to their Egyptian correspondents "if you need them."[6]

Rengstorf also cited an inquiry made in person by Rabban Gamaliel I (i.e., Paul's teacher) to Nahum, an official Temple scribe; he observed that according to a later rabbinic tradition "the book correctors"—i.e., those who made sure the copyists of holy writ had done their work accurately—"in Jerusalem were paid from the Temple treasury,"[7] a statement implying that "their work was quite officially regarded as of the greatest importance in the interests of the whole people, indeed of the whole of Judaism." Priests and Levites (as well as Israelites) were even referred to as among the correctors of Torah scrolls (*Tosephta, Sanhedrin* **4**.7). Josephus himself had mentioned books stored in the Temple.[8] Rengstorf concluded with this observation:

> If all this is taken together it is impossible to doubt that these pieces of information leave plenty of room for a library of the type . . . [found in] the Qumran caves. Many things about this library would even be easier to explain by assuming it to be part of the Temple library than by assuming that it is the library of an Essene monastery. This would account for the mixture of leather and

---

*The actual names of the authors are unknown, but in 2 Maccabees **1**.10b the greetings sent to the recipients are from those who are "in Jerusalem, and . . . in Judaea and the senate and Judas [Maccabeus]," the recipients being "Aristobulus, king Ptolemy's teacher, who is also of the stock of the anointed priests, and . . . the Jews that are in Egypt. . . . "

papyrus manuscripts; the presence of Greek and Aramaic biblical texts; the appearance of manuscripts in the ancient Hebrew script alongside others in the later square characters; the texts which deal with questions of public worship of general importance, including calendar problems, and with questions peculiar to the priesthood; and finally the general breadth of this library which has been rediscovered in such remarkable circumstances. For if the Temple of Jerusalem had a large and important library—and this cannot be doubted—it will have contained the whole Jewish literature that existed, so far as it was obtainable, including, of course, heterodox writings.[9]

Having delivered a lecture in Jerusalem with a similar message only several months previously, I was more than a little stunned by the revelation of Rengstorf's treatment of the problem and the boldness of his solution. What was yet more surprising was the fact that we had arrived in entirely different ways at certain conclusions sharing much in common, although with basic differences. While I had emphasized the military nature of Khirbet Qumran, he had posited that it could have been a priestly landholding. In opting for the origin of the scrolls in Jerusalem libraries, I had stated that, with the exception of the *Copper Scroll*, no substantive autographs, either documentary or literary, had been found in the caves; Rengstorf had proposed that the scrolls came from a Temple library he associated with the Temple archives, without showing an awareness of the problem of lack of autographs. Citing the earlier discoveries in the time of Origen and Timotheus, I had spoken of the wide-ranging phenomenon of dispersal of the scrolls—further confirmed by the discovery of fragments at Masada—and of the many texts and places of discovery, as showing that the scrolls had come from various libraries of Jerusalem, hidden away by the Jews preparing for the Roman siege. Rengstorf, on the other hand, having no prescience of the Masada discoveries, and not having taken into account the earlier scroll discoveries near Jericho, had focused narrowly, but with great erudition, on the evidence of the Temple library, scribes, and correctors, putting the main site of Jewish worship and the priestly retinue in the center of the picture.

Thus according to Rengstorf, the priests had saved the literary treasures of the Jews, while in my own reading of what had become a greater amount of evidence a decade later, it may have been the priests who hid the Temple treasures described in the *Copper Scroll*, along with the scrolls mentioned in that document, but it was other Jews, both individuals and those associated with houses of study in the city, who had hidden most of the Dead Sea Scrolls. While a number of texts did give prominence to the sons of Zadok and the priestly order, many did not, so that Rengstorf's assignment of all of the scrolls to the Temple's library was rather arbitrary, tending to diminish the breadth, as well as the tumult, of Jerusalem's intellectual and religious life during the century before the First Revolt. And yet, in the very first decade of scroll research he had provided Qumranologists with an unusual opportunity to rethink their position and carefully weigh the evidence once again.

With the exception of the appearance of one or two German articles whose authors actually sought to debate the issue in the 1960s, Rengstorf's view was treated with disdainful silence and by 1970 was virtually forgotten. He did not again return to the subject, and many years later, shortly before his death, confided to a younger colleague in Germany that, because the reaction was not what he had hoped for or expected, he had ended up despairing of convincing the traditional Qumranologists that they had blundered.[10] In the summer of 1970 I spent hours at the Cambridge University Library fruitlessly trying to find some serious American, English, or French discussions of Rengstorf's hypothesis. Edmund Wilson had not as much as mentioned his name in the enlarged second edition (1969) of his book on the scrolls.

At the start of 1971, I had been back in Chicago for several months and returned to the study of the Genizah documents. I had intended to put aside the problem of the scrolls for a period of several years, hoping that in the meantime new evidence on the question of their origin would come to light. But the memory of the coldness that had greeted my seminar presentation in Jerusalem kept pressing itself upon me, and I could not dispel the subsequent revelation of Rengstorf's confrontation with the cherished belief of the Qumranologists. So on 25 February I wrote to Edmund Wilson, describing my encounters in Jerusalem and my surprise upon learning of Rengstorf's earlier theory.

By then, the new edition of Wilson's book had been out for well over a year. I congratulated him on the lucid way in which he had summarized the prevailing approach to the scrolls' origin, and

described Rengstorf's interpretation and its points of similarity
with my own. "What I find particularly interesting in the congruence
of our respective views," I wrote, "is that they were arrived at on the
basis of entirely different considerations, Rengstorf's on the . . . evidence supplied by certain Hellenistic and early rabbinic texts, my
own on the basis of the heterogeneity of the contents of the scrolls,
certain of their scribal characteristics, the new geographical pattern
created by the discovery of Qumran-like texts at Masada, and
other equally weighty considerations. . . . Dr. Yadin's explanation that
Essenes from Qumran brought manuscripts to Masada does not
seem to be very convincing, especially in view of the fact that
ancient writers mention still other discoveries of Hebrew manuscripts 'near Jericho,' although none of them qualifies his statement by adding 'by the shore of the Dead Sea.'" Since Wilson had
detailed his interviews with many scroll scholars, I expressed puz-
zlement that he nowhere mentioned Rengstorf's work.

Wilson wrote back several days later: "I knew nothing about
[the Rengstorf] theory at the time I wrote, or I should have tried
to deal with it. It seems to me, though, that it is hard to account
for the presence of sectarian documents—the *Manual of Discipline*, for example—if the whole library came from the Temple."

Although a terse reply, it revealed much: Never during Wilson's
many years of active interest in the scrolls and his lengthy meetings with the principal figures engaged in their study had he as
much as been informed of Rengstorf's interpretation, which yet
relied on powerful evidence in its fundamental opposition to the
prevailing view. I then perceived the source of the impassioned
rejection of the *Copper Scroll*'s authenticity, broadcast internationally by Père de Vaux and his associates several years in advance of
the text's publication—several years, that is, before historians
would be able to evaluate the text for themselves. The Jerusalem
team had clearly recognized the menace the *Copper Scroll* posed
for the interpretation of the scrolls they were championing, and
tried to counter it by declaring the text an ancient figment of the
imagination; when Rengstorf perceived the possible historical
implications of the document, and drew entirely reasonable conclusions from it and other textual evidence, they buried his view
in neglect until de Vaux, a dozen years later, acknowledged it by
dismissal, attacking precisely what was the weakest, and at the
same time least essential, aspect of the theory—the identification
of Qumran as an agricultural outpost of the Temple priesthood.

The whole chapter of events was a salient one in the saga of the scrolls, forming a telling lesson in the politics of scholarship.

Wilson discusses the *Copper Scroll* in his book, pointing out that

> Allegro came to believe that the Essenes had nothing to do with these scrolls [= the two sections of the *Copper Scroll*] except, no doubt, to allow them to be hidden in a cave near the monastery, and that the treasure was that of the Temple in Jerusalem, which the priests there had taken the precaution of putting out of the reach of the plundering Roman invaders, just as the Essenes had hidden their library.[11]

These are views that Allegro expressed both in his correspondence and in his 1960 book on the *Copper Scroll* (that is, just one year after Rengstorf's lecture in Leeds). Wilson also acknowledges that, even though de Vaux made clear to Allegro "that [it] . . . had been assigned for editing to J. T. Milik," it was "Allegro [who] had been the first to decipher" the text.[12] Beyond this, after explaining that Milik shared de Vaux's view that the treasure list was imaginary, Wilson actually states that "I agree with Allegro that this list is too terse and particularized—in its way, too businesslike—not to indicate genuine treasures."[13] Wilson was thus, it seems, on the verge of seeing the possible historical implications of this scroll, but since he knew nothing of Rengstorf's interpretation, and was not himself in any sense a scholar of antiquity, he fell short of doing so.

Wilson nowhere describes the role of de Vaux in publicly characterizing the *Copper Scroll* as a false or imaginative document, although it was de Vaux, rather than Milik or Lankester Harding, who had taken the primary role in publicizing this interpretation in 1956. He had seen to it that the news release concocted in Jerusalem would be read before two of the world's most prestigious academic bodies. Wilson's failure to pursue the question of the scroll's implications was quite evidently linked to his great admiration for de Vaux, who, it will be remembered, had written a blistering—albeit misleading—attack on Allegro's 1960 edition of the text. By the time I corresponded with Wilson he had apparently put the question totally out of mind. No doubt steadfast in his support of the basic theories of the official editors of the Qumran texts, he was content simply to dismiss Rengstorf's hypothesis.

Wilson's answer disappointed me. Despite errors of judgment, he had seemed, from his book as a whole, quite open minded, and I decided to press the issue with him a little further, in the hope that he might reconsider his position and acknowledge that he had perhaps not thought the matter through to the end. I therefore wrote back to him (11 March 1971), indicating that even if one insisted on the strictly sectarian nature of the *Manual of Discipline*, it was difficult to see how Rengstorf's explanation or my own came into conflict with that view. Both the Temple library and other large collections of books in Jerusalem would have included at least some heterodox writings, as well as the more "standard" apocryphal and apocalyptic texts of the sort found in good number among the Qumran scrolls. The very abundance of writings at Qumran that were not in any sense sectarian seemed to be a far more basic problem for advocates of the Qumran-Essene hypothesis than the presence of certain heterodox texts was for Rengstorf's approach or my own. I indicated to Wilson that the *Manual of Discipline* appeared to be a most enigmatic text, despite Dupont-Sommer's exegesis of it: Many scholars had by then begun to recognize its composite nature—one even attempted to harmonize its parts by adapting them to the archaeological sequence at Qumran. "But the shoe," I said, "does not really seem to fit, no matter how stretched or squeezed." I mentioned to Wilson that some years earlier Chaim Rabin had presented an interesting case for the origin of the *Manual* among "purity brotherhoods" of the type described in early rabbinic texts. I asked him whether he was by chance familiar with Rabin's view.

To this Wilson replied briefly (18 March) that "I still cannot believe that the Library of the Temple would have collected all that heterodox literature. As for the non-heterodox [illegible] at Qumran, they would have had to have the Bible as well as the so-called intertestamental texts"—the same argument conveyed, in fact, by Dupont-Sommer's charismatic rhetoric. Never mind that relatively few among the virtually six hundred noncanonical writings discovered in the caves showed characteristics comparable to the separatist tendencies reflected in the *Damascus Covenant* or in the *Manual of Discipline*. For Dupont-Sommer, since all the books derived from the legendary Essenes of Khirbet Qumran, they all had to be the secret products of those sectarians. It was this very belief that Wilson was expressing in his letter.

In saying that the "sectarians of Qumran" would have had to have the Bible and the so-called intertestamental texts, Wilson expressed an utterly confusing idea. On the one hand, even beyond the first century A.D., the Jews did not have a unified work which they called "the Bible," but only individual "holy writings" (Hebrew, *kitbé haqodesh*), and the various Jewish sects were not in total agreement about what books were to be regarded as holy. The Samaritans, for example, considered only the Pentateuch as such, while the authors of the *Damascus Covenant* apparently accorded Jubilees—later treated as a pseudepigraphic work—that status. We will eventually know (but perhaps never fully) what ancient group sanctified which writings only by patiently studying all of the *citations* from such writings in the various individual works found in the Qumran caves. Among the fragments discovered at Qumran, a minority had canonical status; others were officially selected (by the Tannaitic authorities) as worthy of it as late as the second century A.D. (It may be noted that Rengstorf himself, in speaking of the "One Book," showed considerable insensitivity to this fact of the gradual development of the biblical canon.)

On the other hand, there is no proof that the books Wilson called the "intertestamental texts," that is, the so-called Apocrypha and Pseudepigrapha, were recognized by the Palestinian Jews themselves, either before or after the destruction of the Second Temple, as a special collection of writings. The only way that these previously known works can be distinguished from scores of others fragmentarily interspersed with them in the Qumran caves is by the very fact of their having been portrayed, in Christian Bibles closely following the Septuagint, as having a special status or degree of sanctity, and not at all because of any distinguishing quality of their content.[14]

A vast variety of ancient Hebrew literature was hidden away in the caves. The texts included many works that would be entirely lost or forgotten until their rediscovery, some others—a small minority—already deemed holy, and still others that would eventually be so considered. Wilson appeared to be confused on this basic point. In the process, he attributed to the Essenes various types of texts that neither Josephus nor other ancient authors ever mentioned as having been Essenic. Any important library of an ancient Jewish group or individual collector would have contained such writings; and separatist groups including the Essenes would of course in addition have had their own writings expressing the beliefs peculiar to them.[15]

I wrote some words along these lines to Wilson, received a yet terser answer, and in this way our brief correspondence came to an end. I had the impression that he felt himself finished once and for all with the Dead Sea Scrolls, having by then become more interested in other topics. He passed away the year following our correspondence. His final book, published while he was still alive, had no relation to the scrolls.[16]

Writing privately in 1954, Wilson had jested at what he called the "puerility" of Ernest Hemingway, and then observed:

> yet when I read . . . his article . . . on his African adventures, I couldn't help finding it stimulating. He lives in an adventure book for boys, but there's something in myself that responds to it. There may be an element of this in my pursuit of the Dead Sea Scrolls, my visits to Zuñi and Haiti, my love of acquiring new alphabets. . . ."[17]

The scrolls had been an adventure for Wilson, one of many in his memorable life. Encouraged by the world's acclaim, he could hardly have seen how, by his warm embrace of the Qumran-Essene hypothesis, he might have misled the public. Nor would he have had the occasion to ask himself whether, by his own writing and the overwhelmingly positive world reaction to it, he had possibly encouraged the traditional Qumranologists to sink still further into a historiographical morass. Yet more books about the scrolls were appearing, more encyclopedia articles, more doctoral dissertations—and they all bore the same basic message. A new generation of scholars had now drunk deeply from the waters of the Essene theory, and I wondered how I could contribute anything further to a debate that had been discouraged virtually to the point of becoming extinct.

During my stay in Jerusalem and thereafter, I did not waste time on lengthy polemics concerning the origin of the scrolls. I felt discouraged whenever I considered the strange history of Qumran scholarship, and preferred for the most part to engage in less frustrating work that might be free of presumption and hubris. Nonetheless, this very work—on the history of the Jews in mediaeval Normandy—likewise produced a basic conflict over facts and methods of study, offering striking parallels with the unfolding struggle over the meaning of the scrolls.

Earlier in the 1960s, while working with the Genizah manuscript collections in England and later with other texts, I had come upon evidence that there had been a major Jewish cultural presence in Rouen, the capital of mediaeval Normandy.[18] Literary evidence for this culture was scattered in various libraries, while the archives at Rouen still stored plans of a striking mediaeval synagogue. A nineteenth-century historian had once cited an old document referring to a "School of the Jews" that once stood to the east of the synagogue. In 1976 I suggested that this structure had been destroyed to make way for Rouen's magnificent Palace of Justice on the northern side of the Street of the Jews.[19] That same year, a bulldozer clearing debris from the courtyard of the Palace of Justice hit upon a mediaeval structure, and soon upon another building, of monumental proportions and with Hebrew graffiti on the interior walls. Through comparison of decorative aspects of the building with other Romanesque remains in the city, architectural historians arrived at a date of approximately A.D. 1105–1110 for its construction—the very time of the revival of the Jewish community of Normandy, after William Rufus had allowed its return to Judaism around 1099 in the wake of earlier persecutions during the First Crusade (A.D. 1096).

The first traces of the building had been discovered in mid-August of 1976, and three of its four sides were partially cleared during the following ten days. Perhaps inevitably, the local archaeologists began to surmise that it was an ancient synagogue, and invited Michel de Bouard, then a member of France's Académie des Inscriptions et Belles-Lettres and the dominant figure in archaeological studies in Normandy, to study the site. Contemplating the building, he declared that "if we are dealing with a synagogue, the discovery is sensational":[20] an impression arrived at apparently with no knowledge of the plans of the ancient Jewish quarter that I had published. Telegrams were sent to me soon thereafter; I arrived in Rouen in September without fully understanding precisely what had been found or where. The uncovered ruin was situated approximately where, on the basis of documentary hints, I had surmised the School of the Jews once stood.

At a meeting the same day, I explained to the archaeologists that the monumental synagogue had stood on the opposite (southern) side of the Street of the Jews. I showed them the details in old plans of the quarter, describing the process that led me to conclude that the "School of the Jews" must have been another monumental building on the northern side of the street. Given the evidence, the newly discovered building could only be that school—and hence the one known academic building of the mediaeval Jews ever to have been unearthed.

There was thus every reason for the local archaeologists to take pride in their discovery—after all, other mediaeval synagogues were known, while a building evoking the literary and scholastic culture of the Jews in mediaeval times was archaeologically unique.

The archaeologists, however, raised objections, insisting that the Rouennaise edifice could, after all, have been what they first announced it to be: a synagogue nonetheless—a second one rivaling in grandeur the first across the street. I pointed out, on the basis of well-known plans and archaeological remains, that one of the early mediaeval European synagogue's most prominent features was a convex protruding apse on its eastern wall, in which the scrolls of the Torah were kept, and facing in the direction of Jerusalem. With the eastern wall of the edifice still entirely covered by earth—and thus forming the chief underpinning of the grand staircase of the Palace itself—we then agreed that the issue could only be firmly resolved through removal of the staircase, so that the eastern wall might be excavated without danger. But time was crucial; a member of the Commission Supérieure des Monuments Historiques in Paris was agitating for the reburial of the building, which, as was reported to me, he believed had no great value "for the history of France."

Once back in Chicago, I wrote a report on the historical importance of the building in which I urged its preservation—and the excavation of the eastern wall.[21] The Ministry of Culture approved this plan in October 1976, and by the following spring the great staircase had been removed, stone by stone, and the wall cleared away. It proved to have no apse, but was blank and straight.

I was mistaken, however, in thinking this would mark the end of the dispute. Having meanwhile been offered support for their initial stance from an indignant historian in Paris,[22] the archaeologists continued their quarrel, now claiming that there was no absolute necessity that a Romanesque synagogue have an apse. There could have been, they suggested, two rival synagogues across the street from each other, one with an apse and one without. The process of official designation of the building was thus further delayed.

This debate took place in the late seventies—in advance, that is, of the rediscovery of a French manuscript of 1363 placing the "School of the Jews" *precisely* where the monument had been discovered.*

Not yet aware of this manuscript (actually published decades earlier), various proponents of the "two synagogues" hypothesis expressed doubts as to whether there had ever been independent schools of higher Jewish learning in mediaeval France, whether the capital of mediaeval Normandy had possessed so important a Hebraic culture as to warrant such a school, whether the Normannic rulers would ever have tolerated it, whether after the First Crusade the Jews of France would have possessed enough books to have schools, and other such proposals. The obvious motivation for this stance was simply to show that a glimmer of reason still characterized the "two synagogues" claim. The apse, the archaeologists suggested, could perhaps have been on the second floor of the building. That floor, of course, had been totally destroyed at the start of the sixteenth century, to make way for the Palace of Justice.

On reading this argument, I was struck by its parallel with that of Père de Vaux and his scholarly supporters in favor of the presence of a scriptorium at Khirbet Qumran, claiming as they did that it had occupied the completely destroyed second story of a building. When at the 1970 winter presentation in Jerusalem I had asked how such an identification was tenable when not a shred of parchment or other materials compellingly associated with the scribal art had turned up in the rubble, the answer given by Père Benoit, second in command to de Vaux, was that the weather had simply destroyed every last bit of evidence. The answer in both cases was specious; the underlying effort both times was transparently to defend the archaeologically generated theories at all costs.

In each case, the archaeologists had discovered a treasure of the past; their own spades and fingers had cleared it away. They had used what they believed were the best archaeological techniques; the uncovered finds were clearly of historical importance; and the archaeologists believed that they had both the best qualifications for, and the inherent right to, the historical evaluation of

*See Lucien Delsalle in *Etudes Normandes* (1985), pp. 80–83; Lucien Valin, *Le roule des Plès de Heritage de la mairie Jehan Mustel* (Rouen, 1924), pp. 99–101.

the discoveries. For them, stones had taken on a living quality that texts did not quite possess: It was as if the culture evoked by these stones could be comprehended through their empirical observation, without need for recourse to the precise meaning of that culture's written words—beliefs that represented an obvious danger to the impartial investigation of the past.

But there were yet greater stakes involved in both debates. On a deeper level, the impetus for the stance of both groups of scholars was the entrenched belief that the culture of the Jews mattered relatively little, and that urban civilization was a force inimical to it. So deeply rooted was this distortion of the history and culture of the Jews that it had influenced the thinking of numerous scholars and a large lay public in France and elsewhere. The apparent incapacity of the French archaeologists to picture in the capital of Normandy an active Hebraic culture sparked by a school of higher learning reminded me forcefully of the still-dominant interpretation of the manuscripts of the Judaean Wilderness: an interpretation persistently holding that these scrolls had nothing to do with the capital city and the site of the Holy Temple of the Jews, nor with the ancient literary culture of that city, being rather the mere products of a small celibate sect headquartered in a desert monastery.

We shall observe later how an increasingly adamant attempt to impose this view on the public gradually led to stringent measures, within official scroll circles, to prevent study of the unpublished scrolls by those who disavowed this conception. We will confront as well further significant distortions, by figures in the world of traditional Qumranology, of scientific findings concerning the texts, along with the related effort to devalue the scrolls of their literary, spiritual, and historic significance. This process followed upon two of the most important text discoveries in the Judaean Wilderness—writings that in effect highlighted the heterogeneity of the scrolls. These discoveries removed any lingering credibility from the traditional view of Qumran origins.

PART II

SCIENCE, POLITICS, AND THE DEAD SEA SCROLLS

CHAPTER 7

The Temple Scroll, the Acts of Torah, and the Qumranologists' Dilemma

❖

By 1977, Yigael Yadin's publication of another Qumran manuscript, and his explanation of its contents, had convinced me of the need to return to the problem of the scrolls. A decade earlier (October 1967) Yadin had issued an announcement in Jerusalem of the recovery of a scroll containing, among other things, rules relating to an idealized Temple of Jerusalem, and which he hence endowed with the title *Temple Scroll*. In the first news release pertaining to it,[1] Yadin was cited as indicating that the scroll also treated previously unknown rules for preparedness and mobilization, differing "entirely from the description in the . . . 'War of the Sons of Light against the Sons of Darkness'"—and that, unlike the other scrolls, "the words are given as those of God and are written in the first person in most cases." In later statements Yadin confirmed the view he had already expressed at the time of his announcement of the discovery: that the scroll in any event belonged, like the others, to the "Qumran-Essene sect."

During this period, Yadin had put aside both the Bar Kokhba texts found near En Gedi and those Masada scrolls that were still unpublished. (He had apparently appointed himself editor-in-chief of all these manuscripts.) Instead, he concentrated his attention on producing an elaborate edition of the *Temple Scroll*, replete with extensive commentaries whose main thrust was to defend the standard version of the Qumran-Essene theory.*

---

*Regrettably, while working by himself for a full decade on his text edition, Yadin did not transfer the responsibility for other manuscripts to any other party; it was only after his death that they started to become accessible to some scholars in Jerusalem.

The origin of this scroll, although it was widely asserted to have come from Qumran Cave 11, in fact appears to be a mystery. While Yadin often referred to it as a "Qumran scroll," he never offered proof of such provenance, even refraining from revealing whether the anonymous East Jerusalem/Bethlehem seller indicated as much.[2] Since the antiquities dealer was paid $105,000 for this scroll, it is remarkable that Yadin and his associates did not at least require him to divulge the place of origin of this text, or who had brought it to him. We have no record, at all events, of whether this information was divulged, or specifically on what basis Yadin claimed that the scroll was from the Qumran area rather than from some other locality of the Judaean Wilderness.

The Hebrew text of the *Temple Scroll* and Yadin's commentary appeared in 1977,[3] with the by now predictable view being urged upon its readers. However, the view was not borne out by the text, which contained abundant laws—clearly of a theoretical nature and written by an apocalypticist—that, while resembling those of the Essenes in a few details, also resembled those of other ancient Jewish groups in additional ones. The majority of the laws could not in fact be traced to any known Jewish group of antiquity. Baruch Levine of New York University thus urged caution

> in assuming a particular sectarian provenance for the *Temple Scroll*, as though in this instance, we were certain that its provisions reflected Qumranic calendation. The scroll's formulations of the *mo'adim* [festival laws] represent, on the first level, reworkings of the Torah laws. Their proper interpretation should, therefore, be contingent on a thorough investigation of these particular sources. . . .
>
> On the other hand, comparisons with the renderings of the Septuagint and with later rabbinic hermeneutic indicate that what became the normative rabbinic interpretations were known and accepted quite widely long before halakhic Midrash took final form.
>
> How the *Temple Scroll* fits into the development of Judaism remains uncertain. . . .[4]

Disregarding all such caution, however, Yadin felt free to conclude, in answer to his own question as to whether the text was written by members of the "Qumran sect," that the question could

> be answered, it seems to me, positively, even though the possibility should not be denied that within the scroll is embedded—to a greater or lesser extent—also the teaching of a wider movement

which is not to be defined as a sect, a movement from which in the course of time developed the sect of Qumran.[5]

Precisely as in the case of Sanders' treatment of the apocryphal psalms,[6] there was here an implicit acknowledgment of the differences that existed between this important scroll and known "sectarian" doctrine (i.e., that associated with the Essenes or those who wrote the *Manual of Discipline*), but the fixed dogma of a Qumran-Essene identification had prevented the author from drawing appropriate conclusions.

That Israel's most renowned archaeologist should hazard such an approach to the *Temple Scroll,* after also having arbitrarily proposed that the Masada discoveries were somehow related to the "Essenes of Qumran," prompted fresh concern on my part regarding the direction being taken in what was an obviously expanding area of studies. But the central issue at stake, as I perceived it, transcended this concern. It involved a conflict between two different conceptions of scholarship—the search for partnership in a coalition of authorities claiming correct ideas, on the one hand; and, on the other, inductive investigation of evidence linked to a fundamental requirement of reasonability, without regard for the sanctity of cherished scholarly beliefs, by individual researchers.

No Qumranologist responded to my presentation in 1980 of the theory of Jerusalem origin of the scrolls and the accompanying list of anomalies inhering in the old hypothesis.[7] This represented, of course, a studious reticence that, over the next few years, sometimes made me think of the reception accorded to Rengstorf's views and his fall into silence. But I had begun receiving correspondence from historians and philologists working outside the parochial boundaries of Qumranology who articulated a shared skepticism in the face of questionable historiography. In any event, a malaise had apparently been setting in for some time among the members of the official publication team. This was surely due in no way to sheer incompetence nor to the questions I had been raising, but, one might suggest, was perhaps attributable to the ever more glaring difficulties with the old theory that some of the editors themselves apparently perceived as they pored over more and more of the texts.

By the early 1980s the team seems to have virtually stopped working on the scrolls. In the summer of 1982 one member wrote to a former colleague to bring him up to date on what the others were doing: Father Patrick Skehan had died in 1980; he was thought to have finished preparing his volume of biblical texts for the Oxford Discoveries in the Judaean Desert series, but a successor, Dr. Eugene Ulrich, had nevertheless been named. (The volume eventually appeared in 1993.) Josef Milik had left the priesthood some years earlier and had married; he had become a member of the Centre Nationale de la Recherche Scientifique in Paris. (Through the 1980s and until 1993, no further volume by Milik appeared.) C.-H. Hunzinger had produced nothing; de Vaux replaced him on the team with Maurice Baillet, who published his own volume of texts from the fourth Qumran cave in 1982. Having been unwell, John Strugnell planned to spend a year in Jerusalem preparing his volume of texts. (The volume has never appeared.) Whether Frank Cross was preparing his volume was unclear, but Skehan had indicated that he was not. (This volume has never appeared.) J. Starcky had become an honorary director of research at the C.N.R.S.; but since he had left his own volume unfinished, Emile Puech was chosen to succeed him. (As of early 1994, his volume also had not been published.)

We thus observe the impasse in scroll scholarship in the early 1980s. New volumes of Qumran texts had stopped appearing, and word was circulating that some of the photographs of the scrolls were being passed from teachers to students for use as the basis of doctoral dissertations. The ensuing years would witness the outbreak of a great debate over the meaning of the Judaean Wilderness discoveries, accompanied by the general public's growing awareness of it. While this contest was many faceted, one text occupied center stage during much of the debate.

This was a work of highly interesting content, pieced together from fragments of six different manuscripts found in Qumran Cave 4. The name given to the work by Elisha Qimron, one of the scholars studying it, was *Miqsat Ma'asé Torah*: the *MMT* text—at the time translated "Some of the Precepts of the Law." The Hebrew words actually occur in the text, and serve adequately as a working title. Analysis of the text, however, shows that it may equally well be translated as "Some of the Acts of Torah" or, more succinctly, *Acts of Torah*, the title we will use here.

The work would not only come to occupy a central place in the controversy over the Dead Sea Scrolls, but would even serve as the basis of lawsuits of international dimensions. By carefully following the stages of its investigation, then observing its contents and the way they were interpreted, and, finally, reviewing the struggle over the rights of individual scholars to study and publish this text, we shall be in a position to understand the essential value of this work more clearly, and its role in our understanding of the origin and nature of the scrolls.

The thousands of manuscript fragments unearthed in Cave 4 in 1952 were for the most part brought to the Rockefeller Museum and deposited in a ground-floor workroom. There the team assembled by Père de Vaux began cleaning and sorting them. The team's most gifted scholar, Father Josef Milik of Poland, was attached like de Vaux and other colleagues to the nearby Ecole Biblique. The team started by separating fragments of biblical texts from the nonbiblical ones; the lion's share of the latter fell to Milik, who was not only a talented palaeographer but would eventually prove to be the most productive member of the original team.[8]

Apparently at some time between late 1952 and mid-1954, Milik identified some fragments of the *Acts of Torah* which he would later refer to as "4QMishn" (i.e., "fragments of a work in early rabbinic [= Mishnaic] Hebrew found in Qumran Cave 4").[9] In mid-1954, John Strugnell, C. H. Hunzinger, and J. Starcky were added to the Jerusalem team, and joined in the effort of further sorting out the fragments and piecing them together. Strugnell had received his B.A. at Oxford in 1952, and at age twenty-four he showed considerable facility for such detailed work. In the team's joint report on the work in progress (1956) he stated that the 4Q fragments he was preparing for publication "fill about 80 glass plates, containing the remains of almost an equal number of non-biblical manuscripts."[10] He described fragments "represented by four manuscripts" of a text having "certain peculiarities of vocabulary and doctrine which suggest that we may have here a sapiential work composed by the Qumran sect suitable to aid us in reconstructing its moral theology." This was Strugnell's first description of the *Acts of Torah*.

In 1956–57 Strugnell spent some months at the Oriental Institute in Chicago, and then returned to the Rockefeller, working there on his assigned lot of material until mid-1960. He and other members of the team prepared transcriptions of their work, and these became the basis of a card catalog of all legible phrases in the new manuscripts. (This catalog would later be turned into a concordance of the 4Q vocabulary and, beginning in 1991, into printed texts of the so-called Unauthorized Version of the 4Q scrolls by Ben-Zion Wacholder and Martin Abegg.)

During 1960 Strugnell left Jerusalem for an American academic appointment, taking photographs and transcriptions of his assigned lot with him. Milik, for his part, had been working on various Qumran projects; in 1962 his interpretations of the manuscripts of the "minor caves" appeared in the extensive third volume of the Oxford series. Discussing certain linguistic features of the *Copper Scroll*, he compared them to analogous ones he had noticed in the text that he referred to as "4QMishn," and gave several quotations from the latter showing its special idiom and content. He did not refer to Strugnell's editorial responsibility nor to Strugnell himself in his discussion of this text, but seems to have been working on it separately.

Accordingly Milik's description of the text was somewhat different than Strugnell's: "Angels, speaking in the first person, reveal to the visionary, unfortunately anonymous, the laws concerning the purity of Jerusalem and of the Temple and, at the end of the work, about the end of time. . . ."[11] Milik had given a shorter description of the fragments in 1957.[12] Thereafter, in 1961, one of the manuscripts was used by F. M. Cross for his study of the palaeography of the scrolls. He described the handwriting of this fragment as "a late Hasmonaean semicursive script from an unknown work in Hebrew to be edited by J. Strugnell."[13] As events would later show, Strugnell had managed to transcribe virtually all of the extant words by the time he left Jerusalem in 1960 for his first American post, at Duke University. What remained to be done was the restoration, by educated guesswork, of the missing portions to the extent this might be possible, and the proper joining together of the fragments—seemingly a year's work at most.

Many years, however, passed, and the *Acts of Torah*, along with most of the other texts assigned to Strugnell, seemed to fall into oblivion. In 1968, Strugnell moved on to Harvard, where he joined forces with Frank Cross. No other American university at the time could boast of the presence on its faculty of two official members of the scrolls editorial team, and in the ensuing years the pair attracted many students who aspired to a future in Qumran studies. Although Cross was located in Harvard's Near Eastern department and Strugnell in its Divinity School, the two, sharing as they did all of the major assumptions concerning the nature and origins of the scrolls, worked well together.

Even before Strugnell's arrival, Cross had been especially keen to encourage his students in the view that the scrolls had been written by Essenes living at Khirbet Qumran. To this idea he added his own claim (adopted subsequently by the other members of the official team) that many of the scrolls could be dated narrowly to specified twenty-five- to fifty-year time spans (e.g., 50–25 B.C., 25 B.C. to A.D. 25, etc.). Strugnell's arrival, and the support he offered Cross, quite naturally encouraged the Harvard students to believe in both the Qumran-Essene theory and Cross's dating method as truths—ideas that came to be a characteristic feature of doctoral dissertations on the scrolls produced at Harvard. The students, as they graduated, took up their own academic posts and further propagated the theory and with it Cross's palaeographic ideas.

This system worked well until the early seventies, succeeding apparently without the students' direct use of the unpublished Qumran texts assigned to their two teachers. In 1971, however, Père de Vaux died, and the chief editorship of the scrolls passed on to his associate at the Ecole Biblique, Père Pierre Benoit, who was not quite as academically militant as his predecessor had been. Employing a policy of benign neglect that lasted until his death in 1987, he apparently offered no objection when some of the editors began reassigning their texts to others. Both Strugnell and Cross decided to do precisely that. However, they offered individual texts not to already seasoned scholars but to their own students for use in their doctoral dissertations. This gave Harvard students a decided, if inappropriate, advantage, enabling them to publish scrolls that were denied to virtually all others, students and professors alike. Some of the most interesting texts assigned to Strugnell were either published or prepared for publication in this way, but he seems to have made no effort to do this with various other fragments in his possession, including the *Acts of Torah*.

Strugnell had many years to puzzle over these fragments, and must have understood that they constituted a text of heavy, significant legal content, recounting ancient practices related mainly to ritual purity that stemmed from the priestly and levitical legislation of the Pentateuch. The subject on the surface seemed dry enough, but Strugnell evidently recognized, correctly, that the text could reveal an ancient Jewish group's legal opinions at the time of its emergence. His curiosity about the text's significance was undoubtedly piqued by the publication (in 1980) of a study by

Professor J. M. Baumgarten that discussed one of these ritual laws, which Milik had cited by chance virtually two decades earlier.[14] Baumgarten tentatively translated the passage as follows:

> . . . concerning liquid streams we say there is no purity in them, for the moisture of liquid streams and that which acts as a receptacle for them is considered like one.

To an expert in Jewish law, the sense was quite clear: A known point of dispute between Sadducees and Pharisees in early rabbinic times (ca. second century A.D.) concerned the ritual purity of a vessel whose liquid contents were poured into a ritually impure receptacle. The Pharisees held that the impurity could not "travel upward," so to speak, from the receptacle into the vessel from which the liquid was being poured, whereas the Sadducees were of the opposing view. The viewpoint expressed in the translated passage was that of the Sadducees, and Baumgarten concluded that "the Qumran ruling would be an explicit affirmation of the Sadducean position." He described this law in such a way as to make clear, however, that in his view all the legal texts found in the Qumran caves could be associated with the "Essenes of Qumran."

Strugnell, of course, also labored under the view that all of the Qumran nonbiblical and nonpseudepigraphic texts were the product of these same "Essenes," a view not exactly in harmony, as we shall see, with the contents of the *Acts of Torah*. Baumgarten's observations on the sentence published by Milik may have served as a catalyst for Strugnell to take some action regarding the precious text he had been holding on to for so long. For whatever reason, beginning in 1982, he sought the aid of a scholar of rabbinic law, Jacob Sussman of the Hebrew University, to help him elucidate the legal content of the text. He also turned to Elisha Qimron of the University of the Negev for help in further reconstruction of the text itself and for a better understanding of its Hebrew idiom. The latter was particularly important in view of Milik's earlier unalloyed characterization of the language as "Mishnaic"—that is, having the characteristics of the idiom used by the earliest rabbinic figures, the Tannaim, in their legal writings, particularly the *Mishnah* and *Tosephta*. These works were not actually edited until the beginning of the third century A.D., but contained legal texts that had accumulated among the

Tannaim at least since their assumption of spiritual hegemony at about the beginning of the second century A.D.

The importance of Milik's observations about the idiom of the *Acts of Torah* resided in the necessary implication that the work was written during the early or middle first century A.D., before which no evidence could be found for the existence of such an idiom. Indeed, Milik had made use of passages from the *Acts of Torah* to elucidate his discussion of a first-century A.D. documentary work composed in the same idiom—the *Copper Scroll*. The only other manuscripts written in essentially the same form of Hebrew were the early second century A.D. Bar Kokhba documentary texts. The idiom appears in no written testimony from before the turn of the era, and the texts of the first and early second centuries A.D., where it does appear, illustrate how in the course of two centuries the jurisprudential Hebrew of the early rabbis had become what it was.

It was therefore important for Strugnell, with his newfound colleague Qimron, to study this aspect of the *Acts of Torah* with the greatest care. This was especially true in view of the fact that (as Strugnell must well have appreciated) Milik's description of the nature of the work's idiom in effect clashed with an assertion by his own colleague Cross, who had written, in his study of the palaeography of the Qumran texts, that the handwriting characteristics of one of the *Acts* manuscripts showed that the text had been copied between 50 and 25 B.C.—unimaginably early for a text verging on early rabbinic idiom. What is more, since what Cross had dated was, as usual, only a *copy* of the lost original of the work, one would have to project back, taking the year 50 B.C. as a starting point, perhaps as much as fifty or seventy-five years more, i.e., into the second century B.C., in order to define the hypothetical time of actual composition of the work. However, this was a period otherwise represented by no text written in an idiom approaching that of the *Acts of Torah* or the *Copper Scroll*. There was thus a certain clash between the dating of this text by linguistic criteria to approximately the early first century A.D., and Cross's dating of what was merely a copy of the original text, by his own system of palaeography, to the mid–first century B.C. Strugnell, ever faithful to the view of his colleagues of the editorial committee, had a difficult problem on his hands and perhaps hoped that, with Qimron's aid, it would turn out to be resoluble.

The problem was to determine how this text, written in an idiom so different from that of the scrolls ascribed to the *Yahad* group, could be made to fit the (imagined) picture of a unified sect already living at Khirbet Qumran in the second century B.C.

As Strugnell and Qimron continued their study of the *Acts of Torah* between 1982 and 1984, translating various portions in the process, they must have become increasingly surprised and even intrigued by their findings. They were confronting a group of approximately twenty laws, mostly concerned with ritual-purity, that had no parallels in the other scrolls attributed to the "sect of Qumran" at that time. Thus, they had the additional dilemma, as they proceeded to write their first joint articles on this text, of explaining how the "sect" could have produced a work not only written in a distinctively different idiom but also containing so many ritual laws not found among the *Yahad* writings.

Their effort to solve these problems, while yet portraying the text as a significant Qumran document, was expressed in a paper that Qimron delivered at an archaeological conference held in Jerusalem in 1984, and that was published in the form of an article the following year.[15] The article made clear that the goal of the authors was, above all else, to preserve the integrity of the traditional Qumran-sectarian hypothesis. There was no other way to explain the contradictory nature of their assertions.

What they described was a most interesting text indeed. The authors acknowledged the correctness of Milik's observation concerning the nature of the language, and even quoted several passages of the text that revealed the nonbiblical, proto-rabbinic character of the idiom. They also briefly discussed the ritual laws contained in the text. They mentioned not all of them but a total of twelve, asserting that one having to do with the "ashes of the red heifer" was found also among the Sadducees and Samaritans, as well as in the *Temple Scroll*.* They drew no parallels between

---

*See Numbers **19**.2–10. In this passage Moses is commanded:

> Tell the people of Israel to bring you a red heifer without defect . . . and upon which a yoke has never come. You shall give her to Eleazar the priest, and she shall be taken outside the camp and slaughtered before him; Eleazar the priest shall take some of her blood with his finger, and sprinkle some of her blood toward the tent of meeting seven times. The heifer shall be burned in his sight; her skin, her flesh, and her blood, with her dung, shall be burned; the priest shall take cedar

additional rules in the *Acts of Torah* and ritual laws found in other Qumran scrolls.

Yet although the language of the text was highly unusual, and only a few isolated parallels could be drawn between the ritual practices and laws of this work and those of the other scrolls, the authors asserted, as we might expect, almost at the very outset of their remarks that the *Acts of Torah* was nothing other than a writing of "the sect of Qumran." The language they used to do this provides an exemplary case study in one type of scholastic persuasion, revealing the extreme to which authors may at times be ready to go in order to defend their favorite tottering hypotheses.

The authors first proposed that the work was a halakhic (i.e., ritual-legal) work "from Qumran," which we could interpret, if generously inclined, as meaning nothing more than that the text derived from one of the Qumran caves. In the next sentence, however, they stated that it was "one of the most important documents," repeated that it was "from Qumran," and immediately thereafter made the following connection:

> That it was highly considered by *the sect itself* can be inferred from the fact that six manuscripts of the work have been found in 4Q.[16]

It thus became evident that the authors had not set out to demonstrate that the *Acts of Torah* belonged to the *Yahad* sectarian group. They rather *assumed* as much, suggesting in the same breath that its importance for "the sect" revealed itself in the fact that six copies of the work had been found in one of the caves. The statements were strikingly gratuitous: The presence of the six copies could, objectively speaking, show nothing more than that the work was widely read at the time the scrolls were hidden.

---

wood and hyssop and scarlet stuff, and cast them into the midst of the burning of the heifer. Then the priest shall wash his clothes and bathe his body in water, and afterwards he shall come into the camp; and the priest shall be unclean until evening. He who burns the heifer shall wash his clothes in water and bathe his body in water, and shall be unclean until evening. A man who is clean shall gather up the ashes of the heifer, and deposit them outside the camp in a clean place; and they shall be kept for the congregation of the people of Israel for the water of impurity, for the removal of sin. He who gathers the ashes of the heifer shall wash his clothes, and be unclean until evening. This shall be to the people of Israel, and to the stranger who sojourns among them, a perpetual statute.

Seeking, however, to establish plausible interconnections between this text and the other scrolls, the authors asserted, again without substantiation, that the *Acts of Torah* was "a letter from a leader of the Qumran sect (possibly the Teacher of Righteousness himself) to the leader of its opponents. . . ." Acknowledging that they could "only guess" precisely who this "leader" was, since the beginning of the "letter" was missing, the authors nevertheless sought to place the text in the earliest period of the putative sect's existence. To do this, they merely *set aside* the linguistic criterion—which showed the text to be a relatively late product—and reasoned that, since the tone of the writer's polemic was moderate and he hoped that his opponent might become convinced of the truth of his view, "we assume that the text is of an early date in the development of the Qumran schism."

This argument, however, was entirely arbitrary—another example of amateurish historiography. The first stage in the creation of a new schism is often characterized by violent polemics. Had the goal of Qimron and Strugnell been to show that the text was late, they could have simply asserted that the moderate tone of the polemic and the hope for possible reconciliation revealed the "sect" at an advanced stage in its development, after the heated polemics of the earlier times had cooled. Their purpose was to show that the text was of the greatest possible significance: Their "assumption" that it was early was "not inconsistent with the palaeographic results." The work might "then be the earliest Qumranic work, probably written after the separation of the sect."

There were, however, no grounds in logic or fact for any of these inferences. As the first-century idiom of the text showed, Cross's dating of one of the manuscripts to 50–25 B.C. had been a blunder. Strugnell and Qimron were attempting to transmute that mistake into a bona fide criterion for their early dating of the composition. By suggesting that the text from which the copies found in the caves were made was the "earliest Qumran work" and possibly written by the Teacher of Righteousness himself, they were clearly seeking to swell the value of the work, while defending the integrity of the old hypothesis and, with it, the value of Cross's system of palaeographic dating to twenty-five-year periods. And they were doing so without offering a semblance of proof for their propositions. Faced with the problem of the first-century idiom of the text, they suggested that, in view of their other arguments, the language was simply earlier than anyone had thought. It was not, however, the idiom of any sizable area of Judaea, but of one place alone: "We believe," stated the authors, "that the language of MMT, more than that of any other Qumranic text, reflects the spoken Hebrew of Qumran. . . ."[17]

There was, of course, no proof of this proposition either. That an individual locality of the Judaean Wilderness would have possessed this special dialect two centuries before it was otherwise attested, that this dialect would not have turned up in any of the other scrolls attributed to the "sect of Qumran," and that this was in fact the *earliest* composition of "the sect" and perhaps written by the Teacher of Righteousness himself, were outlandish assertions, flying in the face of the reasonable methods that scholars characteristically employ in attempting to date and interpret ancient texts. To all appearances, the *Acts of Torah* represented yet another trend in ancient Judaism, supplying new evidence for the multiform character of the Dead Sea Scrolls and hence their derivation from important libraries. But if readers could be convinced that the Teacher of Righteousness himself had written this text, they would hardly even begin to worry about other possible meanings of the work. That Strugnell and Qimron seriously entertained this obscurantist agenda soon became apparent.

Since their joint article did not meet with immediate widespread reaction, Strugnell and Qimron agreed in consultation with curator Broshi of the Shrine of the Book to arrange for publication of a popular article on the subject that would include a clear photograph of one of the fragments. This article, by Abraham Rabinovitch, appeared as a full-page story in the *Jerusalem Post* on 14 June 1985. Imbedded in the article, in which Rabinovitch essentially related the views of Strugnell, Qimron, and Broshi regarding the work, was a paragraph revealing their purpose: "Among the mass of material from Qumran," Rabinovitch explained,

> no letter has ever before been identified. This has led one scrolls scholar to question whether the documents were in fact from a local Qumran archive, since such an archive might be expected to include correspondence. However, [the editors of the text] maintain that the use of the second person clearly establishes their document as a letter.

This manner of alluding to my critique of the traditional theory was a way of telling readers that the new Qumran text in some way put an end to the problem. Yet the *Acts of Torah* was no more a genuine original "document" or "letter" than were any of the other known Qumran texts, except the *Copper Scroll*. Reflecting a somewhat brazen lack of concern for the values of traditional humanistic scholarship, Strugnell and Qimron had not made available an edition of the new manuscript fragments. It was nonetheless evident, from both the article's description and an accompanying photograph of a part of the text, that the editors had simply identified a *literary epistle*, such as those found for example in the Apocrypha and the New Testament—not, to be sure, the original autograph, but rather fragments of scribal copies of it.

My criticism, however, had been unambiguous from the start: Excluding the *Copper Scroll*, no *original* legal instruments, personal letters, or other autograph documents of a sect—such as those of Bar Kokhba and contemporaries of his discovered elsewhere—nor any autographs (as opposed to scribal copies) of literary texts had ever been identified at Qumran; and that included these new fragments as well—which Qimron himself had shown me in the summer of 1983 at the Rockefeller Museum. The lack of autograph sectarian texts, as much as any other factor, continued to vitiate the hypothesis of Qumran-Essene origins of the scrolls.

By 1984 the climate in Jerusalem had changed somewhat, and after a few negotiations back and forth I was asked to give a lecture at the Rockefeller Museum on the scrolls and the theory of Jerusalem origin. Among other things, I emphasized the problem of lack of autographs. That same evening I found myself back at the Albright Institute, in a closed colloquium devoted to my interpretation of Qumran origins. During the increasingly animated debate, curator Broshi earnestly announced to a large group of assembled scholars, including affiliates of the Ecole Biblique and some well-known Israeli Qumranologists, that an original letter of the sect (i.e., the letter on which Qimron and Strugnell were working) had indeed been preserved in Cave 4—and that this discovery refuted my interpretation. When I responded that Qimron had shown me the manuscript fragments at the Rockefeller in 1983, and that what I meant by an "autograph letter" was the original author's own hand-copy, not something else, and then proceeded to explain the characteristics of an autograph, Broshi was visibly shaken. And yet, despite my having clearly explained the text's status at the Albright Institute meeting, Rabinovitch—

who had been present at that meeting and later wrote his piece with Broshi's input—obscured this essential point in his eventual article on the *Acts of Torah*.

The article also revealed other paradoxical efforts to harmonize the contents of the epistle with the old idea of the scrolls' origin. For example, its headline declared that the authors had pieced together "an astonishing letter written by the founder of the Dead Sea Sect to the 'Wicked Priest' in Jerusalem." The story went on to state that the text was "astonishing less for its contents than for its writer and addressee." Later, however, it asserted that the "opening salutation is missing. This presumably included the identities of both sender and addressee." The only thing, however, that could legitimately be called "astonishing" was the editors' notion that the writer was somehow the Teacher of Righteousness and the addressee the "Wicked Priest" mentioned in passages of several *other* Qumran texts. The text named no personalities at all, and the effort of Qimron, Strugnell, and Broshi had blossomed into a quintessential example of what J. L. Kraemer of Tel Aviv University has, in another context, succinctly described as "the fallacy of over-identification."[18]

Rabinovitch's article also asserted that the author of the text spelled out "the religious rules . . . followed by the breakaway sect at Qumran." Yet it also explained that according to curator Broshi, "the [twenty] specific differences listed *are all new* [my italics] but no more significant than the differences already known"—thus turning the initial claim about the putative sect's "religious rules" into an unfathomable conclusion. For if the religious rules of the new manuscript were mostly not identical with those in other Qumran texts, if the identity of neither the sender nor the recipient of the original epistle was actually known, and if in addition there was no geographical term in the text that might localize either sender or receiver, then any claim that the text was doctrinally related to other scrolls, and like them originated at the Khirbet Qumran site, was scientifically groundless and unreasonable. The fact that a few laws in the new text were (as the article itself suggested) identical with legal views of the Sadducees, while none seemed comparable with regulations attributable to the Essenes, pointed unmistakably to conclusions much different than those urged in the *Post* article.

There is a great difference between attributing a particular notion to a group of scholars, and treating that notion as though it were an established fact. In statements such as "the archaeologists would in time recognize that Qumran had been the headquarters of the sect which wrote the scrolls. . . . Cave Four had been the sect's library. . . ." the author of the *Post* article had clearly opted for the second choice. Still more unfortunate was the fact that the curator of the Shrine of the Book appeared there not as an objective observer but as one actively supporting the editors of the text in their questionable position. How, I wondered, could the curator of an important museum collection, and as such someone entrusted with the basic obligation of impartiality, allow himself to take sides in this obvious way, particularly when the hypotheses he was championing were so ill-founded?

Without forced exegesis, the new manuscript fragments clearly illustrated the doctrinal diversity of the scrolls. Nevertheless, the *Post* article succeeded in promulgating the bizarre idea in Israel, America, and Europe that a letter by none other than the Teacher of Righteousness had been found by Strugnell and Qimron in the Qumran Cave 4 material.

Still, in 1985 these authors had announced that they planned to finish a "preliminary edition of the whole document . . . within a year or so."[19] They now set about to accomplish this goal, no doubt heartened by the wide uncritical acceptance of their idea. In 1986, Qimron spoke of an article on the text written in collaboration with Strugnell, indicating that it was to be published in the *Revue de Qumran*; by citing specific paragraphs, he conveyed the impression that it was substantially complete and would soon be published.[20] However, during the next few years it did not appear. Instead, in a list of planned publications of Qumran texts put out by the Israel Antiquities Authority on 25 January 1989, the text was described as being ready to send to the printers in the summer of 1989, while the title given to it was "4QMMT. 'Letter of the Teacher of Righteousness'"—a title encouraging still wider acceptance of the unfounded theory the authors were proposing.

Much had happened meanwhile. The authors' failure to publish their promised preliminary edition of the text by 1987 had caused quite a few scholars to begin wondering about the reasons for the delay. Those of a critical mind wanted to examine the text for themselves, rather than continuing to rely on the judgments of others for their information about the work. Disturbingly, Strugnell had been holding on to the text since the 1950s, not only since 1984. Between 1985 and 1989 I published additional articles questioning the prevalent idea of a uniform "Qumran sectarianism"; in them I urged the general academic community, as well as the public, to be thoroughly skeptical about the propositions that the Qumranologists were pressing.[21] I indicated that Strugnell's and Qimron's claims about the *Acts of Torah* were baseless.[22]

Although one author has suggested that the absurd delays in publication of the text resulted from my criticism of the "Teacher of Righteousness" theory, this was not necessarily the case.[23] For what Strugnell had sought in the early 1980s was the aid of scholars who might help him elucidate the text in a way that did no damage to the basic suppositions of the traditional Qumranologists. Qimron appeared to be ready to cooperate at once, falling into line on all the well-worn assumptions, and showing full willingness to inflate the value of the manuscript as best he could. Professor Sussman of Jerusalem, as we have seen, had been asked to contribute to an explication of the ritual laws of the text, and on agreeing to do so, was given a copy of the edition in progress. In 1986 or early 1987, Lawrence Schiffman of New York University was also asked to comment on the ritual laws; thus he too was given a copy of the same edition. Most scholars, of course, still had no access to it or to photographs of the manuscript fragments.

Professor Schiffman had built his career on the study of legal passages in the Qumran texts. He had examined such passages in the *Damascus Covenant* and the *Manual of Discipline*, and in 1975 had published a book entitled *The Halakhah at Qumran*. This book reflected the conventional wisdom of the mid-seventies regarding Qumran origins: The writings were those of a sect, and analysis of its known legal texts could tell us more about the identity of this heterodox group supposedly living on the Qumran plateau. A few years later, however, the *Temple Scroll* was published, revealing a program of ritual observance that did not square with the rituals described in the scrolls published earlier. A subsequent study by Schiffman (1983) was therefore more prudently titled *Sectarian Law in the Dead Sea Scrolls*—without the expression "at Qumran." This was eventually followed, *inter alia*, by an essay, "The Temple Scroll and the Systems of Jewish Law of the Second Temple Period" (1989), in which the author reached the conclusion that, while one could point to an occasional exception (for instance, parallel rules prohibiting sexual relations in the

Holy City found in both the *Damascus Covenant* and the *Temple Scroll*), it was "impossible to show direct correspondence between the *Temple Scroll* and the other systems of Jewish law as known from available sources."[24] Even the calendar of the *Temple Scroll* was "in accord with the later rabbinic calendar" and *did not agree* with that of "the Qumran sect." By way of acknowledging the implications for the Qumran-sectarian hypothesis of the discovery of a scroll containing mostly non-"Qumranic" laws, Schiffman referred not simply to "the Qumran sect" but to "the Qumran 'sect'"—putting the last word in quotes to indicate the increasingly problematic quality of that expression.[25]

Appended to this study of the *Temple Scroll* was a discussion of the *Acts of Torah*, a transcription of which Schiffman had received earlier. Here was a challenging new legal text from Cave 4, whose laws had only begun to be touched upon by Strugnell and Qimron. They had already claimed that "two or three of the halakhot on ritual-purity expressed in our work are cited also in early rabbinic literature as the opinion of the Sadducees in their controversy with the Pharisees." For them, the work thus became "an important piece of evidence in establishing the identity of the Sadducees . . . mentioned in Rabbinic sources."[26] The Sadducees and Pharisees were evidently the two largest groups or parties among the Jews during the first century B.C. and the first century A.D., and it was of obvious importance to know whether the new manuscript cast light on either of them.

In the final analysis, Schiffman's discussion did not clarify this question. He had perceived that the contents of the *Temple Scroll* were in no significant way related to the other scrolls, and had also asserted that "we are only now realizing the extent to which the library at Qumran was eclectic."[27] But rather than proceeding objectively to a study of the *Acts of Torah*, without prior conceptions as to how the text could fit into the expanding picture of an eclectic library, he declared at the very outset that the work was essentially what Strugnell and Qimron had said it was—"a letter . . . which purports to be from the leaders of the sect. . . ."[28] He thus disregarded, without explanation, the conclusion he had reached earlier in the same article, failing in the process to mention the problem of the relatively late proto-rabbinic idiom of the text, which pointed not to the second century B.C., when the Teacher of Righteousness lived, but to the first century A.D.

While Schiffman nowhere indicated what had led him to his

conclusion—or even precisely what he meant by his reference to "the sect"—he described a score of laws in the *Acts of Torah* that represented points of dispute between the group represented by the anonymous author and the group's opponents. For these descriptions, he relied—in a departure from the norm in manuscript study—not only on Strugnell's original transcriptions of the fragments but also on Qimron's restorations of words in the holes of the manuscript. The result was not a study of the manuscript *per se*, but of the text as two other scholars had transcribed and restored it.

In the end Schiffman asserted the presence of several ritual laws in the text whose traces were uncertain and based on guesses. This was not understood when he gave his first lecture on this text in Jerusalem in the summer of 1987, but became evident after scholars in various countries began receiving by mail, from one or more anonymous sources, *samizdat* photocopies of a handwritten reconstruction of the text (autumn 1987), and were able to compare it with the list of laws drawn up by Schiffman. Thus, where Schiffman asserted that the work contained a prohibition of cooking sin-offerings "in copper vessels,"[29] the transcription of the manuscript itself only stated: "[. . .][36] to come to the holy place [. . .] that they cook [. . .] in a vessel of [. . .] the flesh of their offerings. . . ." The "copper" was only Qimron's restoration; the law itself may not at all have focused on the character of the vessel, but on the particular class of people who came to sacrifice. Several of the reputed laws of the work were in this dubious category, and no well-grounded judgment about their specific contents was possible.

Other laws, however, were better preserved and often quite fully intelligible. They included the following: (1) Grains produced by the gentiles are prohibited in the Temple precincts. (2) Gentiles themselves are to be discouraged or forbidden from bringing sacrifices as these both contain and cause impurity, while the religious motives of such worshippers are suspect. (3) The Temple priests are not to allow whole offerings of thanks to be kept overnight; rather, they are to see to it that those portions permissible as food are to be eaten during the very day that sacrifice of the animal takes place. (4) Those who take part in the preparation of the ashes of the red heifer (see Num. **19**.2 ff.) are afterward to be certain that they purify themselves "by the setting of the sun, so that the pure might sprinkle [the purifying waters] upon the impure." (5) All the laws of the Torah relating to the "encampments" of the Israelites in the desert apply by analogy to Jerusalem, with the sanctuary taking the place of the Mosaic "tabernacle of the Tent of Meeting" (Ex. **33**.32 and *passim*); slaughter of animals for personal consumption, and the burning of the fat-portions of the sacrificial offerings, are to be performed strictly in accordance with those rules. (6) As in the Torah (Lev. **22**.28), an animal and its offspring are not to be slaughtered the same day. (7) The sexually impaired, as well as Ammonites, Moabites, and illegitimate offspring, are not to be allowed to mix with others in the Temple precincts; and the blind or deaf, unable to understand how to perform the laws of purity and holiness, are by right not to be allowed into the Temple precincts "although they come to the purity of the Temple."* (8) Pouring liquids from a pure container into an impure one results in the impurity traveling upward and defiling the first container. (9) Dogs are not to be brought into Jerusalem, as otherwise they will snatch away the animal bones with sacrificial meat still upon them. (10) The "first fruit," or fourth-year harvest, of trees newly planted in the Land of Israel belongs to the priests, as do the tithe of all the sheep and cattle. (11) Those recovering from skin afflictions are to be excluded from Jerusalem and from participation in consuming the allowable portion of the offerings until they have completed a full eight-day period of purification (Lev. **14**), contrary to the laxity in this matter prevailing in the Temple precincts. (12) Impurity can be incurred by contact with a (human) bone to the same extent as by contact with a dead person. (13) "Harlotry" is defiling to the people, who are "holy," and the priests, who are "most holy"; and the rule of their conduct is to be set by the principle of unmixed kinds applied to clothing and to the plowing of fields (Lev. **19**.19; Deut. **22**.9–11). Thus the priests are, by analogy, not to intermarry with members of nonpriestly families.

Despite the sense of strangeness that the laws of the *Acts of Torah* may well induce in today's reader, we should bear in mind that to the Jews of intertestamental times the various rules and prohibitions laid down in the legal portions of the Pentateuch were a matter of vital concern. The Torah itself did not provide sufficient guidance or explanation for the observance of these

---

*The author means to say that the blind and deaf obstinately come to the Temple precincts even though they should not.

sometimes contradictory laws, which in Second Temple times priests or other interpreters had to explain. It was thus natural for various groups to form and gradually to develop differing interpretations of theological and ritual issues that were felt to bear particular significance.

The writer of the *Acts of Torah* states in the course of his epistle that "We have separated from the majority of the na[tion]" as a result of the specific differences in ritual practice that he lists. The Hebrew term which he uses for "we have separated"—*parashnu*—shares its root with the term that has come down to us as Pharisees (Hebrew, *perushim*), meaning "separatists." No one knows why this term was applied to the historical Pharisees, some writers suggesting it was because of their studied observance of the biblical laws of purity (which required separation from those who did not scrupulously observe those laws), and others that it was only a term of opprobrium used by their opponents.[31] The use of the expression "we have separated," which occurs in none of the other Qumran scrolls, would thus seem to point to a group related to the Pharisees. While the enumeration of several laws of purity in the text reinforces this interpretation, it is particularly abetted by other characteristics of the epistle.

The language, for example, is idiomatically closer to that used by the Pharisees' heirs, i.e., the Tannaim or earliest rabbis, in their first known legal writings, the *Mishnah* and *Tosephta* (second century A.D.). Furthermore, one of the most unusual features of the *Acts of Torah* is its use of pietistic circumlocution in alluding to God, in keeping with the warning of the Ten Commandments not to "take the name of the Lord . . . in vain" (Ex. **20.**7). We now know, thanks to the scrolls, that in at least one trend in intertestamental Judaism this was accomplished by writing the Tetragrammaton YHWH in archaic Hebrew letters (as, for example, in the *Pesher Habakkuk*). The author of the *Manual of Discipline* and several other writers, by contrast, refer to the Lord consistently without employing the Tetragrammaton, but rather by use of the brief *el*, "God," rather than other possible designations, e.g., *elo'ah, elohim, shaddai*, and so forth. The author of the *Acts of Torah*, however, uses no direct designation whatsoever, only alluding to the Deity or referring to Him by the oblique "He" or "Him"—a form of pietism also occurring in early rabbinic literature, but unknown in the heterodox *Yahad* texts or in other literature found in the Qumran caves.

We can further assess the character of the author's thinking and its proximity to prerabbinic Pharisaism or other trends in ancient Judaism by carefully examining the legible portions of what seems to be the last part of the *Acts of Torah*. These represent a summation of the author's message, following the enumeration of the disputed laws. I translate here somewhat literally:

> [. . . from] violence and fornication have [we] lost [. . .] places
> [. . .]. It is writ[ten in the Book of Moses that you should no]t bring
> abomination t[o your house, for] abomination is hateful [. . .]. We
> have separated from the majority of the na[tion and have refrain-
> ed] from intermingling with these matters or from entering

Figure 13
Fragments of one scribal copy of the *Acts of Torah*.

[. . .] as concerns them. You[32] [. . .] find in our keeping iniquity, deceit and evil; yet concerning [these] do we give [. . .]. We have [. . .] to you, that you might gain understanding of the Book of Moses, [the . . . of the p]rophets and of Davi[d . . . ,] every single generation. In the Book is written . . . that not . . . and it is further written [that if you part] from the w[a]y, evil will befall [you]. It is written thus, that [there shall com]e upon you [al]l these thing[s] at the End of Days, the blessing [and] the curse [that I gave unto you; you shall ponde]r (them) in your h[ear]t and return to Me with all your heart and with [a]ll [your] soul [. . .], and [you] will l[i]ve.[33] [. . .] Moses and in [. . . of the prophet]s that there shall come[. . . .] The [ble]ssing[s that] came [. . .] in [his days and] in the days of Solomon son of David, and moreover the curses [that] came unto (Israel) from the d[ays of Jer]oboam son of Nebat until the Exile of Jerusalem and Zedekiah king of Juda[h, that] they should b[ring] them [. . .]. Now we perceive that some of the blessings and curses have transpired as written in the B[ook of Mo]ses.This is the End of Days—that in Israel they should return[to His way . . .] and not backslide. The wicked will then be jud[ged w]icked.[. . .]. Remember the kings of Israe[l], ponder their deeds; for whoever among them feared [the To]rah was saved from calamities. These were see[k]ers of Torah, [and] sins were [forgiven]. Remember David, who was a man of lovingkindness; he also was [s]aved from many calamities and was forgiven (by Him). We have moreover written to you some of the acts of the Torah, as we deemed it good for you and your people; for we perceive that you possess cunning and knowledge of Torah. Understand all these things, seek from before Him that He should make your counsel steadfast, and keep far from yourself wicked thought and the counsel of Belial, so that you might rejoice at the End of the Season, when you find some of our words to be correct. Then shall it be reckoned unto you as righteousness—when you do what is straightforward and good before Him—(and) as goodness unto you and Israel.[34]

These passages reveal additional aspects of the separatist's mentality and spiritual outlook. We may observe first of all the politeness and reserve with which the author addresses himself to the anonymous royal figure implied by the wording of the epistle. There is no polemical harshness in this work, but rather a dispassionate accounting of the points of difference that had led his group simply to "separate from the majority of the na[tion]." This calm and reasoned tone of debate would later be observed by Josephus as a salient characteristic of the Pharisees, as contrasted with their opponents, the Sadducees:

> The Pharisees are affectionate to each other and cultivate harmonious relations with the community. The Sadducees, on the contrary, are, even among themselves, rather boorish in their behavior, and in their intercourse with their peers are as rude as with aliens.[35]

The author of the *Acts of Torah* calls the Pentateuch by the title "Book of Moses," an expression otherwise unheard of in any of the scrolls. The other writings which he especially reveres are the prophetic books and (the writing or Book of) David, apparently a designation of Psalms. He makes a special point of referring to the blessings that were David's and Solomon's; he states that David, as some later Israelite kings, was forgiven by the Lord for his sins. This is of course a startling assertion in view of the many acts of a wicked nature attributed to David in Second Samuel— descriptions that contrast egregiously with the picture of a pious and God-fearing David that emerges from those psalms attributed to him. The author sought to harmonize the conflicting portraits by suggesting that David's sins were forgiven in view of his overall piety and pursuit of Torah—precisely as did the early rabbis when faced with this problem.[36] Even more remarkable are the author's statements concerning the End of Days: In his view, they were fast arriving, for some of the blessings and curses foretold by Moses had already come to be. The End would bring the peoples' return to the Lord, when the wicked would be justly punished by Him. The author exhorts the recipient of his epistle to seek the Lord's guidance so that he might eventually find bliss "at the End of the Season."

These exhortations reveal the author as a follower of the view that there would be a final reckoning for the Jews; but he does not spell out his specific conception of it, other than that the righteous would find bliss and the wicked punishment. He first writes that the "End of Days" (*aharit hayamim*) was upon the people, that Israel would be returning to the Lord and the wicked would then be punished, and the addressee would hopefully rejoice in the "End of the Season" (*aharit ha'et*). According to the views of man's fate that Josephus attributes to the major "philosophies" of the Jews, the idea expressed here conformed most with that of the

Pharisees, less with that attributed to the Essenes, and least with that of the Sadducees. It was the Pharisees who, as Josephus writes,

> believed that souls have power to survive death and that there are rewards and punishments under the earth for those who have led lives of virtue or vice, while the good souls receive an easy passage to a new life[37]

—a doctrine that appears with vigorous nuances in rabbinic literature. Josephus does not speak of any particular time frame for the Pharisees' eschatological doctrine. The scrolls that treat this matter, for their part, generally imply that a final cataclysm was soon to happen; but the stark eschatological imagery of such writings as the *War Scroll* and the *Habakkuk Commentary* contrasts sharply with the language of the *Acts of Torah*, which lacks all the bizarre elements of those other works. The author conceived of an impending End that would bring with it the tranquillity of the righteous and the punishment of the wicked. However, this finality was not to be achieved by avenging armies or battles of mythic proportions, but only by the will of the Lord, whose moral imperative could indeed be heeded if one but abjured the counsel of an ever-lurking spirit of evil. We seem to be dealing with an early form of the Pharisaic eschatology. Josephus would later state of the Pharisees that they

> attribute everything to Fate and to God; they hold that to act rightly or otherwise rests, indeed, for the most part with men, but that in each action Fate cooperates. Every soul, they maintain, is imperishable, but the soul of the good alone passes into another body, while the souls of the wicked suffer eternal punishment.[38]

The Sadducees, on the other hand, according to Josephus rejected the concept of fate altogether. They

> remove God beyond, not merely the commission, but the very sight of evil. They maintain that man has the free choice of good or evil, and that it rests with each man's will whether he follows the one or the other. As for the persistence of the soul after death, penalties in the underworld, and rewards, they will have none of them.[39]

The Gospels and Book of Acts affirm that the Sadducees had no belief in a compensatory afterlife or End of Days, in contrast with other Jewish groups.[40]

It is thus unlikely that a Sadducee would ever have employed expressions such as "the End of the Season" in a moral or religious context, or spoken of a future reward for the righteous and punishment for the wicked, and particularly so in the context of the Lord's benevolence.

The Essenes' conception of an afterlife as related by Josephus also does not satisfactorily fit the picture created by the author of the *Acts of Torah*. According to Josephus, the Essenes held that the body was finite and perished, while the soul was immortal. They believed that

> emanating from the finest ether, these souls become entangled, as it were, in the prison-house of the body, to which they are dragged down by a sort of natural spell; but when once they are released from the bonds of flesh, then, as though liberated from a long servitude, they rejoice and are borne aloft. Sharing the belief of the sons of Greece, they maintain that for virtuous souls there is reserved an abode beyond the ocean, a place which is not oppressed by rain or snow or heat, but is refreshed by the ever gentle breath of the west wind coming in from the ocean; while they relegate base souls to a murky and tempestuous dungeon, big with never-ending punishments.[41]

Thus, for the Essenes, the souls of the good had bliss in an abode beyond the seas, while the souls of the wicked were chastised in a murky dungeon—terms that are not at all characteristic of the author of the *Acts of Torah*. He does not express the hope that the *soul* of the royal personage to whom he addressed his epistle should find eternal bliss, but that the recipient himself will find happiness "in the End of the Season," foreshadowing the eschatological position not only of the Pharisees as implied in the New Testament and of the early rabbinic Tannaim, but of the early Christians as well.[42]

The characteristics discussed until this point thus favor the attribution of the *Acts of Torah* to early first-century A.D. Pharisees or a group close to them. The ritual laws of the text, however, present a more confusing picture, and for good reason. Students of Jewish law have long been aware that various rulings of the early rabbinic legislators were drawn directly from earlier Pharisaic legislation, while others were not; different schools and individual scholars among the Tannaim themselves maintained varying degrees of severity in the observance of ritual laws of purity and other genres of precepts. Over three centuries, dynamic changes occurred in the interpretation of the Pentateuchal law, changes that affected all parties and sects among the Jews. The laws preserved in the *Acts of Torah* reflect aspects of Jewish legal practice as interpreted by a particular separatist group during a specific period of its existence. As with the history of schisms, sects, and parties in general, this group's legal ideas undoubtedly developed and changed during the course of time. Traces of them can be found later in the early rabbinic corpus, some being approved by a consensus of the Tannaim and others not.

Neither the group behind the author of the *Acts of Torah* nor the early rabbis, for example, approved of the admission of people with skin diseases (the so-called lepers of the standard Bible translations) into the precincts of the Holy City, since such diseases rendered those individuals ritually unclean.[43] In the conception of both groups, the Pentateuchal "encampment" of the Israelites in the desert signified Jerusalem as a totality, and the laws applying to the one were relevant to the other.[44] By contrast, certain laws espoused by the author show a greater severity than that later endorsed by Tannaitic figures. The so-called fourth-year produce had to be given to the priests, as did the tithe of cattle and sheep. Even fragments of bones could render one impure. The author criticizes the priests for allowing portions of certain offerings to be eaten (whether by gentiles or Jews is uncertain) on the day following the sacrificial ceremony; whereas the later Tannaitic view* was that such sacrifices could in principle be consumed as late as the dawn following the day of the sacrificial ceremony, although generally they were to be consumed by midnight of the same day—"in order to distance people from sin."[45] Blind and deaf people, the author asserted, were unable to understand or even follow all the laws of purity, and thus should be excluded from the Temple precincts. The author—but not the Tannaim—frowned upon sacrifices by gentiles. His overriding concern was to institute, or reinstitute, scrupulous observance of the laws of purity and holiness in the Temple ritual practice, and to protect

---

*The early rabbinic views on sacrifice were only theoretical, since the Temple had already been destroyed before they were put into the *Mishnah* and *Tosephta*. The rebuilding of the Temple was never carried out, although the emperor Julian the Apostate (ruled 361–363) is reputed to have promised the Jews he would allow them to rebuild it.

the holy status of Jerusalem through full imposition of the purity laws on its inhabitants, pilgrims, and visitors. Failure to secure this compliance had led to the self-imposed separation of the author's group, both as a protest and so that they themselves might practice the laws of purity to the fullest extent. It was this same mentality that gave rise to the "friendship" groups that were later to occupy so singular a place in the hierarchic configuration of Tannaitic Judaism.

One or two of the laws of the *Acts of Torah*, however, appear to be identical with those of the Sadducees as described in later rabbinic texts. This is the case, as we have seen, for the severe rule concerning retrograde impurity proceeding from poured liquids. The law concerning the ritual status of those responsible for preparing the ashes of the red heifer is, however, more problematic; the author of the *Acts of Torah* states that they were to make themselves pure *by evening*—i.e., by a ritual bath—so that they could then sprinkle the waters containing the ashes on those who were impure. The Sadducees, by contrast, claimed that they should remain *impure* until evening (see Num. **19**.7–10). Although some have seen in the law of the *Acts of Torah* a Sadducaean rule of purity, the author's words are in fact closer to the position of the Pharisees as described in rabbinic sources, who held that those who prepared the ashes were to be considered as pure from the moment they immersed themselves, *without waiting* for sunset.[46] A priest involved in the preparation of the ashes who immersed himself before sunset could not yet engage in certain sacrificial proceedings, but was considered to have a sufficient degree of purity to sprinkle the waters containing the ashes on those who were impure. An approximate ruling is endorsed by the author of the *Acts of Torah* who explicitly calls upon the preparers of the ashes to be pure "by evening so that the pure may sprinkle upon the impure."

For enigmatic reasons, however, both Schiffman and Sussman pointed to this rule as proof of the presence of Sadducaean laws in the *Acts of Torah*.[47] Schiffman in fact claimed that, of five disputes between Pharisees and Sadducees recorded in a particular tractate of the *Mishnah*, "four have echoes in MMT."[48] Yet of these four rulings, only one—that pertaining to retrograde impurity of liquids—has a palpable counterpart in the *Acts of Torah*. The other points of difference given between Pharisees and Sadducees have to do with the latter's insistence that:

(a) if a stream flows through a cemetery, the water in that stream is rendered impure;

(b) if a servant causes damages, his master is responsible for the loss;

(c) all books, including holy writings, cause ritual defilement to the hands;

(d) all bones, animal or human, may render one impure.

Schiffman claimed that all these laws had "echoes" in the *Acts of Torah*, whereas none of them do; there is nothing in the *Acts* concerning *any* of these rules. In their edition of the text, Qimron and Strugnell reconstructed a few lines in such a way as to reflect the fourth of the Sadducaean rulings, but the actual preserved words reveal no such connection:

> Moreover concerning skin[s. . .] and from their sk[ins] handles of v[essels . . . sk]in of the carcass of the pure [. . .] her, her carcass [. . . br]ing to the purity of the [. . .].

There is nothing at all about bones in this passage, only about the impure skins of animals.

Schiffman, however, appears not to have been content with this exaggeration, but went on to one that was even more remarkable: that the "MMT text took the 'Sadducee' position," that it was also "clearly related to the Temple Scroll" and that hence "we must reopen the question of the relationship of the Sadducees to our sect."

The claims were baseless. Schiffman had found only a few instances at most where the laws of the *Temple Scroll* and of the *Acts of Torah* were closely related.* He moreover pointed out only one law of the *Acts of Torah* demonstrably parallel with that of the Sadducees, as known from later rabbinic texts. Yet even taking for granted his claim of additional parallels, his conclusion repre-

---

*In the article under review (see endnote 24 to this chapter), Schiffman claimed (p. 250) that his "comparison has shown . . . that MMT and the Temple Scroll have much in common, while exhibiting some incongruities." In the preceding pages, however, his discussion described numerous divergences between these two texts, the one case of an apparent bona fide agreement being that concerning fourth-year agricultural products and the tithe of cattle, which, Schiffman claimed, are assigned by the authors of both texts to priests. As the Temple Scroll text is fragmentary at the crucial point, however, this parallel is not certain.

sented an enigmatic about-face from the position he had taken earlier in the same essay, when he recognized that the *Temple Scroll* was basically unrelated to the texts of the *Yahad* group and encouraged the view that the "library at Qumran was eclectic." He had found in the *Temple Scroll* virtually no ritual laws that could conceivably be termed "Sadducaean," making the conclusion all the more egregiously self-contradictory.

Schiffman had first presented this article as a lecture in December 1987—six months, that is, after Sussman had reported on his own findings concerning the *Acts of Torah*, having received his copy of the text from Strugnell a few years earlier. Sussman's report was delivered at a conference in Jerusalem celebrating the fortieth anniversary of the discovery of the scrolls. He too had come to the conclusion that the text was heavily Sadducaean. His paper was first published toward the end of 1989, giving the wider body of scholars the first opportunity to examine the author's reasoning. The proofs he offered turned out to be quite similar to Schiffman's. He too had based his interpretation on the prior supposition of the existence of a sect at Khirbet Qumran. The legal texts discovered in the caves, he claimed, represented the law "of the sect of the Judaean Wilderness"; there was no doubt "that in any future study of the laws of the sect, its identity, or the history of Jewish law in general, this scroll would stand in the center of discussion." The legal system accepted by the author of the *Acts of Torah* was "to the extent we have material for comparison . . . in general identical with the legal system in the other writings of the sect of the Judaean Wilderness."[49] The writer made these statements, and others to the same effect, in advance of discussing any of the specific laws stated in the text. When he came around to citing the text, however, the laws he quoted turned out to be precisely those few that Schiffman also would soon claim to show an affinity with the practices of the Sadducees. Sussman argued that, in light of these parallels, and since both the author of the *Acts of Torah* and the Sadducees as described in rabbinic sources showed greater severity in the interpretation and application of Pentateuchal law than did the spiritual heirs of the Pharisees (i.e., the early Tannaim), the text was clearly Sadducaean. And since, in his view, this was a writing of the "sect of the Judaean Wilderness," the "sect" was perforce Sadducaean.

The fallacy in this line of reasoning, however, is embarrassingly apparent. Virtually all of the laws of the *Acts of Torah* are unique to that text, and not known from the other Qumran scrolls. Only one of the twenty laws can demonstrably be shown to be Sadducaean *per se*. Sussman had focused narrowly on only a few of the laws and, from this paucity of evidence, drawn a large conclusion, emphasizing the phenomenon of severity that he had perceived in both groups. Yet this same severity characterizes, albeit with notable inconsistency, the rabbinic law itself. Although neither the school of Shammai nor that of Hillel was connected with the Sadducees, both were characterized by their different severities and leniencies. Among the rabbis of the early Tannaitic generations in Palestine, some were far more severe than others in their interpretation of the biblical laws—and the opinions of all, whether lenient or severe, were ranged against one another in the pages of the *Mishnah* and *Tosephta*. The Pharisees themselves were not a monolithic bloc, but were divided into schools and groups whose varying and contradictory opinions were often recorded in the early rabbinic texts.

Josephus, writing *circa* A.D. 75, describes two fundamentally different groups among the Essenes—those who were celibate and those who were not; while in addition to them, as well as the Sadducees and the majority of the Pharisees, he speaks of a "fourth philosophy" (led by an otherwise unknown "Judas the Galilean") that

> agrees in all other respects with the opinions of the Pharisees, except that they have a passion for liberty that is almost unconquerable, since they are convinced that God alone is their leader and master. They think little of submitting to death in unusual forms and permitting vengeance to fall on kinsmen and friends if only they may avoid calling any man master.[50]

There were also the Zealots and *sicarii*, whom Josephus also described as sectarian groupings. The scrolls, however, make it abundantly clear that the number of religious groupings among the Jews was still greater than that given by Josephus. The author of the *Acts of Torah* evidently belonged to a group aligned with the Pharisees. We have already observed the Pharisaic quality of the final section of the work, but may gain further insight into the group's identity by comparing the author's outlook on the interpretation and practice of the law with that of the Pharisees and Sadducees as described by Josephus.

The Pharisees, according to Josephus,

had passed on to the people certain regulations handed down by
former generations and not recorded in the Law of Moses, for
which reason they are rejected by the Sadducaean group, who hold
that only those regulations should be considered valid which were
written down (in Scripture), and that those which had been handed
down by former generations need not be observed.[51]

Josephus describes the Sadducees as observing only the letter of
the law, in contrast to the Pharisees who added accumulated oral
tradition to it. Had the author of the *Acts of Torah* been of the
Sadducaean persuasion as Josephus here describes it (ca. A.D. 75),
how could he have endorsed the many nuances discernible in his
legal rulings? The innovative leap from the Pentateuchal
"encampment" to Jerusalem—i.e., the author's claim that the laws
of the Pentateuch pertaining to the Israelites' encampments in the
desert applied equally well to the holy city of Jerusalem—was, as
we have seen, a rabbinic conception, while such laws as that of
retrograde liquid impurity, prohibition of dogs from entering
Jerusalem, the application of the Pentateuchal law of "mixed
kinds" to priestly marriages, and others in the text of the *Acts of
Torah*, point to a distinct accumulation of traditional interpretation being added on to the letter of the biblical law.

After the destruction of the Second Temple and the eventual
rise of Tannaitic hegemony, however, the Sadducees lost their
power and were reduced to a minority sect that adopted the basic
rabbinic principle of innovative interpretation of the Law. What
we perceive in the second-century A.D. rabbinic texts that concern
the differences between the Pharisees and Sadducees is a relatively late record of their debates, and thus one that can hardly be
forced to apply specifically to conditions in the early first century
A.D. or earlier, when the *Acts of Torah* was written. Josephus too
was a relatively late observer, but he had lived a long time in
Palestine and, while surely simplifying much of his description so
as to make it accessible to his Greek-speaking and non-Jewish
readers, can be considered a more reliable witness for the beliefs
and practices of the Jewish sects as they were in the earlier first
century A.D.

Sussman, unfortunately, had not dealt with these basic underlying factors when pressing his view of the Sadducaean origin of
the *Acts of Torah*. Beyond this, he leaped from this single text
to the whole of the Qumran manuscript discoveries by declaring

their authors to have been a sect of Sadducees. A group known as the Boethusians sometimes appears in Tannaitic texts along with the Sadducees, and has often been thought to be a subsect of the latter. Recently, however, these same Boethusians (Hebrew, *betosin* or *betisin*) have been connected with the Essenes because of the way the last two syllables of their name are spelled. For Sussman, therefore, the "Sadducees" of the *Acts of Torah* were perhaps Boethusians and thus related to the Essenes.[52] In this way he regrettably plunged the study of the *Acts of Torah* into confusion. He, like Schiffman, offered no proof for an organic connection between this work and other Qumran writings, but instead presented it as an *a priori* assertion. He then went on to build his own theory on the foundation of what was no more than a scholarly dogma. Throughout his study he failed even to hint at the possibility of multiform origins of the scrolls—a view obviously strengthened by the contents of the *Acts of Torah*—instead revealing not merely an uncritical loyalty to the old Qumran-sectarian theory but a design to defend the theory at all costs.

These attempts to harmonize the *Acts of Torah* with the traditional Qumran-sectarian hypothesis showed that a turning point was occurring in the study of the scrolls. While appeals were beginning to be heard for free access to the texts, those who controlled them were apparently developing a marked lack of enthusiasm about publishing their assignments, and at the same time were attempting to use some of the suppressed items to shore up the traditional theory. Those scholars who questioned the theory were being excluded from conferences on the scrolls, and the overall tone of debate was becoming increasingly strident. By way of reaction to these circumstances, and after consultation with colleagues at Chicago in the winter of 1990, I proposed to the New York Academy of Sciences that they hold an international conference on the topic of the scrolls. We had conceived of such a conference as one that would bring together various parties who, however opposed they might be to one another's ideas, might still be willing to debate their differences in a spirit of scholarly decorum. The Academy immediately showed interest in the project.

While these steps were being taken, Schiffman was transmuting his earlier idea of the text into a more fully blown Sadducaean hypothesis of his own. In June of 1990—by which time the *samizdat* version of the manuscript fragments had come to be widely circulated among scholars—he published the further fruits of his thinking on the subject.[53] Thanking Strugnell and Qimron "for graciously making available" to him their "soon-to-be-published edition and commentary of this text,"[54] Schiffman began by stating that the text was important because of the issue of "the origins of *the sect* and the early history of *the Qumran community*." He asserted that the scroll "purports to be a letter of the *nascent* sect" and that the laws contained in it "clearly represent the views of the *founder* of the sect. . . ."[55]

There was, of course, no support for these assertions in the manuscript itself. Neither the legal portion of the text nor the admonition contain evidence of important affinities with either the *Yahad* texts, the *Damascus Covenant*, the *Temple Scroll*, or any other single grouping of Qumran manuscripts. Reflecting, it would seem, an incipient realization of the gravity of the problems facing the standard hypothesis, Hartmut Stegemann, a member of the inner circle of traditional Qumranologists, had already acknowledged in 1989 that at the most only 20 percent of the scrolls found in the caves could have originated with the inhabitants of Khirbet Qumran;[56] in the same volume, Schiffman himself, as we have seen, had recognized the eclectic nature of the "library" at Qumran. And yet here Schiffman, like Sussman before him, did not bother explaining on what grounds he connected the idiosyncratic *Acts of Torah* with the claimed "sect of Qumran." Moreover, nothing in the surviving text of this work implied that at the time of its writing the group it represented was "nascent."

Schiffman, to be sure, added the nuance that the letter, although it "purported" to be from the original founder of the "sect," might also have been "an apocryphal text written years, or even decades, later. . . ." From the text's preserved words, however, it is quite clear that its author is only speaking for himself, and may be defending either views first formulated by predecessors as long as a century or more before him, or ideas of his own group as they developed subsequently. Schiffman's suggestion that the text might have been an apocryphal letter merely *imitating* the founder's ideas simply seemed to reflect a desire to make the "Teacher of Righteousness" theory of Strugnell and Qimron more palatable, by suggesting that while not necessarily true literally, it was true in its basic thrust. At the same time, by pressing for an early date, Schiffman, like Sussman, eradicated the criterion of language. In this manner the two scholars, while each entertaining a grossly different conception of the nature of the manuscript groupings found in the Qumran caves, maintained a surprisingly unified position on the *Acts of Torah*: Except for their joint reluctance to explicitly acknowledge the presence of the Teacher of Righteousness in the text, their position did not differ in the least from the views of the two scholars who bestowed upon them the singular right to study their transcription of the manuscript in advance of its publication.

In subsequent paragraphs of his new article, Schiffman attempted to flesh out his view—but always without defining in a clear-cut way what he meant by the "sect of Qumran" and what manuscripts had been their own. He declared that, because fragments of six manuscripts of the work had been found in Cave 4, the text "was indisputably significant in the life of the sect."[57] And yet multiple copies of other writings having no demonstrable sectarian affinities had also been found in the caves, including the *Songs of the Sabbath Sacrifice* (eight copies); *I Enoch* (seven copies), *Vision of Amram* (five copies), and others. The most that the multiple copies could indicate, in the absence of *proofs* that they were all possessed by a single organization dwelling at Khirbet Qumran, was that they appear to have been relatively popular works among Jewish groups of the time.

With similar carelessness, Schiffman proceeded to elaborate a series of increasingly remarkable suggestions, among them the following:

1. *The group represented by the author consisted of "dissatisfied priests" who had withdrawn from participation in the Temple ritual.*[58]

Nothing in the *Acts of Torah* supports this notion; the author and his group can equally well have been Israelites who believed the Temple priesthood was lax and iniquitous, and for this reason withdrew from "the majority of the na[tion]." If they had been priests, the writer would more likely have spoken of a withdrawal from "our brethren the priests," or from "the seed of Aaron."

2. *The "major conflicts of Second Temple Judaism did not result from disagreements over . . . theological matters but, rather, from issues of Jewish law."*[59]

There can be no doubt that disputes over the interpretation of Jewish law occurred among the parties and sects of the period, but fundamental conflicts of a theological nature were also widespread—as the *Manual of Discipline*, among other manuscripts, itself proves. Schiffman's dogma was based upon some of the Qumran texts only, to the exclusion of others, and in complete disregard of Josephus's description of the Jews of his and earlier times contained in the *Jewish War* and the *Antiquities of the Jews*.

3. *The letter was written to the head of the Jerusalem establishment, or "high priest," who saw himself as almost a royal figure. This would explain why the letter addresses him as royalty. Because the Hasmonaeans took on the true trappings of royalty, the letter is "either written to or purporting to have been written to a Hasmonaean high priest."*[60]

To begin with, the opinion that the epistle was addressed to a *priestly* figure is capricious: Its wording actually carries no such implication. Secondly, its evocation of the deeds of past kings— and not, for instance, the deeds of Aaron and his descendants, which the author could easily have added—indicates that he was addressing not a sacerdotal figure, but rather a royal one who was *not* a priest. In addition, the epistle reveals no demonstrable connection at all with Hasmonaean (i.e., second- and first-century B.C.) figures. The language of the text indicates that it was written around the beginning of the first century A.D., and its specific wording shows that it was addressed to a royal personage of that time.

4. *The author of the* Acts of Torah *was addressing not simply "the head of the Jerusalem establishment" but indeed the "ruler of the nation" himself.*[61]

In this statement, Schiffman contradicted the point he made just beforehand, that the letter was addressed to the high priest who saw himself "as almost a royal figure." This shows how, in what may only be characterized as a weak and inadequate treatment, one confusion has led to another. It is known, of course, that the roles of king and priest were occasionally combined in one person during Hasmonaean times, and as Schiffman, following Qimron and Strugnell, sought to place the text in this earlier period, such an identification would have suited his purpose. But just as nothing in the text indicates that the addressee combined a priestly with a royal role, nothing indicates that he was actually *the* "ruler of the nation."

5. *The absence of the Teacher of Righteousness from the* Acts of Torah *is due to the "fact" that the text was composed* before *the Teacher's time.*

For this proposition, Schiffman, outdoing Strugnell and Qimron, relied on the fact that the *Damascus Covenant*—which he described as containing the "official history of the sect"—includes a statement that the Teacher of Righteousness emerged twenty years after "the sectarians' initial separation from the main body of Israel."[62] Now the laws contained in the *Acts of Torah* are virtually without parallel in the *Damascus Covenant*; no textual evidence indicates that the two works derived from the same sectarian group. The *Covenant* describes the members of its group as being comprised of "blind ones and those groping for the road for twenty years . . . until (the Lord) established for them a Teacher of Righteousness to lead them in the way of his heart."[63] The calm style of the *Acts of Torah*, and the author's full command of the issues that had brought about the separation of his group, do not reflect such a period of initial turbulence. Both the idiom of the *Acts* and the issues its author discusses indicate a period at least one hundred years *later* than that of the *Covenant*'s Teacher of Righteousness. Schiffman failed to show any evidence in the manuscripts that might justify using the expression "the sect" to describe, in one breath, such dissimilar writings.

Relying on his earlier unproven generalization that the *Acts of Torah* reflected the laws of the Sadducees, Schiffman then created a new hypothesis to explain the origin of the scrolls: "The earliest members of the sect," he explained, "must have been Sadducees," with disaffected members of this group parting from their fellow Jerusalem Sadducees, in protest at "the following of Pharisaic views in the . . . Temple under the Hasmonaean priests." The authors' polemics, Schiffman declared, were "aimed at their Sadducaean brethren who stayed in the . . . Temple and accepted the new order"—a discovery leading Schiffman to a reassessment of older theories about the scrolls. On the one hand, the "dominant Essene hypothesis, if it is to be maintained, would require a radical re-orientation." On the other hand, the "notion that the collection of the scrolls is in no way representative of a sect . . . must also be abandoned." Henceforth, Schiffman concluded, any theory of sectarian origins of the scrolls had to "place the earliest, preteacher stage of the history of the Qumran sect in the offshoots of intrapriestly contention" and also had to "reckon with the Sadducaean view of those who formed the sect."[64]

Thus Schiffman had progressed from a single law in the *Acts of Torah* to a general theory of the scrolls' origins that was rationally connected neither with the evidence contained in the scrolls themselves nor with the known characteristics of the Khirbet Qumran site.*

Despite the fact that his interpretation completely disregarded Josephus's description of the beliefs of the Sadducees and Pharisees, and was based on a text written in proto-rabbinic idiom, Schiffman apparently received encouragement from a group of Qumranologists gathered in Jerusalem in 1989–90 for a year of study of the scrolls at the Hebrew University's Institute of Advanced Studies. A further development of his views appeared in a 1990 article, where he declared that a new generation of researchers—presumably including himself—were not "bound to the original theories . . . [and] had opened anew all kinds of questions pertaining to the origins of the texts."[65] Nevertheless, in the course of his discussion he repeatedly referred to "the sect" living, so he believed, at Khirbet Qumran.

This replacement of the Essenes of Pliny and Josephus with postulations of one or another "Qumran sect" was in fact a strategy shared by many scholars. As in his earlier articles, Schiffman offered no evidence that the sect he had in mind actually had lived in the Judaean Wilderness at Qumran.

Explaining that the original Essene theory had had "a certain surface attractiveness," he asserted that the new "non-consensus" which, he claimed, he had instigated,"calls for postponing definite conclusions on the identity of the sect until the publication of the entire corpus [of the scrolls]."[66] Then he baldly defied his assertion

---

*In "Sadducees in the Dead Sea Scrolls?" (Z. Kapera [ed.], *Qumran Cave 4—Special Report* [Cracow, 1991], pp. 89, 90, 94). Philip Davies of Sheffield University has examined Schiffman's reasoning. He concludes that it is "not simply hard to *accept* [but] . . . even hard to *understand*." Davies indicates that, rather than refuting my argument for the scrolls' multiple origins, Schiffman "provided a good deal of support for that view"—unfortunately in the course of a presentation "at best contradictory and at worst verging on nonsense." Acknowledging that my explanation of the scrolls' origin "coped with [the *Acts of Torah*] rather better than any other," Davies concludes that "the rather cavalier exploitation of 4QMMT by Schiffman seems . . . to offer little but methodological chaos."

by urging, on the basis of his own conclusions, the identification of the "sect" with a group of dissident Sadducees.* (Schiffman stated that the surface attractiveness of the Essene theory was due to the fact that "Josephus, Philo, and Pliny all describe the Essenes on the shore of the Dead Sea."[67] However, neither Josephus nor Philo anywhere mentions Essenes near the Dead Sea.)

Strangely enough, in the course of what can only be termed another incoherent argument, Schiffman implicitly called his Sadducaean proposition into question by echoing my own version of "non-consensus." He stated, for example, that the Qumran writings included not only "the sect's special texts" but also "a whole variety of other texts collected by the people who lived at Qumran." These were "apparently brought to Qumran from elsewhere," and could not be "regarded as representing the Qumran sect itself. . . ."[68] Given this concession, Schiffman's own recourse to the idea of a "Qumran sect" became even more enigmatic. The score of writings of the *Yahad* group could no more be pinned upon a particular Judaean Wilderness settlement than could any of the other scrolls. The mental construction of a particular sectarian group actually living on the Qumran plateau and bringing in "outside" manuscripts reflecting different ideologies was an entirely arbitrary one, unsupported by the available evidence, and having no other apparent purpose than to defend the essence of the Qumran-sectarian theory.

Having conceded the importation of texts to Qumran "from elsewhere," Schiffman went further, explaining that

> Very recently several fragmentary texts were published from Masada . . . , occupied by rebels during the . . . Revolt against Rome. In addition, a manuscript of the Sabbath Songs (angelic liturgy), known in several manuscripts from Qumran, was found at Masada. Thus, the Jewish defenders of Masada possessed books of

---

*Schiffman claimed in this same article that opposition to the Essene identification was first voiced in a 1985 conference he had organized at New York University. See the conference proceedings in L. Schiffman (ed.), *Archaeology and History in the Dead Sea Scrolls* (Sheffield, U.K., 1990). A perusal of the papers in this enigmatically titled volume, which contains virtually nothing about archaeology, fails to reveal any notable departure from the mode that the sectarian theory had by then assumed; there is also no perceptible attempt to explore the nature of the Khirbet Qumran site, which throughout the various discussions is rather assumed to have been the habitation of a sect.

the same kind as those in the Qumran collection, but that were not directly associated with the sect itself. In other words, many of the works found at Qumran were the common heritage of Second Temple Judaism and did not originate in, and were not confined to, Qumran sectarian circles.[69]

Now these words read like a close paraphrase of an essential part of my first published treatment of the problem of Qumran origins, that is, my discussion of the Masada fragments.[70] Minus the vexatious problem of identification of the Khirbet Qumran site, and despite Schiffman's cosmetic excision of the word "Jerusalem" from his formulation, he was in essence expressing the same view of the nature of the scrolls that I had proposed in 1980, and doing so, *inter alia*, on the basis of the same evidence discovered at Masada that I had then adduced. Thereupon, developing his argument, he stated, just as I had earlier suggested, that

> It is now becoming increasingly clear that the Scrolls are the primary source for the study of Judaism in all its varieties in the last centuries before the Common Era. In short, this corpus does not simply give us an entry into the sect that inhabited the nearby settlement, but also has an enormous amount to tell us about the *widely varying Judaisms* [my italics] of the Hasmonaean and Herodian periods . . . these documents are providing a critical background for the study of the later emergence both of rabbinic Judaism and of the early Christian Church. . . .[71]

This latter idea concerning Judaism and Christianity was, of course, none other than what I had suggested in 1985, in stating that what was by then understood of the contents of the scrolls was "more than sufficient to show the mentality and religious outlook of various groups within Palestinian Judaism" before A.D. 70. This, I suggested, had already "cast important new light on aspects of that period's history, particularly on the question of the influence of the beliefs and practices then current in Palestine on both the nascent rabbinic Judaism and the earliest forms of Palestinian Christianity."[72]

These similarities, which Schiffman published without attribution, were abetted by yet another. The influence of the apocalyptic texts of Qumran, he suggested, could be observed

> in the messianic pressures for Jewish resistance against Roman rule *that were factors in fueling the two Jewish revolts*, the First

Revolt of 66–70 C.E., and the Second Revolt, the so-called Bar Kokhbah revolt, of 132–135 C.E., both of which had messianic overtones.[73]

Arguing against the idea that the apocalyptic Qumran texts were all attributable to the Essenes or any other particular sect, I had stated in 1980 that the mentality of Palestinian Jewish groups prior to A.D. 70 were "factors which may . . . help to explain the zeal which led to the Jewish War."[74]

Schiffman failed to refer to any of these published views of mine, which had played a large role in the development of the theory of Jerusalem origin. His confusion about the nature of the "sect" whose presence at Qumran he persisted in espousing would later be reflected in an interview with Avi Katzman in the newspaper *Haaretz* (29 January 1993). After publishing a Hebrew book under the express title *Law, Custom and Messianism in the Dead Sea Sect*, Schiffman was asked by the journalist why it was that "in different articles you have published, you have not hesitated to take over portions of Golb's theory without acknowledging as much, and without giving him appropriate credit?" Schiffman responded: "This isn't the issue. There's no innovation in Golb's theory. He can say what he wants. *The idea that we're not dealing with a sect is self-evident.* Does he think that he wrote the Bible?"

Thus Schiffman himself revealed his own basic confusion about "the Dead Sea sect," while also failing to respond with candor to the question that Katzman had asked him. The response nonetheless pointed to a likely source for a variety of egregious misrepresentations of my theory that had accompanied his appropriation of several of its most essential elements:[75] Playing out a hopelessly confused and self-contradictory version of the doctrine of Qumran-sectarianism, Schiffman was caught between the need to acknowledge the multiform nature of the scrolls and the need to deny the annoying implications of this reality. His adding, to the resulting pastiche of inconsistencies and innuendos, the complaint that I had argued for the scrolls' Jerusalem origin "in an aggressive way,"[76] did not confront the dilemma into which he and others had plunged traditional Qumranology by their overt inability to harmonize the *Acts of Torah* with the theory of the scrolls' origin. John Strugnell must have himself perceived, in the course of time, at least some of the problems growing out of this effort, for in 1993 he retracted his view that the famous Teacher of Righteousness had composed the work.[77]

As increasing numbers of independent scholars around the world called for access to this manuscript, others continued efforts to prevent them from studying it. The clash of wills would eventually result, as we have seen, in bitter lawsuits. In the meanwhile, growing discontent with the treatment of this text fed into a general tide of resentment that had been rising since the early 1980s. With each passing year, it had become clear that the editorial committee was not living up to its basic responsibilities. Various scholars had begun calling for release of photographs of all the Dead Sea Scrolls. The growing controversy over the question of origin and meaning of the scrolls intersected increasingly with the problem of control over the manuscripts. The monopoly seemed to have developed to its full capacity, but a confluence of circumstances was starting to diminish its power.*

---

*As this book was going to press (mid-1994), the text of the *Acts of Torah*, together with translation and commentaries, was finally published in the official *Discoveries in the Judaean Desert* series: E. Qimron, J. Strugnell et al., *Qumran Cave 4. V. Miqsat Ma'ase Ha-Torah* (Clarendon Press, Oxford: 1994), 235pp. + 8 plates. The work as it now stands is in large part written by Qimron and in smaller part by J. Strugnell, with additional contributions by A. Yardeni (on paleography) and by Y. Sussman (on Jewish law). Sussman's main contribution to the volume consists of a verbatim English translation (pp. 179–99) of his 1987 Hebrew lecture discussed above. While the book contains various useful observations on the Hebrew text, it also reveals a fervent determination by Qimron to stand by almost all of the ill-founded ideas discussed above, and indeed to confound them with further qualifications. Only with respect to Qimron's headline-producing claim that the text was written by the Teacher of Righteousness does the author now belatedly express second thoughts: "Our initial description of MMT, as a letter from the Teacher of Righteousness to the wicked priest, pleasantly startling though it was [*sic!*], is probably to be modified. Rather than a personal letter, it is probably a treatise on certain points of traditional Zadokite legal praxis . . . a group composition originating in the Qumran group, or in one of its antecedents . . . when their leader was probably the Teacher of Righteousness. . . ." Qimron's unfounded claims continue without abatement throughout the volume, impelling Strugnell himself to issue a disclaimer in which he rejects the most egregious of them (ibid., pp. 203–6), adding the observation that the volume "does not contain a chapter on the theology and tradition-history of Section C" of the *Acts of Torah* (ibid., p. 205). The work is thus, after ten years of assurances, basically incomplete.

Shortly after publication of the Oxford volume, there appeared the new book by Lawrence Schiffman, *Reclaiming the Dead Sea Scrolls* (Philadelphia, 1994), in which the author repeats and amplifies his self-contradictory proposals examined above.

CHAPTER 8

Power Politics
and the Collapse
of the Scrolls Monopoly

❖

In 1985, I received an inquiry from Zdzislaw J. Kapera of the Jagiellonian University in Cracow about the growing problem of scroll origins and my role in exposing it. Out of our ensuing correspondence came the idea of an independent conference devoted to the problem and it was eventually held, under the auspices of the Polish Academy of Sciences, in Mogilany, near Cracow, in the summer of 1987. This meeting constituted my first European forum for a detailed face-to-face presentation of the issues concerning the scrolls' origin. The audience consisted mainly of traditional Qumranologists—from both Western and Eastern Europe as well as the United States—and yet the tenor of the conference was remarkably cordial. We agreed to reconvene every other year and continue the dialogue; the meeting gave me hope, for the first time since 1970, that collegial debate on the origin of the scrolls might still be possible.

During this period, Hershel Shanks of the *Biblical Archaeology Review* had begun a campaign to wrest free the still-unpublished scrolls from the hands of their original editors, several of whom had still not published the texts assigned to them despite the passage of thirty years. Geza Vermes stated in 1987 (consonant with an earlier assessment of his that the situation constituted the scholarly scandal of the century) that if his translation of the scrolls into English was not yet all-inclusive, the "guilt lies elsewhere, in the slackness of those responsible since the early 1950s for the publication of the many fragments found in Qumran Cave 4."[1] Robert Eisenman of California State University, a proponent of the view that the scrolls originated with early Judaeo-Christians, had by that time also begun his own campaign for

217

open access to the texts. By 1989, the Israel Antiquities Authority had established a "Scrolls Oversight Committee." Its ostensible purpose was to supervise the editorial committee and to encourage its members to publish their work in a timely manner.

In a news release from Jerusalem of 26 June 1989, Nicholas B. Tatro of the Associated Press described an interview he had with General Amir Drori of the Authority on this issue. According to Tatro, Drori "said he set up a program to require annual progress reports [on publication of the scrolls] and got the scholars to agree on publishing all their finds in seven years." The report indicated that the number of participants in the editorial project was by that time twenty. Tatro continued: "To speed the process, he [Drori] said scholars had been urged to share the workload with students and other researchers, and a special study program has been set up by Hebrew University for leading Bible scholars next fall. A $350,000 grant from an offshoot of the Wolfson Foundation also has been obtained. 'For the first time, we have a plan, and if someone does not complete his work on time, we have the right to deliver the scrolls to someone else,' said Drori, the former commander of troops in Lebanon during Israel's 1982–85 invasion."

Beside the reference to a generous research grant from a British charitable foundation, which at the time seemed to be an appropriate and positive development, an important element stood out in this report. This was General Drori's striking defense of the decision to close the doors to some scholars, on the grounds that, to quote Tatro's story, "free access was unfair to those who had 'devoted their life' to the research." This, of course, contradicted the fact that, by the time of the interview, at least twenty researchers had been included in the team. Beforehand, in the late 1980s, the core team had consisted of no more than five or six members, and approximately seven of their students were by then working on scrolls for their doctoral dissertations; thus at least seven new members were being added, among them some who had virtually no prior experience with advanced research on the scrolls. It was this arrangement that Drori had alluded to in explaining that "scholars had been urged to share the workload with students and other researchers." (Eventually the number of participants in the project would virtually triple, the new ones including some who had done advanced research on the scrolls and others who had not, but all being handpicked by the editorial and oversight committees.)

Also apparently at odds with Drori's statement was the increasingly proffered assertion by members of both committees that granting independent scholars access to the manuscripts would result in inferior editions of the texts. By the summer of 1989, it was becoming obvious that such explanations were merely foils for a basic intent on the part of the two committees to control the study of the scrolls and thereby predetermine the outcome of the debate on their origin and meaning. In a word, the intellectual monopoly of the earlier editorial group under Père de Vaux and his successors was being renewed and expanded.

This was the material of an emerging scandal. We discussed it at length during the second conference in Poland (September 1989) and, despite the opposition voiced by Jonas Greenfield (a newly appointed editor and member of the oversight committee), we passed a resolution calling for publication in advance of photographs of all the unpublished texts. It was the first such resolution debated by an assembly of scroll scholars, and was only passed because the conference was not under the usual control of traditional Qumranologists intent on guarding the sanctity of the old hypothesis.

Two months later (November 1989), Ephraim Isaac of the Institute of Semitic Studies in Princeton—intuiting possible changes in the air—organized a symposium of his own, with John Strugnell and Eugene Ulrich of the official scrolls editorial committee participating, as well as several others including myself. The symposium attracted a large audience, public interest in the scrolls' fate being obviously high, and afterward newspapers carried reports and editorials addressing the issues that had been raised:[2] Was there any legitimate reason for the long delay in publication of the texts from Cave 4? Was the response of Strugnell and Ulrich—that there were many problems in editing these difficult fragments; that other unpublished manuscripts had been around much longer—cogent or disingenuous? Could there be any truth in what I said at the meeting—that there was a *reluctance* to publish the remaining manuscripts, because the ideas found in them might destroy the conventional theory that these texts derived from a sect living near the Dead Sea shore?

This meeting and subsequent press coverage alerted the public

to two interrelated problems: Qumran politics, and the interpretation of the manuscripts' origin and nature. The small group with a
suzerainty over the scrolls continued to let only those sharing
their interpretation see them, as had been the case with the *Acts
of Torah*. As criticism of their delays increased, they sought to
calm it by co-opting new participants—but always those who
were their own colleagues and disciples and could be counted on
to follow the accepted line. Those whose ideas made members of
the official committees uncomfortable or angry were to be kept
out of the process.

I emphasized these increasingly obvious facts in a letter to the
Washington Post (17 December 1989), in response to an editorial
(20 November) attempting to justify the editors' delays in publication. The expanding group of editors—by then numbering twenty-
five—was, I pointed out, still being chosen in such a way as to
ensure that scholars working in certain institutions would be
excluded from participation. In addition, a few of the original
team members had assigned texts to their own students as subjects of doctoral dissertations, thus raising a basic question of
scholarly propriety: namely, should the editing of manuscripts
never before published be assigned to relatively inexperienced
graduate students rather than to scholars whose abilities were
already demonstrated by published work? Meanwhile, those dissenting from the standard interpretation were not being allowed
to examine the manuscripts.

While the *Post* had pointed to the dilatory publication of the
Greek papyri of Egypt, they had failed to note the absence of any
clamor for them. In the case of the scrolls, however, a crucial
issue was at stake: our understanding of early Judaism and
Christianity. There was thus a legitimate and compelling public
interest in the outcome. And while the *Post* had written sympa-
thetically of the fear of "pirated inferior editions," they failed to
justify the implication that the "official" team had superior scholarly gifts. I wrote that what was actually called for was intense
competition, many of the previously published texts having
already appeared in more than one edition to the great benefit of
scholarship. The *Post*'s statement that the scrolls were "unread-
able, decayed to thousands of blackened scraps," was, I suggested, greatly exaggerated; while applicable to some of the
fragments, it was obviously not true of the great majority, "whose

publication [had been] justifiably expected, and should [already] have taken place without excuses."

Afterward, Eugene Ulrich of Notre Dame picked up the theme of competence to justify the committee's actions: "No one, no one will ever expend the same concentration that a good editor of a manuscript expends. No one will ever do right what the editor has failed to do. The vast majority of people who will use these editions—including average university professors and doctoral students—are barely able to judge competently difficult readings. I'm sorry if this sounds arrogant, but it's true" (*Jerusalem Post*, 2 March 1990). What Ulrich failed to state was that the "good editor of a manuscript" he had in mind was not necessarily one of the many specialists in Hebrew manuscripts as such. He was rather someone who had primarily studied the Dead Sea Scrolls and did not necessarily have expert knowledge of other genres of Hebrew manuscripts; in particular, he was one who had entered the fraternity of traditional Qumranologists by studying under those scholars with privileged access to the scrolls, and who had written a dissertation assenting to the basic tenets of the Qumran-sectarian theory.

By this time a number of traditional Qumranologists were suggesting a nuance to the theory. It was that some of the texts found in the caves had perhaps not been composed at Qumran but had been "brought in from the outside." And John Strugnell, still the official editor of the *Acts of Torah*, stated that with the participation of Elisha Qimron, he was completing a six-hundred-page commentary on this brief text. Then he attacked Judaism in a startling diatribe (*Haaretz*, 9 November 1990):

> I think Judaism is a racist religion, something very primitive. What bothers me about Judaism is the very existence of Jews as a group, as members of the Jewish religion. The Sabbath laws are a wonderful excuse for laziness. When I look at the details of the Jewish law, including sex, I think, "That's amusing, it's not religion." These people are acting according to what I would call folklore.

Strugnell, who had been serving as editor-in-chief of the official editorial committee, was, after brief hesitation by his peers, demoted to a lower rank in the Qumran hierarchy. His outburst—which he never subsequently repudiated—elicited a new series of articles in the press, their main thrust being in favor of free access to the manuscripts.

Others, however, stepped in to guard the old hypothesis. An international meeting on the scrolls held in Madrid in February 1991 carefully excluded both dissenters and critics of the editors' policies. My own exclusion had of course been preceded by publication of several "heretical" articles pointing to the futility of the Essenic approach to the texts. Participants in the meeting attempted to defend the Qumran-sectarian theory against my criticisms, but characteristically, only after the organizers saw to it that I would not be there to respond. The organizers did their utmost to impart a sacrosanct aura to the traditional approach, also seeing to it that the Queen of Spain would be present during the conference to award the country's highest medal to Frank Cross of Harvard, a chief exponent of the old hypothesis.

Despite the continuing attempts to obscure the issue, it is evident in retrospect that during this period the balance of power between "insiders" and "outsiders" was shifting. While this was happening, the *Biblical Archaeology Review* continued to stress the theme of freeing the scrolls for universal scholarly appraisal. Then, beginning in the summer of 1991, a number of well-known figures on the scrolls scene who became linked, both institutionally and through their ideas, to the reigning scrolls establishment committed a series of what must now be seen, even from their perspective, as blunders—a reflection, at its least, of the increasing difficulty of that establishment's position.

On 24 June, the *Times* of London announced that the Oxford Centre for Postgraduate Hebrew Studies had made arrangements to accept a complete set of photographs of the scrolls from the Antiquities Authority in Jerusalem; the Centre would open a "Qumran Room," and Geza Vermes was "director-designate of the new archive."* Vermes stated that he hoped "that today's editors will visit the Oxford centre, to lecture and to discuss unpublished texts. . . . *But academic protocol will still apply, and access to such*

---

*We are now informed that the office is not that of director of the archive but director of the Oxford Forum for Qumran Research. See the statement of Ph. Alexander and G. Vermes to that effect in *The Qumran Chronicle*, vol. 2, no. 3 (June 1993), pp. 153–154. In the following pages, the reader should bear in mind the distinction between the Oxford Centre for Postgraduate Hebrew Studies and the Oxford Forum for Qumran Research, which was created by the Centre.

material will only be by permission of its designated editor." (My italics.)

The directors of the Centre and the scroll forum would later correct the wording of the *Times* reporter, saying that "Dr. Vermes would never have chosen the phrase 'academic protocol' to designate the *constraint* imposed on the Centre by the contractual stipulation laid down by the Jerusalem officialdom."[3] From this later statement one learned that there was a contract between the Oxford Centre and the Antiquities Authority stipulating, *inter alia*, that once the Centre had possession of the scroll photographs, it would have to refrain from allowing independent scholars to study them freely. We are not told, however, why the Centre principals allowed themselves to sign such a restrictive contract.

I saw the *Times* statement of 24 June 1991 during a stay at Cambridge, where I had returned primarily to work on the Cairo Genizah manuscripts located at the university library; each day, any that I requested would courteously and efficiently be brought to my desk. This procedure has always been followed in modern times by institutional libraries in England where manuscripts are kept. Researchers on the Genizah manuscripts to this day, it should be noted, look forward to attending meetings, as commonly happens in historical and literary study, for the purpose of analyzing and debating interpretations of difficult texts. It is scarcely necessary to indicate that open access to manuscripts and free debate about them have been notable features of humanistic study in the West, particularly in England.

I perceived that the announcement from the Oxford Centre represented a challenge to these values that had to be answered, and so wrote to the London *Times* (10 July) that this action marked "a surprising departure from academic practice in Britain, where scholars have traditionally enjoyed [the] free and liberal access to ancient manuscripts . . . [that] alone guarantees an open interplay of ideas and prevents a monopoly on them by any one group of researchers." Reiterating my views on the scroll committees' censorship, and expressing my regret that in England, "with its notable record of openness in scholarship . . . , this deleterious policy in the realm of knowledge and opinion should be assented to," I argued that, given all the circumstances, the Oxford Centre should not have agreed to accept the photographs.

Referring to my "attack on the Oxford Centre"—a statement that entirely overlooked the principle I was addressing—the administrator of the project, Alan Crown, replied in his own letter to *The Times* that it was obvious to him that "sooner, rather than later, open access [would] be permitted" and that "it was our intention to prepare for that day by having all the working tools and scroll copies at hand. . . ." Most surprisingly, he added that the "Israel Antiquities Authority *conceded to our request for a set of photographs in exchange for our mediation of funding for the research and publication programme which had ground to a halt for lack of funding*" (16 July; my italics). This was an excuse that, in their public statements justifying the monopoly, the members of the two official scrolls committees had not previously offered; as we have seen, they claimed only that more scholars had been added to the project in the hope of publishing the texts in a timely fashion. I was and remain unaware of any letter sent to me or other scholars expressing either a desperate need for money to rejuvenate the publication project or indicating that our institutions would receive sets of scroll photographs in exchange for large contributions to a Qumran research fund.

Thus, the public first learned from Professor Crown's letter that the Oxford Centre raised a sum of money in exchange for which it received a set of photographs of the scrolls. This arrangement in turn enabled the Antiquities Authority, through the two scroll committees, to allocate portions of these funds to those engaged in editing manuscripts at the Authority's invitation. Scholars, students, or both began receiving grants for their participation in the project. The editors apparently did not wish, at least at that time, to divulge the names of recipients of these funds.[4]

Adding to Dr. Crown's reply was another letter appearing in the London *Times* of 16 July. This one was from the director, or director-designate,* of the Oxford Forum for Scroll Research, Geza Vermes, who until then, like scores of other scholars, had

---

*There is some confusion about what Dr. Vermes's title was at that time. In the aforementioned article in *The Qumran Chronicle*, Drs. Alexander and Vermes first stated (p. 154) that "In June 1991, Vermes was Director of the Oxford Forum. . . ." (and not "director-designate of the archive," as the London *Times* had earlier stated). Yet in attempting to rebut my critique of the Centre's actions, two pages later they stated that "Vermes's appointment as [the Forum's] Director, decided in November 1990, actually took effect on the day following his retirement on 30 September 1991 from his Chair in Jewish Studies at the University of Oxford." The dates and titles seem to be playing musical chairs.

been denied access to the scrolls. Vermes explained that his previous attacks over publication delays did not prevent the Israeli committee from inviting him *"to take charge of the unpublished material relating to the* Manual of Discipline, *one of the most important of the sectarian documents"* (my italics). This invitation to Professor Vermes had not been disclosed in the original London *Times* news article of 24 June. (It was later revealed that this invitation was offered to Vermes by Dr. Emanuel Tov, the new editor-in-chief of the scrolls editorial committee, following the latter's "visit to Oxford, early in 1991.")[5] Vermes's concession appeared simultaneously with Alan Crown's acknowledgment of the transfer of money to the Antiquities Authority in Jerusalem, an agreement also not alluded to in the original news item. In an interview, Vermes acknowledged that he was granted access to some of the unpublished scrolls in consideration of the funding provided. He is quoted as saying: "That is what happened as a sort of offshoot of the operation."[6]

Responding later in *The Qumran Chronicle* to my subsequent criticism of this course of action,[7] Philip Alexander and Vermes stated that Vermes "played no part" in "the Centre's role in the Qumran Project" (i.e., in raising the money) and that I confused the Centre's role with Vermes's invitation to edit Cave 4 materials relating to the *Manual of Discipline*.[8] They claimed that Vermes did not offer the *Times* journalist, George Hill, a "formal announcement" of his new editorial assignment because "the official appointment as editor . . . did not come through till 23 June 1991, several days after the interview with 'The Times.'" Yet, strangely enough, when Dr. Vermes called a press conference on 24 June—the day *following* receipt of his official appointment— the subsequent news report published in the *Times* on 25 June also contained not a word about Vermes's editorial appointment.

Alexander and Vermes then supplied a second reason for the apparent reticence: "The main news release, with heightened dramatic effect, was reserved for the ceremony inaugurating the Qumran Room, which took place before a distinguished audience on 1 July 1991." They do not state, however, whether this main news release itself contained news of the editorial appointment, and to the best of my knowledge no relevant statement appeared anywhere in the press prior to the acknowledgment contained in Vermes's own letter to the London *Times* of 16 July sent in response to my own.

Yet on the basis of the totally unconvincing arguments relative to this matter mustered by Alexander and Vermes, they reached the conclusion that two "serious allegations" they attribute to me were "unsupported by any evidence and . . . absolutely untrue." These "allegations," in their words, were "that Vermes bought, as it were, a share in the Scrolls and then tried to conceal this fact." I never stated or implied, however, that Vermes "bought" a share of the scrolls. Dr. Vermes is a fine scholar, and like others should have been granted access to the scrolls long before 1991. The circumstances show, however, that despite complaints of his own over a number of years, it was only after the Oxford Centre had offered to supply that same Authority with a grant of $350,000 from the funds of a branch of the Wolfson Foundation that Vermes benefited from the largesse of the Antiquities Authority. In my *Qumran Chronicle* critique I cited the acknowledgment of Dr. Vermes as it appeared in print, to the effect that his appointment as editor of unpublished scroll fragments occurred in consideration of the funding the Oxford Centre provided and, in Vermes's quoted words, "as a sort of offshoot of the operation" (*Chicago Tribune*, 11 November 1991).

However, in their reply Alexander and Vermes stated that the *Tribune* quotation was "misleading," that Vermes instead "told the journalist that the provision of the archive, and not his recruitment as an editor, was 'a sort of offshoot' of the operation whereby the Centre acted as a clearing-house between the anonymous trust and the IAA."

This new explanation is quite mystifying on several grounds. Dr. Crown in his own letter to the London *Times* of 16 July 1991 had, as mentioned earlier, acknowledged that the Antiquities Authority agreed to the Oxford Centre's request for a set of photographs "in exchange for our mediation of funding." Indeed, the Centre's interest in funding the Authority's scroll publication project cannot be comprehended on any other basis than as part of a contracted agreement whereby, in direct exchange for the monetary consideration, the Centre would receive the scroll photographs from the Authority. It would be a unique cultural institution indeed that raised money to benefit the activities of another one located far away, without the express stipulation of a benefit in return. This hardly can be construed as a mere "offshoot of the operation." If my own discussion on such an important matter as this impelled Alexander and Vermes to state that I was expressing "serious allegations," why then is there no indication that Vermes wrote to the *Chicago Tribune* to deny the accuracy of its statement? No such letter has ever appeared.

There was, in brief, nothing on record to support the new claim of the authors—at all events, nothing that has so far been made public. If, out of the several news conferences held by the Centre and/or by Dr. Vermes in his capacity as director or director-elect of the newly established forum, not one word appeared in print regarding Vermes's new editorial role, it could hardly have been because he wished to "conceal" this fact, as I am supposed to have alleged, but simply because there was no keen desire on anyone's part to emphasize it, at least until after my letter to *The Times* was published.

No less notable was the statement made by General Drori in 1989, in which he failed to divulge the Antiquities Authority's agreement to send photographs of the scrolls to the Oxford Centre in exchange for the grant of $350,000 mediated by them. Drori's statement had also hidden more than it revealed, rendering still more disturbing the subsequent absence of pertinent information from the London *Times* reports on the granting of photographs to the Oxford Centre.

Some individuals outside the circle of principal players in this unfortunate arrangement were, I may add, already at least vaguely aware of it in 1989. A muffled statement, for example, appeared in the *Biblical Archaeology Review* to the effect that a "set of photographs of unpublished texts will soon be deposited in Oxford University's Centre for Hebrew Studies pursuant to an agreement providing funding for research."[9] A cryptic sentence, strange in a magazine noted for its candor in opposing the scrolls monopoly.

The totality of events thus made manifest a deeply troubling and indeed almost Byzantine pattern of thinking on the part of the Qumran establishment.

It is worth noting that, at about the same time the above events were transpiring, analogous generosity was being shown to still another donor to Qumran research. Dr. Manfred R. Lehmann, who has published occasional articles on the scrolls and has a philanthropic foundation of his own, reported the following in September 1991: "Through my close collaboration with Professor Qimron—our Foundation is funding the publication of a new, improved version of the *Temple Scroll* through Professor

Qimron—I have in my possession the full text of MMT. Because of the intensive interest in this Scroll . . . I find it appropriate to place before the public, in advance of the publication of the full text, some parts of the Scroll to illustrate its importance."[10] An outline of the contents of the *Acts of Torah*, a photograph and excerpts from it, and a discussion of its importance followed.

And yet no one publicly questioned the nature of this remarkable *modus vivendi*, in which money and the privilege of studying ancient manuscripts were exchanged for each other. Up to the end of 1994, the Antiquities Authority had offered no explanation of this or any of the other highly unusual arrangements described above.

Other events, however, were about to take place that irrevocably altered the struggle over access to the scrolls. In September 1991, a pair of Cincinnati researchers, Ben Zion Wacholder of the Hebrew Union College and his student Martin Abegg, published the first 118-page facsimile of what they described as a computer-generated version of previously unpublished Qumran texts. Their edition was based on a privately issued concordance to the texts that in itself had been inaccessible to most scholars.[11] Then toward the end of the same month, William Moffett, the director of the Huntington Library in Pasadena, dramatically announced that the Huntington would make available to all scholars the complete set of negatives of the scrolls fortuitously located there.[12]

The negatives had been contributed to the Huntington in the early eighties by Mrs. Elizabeth Bechtel, who had been philanthropically instrumental in establishing the Ancient Biblical Manuscript Center at Claremont. The executive vice-president of the new center, J. A. Sanders, and she had urged the Israel Department of Antiquities (as the Antiquities Authority was then called) to allow photographic copies of the scrolls to be made for safe storage overseas—i.e., at the Center. After this permission had been secured, Robert Schlosser, at first acting on behalf of Sanders, had gone to Jerusalem in the summer of 1980 and made infrared 5" x 7" negatives of most of the Rockefeller fragments. While this was being done, Mrs. Bechtel had a serious falling out with Sanders, who wished to have her removed from the Center's board of trustees, and Schlosser had ended up doing the photography on her own behalf. While she had subsequently maintained her agreement to give the Center a set of negatives, she had also requested of Schlosser that he keep the master set for her. He had done so (in the process making several duplicate copies) and, after some negotiating with the Huntington, Mrs. Bechtel had formally contributed a set to the library in 1983, having agreed to supply the sum of $90,000 for a cold-storage safe to house the negatives. They had thereafter reposed in that chamber until 1991, being augmented in 1984 and 1985 by new images of fragments (approximately 10 percent of the total) that Schlosser had been unable to photograph earlier. Thus the Huntington had come to possess a more complete set of negatives than did the Center at Claremont. In addition, it would appear that Sanders had no clear idea that Mrs. Bechtel had retained for herself a complete set of negatives including not only previously unpublished texts but all of the published ones of Cave 4 as well.*

Moffett's decision to release the negatives followed both a request in writing to the Huntington from Notre Dame's Eugene Ulrich to turn over the entire set of photos to the Claremont Center, and Moffett's almost simultaneous reading of the exchange of letters between me and the individuals at the Oxford Centre published in the London *Times* that had taken place two months earlier.[13] We can thus understand the decision as both a pragmatic statement of library policy and a moral statement of intellectual principle.

Those linked to the scrolls committees were obviously not pleased by such developments, and indignant protests were fast to follow. Emile Puech, by now a member of the official team and a professor at the Ecole Biblique, explained that the Wacholder-Abegg publication was a "violation of international law," while James VanderKam of Notre Dame asserted less unequivocally that "it seems to be a last-ditch ploy by some people who feel they don't have access to the scrolls" (*New York Times*, 5 September 1991). Concerning the Pasadena announcement, J. A. Sanders asserted that "we're very disappointed with the Huntington" (*New York Times*, 22 September 1991). Magen Broshi, the curator of Jerusalem's Shrine of the Book, assured the public that "instead of

*My thanks are due to Robert Schlosser for clarifying many of these details for me in a telephone conversation of 14 March 1993. I have until now been unable to determine when the directors of the Claremont Center first became aware of the fact that the Huntington's collection included negatives of the unpublished as well as published texts.

getting good stuff, we'll be inundated with third- and fourth- and fifth-rate productions." Amir Drori of the Antiquities Authority justified his closed-door policy by claiming that "definitive interpretations" on the part of the forty handpicked editors by then working for the editorial committee would soon materialize.[14] According to Harvard's Frank Cross, the action "involved the theft of scholarly work" (*New York Times*, 22 September 1991). It is intriguing to note that, in contrast to his earlier passionate defense of the committee's policies, and in apparent conflict with the import of his letter to the Huntington, Eugene Ulrich now protested that "in the last few years, our committee has been taking steps to open up access to the scrolls" (*Chicago Tribune*, 22 September 1991)—a cryptic allusion, it would seem, to the forty handpicked experts. And regrettably, Alan Crown of the Oxford Centre, having earlier justified the Centre's acquisition of scroll photographs by stating that this was done in the hope and expectation that the scrolls would soon be open to all scholars (*The Times*, 16 July 1991), now expressed "anger at the Huntington's release of the photographs" (*New York Times*, 27 September 1991).

By that time, news had apparently reached Jerusalem of the London *Times* correspondence and its effect on the Huntington's decision. Curator Broshi, a member of the oversight committee, thereafter declared in an interview that I was "a revolting argumentalist, a polemist, an opinionated trouble-maker" who had "filled the world with his filth. . . . When will we be free of [him]?—When he dies" (*Haaretz*, 4 October 1991). In the meanwhile, although not known as an expert in Hebrew manuscript studies, Broshi had become one of the "official" scroll editors.

The Antiquities Authority principals were by now having second thoughts about their published threats to sue the Huntington. Instead, they were reported to "have invited participants in the bitter controversy to a meeting in Jerusalem on December 4th to attempt to negotiate a compromise" (*New York Times*, 27 September 1991). Those locked out of the inner sanctum of scrolls scholarship began to think that this meant, finally, that the members of the oversight committee were possibly willing to engage in discussion with them about studying the manuscripts; but word was soon sent out that the invitation was only for representatives of the few institutions then possessing scroll copies. (These included Hebrew Union College, Claremont, and the Oxford Centre.)

This stonewalling effort itself received a setback in October 1991 when the head of the Knesset education committee, Michael Bar-Zohar, declared, against the urging of the scrolls oversight committee, that he would recommend the opening of the texts to all scholars wishing to study them. The scroll authorities thereupon canceled their planned meeting, while continuing to assert that the right to edit and publish the texts still resided with the handpicked editors. Open access to the scrolls, they conceded, would henceforth be granted—but on condition that quotes be limited to "portions therefrom." The access was to be "for personal research and not for the production of a text edition," and the right to production of text editions was to remain solely with those honored by the committee (*New York Times*, 28 October 1991).

Another headline-producing move, however, soon obliged the committee to change its stance again. This was the announcement on 20 November 1991 of the publication, in two volumes, of black-and-white photographic facsimiles of all the Cave 4 manuscript fragments that had previously remained under wraps. It was published, under the editorship of Robert Eisenman and James Robinson, by the Biblical Archaeology Society.[15] Emanuel Tov, the editor-in-chief of the scrolls editorial committee, then announced that there would no longer be legal opposition to the free use of the manuscripts.[16] Yet even his quoted statements would in time become the subject of tortured exegesis.

Tov's announcement, made in a special session (25 November) of the 1991 annual meeting of the Society of Biblical Literature held in Kansas City, was reported by three leading American newspapers (among many others). According to all of them, the gist of his statement was that scholars who studied the texts might henceforth feel free to publish them in full if they so chose.[17] One article indicated that Tov had also said his "international team would press forward in its effort to produce scholarly editions . . . rather than preliminary translations and interpretations"; the conference at which the announcement was made "sometimes seemed more like a ceremony marking a peace settlement" (*New York Times*, 27 November). The then president of the Society, Dr. Helmut Koester, was quoted as saying, "This is a historic moment, a moment all of us wish had occurred earlier."[18]

At the same meeting, a "Statement on Access to Ancient Written

Materials" drawn up by the Society's research and publication committee was read by James VanderKam and approved by members of the Society who were present. This statement made clear the liberal position that the committee had arrived at regarding such access. It emphasized that:

> Those who own or control ancient written materials should allow all scholars to have access to them. If the condition of the written materials requires that access to them be restricted, arrangements should be made for a facsimile reproduction that will be accessible to all scholars. Although the owners or those who control may choose to authorize one scholar or preferably a team of scholars to prepare an official edition of any ancient written materials, such authorization should neither preclude access to the written materials by other scholars nor hinder other scholars from publishing their own studies, translations, or editions of the written materials. . . .

The committee emphasized that further distribution of the statement be made "as widely as possible." In this way the voice of the small group of scholars meeting in a village near Cracow in 1989 was finally translated into a meaningful policy of action and moral principle.

In Jerusalem on 28 November, I wrote to General Drori requesting to see the scroll texts themselves for purposes of a palaeographic examination. The response to this request was that I would be permitted to see "photographs" of the manuscripts. For palaeographic study, the use of photographs of manuscripts instead of the manuscripts themselves leaves much to be desired, as I wrote back to Drori on 12 December. On 17 December, I received the response that, I thought at the time, signaled the final freeing of the manuscripts: The fragments themselves would henceforth be available to me for study, as long as classification numbers of the requested pieces were submitted in advance.

But this was not to be the end of the story. Despite the impression conveyed to the public that the scrolls were now fully available, in the winter of 1992 it became evident that the two committees, in conjunction with the Antiquities Authority, were still pursuing efforts to maintain control over publication of the Qumran texts—now, ironically, using the device of moral suasion. This began in the pages of a scholarly newsletter on Aramaic studies. In an editorial piece entitled "The Ethical Issues—A Position

Statement," Steven A. Kaufman argued that (a) the Wacholder-Abegg reconstructions were "done in a superficially ingenious manner" and were "totally devoid of scholarly value"; (b) the Huntington's photographs had been "illicitly obtained," and it was wrong to release them because earlier scholars had labored for "tens of thousands of hours" to join small fragments together into more comprehensible units: "to publish their work without permission is theft, pure and simple!"; (c) the Antiquities Authority had the right to assign manuscripts of theirs to individual scholars for publication in the same way that libraries did; while the majority of scholars "clamoring for access to the Scrolls" had "never dealt with original antiquities" and thus might be "forgiven their enthusiasm," institutions such as libraries, museums, and journal publishers were "expected to know better." Therefore, Kaufman concluded, publication of the scrolls should be left "where it belongs, to those to whom the texts have now been assigned" by the Antiquities Authority.[19]

Each of these assertions was, however, misguided and highly dubious: When used with the newly published photographs, the Wacholder–Abegg transcriptions, however tentative, were not at all devoid of scholarly value, and there was absolutely no indication that the Huntington photographs were illicitly or improperly obtained, except perhaps by those standards of judgment that would hold virtually all manuscripts in libraries to have been primevally acquired under suspicious circumstances. The process of piecing together fragmentary texts is one often employed in Genizah and papyrological studies, and does not secure publication rights for some to the exclusion of others; furthermore, the same argument could be used to show that the current editors of the scrolls, who for the most part are not the ones who originally pieced the fragments together, were, in the absence of the original editors' explicit permission, stealing their work by accepting photographs of the joined fragments as the basis for their planned editions. Libraries do not generally have the kind of restrictive policies that Kaufman attributed to them, except, for example, in the case of a particular scholar who, while studying a manuscript to which others have had free access, makes a unique discovery that then gives him a moral right to reserve first publication of that text, within a reasonable time span. This circumstance is irrelevant to the case of the editors of the Qumran texts, who were merely awarded their editorial roles for whatever reasons of academic politics the Antiquities Authority cared to entertain.* Kaufman's suggestion that most scholars are manuscript illiterates reads strikingly like the earlier suggestion of Eugene Ulrich (see page 221). Both assertions clashed awkwardly with the startling fact that among the almost sixty privileged scroll editors (the figure that had been reached during the three months preceding Kaufman's statement) were many who had no previous experience editing ancient manuscripts. The sad fact is that Kaufman's forced arguments had to be understood in the light of his own selection by the Antiquities Authority to participate in the scrolls project—something he did not divulge to his readers in the editorial.

Another newfound scrolls editor who attempted to shore up the credibility of the Antiquities Authority's procedure was Geza Vermes, who, as we have seen, had already played a prominent role in announcing the Oxford Centre arrangements. We must now examine that episode more closely.

In the spring of 1992 (i.e., several months after the Authority had announced its shift in policy) Vermes explained in the *Journal of Jewish Studies* that, "thanks to the generosity of an anonymous British charitable trust, the Oxford Centre . . . has been able to acquire an archive of 3,300 photographic plates representing all the manuscripts from the Judaean Desert housed in the Shrine of the Book and the Rockefeller Museum in Jerusalem"[20]—a formulation that strongly suggested the charitable trust's contribution was for the purpose of paying for the actual process of making photographic duplicates of the scrolls, and then having them sent to the Oxford Centre. The $350,000 sum involved, however, was at least one hundred times the amount necessary for photoduplication of the manuscripts, and its primary use had nothing to do with the manufacture of photographs.

Corresponding to the earlier reticence of General Drori and Professor Crown, Dr. Vermes here regrettably failed to indicate what we have already observed: (a) the Antiquities Authority's agreement to furnish the Oxford Centre with scroll photographs

*See the trenchant question posed by James Robinson (*The Qumran Chronicle*, vol. 2, no. 3, June 1993, p. 143): "Why did not those young scholars [who agreed to join the official editorial group], with the lessons of the past generation staring them in the face, face up to their ethical responsibilities to their excluded colleagues, rather than excluding them still again so as to advance their own careers at the expense of the rest of the academic community?"

only upon receiving assurances of the receipt of a very large sum of money; (b) the agreement to make Vermes himself an official editor of unpublished scroll fragments; (c) the Authority's use of the mediated funds as grants to individual editors to facilitate the production of editions of and commentaries on the scrolls under its direction—precisely the single element, to the exclusion of the others, emphasized in Drori's Associated Press interview of June 1989. Consistently, then, we find the absence of a public statement up front, either by the Antiquities Authority or the Oxford Centre, frankly describing all the elements of these transactions—resulting in the necessity of piecing together the story of what had actually occurred from hints and admissions appearing sporadically in a variety of publications.

This task was made no lighter by remarks of Professor Vermes immediately following those in the *Journal of Jewish Studies* cited just above. Referring the reader to his earlier "account of the events within a historical perspective" that had appeared in November 1991,[21] he stated that "the lifting of the ban by the Israel Antiquities Authority on access to unpublished documents, first announced on 25 September and finalized on 27 October 1991, *happily coincided* with the establishment by the Governors of the Oxford Centre of a Forum for Qumran Research. . . ." (my italics).*

This statement did not, regrettably, conform with the facts, which are a matter of public record. As we have seen, the 24 June 1991 announcement in the London *Times* indicated that the Centre's scroll research activities would officially begin in *July*—that is, while the struggle to free the scrolls was raging, and four months before they would be freed. Vermes made a public announcement in the same vein that very day, which was not only noted afterward in the *Times*, but also televised on July 4 on the BBC's "Newsnight" program. He also stated in his July 16 letter to the *Times* that he had already been appointed director "of a new forum for Qumran research,"—an appointment, we need hardly mention, thus made over *three months* before the Authority's announcement of its change of policy. And as pointed out above, both the new president of the Oxford Centre, Dr. Philip Alexander, and Vermes himself subsequently stated that the deci-

---

*As indicated above, p. 224, the italicized expression was thereafter defended by Alexander and Vermes.

sion to appoint Vermes as director of the Forum took place as early as November 1990—the year following General Drori's announcement of the $350,000 grant, which was mediated by the Oxford Centre. By this time Vermes could not possibly have avoided knowing of the financial agreement that facilitated the transfer of photographs, an action lying in turn at the heart of the establishment of the Forum. The conclusion is thus inescapable that Vermes accepted this privileged arrangement for Oxford in the face of his earlier criticisms directed against the scroll monopoly.*

Dr. Crown's explanation in his letter to *The Times* of 16 July 1991, i.e., that this arrangement was only a temporary measure carried out in the hope that the scrolls would soon be opened up to all scholars (an explanation thereafter taken up by Alexander and Vermes) is vitiated by a disturbing fact: Dr. Crown's reported anger upon hearing of the Huntington's decision to free the texts. If the goal of the Oxford Centre had been to free the texts for the

---

*On p. 156 of their *Qumran Chronicle* reply, Alexander and Vermes state that "The facts of the matter are [that] The Oxford Forum . . . came into being on 1 October 1991, happily coinciding with the lifting of the ban on unpublished documents. . . . Vermes's appointment as its Director, decided in November 1990, actually took effect on the day following his retirement on 30 September 1991 from his Chair in Jewish Studies at the University of Oxford." By acknowledgment of Alexander and Vermes themselves, however, we know that the latter's appointment as director of the forum was decided as early as November of 1990; it was thus no later than this time that the decision was made to establish the forum. As to the actual time that it began to function, the London *Times* reporter, George Hill, specifically wrote on 24 June 1991 that "Next month, Britain is to become a centre of international research into the scrolls. A study centre will open at Oxford, marking a new stage in what scholars hope will be an era of greater openness in the field." The centre would have a "Qumran Room" housing the new photographic archive of the scrolls. A similar announcement appeared in the *Times* on 1 July 1991. Alexander and Vermes, however, subsequently supplied a new fact—that Vermes's actual appointment as director of the forum "took effect" on 1 October, the day after his retirement from the chair he held at Oxford. Until that time he was, technically speaking, only the "director-designate" (the term used by Mr. Hill, but not by Vermes himself in his letter of 16 July). Alexander and Vermes confuse readers by pointedly linking the two expressions "came into being" and "took effect," and then tying in the conjoined concepts with Dr. Vermes's changed status as of 1 October. Despite this smokescreen of verbiage, it is clear that the Oxford Forum was established by the Governors of the Oxford Centre long before Vermes's change of status.

use of all scholars, Crown should have expressed nothing but pleasure at the Huntington's move.

Thus, it is impossible to see how Vermes's assertion of a happy coincidence of events can be reasonably maintained.[22]

An examination of Vermes's earlier "account of the events within a historical perspective," which appeared in the London *Times*'s "Higher Education Supplement" on 8 November 1991, raises a further problem. As with earlier statements, this account omitted the most significant of the events. While mentioning various occurrences taking place before June and after August 1991, he says nothing of the crucial period in between: nothing of the announcements at the end of June and beginning of July regarding the Oxford arrangements, nothing of the statements contained in that announcement that resulted in the published exchange of correspondence between me and the Oxford principals. And, to be sure, we find no reference to the correspondence itself—centering around my *objections* to the procedures acquiesced in by the Oxford Centre—nor to the role that the correspondence played in the Huntington's decision to free the scroll photographs for scholarly use.

Strikingly, however, Vermes did acknowledge in this article that "protectionism or 'scholarly closed shop' is incompatible with academic freedom. . . . No keeper of manuscripts in a self-respecting British or American library," he emphasized, "would refuse a scholar access to an unpublished document simply because another scholar was in the process of editing it." This is of course a paraphrase of my own criticism of the Oxford Centre's very policy, as expressed in my letter to the London *Times*. Written only *after* the Antiquities Authority had announced the qualified freeing of the texts on 27 October, not beforehand, Vermes's statement directly contradicted the position taken by him and the Centre in the *Times* correspondence published three months earlier, supporting as it did the essential elements in the stance of the Antiquities Authority and of various traditional Qumranologists regarding limitation of access to the texts.

The article which provoked our exchange, published 24 June in *The Times*, had described Dr. Vermes's hope that the official editors would visit the Oxford Centre to lecture, making clear that access to the scrolls would only be by their permission ("in the last resort, editors determined to play dog in the manger will be able to continue doing so"). While the official editors of the scrolls would thus be the ones to *deliver* the lectures, other scholars lacking prior access to the particular texts on which the lectures were to be based would merely be auditors. While the official editors might, if they so chose, share their texts with less privileged colleagues, it was clear that a situation of gross inequality would prevail at the planned meetings. Stated simply, the Oxford Centre had entered into a collaboration with the Antiquities Authority whose practical effect was to provide for arbitrary denial of access to the texts. This denial might be directed either to those scholars whose fundamental views on the origin and significance of the scrolls might clash with those of the members of the two official scroll committees, or to others for whatever reasons the "official" editors might wish to entertain.

While claiming the cachet of a primary, independent research center for the scrolls in Europe, in practice the Oxford Forum had emerged as a center devoted largely to maintaining variations on the old, ever more unbelievable "Essenic" theory of their origins. What this amounted to was an ongoing effort by the Forum's organizers to have it both ways: to acquire the stature befitting distinguished academic bodies devoted to freedom of inquiry and scholarly debate, while in fact quietly proceeding with an ideological agenda.

This was the context for Alan Crown's assurances, in his reply to my London *Times* letter, that "several signs have emerged that our faith in the future opening out of Scrolls scholarship is justified. When our Qumran [Scrolls] room was opened on July 1, Professor Emanuel Tov, the editor-in-chief, and Professor Geza Vermes of Oxford both gave public lectures to a large gathering of scholars on unpublished materials on which they were working." This only reinforced the original *Times* announcement to the effect that *official* editors of the texts would henceforth give lectures about their findings to others not so fortunate. And in a continuation of the characteristic reticence, Dr. Crown did not mention that Vermes and Tov shared the traditional view that the scrolls in whole or in part originated with a sect supposed to have lived at Khirbet Qumran. Even after the Antiquities Authority's forced concession—due to actions transpiring overseas—that it would no longer attempt to prevent open study of the scrolls, and Vermes's subsequent acknowledgment of the general need for free access to ancient manuscripts, the Forum's policy did not fundamentally change. One looked in vain for some word from the director that in the future bona fide scholars working on the Qumran texts would be invited by the Oxford Forum to lecture entirely without regard either to their views on the fundamental issue of the scrolls' origin or to the side they were on in the struggle to free the texts.

A separate development, in fact, soon suggested that the opposite was the case. Vermes's acknowledgment appeared in the London *Times* simultaneously with publication in the *New York Times* of a report on a scroll fragment freshly deciphered by Professor Michael Wise of the University of Chicago (8 November 1991). Working in collaboration with him, Professor Robert Eisenman of California State University had concluded that its six broken lines contained a reference to the death of a messianic figure by "piercings." In one possible translation, the crucial line of the fragment read, "And they shall slay the Prince of the Congregation," which could be taken to describe a messianic figure. This line, when considered with other new scroll texts, could possibly cast further light on messianic thinking among the Jews just prior to the birth of Christianity. Being well aware of assertions by traditional Qumranologists that nothing new would be found in the newly freed texts, Eisenman had decided to make an early, public announcement of his interpretation of this text. Following the appearance of reports on the subject in Britain, Vermes called a special session of his seminar, publishing the results in the same issue of his journal that contained his remarkable chronological assertion. In this report he announced that "a special session was held on 20 December [1991] for experts from Oxford, Cambridge, London, and Reading Universities" to examine this text "which had recently gained international notoriety."

In the report, not unexpectedly, Vermes faulted the interpretations of Wise and Eisenman, claiming that the crucial line of the text should be translated as "The Prince of the Congregation will slay him." Vermes thereafter triumphantly stated that he and his assistant were supported in their own view by participants in the seminar. Indeed, a subsequent Associated Press news release, compiled after an interview with Vermes,[23] stated that scholars from the above-mentioned universities "concluded the fragment does not speak of a slain leader but of a triumphant Messiah. . . ." Since the article written by Professor Vermes and his associate was of a scholarly nature, with footnotes and citations of several

Qumran texts, the uninitiated public might well have concluded that the interpretation of Professors Wise and Eisenman had been disproved: The "refutation" was even headlined in the popular *Biblical Archaeology Review* of July 1992 with the words, "The Pierced Messiah Text—An Interpretation Evaporates."

Let us note that no scholarly article by Wise or Eisenman had yet appeared when the Oxford group offered its refutation, the American scholars having only given a preliminary report on an until then unpublished text. Seizing upon this fact, Vermes wrote that "since Eisenman and Wise have not published their theory in a scholarly journal and the media emphasize their claims without arguments to support them, the present paper . . . will not be polemical [but] . . . will seek to understand this badly truncated fragment in its wider Qumran context."

The logic underlying this announced action might upon reflection seem odd to those uninitiated into the arcane struggles attending Qumran politics: In view of the counsel of scholarly fellowship that Vermes expressed in his letter to the London *Times* of 16 July, why did not the Oxford Centre simply invite Eisenman and/or Wise to present a detailed version of their view at the meeting of 20 December, or why were not Eisenman and Wise invited to publish their interpretation in the same issue of the journal in which Vermes's critique appears? (We will recall that Vermes himself is the editor of this journal.) It was, after all, Wise and Eisenman who first publicly pointed to the text's importance—prompting Notre Dame's Eugene Ulrich to announce that "the same text was discussed last March in a closed-door meeting of the official Scrolls scholars" (*New York Times*, 8 November 1991). It was then thought to be an important text by the "official" scholars, who kept it secret until Professor Wise independently deciphered it. Yet one finds no acknowledgment in Vermes's article of the contribution of Wise and Eisenman in bringing it to public attention.

What was actually at work in this process—as in a game played only to win, devoid of principle—was the removal of the initiative from Wise and Eisenman with respect to the study of this text. Although it was they who had independently perceived its importance, it was developed by Vermes into an issue and then into a subject of his own study. In addition, Vermes's refutation was, despite his disclaimer, indeed polemical in nature. He offered his observations in great detail, but did not provide a forum for the scholarship of those he wished to refute, thus appearing to suggest that they had nothing to offer.

Despite the disdain he had shown for Eisenman's turn to the popular press, Vermes had resorted earlier to the very same kind of contact to promote his support for the traditional Essene hypothesis. In that case he adduced new and, as of then, yet-unpublished findings of Swiss specialists in radiocarbon dating. In "a gesture of scholarly showmanship," according to the London *Times* article of 24 June 1991, "[Dr. Vermes] means to announce . . . the results of recent carbon-14 dating tests on major documents in the collection."* Behind this gesture was his contention, and that of many other Qumranologists, that the great majority of the scrolls were of the pre-Christian period—in opposition to the claim by other scholars that a substantial number might derive from the early first century A.D. "Modern carbon-14 techniques," we are informed in the same article, "could answer the question with a high degree of certainty. The betting is that when the test results are announced . . . , the conventional view will prevail."

The test results were indeed announced by Vermes the same day and, according to him, supported the view that "most of the . . . Scrolls date to the last two centuries B.C." The London *Times* article on this new announcement went on to emphasize that he "and his fellow palaeographers are gratified that in almost all cases their estimated dates have been corroborated by science." Then came a sweeping endorsement of Vermes's views: "The *firm*

---

*Radiocarbon-14 measurement is a process of determining the approximate age of certain materials, including parchment and other ancient writing surfaces. The sample (in the case of scroll fragments, a piece of the parchment or papyrus to be tested) is cleaned and heated in an oxygen atmosphere, during which process all the carbon in the sample is converted to carbon dioxide. This is then reduced to graphite. The material is thereafter placed into an accelerator mass spectrometer, where an isotope ratio of $^{14}C/^{13}C$ and the radiocarbon age of the sample are determined. The radiocarbon age is then converted into a calendar age by using calibrations obtained from tree-ring measurements. This process, according to specialists in the technique, can in the end, after two or more independent measurements have been made, produce calendar datings that have a final uncertainty of as little as ±25 or 30 years; i.e., if the radiocarbon age obtained is, let us say, 1900, the corresponding calendar age of the sample would be between approximately A.D. 10 and A.D. 70, optimally speaking. However, the actual range of possible calendar ages can be 100 or more years.

dating of the Scrolls to the pre-Christian era will end speculation that they reflect clashes within the early church. *The Essene community that wrote the texts* seems rather to have been one of many participants in an intellectual milieu into which Jesus of Nazareth brought some new and radical ideas" (my italics).

All of this, however, was accompanied by the statement that "the most recent [of the scrolls] were probably written *during the lifetime of Christ and the Apostles,* according to [the] new radiocarbon dates on eight of the documents . . ." (my italics). In brief, to the extent that they might be considered accurate, the carbon-14 tests had *not* resulted in a firm dating of the scrolls to the pre-Christian era, but rather had shown that some of them dated to the pre-Christian era and some did not.

The scientific findings ostensibly forming the basis for Dr. Vermes's claims to the press would subsequently be published.[24] The results were quite graphically tabulated, but, as we shall observe in the following chapter, only revealed the absence of any solid basis for all three central assertions of his press announcement: They would neither prove a "firm dating of the scrolls to the pre-Christian era," nor that the estimated palaeographic datings of the individual scrolls "have been corroborated by science," nor that it was an "Essene community that wrote the texts."

The Antiquities Authority, in sending out advance copies of this radiocarbon study (6 November 1991), stated that the "scroll fragments being newly released for scholarly consultation will be available simultaneously in Oxford and Jerusalem."[25] But then on 20 November, as we have seen, photographs of the previously suppressed scrolls of Cave 4 were published, and on 25 November Dr. Tov made his famous announcement that all scholars would have access to the manuscripts without restrictions. Yet no official written statement of the Antiquities Authority actually underlay Tov's announcement, and none would ever be promulgated by the Authority. Instead, Tov would, a few months later, publish—in Vermes's *Journal of Jewish Studies*—a list specifying the scroll assignments of all of the members of his editorial team (by this time numbering approximately sixty) along with the names of those members—without as much as mentioning his announcement made at the Society of Biblical Literature meeting.[26] For this reason particularly, I asked him early in December 1992 to send me the statement he had read, as I wished to include it in a discussion on the ethics of manuscript publication planned for the international conference on the scrolls to be held in New York City later that month. This request, however, was refused. Tov said that he had found only a handwritten copy of his statement and that he did not think it would be worthwhile to send the text "which should be viewed in the light of the then-heated discussion about the issue of free access to the scrolls."[27] He also stated that different matters entirely were at issue,

> mainly scholarly honesty and unauthorized and inappropriate quoting from unpublished and published transcriptions and scholarly discussions, which are the intellectual property of the scholars who had carried out the research and who now see their work in print without their names attached or improperly quoted.

The implication of Tov's statement was that members of his team who distributed transcriptions of the texts assigned to them, or described the texts orally at scholarly meetings, thereby established for themselves certain moral or legal rights of first publication of those texts—even though they were merely text assignments, and not in their keeping as the result of discoveries made by them. This view represented an apparent about-face from Dr. Tov's own quoted statements in news reports of November 1991. I therefore wrote back to him on 22 December 1992, pointing out that the quoted statements in effect meant that

> you did not fully intend what you stated at the meeting. . . . This perception is additionally reinforced by the fact that in . . . the *Journal of Jewish Studies* . . . you published a list of all of the participants in the Jerusalem project, with their manuscript assignments—but did not as much as allude to your earlier quoted Kansas City statements. Your publication of this list without accompanying publication of the statement in question could not but create the impression that you are now attempting to qualify that statement, and to assert, on behalf of the assignees, a prior right of publication.

Tov wrote back the following month (17 January 1993) that "the members of the international team, with the support of the IAA [= Israel Antiquities Authority], simply ask their colleagues not to" publish text editions of scroll fragments, but only to limit themselves to an occasional quote from such texts. To this he added that some members of the "international team are more liberal than others" and might indeed subscribe to the view that the scrolls were open to all scholars to study and publish as they saw fit. Tov then added that his own view had not changed since November 1991; he had meant every word expressed in Kansas City, and had emphasized that there was a "new spirit of openness." He went on to say that colleagues were merely being asked "to refrain from full-fledged text editions (as opposed to studies of texts and quotations from them.)" He stated that this was the view reflected in his speech, "which was correctly quoted in the *Religious Studies News* 7, 1 of January 1992 . . . but not in the *New York Times* of 27 November 1991." He had not written a letter of correction to the *Times* "for if I were to keep track of all the statements in the papers in which mistakes were made concerning the scrolls, I would never be able to do my work as editor-in-chief."

Thus Tov claimed, as of January 1993, that at the Kansas City meeting he had been consistent in his position that independent scholars should refrain from text editions of scroll fragments. The statement from the *Religious Studies News* that he enclosed with his letter did indeed appear to reflect that view; it was to the effect that the Antiquities Authority had

> full copyright jurisdiction over the Scrolls [and] had taken the step of authorizing free access to the photographs. . . . Initially, this access carried with it the requirement that users declare their willingness to quote from, but not produce text editions of, the photographs. In a subsequent move, the [Antiquities Authority] dropped all institutional restrictions against publication, *although it continues to hope that moral pressure will produce the same results.*[28]

This description of Tov's statement obviously contradicted the one that had appeared not only in the *New York Times* but also in other press accounts during the days immediately following his announcement. Puzzled by this discrepancy, I wrote to the editor of *Religious Studies News*, E. H. Lovering, Jr., requesting more information about the meeting. He eventually located a recording of the session, had it transcribed, and sent it to me. According to the transcript of Tov's address, he stated that the Antiquities Authority (IAA) acted twice. First, it decided to allow free access to all photographic images of the scrolls. . . . At that stage, it was expected from the users . . . to sign a declaration stating that the content of the text may be quoted in all publications, but not including a text edition. At a second stage which has not been publicized so far, the IAA realized that this request was not practical. Thus two weeks after the first [announcement] the IAA relieved the institutions holding the photographs from the request to institute such a declaration. It was and is believed that moral pressure is the only possible approach in this time and age. That is, anyone asking for access to any or all of the photographs will automatically get permission to do so without any limitations, both in Israel and at the institutions abroad.[29]

Tov went on to state—again according to the transcript—that he "agreed that the IAA had no choice but to change its policy" and that he was "in full agreement with that change. Obviously," he continued, "many of my colleagues who edit texts on behalf of the international team have mixed feelings. Only the future will teach us whether the recent developments were good or bad for scholarship."

Although the *Religious Studies News* article portrayed Tov as stating that the Antiquities Authority, in dropping all institutional restrictions against publication, continued "to hope that moral pressure *will produce the same result*" (my italics), the ambiguity in Tov's recorded statement hardly warrants that reading of his remarks. Tov expressed no disagreement anywhere in his address with the Society's "Statement on Access to Ancient Written Materials" read a few minutes beforehand at the very same meeting—a statement specifically stipulating that authorization of teams of scholars to prepare official editions of texts should not *"hinder other scholars from publishing their own studies, translations, or editions of the written materials"* (my italics). If Tov knew that the Antiquities Authority disagreed with this statement of principle, or if he himself disagreed with it, it was his obvious obligation to state as much specifically and without ambiguities. His statement about moral pressure as the "only possible approach" was instead followed by a single explanatory sentence, one that makes the words concerning moral pressure appear to have more bearing on the Antiquities Authority for withholding the scrolls than on the individual scholars who fought for access to them.

This was likewise the gist of the positive and conciliatory remarks contributed by all the other participants in the Society's panel session. Dr. Helmut Koester and Dr. Beverly Gaventa addressed themselves to the importance of the Society's statement on access, Koester adding that Dr. Tov "and the authorities of the State of Israel have agreed to cooperate with the policy we are instituting now."[30] Dr. James VanderKam read out the statement. After Tov's remarks, Dr. Ulrich expressed his own assent to the open spirit of fair play that was being expressed: The publication process, he said, "needs not anger . . . [but] the values of scholarship: . . . trust, harmony, and cooperation."[31] J. A. Sanders of the Claremont Center thereupon stated that "we are very happy at the developments."[32] Dr. Abegg, observing the "great events that we see taking place tonight," then spoke of his and Dr. Wacholder's intention to continue publication of the computer-generated version of the scrolls that they had begun earlier.[33] The last speaker was Dr. Moffett of the Huntington, who traced the role of the library in freeing the texts and concluded by saying: "My position was that if you free the Scrolls, you free the scholars. That, indeed, I think is what has happened."[34]

The press reports that followed the meeting were thus based on the general sense of all of the statements made. What is more, not one of the participants in the panel reported afterward on any utterance of Dr. Tov's that was in disharmony with those made by the other speakers. But it remains quite possible that Tov's statement regarding moral pressure, inserted almost as a passing remark, was intentionally ambiguous.

For these reasons, it would appear that in the days following the press reports, Tov's statement at this point was modified or otherwise smoothed over, so that it took on a meaning in the pages of the *Religious Studies News* different from that originally conveyed to the audience at the Society of Biblical Literature meeting: namely, that the Antiquities Authority continued "to hope moral pressure will produce *the same results*"—i.e., *of restricting publication of the scrolls*. By this subtle alteration of wording, the Antiquities Authority was aided in maintaining the essential element of its earlier hard-line position. However, as no retraction was ever made to the national press by Dr. Tov, Dr. Koester, or the Society of Biblical Literature, and as the *Religious Studies News* item never received general press coverage, the reading public continued to believe, on the basis of the national press statements attributed to Tov, the president of the Society, and others, that the scrolls had become fully accessible to all scholars for research and publication purposes without the threat of stigma or retaliation. My request of the Society that it issue a public statement clarifying the matter ultimately met with studied inaction.

CHAPTER 9

Myth and Science
in the World of Qumranology

❖

The scientists of the Institut für Mittelenergiephysik at Zurich who performed the radiocarbon-14 tests on fragments of the Dead Sea Scrolls were obviously uncommitted, at the outset, to any particular view of either the manuscripts' origins or their palaeographic dating. In recording their results, however, they failed, either by choice or instruction, to honor a basic scientific obligation: that of leaving the comparison with palaeographic datings to researchers not involved in the testing process and with no particular commitment to personal datings of the individual scrolls. Whether committed to the Essene hypothesis or not, many scrolls scholars would obviously have wished to assess the findings independently, particularly in order to test earlier speculation on the dates of these texts.

The palaeography of the scrolls—in particular, the examination of the forms of individual letters to determine when the texts were copied—cannot be considered anything like an exact science or even a sophisticated art, since no manuscripts with dates are available, among the scrolls, to serve as standards of comparison. One may discern in the texts a gradual progression from apparently earlier to apparently later forms of individual consonants, but—as manuscript scholars are aware—the less square and more cursive, or rounded, the handwritings are, the more difficult the process of approximate dating becomes. Even texts written in square Hebrew/Aramaic characters—which are somewhat easier to handle as palaeographic specimens—cannot as a rule be dated to anything less than a hundred-year time span, and this is not only because of the absence of dated texts, but also because each individual scribe's hand differs from every other's. Some scholars have attempted to use available dated documents of earlier and later periods as a way to approximate the dates when individual scroll fragments were copied by their scribes, but this procedure has proven to be highly conjectural at best. Of the period of the scrolls themselves, there are no known dated documents.

Even in the case of the much more abundant Cairo Genizah manuscripts, the approximate dating of undated texts to periods of less than seventy-five to a hundred years on the basis of palaeographic considerations alone is hazardous and uncertain— although there are *numerous* dated texts with which to compare them. More precise dating in such cases becomes possible only when the handwriting is identifiable as that of a particular writer or copyist known already from dated documents, or where clear internal evidence (i.e., names and events mentioned in the text) establishes specific historical limits.

The difficulty of dating Genizah texts to limited time frames of twenty-five or even fifty years may be illustrated by an incident that occurred at the Oriental Institute approximately two decades ago, during the visit there of Professor Philip Birnbaum of the University of London. His work was principally in the field of Hebrew palaeography; he had by then devoted much time to the study of scripts in the scrolls as well as mediaeval Hebrew manuscripts. After a lecture he gave, I invited him to my office for a discussion of problems of palaeographic method. During the conversation, I pointed out a large stack of photostats of Genizah manuscripts on which I was then working, and expressed frustration at the lack of a detailed handbook to help in the dating of the various texts. "Then again," I said, "even the dated texts themselves show how difficult it is to supply dates to the much more numerous undated ones—there's no demonstrable linear progression in the dated texts from so-called earlier hands to later ones." We discussed this point for some time, and then I asked him to help me perform an experiment: I would select a dozen or so Genizah photostats that contained dates, cover the dates over, and then hand the photostats to him one at a time for his palaeographic appraisal, after which we would uncover the actual dates and make a graph to delineate the accuracy, or lack thereof, of the palaeographic estimates. Birnbaum, however, declined to do this, saying it was obvious that the results would not be satisfactory. The experiment would have been interesting, but he was surely wise to decline the proposal.

Since then, scholars around the world, because of the increasing quantity of Genizah texts they have studied—including a relatively large number of dated documents—have become more adept at judging the approximate age of various undated documents from this hoard. Dating unique or otherwise unknown Genizah handwritings, however, remains a challenge difficult to meet, unless very good internal evidence (e.g., allusions to known historical events) occurs in the texts. What gives this effort its basic stability are the dated documentary texts, and also those occasional literary texts that bear dates—especially where the latter may contain an occasional *colophon*. This is a record made by an author or scribe that gives his name as well as the place and date of composition, or copying, of a literary work, and is usually found at the end of the work in question.

As indicated, the Qumran scrolls are only *undated* scribal copies of literary writings. They do not have colophons, and originated a full millennium earlier than the Genizah manuscripts. More remote in time and offering only five or six hundred examples of Hebrew handwritings spread over three centuries, they are much less suitable for limited time-span datings than are the Genizah texts, which, also spread mainly over three centuries, include well over twenty thousand different handwritings. The relative paucity of Dead Sea Scroll handwritings, however, has not prevented scholars from proposing such limited time spans—as little as twenty-five years for individual scroll fragments.

The best-known palaeographic work on the scrolls is that of Frank M. Cross, who offered strikingly specific dates for numerous texts, dates then endorsed by colleagues, students, and many other writers.[1] A somewhat more cautious palaeography of the texts, with time-span estimates far greater than those of Cross but dealing with a more limited number of texts, had earlier been worked out by Nahman Avigad of the Hebrew University.[2] What the two writers did agree on was the general delineation of some of the scripts as "Hasmonaean"—that is, belonging approximately to the period of the Hasmonaean rulers, from 167 to 37 B.C.—and "Herodian," belonging to the period of Herod the Great, his successor Archelaus, and the Roman procurators who ruled Palestine until the destruction of the Second Temple (37 B.C.–A.D. 70). However, there is still no exhaustive palaeographical work on the more than five hundred scripts represented in the scroll fragments. Nor, in the absence of dated documents, can the datings that have been provided for Qumran texts be considered anything other than educated guesses.

Now the authors of the study recording the Zurich radiocarbon test results included not only the scientists who performed them but also two exponents of traditional Qumranology, namely, Strugnell of Harvard and Broshi of the Shrine of the Book and the Antiquities Authority's oversight committee. From the beginning they had been firm supporters of Cross's specific palaeographic datings as well as the attribution of the manuscripts to the Essene sect, and no other point of view was represented in the study in question. Accordingly, near the beginning of the article readers were soberly informed that "the history of Jewish scripts can be delineated in great detail, and palaeographers are in a position to ascribe dates within ranges of a half, or even a quarter, of a century"—a highly dubious statement, abetted at the end of the article by the conclusion that "our research put to test both the radiocarbon method and palaeography; seemingly, both disciplines have fared well." This conclusion is not borne out even by a cursory examination of the article, while detailed scrutiny of the data encourages yet deeper doubts, extending both to the accuracy of the radiocarbon dating method itself and to the trustworthiness of the narrow-span palaeographic method promoted by Cross.

A total of fourteen ancient Hebrew texts were tested, eight from Qumran, two from Masada, and four from other sites that do not bear on the question of the dating of the Qumran and Masada fragments.[3] The scientists in Zurich, who performed the radiocarbon tests on small pieces of the parchments, stated that of the two Masada texts, there was a 68 percent probability that the date of one fell between 169 and 93 B.C., whereas the commonly theorized *palaeographic* dating was between 30 and 1 B.C. The separate datings of the other Masada text did not indicate as wide a discrepancy, but the palaeographic dating of 30–1 B.C. intersected only with the first third of the radiocarbon dating of 33 B.C.– A.D. 74. The most that could be said for this kind of "corroboration" was that the radiocarbon datings did not entirely disprove the suggested palaeographic ones. It must be noted that although both of the tested Masada fragments were palaeographically dated to within the same time frame of 30–1 B.C., the radiocarbon datings differed from each other radically.

The eight testings of Qumran fragments yielded results similar to those obtained for the two Masada texts: Only one of the tested manuscripts, the *Thanksgiving Scroll*, showed a highly positive corroboration between radiocarbon and palaeographic datings; the former dating was between 21 B.C. and A.D. 61, the latter between 50 B.C. and A.D. 70. None of the other Qumran texts yielded this degree of corroboration. In two of the fragments, there was no overlapping whatever between the paleographic and radiocarbon datings, and in four others the overlapping was insignificant, a considerably greater part of the radiocarbon probability range being outside the surmised palaeographic range than within it. In the case of one of the eight fragments, the chance that the radiocarbon dating range even touched the surmised palaeographic range was extremely slight. One could, then, infer no more from the supplied radiocarbon data than that in a few cases corresponding palaeographic surmises were irrelevant to them, in several cases they were of meager import, while in one case only (that of the *Genesis Apocryphon*) were the data firm—a case, it will be noted, where the palaeographic surmise covered the unusually long range of one hundred and twenty years.

If the tests showed anything, it was that the relatively precise palaeographic datings of the scrolls proposed earlier by Frank Cross and his associates were largely guesswork and basically unfounded—and not the opposite, as the press announcement of Geza Vermes (see pages 241–242) had led one to believe. Vermes's claim, in the same announcement, that the radiocarbon dating proved that "most of the . . . scrolls date to the last two centuries B.C.," was based on tests conducted on a mere *ten* of over eight hundred manuscripts—only six of the ten being dated to the pre-Christian period; and this was hardly the kind of data to provide conclusive support for such a claim. Particularly in light of the radiocarbon probability range of 68 percent, what could soundly be made of such data was that it supported, in a general way, the commonly held and well-founded view that the scrolls are not mediaeval manuscripts, but rather ancient ones, dating roughly between the third century B.C. and the first century A.D. While correct within that range—accepting the authority of the radiocarbon testing that, as we will see, is not entirely authoritative—all that can be concluded is that the radiocarbon datings of the scrolls were correct only to within approximately a century or a century and a quarter, certainly not to any shorter period. No "substantiation" or "validation" of the palaeographic surmises could be perceived in this data,* if such terms mean anything like the twenty-five-year range originally claimed by Cross.

Perhaps the most unusual aspect of Vermes's press announcement concerning the radiocarbon dating was the step he took of interweaving the Qumran-Essene hypothesis into it. Already in April of that year, curator Broshi had confidently claimed that "the [radiocarbon] testing, performed in a Zurich laboratory to settle a scholarly argument, appeared to confirm most scholars' belief that the works were those of a Jewish sect, the Essenes,"[4] and it was this very theme, reintroduced somewhat more subtly, that Vermes himself hazarded three months later—after the Oxford Centre had formalized its agreement with the Antiquities Authority and received photographs of the scrolls. And yet, when the article containing the radiocarbon data was published a few months later, it offered—despite the unacceptable fact that such highly partisan figures as Broshi as well as John Strugnell were actually among its authors—no proofs whatever demonstrating that Essenes had written the scrolls, nor any statement showing how the radiocarbon dating might support this view.

The most remarkable disaccord the radiocarbon tests produced was that involving the *Testament of Kohath*, one of several Qumran pseudepigraphs that read as admonitions delivered by forebears of the tribe of Levi. The hypothesized palaeographic dating of this manuscript was 100–75 B.C. (i.e., the period of Alexander Jannaeus). Here the radiocarbon results yielded two time spans: one of 388–353 B.C. and a more probable one of approximately 310–240 B.C. The authors of the radiocarbon study here acknowledged a difference "on the order of 200 years" and

---

*See the chart as published by G. Bonani et al. in *'Atiqot* 20 (1991), p. 31. Of the ten tested Qumran scrolls, the four most often claimed to be sectarian, i.e., the *Hodayot*, *Genesis Apocryphon*, *Temple Scroll*, and *Songs of the Sabbath Sacrifice*—all have calibrated age ranges extending into the first century A.D. Hershel Shanks, in an article entitled "Carbon-14 Tests Substantiate Scroll Dates," *Biblical Archaeology Review*, (Nov.–Dec. 1991, pp. 70–71) published a chart based upon the one produced by Bonani and colleagues, and yet asserts that "In general the C-14 tests appear substantially to validate the paleographic dating." The author fails to indicate what scholars or statisticians he consulted before expressing this untenable view. See further the debate on the radiocarbon results in M. Wise *et al.* (eds.), *Methods of Investigation of the Dead Sea Scrolls and the Khirbet Qumran Site* (New York, 1994), pp. 448–453.

stated that they did "not have a simple explanation for the discrepancy." But rather than admitting that this finding possibly
cast doubt on the palaeographic dating assigned to this manuscript, they instead asserted that "there is no doubt with regard to
the palaeographic date (late Hasmonaean)." The actual content of
the *Testament*, by contrast, indicated a date in the *Herodian* period, when individuals of "mixed origin" such as are mentioned in
this text (i.e., those stemming from Herod's mixed Jewish-
Idumaean parentage) actually controlled the Temple.

The statement of the authors acknowledging "no simple explanation" certainly flies in the face of the ostensible purpose of the
·radiocarbon tests on the scrolls, as implied both in the earlier
news releases and in the Zurich article itself: It was none other
than to determine whether the surmised palaeographic datings
were or *were not* supported by the scientific method in question.
The considerable effort made by the Zurich scientists to explain
away the notable discrepancy by suggesting the possibility of
chemical contamination, after having gone to the unusual length
of testing two samples of the *Kohath* scroll "collected at different
times"—samples on which they felt obliged to perform special
microscopic examinations (pp. 30–31)—does not speak well for
the scientific objectivity of the tests.

Making matters worse, the authors of the article asserted that
"good agreement between radiocarbon and palaeographic dates"
could be seen "in nine of the . . . ten cases, *taking into consideration the fact that statistically up to three dates are allowed to devi-
ate by more than one standard deviation*" (p. 29; my italics). When
referring to these three deviant datings, the authors did not
explain who granted such a statistical allowance—or on what
basis they might term the results of other testings (with the single
exception of the one performed on the *Thanksgiving Scroll*) examples of "good agreement." One could, perhaps, have spoken in
such positive terms if the tests had probed only the soundness of
the general belief that the manuscripts were written over a three-
or four-hundred year period ending approximately in A.D. 70 at
the latest—but not at all if, as the article itself indicated, the primary purpose was to test the narrow time-span methods of Cross
and his followers among scroll palaeographers.

Particularly when these results were read together with the pre-
publication statements of Broshi and Vermes regarding the significance of the tests, it became evident that the chief goal of the

Antiquities Authority in commissioning the tests was to lend scientific legitimacy to the methods of the traditional Qumranologists, including their belief in the old Essenic hypothesis. The lack of objectivity and, particularly, the vested ideological interests at work in this unfortunate episode were already manifest in the inclusion of two traditional Qumranologists on the committee. Scholarly and scientific protocol clearly called for an objective commission of researchers, including those from other but related fields of knowledge, to assess the radiocarbon findings independently. In addition, it obviously required an important *control*: inviting, in advance of the radiocarbon tests, a range of scholars working on the scrolls, regardless of their particular views of Qumran origins, to submit their own independent evaluations of the earlier palaeographic datings, and then to have these evaluations tested anonymously against the radiocarbon findings. It is notable that in the light of the advance claims about the test results and their contrast with the actual results published later, no scientific commission either of the Israel Academy of Sciences or another group has yet been appointed in Jerusalem to investigate the unacceptably embarrassing combination of incidents that make up this bizarre episode in the study of the scrolls.

The remarkable lengths to which traditional Qumranologists appeared willing to go to salvage what had by 1990 become the theoretical equivalent of a sinking ship were also apparent in a series of subsequent developments. In the spring of 1992, as mentioned earlier, Professor Emanuel Tov of the Hebrew University, the new editor-in-chief of the Antiquities Authority's publication project, finally divulged the names of the many new participants in the project. He did this in the very issue of the *Journal of Jewish Studies* containing the Oxford Centre group's interpretation of the by-now-famous messianic fragment.[5] There were now well over fifty editors, divided about equally between university faculty members and former and present students of some of them (including Tov). This configuration reflected the policy employed at Harvard during the previous decade. Among the students were three doctoral candidates, who soon thereafter published a study of a new Qumran text from Cave 4, classified as 4Q448.

A few weeks before publication of this fragment, an article describing it appeared in the *Jerusalem Post* (24 April 1992), from which it became clear that one of the students, A. Yardeni, who had been granted the privilege of studying the text two years previously, now had gotten far enough in her work to perceive that it was a fragment of a liturgical poem in praise of "Jonathan the King." Strugnell, who brought this text to the attention of the students, had earlier on entirely misunderstood its language—underscoring once again the need to free the scrolls from monopolistic control. The *Post* article emphasized that the words "Jonathan the King" constituted "the first reference ever found in the Dead Sea Scrolls to a Jewish historical figure." This was "an identification that would demand extensive scholarly rethinking—about the history of the period, the identity of some of the residents of Kumran, and other aspects. . . ." Another doctoral candidate to whom the text was then shown had determined that this "Jonathan" could be none other than Alexander Jannaeus, who ruled in Judaea from 103 to 76 B.C. The two candidates, together with a third, proceeded to form a committee of their own to publish this text, in the course of their work determining that "this scroll could not have been written by the Dead Sea sect or by Pharisees."

This was, of course, a most intriguing conclusion. Alexander Jannaeus, among other crimes, once massacred eight hundred Jews and their families in revenge for actions they had initiated against him.[6] One scroll fragment, the *Pesher Nahum* ("Interpretation of the Book of Nahum"), contains a possibly unsympathetic account of revenge taken by a ruler known as the "angry lion-whelp"—thought by some scholars to be Alexander Jannaeus—against the "seekers of smooth things," thought to be the Pharisees. With the *Pesher Nahum* deemed to be a product of the "sect of Qumran," it appeared obvious to the editors that this "sect" showed opposition to Alexander Jannaeus, just as had the Pharisees according to Josephus. That either group could write a separate song of praise in honor of Jannaeus was perceived as impossible.

The text's editors, in the course of this process of reasoning, posed a grave puzzle: namely, "Why would the fundamentalist sect living at Kumran, generally believed to be Essenes who were bitter enemies of the Hasmonaean regime in Jerusalem, write a prayer for the welfare of a Hasmonaean king, especially one so cruel and war-obsessed as this one?" (*Jerusalem Post*, 24 April 1992). Let us note that in this formulation two notions were taken as fact: that a sect inhabited Qumran and that this sect composed the writings found in the caves. A third notion—the Essenic nature of the sect—was acknowledged as something "believed." In fact, however, *each* of these ideas was and remains nothing but a belief, unsupported by the evidence. And, in the process of embracing all of these beliefs, the three editors attempted to explain the presence of this fragment among the scrolls in dramatically contradictory ways.

According to the joint explanation of the editors presented in the *Jerusalem Post*, the likely author, since he could be neither a Pharisee nor an Essene, "belonged to the third major ideological grouping within the Jewish nation at the time, the Sadducees. The Sadducees and the Essenes shared a system of Jewish law . . . stricter than the Halacha [ritual-legal observance] followed by the Pharisees. . . . The scroll was probably brought to Kumran by a Sadducee who joined the sect and took his library with him."

Here we may observe one shaky theory being built upon the next in the editors' zeal to explain away their disturbing text. There was in fact nothing of a distinctly Sadducaean nature expressed in the fragment. In adition, far more than three ideological groupings prevailed among the Jews of intertestamental times. And, as we have seen in Chapter 7, it is only because of one or two Sadducaean-like laws among a total of *twenty* found in the *Acts of Torah* that some Qumranologists began claiming that the "Essenes of Qumran" were really Sadducees, or that the two groups must have shared one system of law.

While no proof whatever exists that a Sadducee brought his personal library to the claimed Khirbet Qumran "sectarian" settlement, the suggestion of the editors did make it seem as though they were in effect implicitly embracing an aspect of the theory of Jerusalem origin of the scrolls. We shall see below how, with some aid from the press, they attempted to foreclose this option.

In a detailed, scholarly study in the Hebrew quarterly *Tarbiz* that followed publication of the *Post* article, the editors had somewhat greater difficulty explaining the phenomenon they were confronting.[7] Here they said nothing at all of a Sadducaean library, or of a Sadducee who joined the claimed sect. Instead, they pointed out that the language of the poem was unusual and that the worldview it articulates "opposed that of the people of Qumran who hated the Hasmonaeans"; and, in a refreshingly plain acknowledgment, they admitted that there was "no proof" the text "was written by the authors of the community inhabiting Qumran."[8]

Once this conclusion was arrived at, however, a perception seems to have surfaced that the acknowledgment might create a rather shattering difficulty: namely, the necessary implication that proofs might equally well be needed for the contention that all the other cave manuscripts did derive from a particular community living at Qumran. Until publication of this article, traditional Qumranologists had generally required no such proofs of themselves, relying instead on the sustenance of their overarching sectarian hypothesis. The three authors here found themselves in the awkward position of raising crucial questions about method: the method, that is, of a large body of scholars engaged in constructing sectarian castles in the desert over the past forty-five years.

The authors thus added a qualifying statement: "The compositions of Qumran published *until now* are compositions of the people of the Sect, *or else compositions that do not contradict their views.*"[9] Numerous ideas in the scrolls are in fact mutually contradictory, and no demonstrable sectarian interconnection exists among the vast majority of the texts. The idea lurking in the background of this statement is clear enough: As long as the views in most of the scrolls did not actually *contradict* what were being conceived of as the essential doctrines of the sect—by which the authors meant doctrines found particularly in the *Manual of Discipline*—then no basic harm could befall the Qumran-sectarian theory. It could henceforth be simply qualified by asserting that "the sect" would naturally possess books not of their own making, perhaps brought in "from the outside" as an embellishment to their own sectarian reading. But the authors actually went rather further, stating at this point in their discourse that

> in our opinion *many of the scrolls* discovered at Qumran are the creative fruit of extensive Jewish groups in the Second Temple period that by chance were brought to Qumran by people of the Sect, and the fragment under discussion here . . . is apparently in this category[10] (italics mine).

In this unusually strained argument, what of course stands out most is the authors' newfound readiness to suggest that not just a few, but indeed many, of the scrolls derived from groups of Jews other than those imagined to have lived at Qumran—a basic element in the theory of the scrolls' Jerusalem origin. In 1980 I had already concluded my first presentation of the theory by stating that the manuscripts are remnants of a literature showing a wide variety of practices, beliefs and opinions . . . removed from Jerusalem before or during the siege. . . . Determination of the nature of [their] concepts and practices . . . may best be achieved not by pressing them into the single sectarian bed of Essenism, but by separating them out from one another, through internal analysis, into various spiritual currents which appear to have characterized Palestinian Judaism of the intertestamental period.[11]

It is thus fair to observe that the students had moved, however reluctantly, toward a basic understanding of the scrolls' nature akin to the hypothesis I first expressed in 1980. They did so, however, without acknowledging as much, and not for lack of awareness of the idea. In a footnote to their article they cited my study of that date—but only in connection with a statement that they did not "accept" my view that one should refrain "from interconnecting the manuscripts with the inhabitants of Khirbet Qumran." Having nonetheless arrived at a perception dangerously close to my own by intensive analysis of the scrolls' contents (such as I had originally urged for all the texts) the authors thereupon refrained from fully disclosing my published view. I did not merely state that one should forbear organically interconnecting the scrolls with Khirbet Qumran—but rather that the scrolls derived from libraries of Jerusalem that, with the aid of inhabitants of the area, were eventually sequestered in Judaean Wilderness hiding places before and perhaps also during the Roman siege of A.D. 70.

The reason for this inappropriate omission is self-evident. During the time they wrote their paper, the three authors were doctoral candidates at a university where several faculty members were not only deeply committed to a theory opposing my own but were also responsible for appointing two of the students as editors of Qumran texts:[12] grounds enough, sadly, for their guarded hedging of conclusions, introduction of awkwardly qualifying and self-contradictory statements, and failure to acknowledge or divulge the origin of their fundamental idea.

Having worked out their plan of presentation, the authors sought aid in bringing their views to the attention of a wider readership. The *Jerusalem Post* obliged with an article that, while divulging important information about the text due to appear in the detailed Hebrew study, in the end obscured the basic issue even further. Taking his cue from the writers' own statements, the *Post* reporter began with what was claimed as my view: ". . . that the . . . scrolls were not written at Kumran at all but were brought from elsewhere . . . [and] that . . . Kumran was a fort and not a monastery settlement inhabited by members of an ascetic sect. . . ." This characterization of my theory as constituting nothing more than a vague notion that the scrolls were brought to Qumran from "elsewhere," together with its studied omission of the fact that many scholars have described the military nature of Khirbet Qumran, was by then a favorite ploy of traditional Qumranologists.

The precise nature of my interpretation—with its essential elements of Jerusalem origin and doctrinal diversity—became fully available to scholars as well as the reading public in English- and French-speaking countries during the 1980s, and to the general Hebrew readership in late 1991.[13] Referring, however, not to the theory itself but to its parodic effigy, the *Jerusalem Post* reporter then piously explained that my "view is shared by virtually no other reputable scholar" (apparently a reference to traditional Qumranologists). Then came the article's putative climax: "An increasing number of scholars—including the editor of the official Dead Sea Scroll publications, Prof. . . . Tov of the Hebrew University—believe that some of the scrolls* have indeed been brought from other places by people joining the sect." The three authors, the article then not very surprisingly clarified, believed that the new scroll fragment "has to be one of these."

Unmistakably at work in the *Post* piece was a poor substitution of parochial advocacy for the higher journalism that cogent science reporting requires. Upon reading the piece and comparing it with the scholarly article in *Tarbiz*, I wrote the *Post* with the appropriate corrections, adding, in response to the newspaper's claim that the new manuscript contained the "first reference ever found in the Dead Sea Scrolls to a historical figure," that (a) already in the 1950s the Polish scholar J. T. Milik stated that Queen Salome (Shelamzion), John Hyrcanus, and a certain "Yohanan" were mentioned in unpublished scroll fragments; and (b) that the texts in which these names appeared were among the fragments from Cave 4 already published in photographic

---

*By that time Tov had already written that he believed "many" of the scrolls came from elsewhere, and he would eventually write that "most" of them had. See below, page 295.

facsimile in the autumn of 1991. The *Post* failed either to publish or acknowledge my letter.

One of the authors of the *Tarbiz* study was quoted in the *Post* as saying that the publication of the new text would occur "a year and a half after we got it. . . . *With older scholars, this would have taken years to do.*" (My italics.) As is clear from the *Tarbiz* publication, the several lines of text were indeed fairly well deciphered during those eighteen months, and are accompanied by observations on the palaeography of the handwriting, the historical significance of the fragment, and its poetic content, with each of the three authors concentrating on one of these areas. There is, however, nothing highly remarkable about the fact—enthusiastically heralded, as we have seen—that an advanced graduate student trained in palaeography should have correctly deciphered the phrase "Jonathan the King" after Strugnell's earlier failure to do so; the scrolls are decipherable with proper concentration and the right techniques at one's disposal. The work was, moreover, that of a committee rather than of an individual scholar, and it spent parts of over a year concentrating on a single fragment. It is somewhat difficult to conceive of the resulting thirty-three-page article as having been accomplished with any unusual alacrity, regardless of the ages of the committee's members. Various scholars noted for their palaeographic skills have satisfactorily deciphered much longer texts, and texts no less difficult to deal with, in shorter time.

The reference to "older scholars" thus remains rather a puzzle, unless meant to allude to the failure of some original editorial committee members to publish their assigned work over a period of three decades. Mr. Broshi of the Shrine of the Book had already suggested that the failure arose from the editors' senior academic status, which brought with it the absence of particular deadlines for projects whose completion might be needed to secure tenure. The newer people, he had observed, "still have promotion ahead of them. They are hungry, and we can expect that they will perform at top speed. If they don't publish, they won't get academic tenure or professorships or advancement" (*Jerusalem Post*, 29 September 1989). I had responded to this explanation by pointing out that most scholars fortunate enough to have senior status at universities consider this a hard-earned gift enabling them to continue their research, and that the proffered explanation was no excuse for the scroll editors' failure to publish their work. I also indicated that the depiction of "hungry" scholars as saviors of the scrolls failed to make clear whose table they had to frequent in order to perform the rescue (*Jerusalem Post*, 1 November 1989).

Leaving aside this apparently consensual appeal to the geriatrics of scholarship by the three graduate students, we are left with the more pressing question of the quality of the work invested on the 4Q448 text. We need to consider this matter particularly in view of several earlier claims: Broshi's speculation that the freeing of the scrolls would result in "third- and fourth- and fifth-rate productions" and the committees' contention that only their control of the editorial selection process would assure text editions of high quality, backed up by General Drori's assertion that "definitive editions" could be guaranteed only by this process. The *Tarbiz* article, in fact, revealed both scholarly strengths and grave weaknesses that included unprovable assertions and serious flaws in the method and criteria of investigation. It was the product of a painfully awkward determination to guard basic aspects of the old notion of Qumran origins as well as the highly problematic dating of Qumran handwritings worked out by Frank Cross.

Utilizing these datings without explaining on what grounds they did so, the authors expressed the conviction that the manuscript "is the only one of the documents discovered at Qumran and so far published that may almost certainly be dated to the first half of the first century B.C."[14] Though their painstakingly detailed discussion of the palaeography of individual consonants was excellent, the specific criteria for their dating of this particular scroll did not emerge with any clarity. Some characteristics, according to the authors, were more like those of the "Hasmonaean" scripts, others more like those of the "Herodian" ones, and in the manuscript "there is a confusion of early and late [letter] forms."[15] They properly categorized the script as "semi-cursive," but there are relatively few such manuscript hands among the Qumran texts, making a specific palaeographic dating all the more difficult. The reason for opting for this relatively early, and relatively specific, dating of the text was not revealed until the end of the palaeographic discussion, when we read: "Because of these [palaeographical] characteristics, and since this document includes a prayer for the peace of Jonathan the King and his domain, it appears that it was written in the period of Alexander Jannaeus [104–78 B.C.]."

One has the right to expect considerably more intellectual rigor of doctoral candidates than is revealed in this sentence: With the manuscript being described here without warrant as a "document,"[16] we find—as we have seen, not for the first time—a crucial failure to ask the question required of all palaeographers if they are doing their work correctly, "Is the text I am studying an autograph original or a scribal copy of something composed earlier?"

In fact, from the very beginning of the discussion, the term "document" was used misleadingly, for no proof was offered that the fragment was the original author's own autograph. The text might, indeed, be a *unicum*—i.e., a unique text, not otherwise known—but that did not make it an autograph, and scribal copies of literary texts may not properly be called "documents."

Fragments of two poems are preserved in this text—a portion of a noncanonical psalm in a highly idiosyncratic semicursive handwriting, and the fragment of the hymn of praise to Jonathan (correctly identified by the authors as Alexander Jannaeus) appearing below it in a handwriting that, according to the students, may or may not be identical with the first. There is no signature to indicate authorship, one does not find corrections in the text such as would be expected in bona fide authors' original holographs (the more precise term for a literary autograph), and the fragment, rather than being an individual sheet of papyrus such as we would expect to find in the case of documentary autographs of the period, is a parchment fragment of what was once a scroll,[17] similar to the many others found in the Qumran caves containing scribal copies of literary works.

At the most, the fragment may be characterized as a literary hand-copy *going back* to an autograph that may have been written fifty or even one hundred years before the preserved copy was made. The text may well be characterized as a unique fragment containing a hymn of praise to Alexander Jannaeus—but there is absolutely no evidence that the *copy* we now possess was written anytime during the author's life or that of the king. It could have been written down by the scribe as much as several decades after 78 B.C., when Jannaeus died.

The editors' strength was in *descriptive* palaeography, as we see in their laudable reproduction of all of the text's consonants in tabular alphabetic form, their very careful detailed description of each of the consonants and even their individual variations, and their almost fully correct working out of the preserved textual remnant.[18] Their weakness proved to be in the area of *analytical* palaeography, as seen not only in their treatment of the dating of the text but also in the method of editing: In effect, one author worked out the palaeography and decipherment of the text, another—taking that decipherment as an immutability—offered a literary commentary on the two poem-fragments, and a third offered a historical commentary, taking those other findings as given truths. In this system of shared efforts by a committee, there is virtually no room for analytical palaeography, which requires that a single individual, when working out the meaning of an ancient text, critically balance the various literary, palaeographic, and historical elements that come into play.

The difficulty involved in having a specialist in palaeography produce a transcription of an ancient text while not being also responsible for explicating its literary and historical meaning became clear in two passages of the published version of the hymn to Alexander Jannaeus. The first is the hymn's opening section—in fact an explanatory rubric in prose preceding the hymn itself, not unlike the device used at the beginning of many biblical psalms. (The poem's interpreter, however, made the mistake of considering the introduction part of the poem itself, and on this basis drew the unwarranted conclusion that the poem is not in poetic balance or rhythm.)[19] In the *Jerusalem Post* report, the translation of the Hebrew rubric reads:

> Holy city, for King Yonatan and all the congregation of
> your people Israel who are in the four winds of heaven.

This faithfully reflects the edited Hebrew text, whose interpreter, however, could not satisfactorily explain the indeed baffling connection between the expression "holy city" (i.e., Jerusalem) and the rest of the sentence.[20] The transcriber of the text, working on a purely empirical basis, had not been able to decide whether the middle consonant of the triliteral word signifying "city" was indeed the consonant required for the correct spelling of that word or another, and so published the word with *two* middle consonants, written one above the other, the one giving rise to the word for "city" and the other to a verb which made even less sense in the context.[21]

The tortured treatment of the opening word of this important text was the result of an overly pedantic adherence to the technique of tracing the script. The initial consonant as printed, i.e., the guttural *'ayin* (transcribed usually as '), together with the two following consonants *y* and *r*, do indeed constitute the word for city (*'ir*); but the context of the rubric requires not a "*city* of holiness for Jonathan the King" but a "*song* [in Hebrew, *shir*] of holiness" dedicated to him. The Hebrew consonant representing *sh* (*shin*) is, in this manuscript, formed like the *'ayin*, but has one more stroke on its right, which in the present case was simply effaced in part as the manuscript physically degenerated and assumed its present fragmentary state. The excellent copies given in the article of these two consonants as they appear in the manuscript, when placed next to one another, show how this occurred.[22] On the left side is a sample *'ayin*, and on the right a sample *shin*:

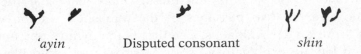

'ayin   Disputed consonant   *shin*

The stroke of the *shin* farthest on its right is the one that, in the instance being discussed, mostly dropped away. In order to draw this conclusion, however, it was clearly not enough to trace the letters as they remained; some slight restoration was needed—that is, of part of a single stroke—but always on the basis of an empirical consideration of the letter forms in conjunction with the meaning of the line as a whole. Palaeography and interpretation fully succeed only in tandem with each other. Palaeography is in effect a subdiscipline of history and text interpretation and not, as a growing number of scholars would want to make it, a field unto itself. By any standard of reasonableness, the rubric of the poem (column B on the parchment leaf) reads:

> A song of holiness unto Jonathan the King and all the community of your people Israel (scattered) to the four winds of heaven. May all be in peace! Over your kingdom may your name be blessed!*

The extant fragments of the poem, which follow the rubric, con-

---

*In the *Times Literary Supplement* of 4 December 1992, G. Vermes proposed that the first two lines of the rubric are *'ir qodesh 'alisat hamelek*, which he translates: "Holy City, Joy of the [divine] King." Vermes stated that he arrived at his reading on the basis of a computer-enhanced photograph of the manuscript. The excellent color photograph of the scroll appearing in *Scrolls from the Dead Sea*, the catalogue of the 1993 American exhibition of

tain many difficulties, since some words are missing from each line. Here as well a blunder marring the transcription has not been corrected by the interpreter, creating a needless difficulty.

In translation these fragmentary lines could read:

> In your love do I . . . .
> By day and unto evening. . . . .
> To be close unto. . . . .
> O visit them blessedly. . . . .
> For a day of war. . . . .
> Unto Jonathan the King. . . . .[23]

---

the scrolls (p. 42), leaves little room, however, for this reading. It is also most difficult to agree with this reading because it would involve several highly forced meanings of the proposed Hebrew words. To match Vermes's English version, the Hebrew would at least have to read *'ir haqodesh, mesos el 'elyon,* or another such combination of words. *'ir qodesh* in the sense of "the Holy City [of Jerusalem]" is anomalous for *'ir haqodesh; 'alisat,* which is supposed to mean "joy of," occurs in ancient Hebrew only as *'alisut;* and *hamelek,* "the king," in the sense of "the King of the Universe," occurs nowhere else in the intertestamental literature extant in the cave scrolls. For these reasons, I do not perceive how Dr. Vermes's reading may be said to hold water.

In *Scrolls from the Dead Sea* (Catalogue of the Library of Congress Exhibition, Washington, D.C., 1993), p. 41, the first crucial line of each column in this poem is given a different order than it has in the Hebrew original or in the transcription supplied by the three editors—this despite the fact that the same three students are credited in the catalogue with the transcription and translation of the poem as it appears there. (The Hebrew transcription on p. 43 is arranged in the same puzzling way.) Their translation in the catalogue of the first four lines of each column of text is as follows:

Column C	Column B
1. Because you love Isr[ael]	1. holy city
2. for King Jonathan	2. in the day and until evening [
3. and all the congregation of your people	3. to approach, to be [
4. Israel	4. Remember them for a blessing [

Printed this way, the text makes no sense whatsoever. The rubrics *Column B* and *Column C* have to be interchanged, as well as the first lines of each column. As it is printed, not only is the meaning of the entire poem obscured, but the fact that *Column B* is a *rubric*—not a part of the poem as such—is lost. Also, the embarrassing unsuitability of the decipherment "holy city" in place of the quite readily legible "a song of holiness" can no longer be perceived. The color photograph of this text appearing in the catalogue quite adequately shows the reading *shir qodesh,* "a song of holiness," at the crucial spot.

Speculation will be endless as to what words belong in the missing spaces and how many lines followed, but, as the explanatory rubric had already indicated, the hymn itself is clearly a song of praise to Alexander Jannaeus, and it is written in elevated poetic style and expresses affection for the king; as such it is indeed an especially important fragment. One strains, therefore, to decipher every word and letter as accurately as possible, but this means doing so only in harmony with the logic of the text as a whole. The opening line requires a verb denoting expression of the feeling of love, and actually all but the last consonant of a verb appears after the expression "In your love." The following verb, however, has been transcribed in the printed edition so as to yield the Hebrew word *etyas[er]*, meaning "I suffer (*or* will suffer) chastisement." An expression, however, such as "In your love I suffer chastisement" makes little poetic sense in this context, and is one that the interpreter, relying entirely on the prior palaeographic decipherment, admits cannot be satisfactorily explained.[24] The last consonant of the enigmatic word is, however, not necessarily an *s* (in Hebrew, *samekh*, s) as the authors posit, but may equally well be an *m* (in Hebrew, *mem*, m) The palaeographic chart supplied by the authors themselves indicates that the *mem* varies considerably from occurrence to occurrence in the text. It cannot be definitively distinguished from the *samekh* except through the contextual analysis of the surrounding words and letters.

Examples of *samekh*   Examples of *mem**

The word is clearly not *etyaser* but *etyamer*, a form of the same verb as is found in the Book of Isaiah connected to the expression "in their glory," and which is construed by the ancient translators to mean "exult" or "boast." "Ye shall eat the riches of the gentiles," the King James version renders the verse in Isaiah (**61**:6), "and in their glory shall ye boast yourselves." The author of the poem praising Alexander Jannaeus straightforwardly wrote the equivalent of "In your love do I exult," and the following line-fragments

*From chart prepared by A. Yardeni and published in *Tarbiz* 60 (1991), pp. 318 ff.

follow logically from this most suitable opening, making a hypothetical poetic reconstruction of the missing words reasonably
possible.

The nature of the scholarship and argumentation at work in the
Tarbiz piece tended to demonstrate a view I expressed in several
forums in the late 1980s: namely, that the Harvard-inspired policy
of co-opting the services of graduate students as editors of hitherto unpublished scrolls—in this way foreclosing the option of open
international competition based on merit—constitutes a practice
unfair not only to the community of scholars specializing in scroll
studies but also to the wider world of letters and to the students
themselves. Taking the present text as a representative example,
the promised "official" editions of the Qumran texts clearly run
the danger of ending up heavily laced with interpretations intended to support the old Qumran-sectarian hypothesis, rather than
simply being editions and translations of the texts. Serious questions arise pertaining to the eventual, overall quality of the work
to be accomplished. There is cause for concern not only in the
area of history, but of text interpretation and palaeography as
well.

Palaeographic skills are not in themselves sufficient for the
decipherment and interpretation of difficult manuscripts, which
rather require an interplay, within a single individual, of various
efforts and skills; whether such talents can satisfactorily be found
parceled out among members of a committee remains problematic. The scholar who best described this interplay was the late
papyrologist of the University of Michigan, H. C. Youtie, who conceived of it as being realizable only in a single individual. The
papyrologist, he wrote,

> has a defensive shield against error-producing accident in his belief
> that the scribes wrote in order to clarify and not obscure. . . . The
> papyrologist who is adapted to his job will also like precision and
> sharp outlines. For reaching these desirable goals, he has at his dis-
> posal three resources which he can and must bring into play simul-
> taneously: experience, logic, and the papyrus. He has acquired his
> experience over the years; he has more or less of it as the years are
> many or few; it comprehends not only what he has learned from his
> own efforts to transcribe and edit papyri, with all that he has
> absorbed on the way of palaeography, language, history, and the
> rest, but also what he has learned from the recorded experience of

his predecessors. What the papyrologist means by logic is in large measure a doctrine of correspondence and coherence, correspondence to the facts and probabilities of ancient life as we know it, coherence of language and meaning through the document; it is a logic which rests on the papyrologist's capacity for imaginative reconstruction of incident, intention, and sentiment—in short of a human situation, as depicted in a stream of words which is often broken; it serves him best when his document is preserved in its entirety, but the more fragmentary the document the more indispensable his logic becomes. The writing on the papyrus is the one stable element in his activity; it controls all his readings as they are suggested by previous experience and by the logic of the document.[25]

The papyrologist's message is one that all manuscript scholars would do well to bear in mind, but we may doubt whether the politics of Qumran studies will soon allow for the consummately apollonian spirit of inquiry Youtie urged to prevail. Without it, on the other hand, the academy will stand diminished, and the larger world of humanistic study eventually will be the loser—reason enough to strenuously resist the process epidemically occurring in "official" circles of scroll scholarship.

During the late 1980s, the spread of the *samizdat* version of the *Acts of Torah* had continued, and in this way an increasing number of scholars were becoming aware of the text's importance. In the summer of 1989, the participants in the second Polish conference on the scrolls agreed that the 1991 meeting should focus on the *Acts*. A typed version was thereafter prepared and distributed in Germany in the 1989–90 academic year by Professor H. Peter Rueger of Tubingen. I received a copy of it in June 1990, during a lecture I had been invited to give there. "Do you then doubt," came the incredulous challenge of one of the students, "that this letter was written by the Teacher of Righteousness?" The text had been studied and discussed during Professor Martin Hengel's seminar that year, but always on the assumption that the one and only Teacher himself had written it: a fable whose pietistic mystique was warmly embraced by some all-too-credulous students of religious history at that center of learning.

At the end of 1990, in consonance with the goal of the coming conference in Poland, and after fruitlessly awaiting the official editors' promised publication of the *Acts of Torah*, the organizer, Z. J. Kapera, distributed a printed version of the *samizdat* text and translation for use by those planning to attend the meeting. A copy of the Polish pamphlet was duly sent to Hershel Shanks of the *Biblical Archaeology Review*, who had attended the second conference as an observer. In the following months Shanks continued to press in the pages of his review for full publication of photographs of the still-unpublished manuscripts. When the two-volume edition of scroll photographs prepared by Robert Eisenman and James Robinson appeared in November 1991, it was found to contain a "Publisher's Foreword" by Shanks. This included photographs of various items documenting Shanks's role in the effort to free the scrolls—as well as a copy of the text of the *Acts of Torah*, without translation, that had earlier been sent out from Cracow. A few remarks regarding the complex question of the propriety of Shanks's quixotic gesture are in order.

On the one hand, his publication of the *Acts of Torah* surprised even the two editors of these volumes, for the *samizdat* version had already been widely circulated, and, as indicated above, another crude edition put out earlier in Germany. With publication, in Eisenman and Robinson's facsimile edition, of actual photographs of the *Acts of Torah* and the prior appearance of preliminary discussions of the text, no impediment any longer prevented scholars from weighing the claims of the two editors and their collaborators: They now had all the necessary resources at their disposal to investigate these manuscript fragments for themselves, and were no longer unable to put out their own independent editions of this text should they so choose.

On the other hand, it is important to note that some months earlier, Kapera had been sent a warning letter (dated 12 March 1991) by General Drori of the Antiquities Authority, urging him to desist from further distribution of the preliminary twelve-page edition and translation of the *Acts of Torah* in his possession. Drori claimed in his letter that Kapera should have applied to the Authority for permission to distribute this text—which, as Drori's persistent policies made clear, would have been denied. The letter indicated that further action would take place if Kapera did not accede to Drori's demand. In light of the obvious imbalance in resources between a governmental agency and a single Polish scholar, Kapera felt he had no choice but to do as requested.

Whatever the wisdom of Shanks's decision—potentially opening, as in fact it later did, a Pandora's box of legal and ethical issues centered on the translation and reconstruction of ancient manuscripts—it may have been this development in Poland that prompted him to print, in a single page of the publisher's foreword, the *Acts of Torah* text. For here, after all, was a notable attempt by an official to suppress direct knowledge of the contents of an ancient manuscript work—precisely that policy which had so fired Shanks with indignation in the past, and whose abolition was, by 1991, being so widely supported in the American press. Let us further recall that those scholars having privileged access to this work had been for years imposing a most peculiar interpretation of its contents upon the public, while refraining from publishing it. The one open effort by an independent scholar to end this mockery of free investigation—made without the backing of any group of power brokers—had been met with official threats of punitive action and, in the end, the suppression of further distribution of the pamphlet.

When the Antiquities Authority had threatened legal action in the wake of the Huntington Library's decision to open scholarly access to the scrolls, the reaction of the American press had resulted in withdrawal of the threat. In the wake of Shanks's action in reprinting the *Acts of Torah*, the Antiquities Authority did not, by contrast, officially associate itself with any legal maneuvering. Rather, a member of the official team of editors—namely, Elisha Qimron— came forward, entering a suit on 14 January 1992 in Jerusalem District Court against Shanks, James Robinson, and Robert Eisenman and claiming damages exceeding $200,000. This sum was described as covering loss of present and future income and academic reputation, as well as personal grief, linked to Qimron's claimed inherent copyright to the transcription of the text. It was his "creation" upon which he had labored an entire decade, so he insisted. In a countersuit entered in Philadelphia District Court, Shanks argued that a scholar could not hold a copyright on an ancient text. During the process of legal discovery, tactical skirmishing, and the trial that followed, the *Acts of Torah* (under the name of *MMT*) received considerable publicity, albeit in a manner obscuring its historical significance. Yet the work would continue to be the focus of international scholarly interest as the debate on the origin of the scrolls intensified.

CHAPTER 10

The Deepening Scrolls Controversy

During the years leading up to the freeing of the Dead Sea Scrolls, the debate on their origin and significance had intensified. By 1992, a number of scholars had begun to question the basic tenets of the traditional belief, reaching out toward more cogent interpretations and an identification of Khirbet Qumran in harmony with the archaeological evidence. This evolution did not occur easily or as a group effort; it began in the workrooms of individual researchers who, as they thought things through, became less satisfied with the standard solutions. The effort to censor new ideas continued, but with lessening effect.

Dissatisfaction with the hypothesis was not, to be sure, a new phenomenon, but had been expressed since the first decade of discovery of the scrolls. We have already seen how, in the late fifties, K. H. Rengstorf in Germany and C. Roth and G. R. Driver in England had proposed their own, in certain respects superior, solutions to the Qumran puzzle. Besides them, and leaving aside the untenable position of those writers who claimed the scrolls to be mediaeval products, there was also Henri Del Medico of France, who in a book published in 1957 had already forcefully exposed some of the fallacious lines of reasoning being pursued by the official team and its supporters.[1] As a substitute, however, Del Medico offered solutions that turned out to be no better than those of the official team. He proposed that the finds constituted a *genizah* (or storeroom) of worn-out and damaged manuscripts, analogous to that kept in the Palestinian synagogue of Fustat (Old Cairo), and not connected with the nearby site. He claimed that the very existence of the Essenes in general was a fiction. Khirbet Qumran, he asserted, had been a military post during the reign of Alexander Jannaeus, but was abandoned during the reign of Herod, and was virtually unoccupied during the time the imagined sect was supposedly living there, except possibly by some

273

insurgents for a brief period of time during the First Revolt; it was mainly used as the site of graveyards adjacent to each other and kept by two separate groups of Jews until the Romans captured it.

Del Medico correctly perceived that an ancient community of observant Jews, especially one regulated by priests (as described in the *Manual of Discipline*), would not have allowed itself to be situated so close to a cemetery; but his insistence that Khirbet Qumran was nothing but a graveyard between the time of Herod and the Roman occupation could hardly invite serious scholarly attention. Likewise, his view that the Essenes were a mere fiction was highly problematic when measured against the ancient descriptions, particularly the very detailed one offered by Josephus. His idea that the hidden scrolls represented a *genizah* (something actually first proposed by Eliezer Sukenik as early as 1948) at first seemed to be supported by his vivid description of the nature of the damage done to them: They had in some cases been badly mangled, and might thus, perhaps, have been stored away after becoming worn out or otherwise losing their usefulness—the very reason given in ancient Jewish sources for the existence of storage chambers for manuscripts. Other writers, however, argued cogently that the damage was due almost entirely to natural conditions prevailing over two millennia. Del Medico, in any event, offered his theory before publication of the *Copper Scroll*—with its references to the hiding of scrolls alongside treasures—and before the discovery of the manuscripts of Masada.

This new evidence, together with Timotheus's description of the "many books" found by eighth-century Jews in a cave near Jericho, did grave damage to Del Medico's argument. Timotheus did not indicate that the books were mangled; and the idea that worn-out or damaged manuscripts would be selected for burial with important caches of treasure or that refugees from Jerusalem would take such writings with them to Masada is strikingly implausible. One of the scrolls found in the third century had even been used as the basis for the sixth column of Origen's *Hexapla* to Psalms. Del Medico's main contribution to the study of Qumran origins remains his proposal—bold for its time in France, at the very height of Dupont-Sommer's immense popularity—that there was no proven organic connection between Khirbet Qumran and the texts discovered in the caves. In addition, Del Medico was the sole French researcher to suggest that members of the Zealot faction may have occupied Qumran during the war with Rome—a view expressed almost simultaneously at Oxford by Cecil Roth.

The opinions of both researchers doubtless made an impression on Rengstorf in Germany—Del Medico's because his views caused a brief storm, particularly in France but also in the rest of Europe, before meeting the ridicule of Dupont-Sommer and the Jerusalem team; and Roth's by virtue of his renown as a historian of the Jews. But while apparently appreciating the temporary break in the Qumranologists' consensus view, Rengstorf perceived that the mass of discovered scrolls had far more the character of a library than a *genizah* of discarded texts. Del Medico's concept of a complete separation between Khirbet Qumran and the cave manuscripts clearly did not appeal to Rengstorf: A connection of some kind could be left intact by assuming that the possessors of the single library he had in mind—that is, the Temple priests—were not only the ones who brought the scrolls to the desert, but also had some kind of habitation of their own at Qumran. Roth had pointed out that the *War Scroll* and some other texts betrayed an apocalyptic militancy not associated with contemporary descriptions of the Essenes, and had traced a line between these texts and the military activities of the Zealots. He concluded that it was in fact they who, at all events during the revolt, had occupied Khirbet Qumran and succumbed there to the Romans.

While Rengstorf disregarded the military nature of the site altogether, Roth's arguments may very well have called his attention to the fact that some texts did indeed reflect militancy and others did not. The texts, in brief, could not be a homogeneous collection belonging to a single sect, but in Rengstorf's view represented a heterogeneous library. The theory he developed was thus remarkably individualistic, based, as I have indicated earlier, primarily on his extraordinary erudition in the field of Hellenistic Judaism and early rabbinic sources. But in the ensuing polemics, his opponents threw it together with the arguments of Del Medico, Roth, and Driver into a single heap, and then dealt with them all together as the improbable meddling of parvenus, regardless of whatever kernels of truth the new ideas might contain.

This treatment, in turn, discouraged the four nonconformist authors from pressing forward with their separate views after the early 1960s. With their fall into silence in the subsequent decades—and with the effort of those in official control of the discoveries to protect the traditional assumptions—the critically valid elements in their work were largely forgotten. There were two reasons why this breach in the consensus turned out to be ephemeral. Partly, the new ideas being proposed were themselves plagued by weaknesses and inconsistencies, with their proponents not fully willing to engage in a protracted *guerre de savants*. Also, much of the accumulating evidence had either appeared only recently or was still under wraps.

This last factor affected the development of my own theory of Jerusalem origin of the scrolls. I did not begin to sense the significance of the Masada manuscript finds until after having read and reread, over a span of many months, Yigael Yadin's explanation of the presence at Masada of a work—the *Songs of the Sabbath Sacrifice*—that was already known from copies found in the Qumran caves. Likewise, the efforts of de Vaux and his colleagues to deny the authenticity of the *Copper Scroll* did not begin to strike me as strange until after I became aware of the oddness of many explanatory placards at the Khirbet Qumran site. Put otherwise: the theory did not emerge from a smooth symmetrical blend of individual concepts, but developed sporadically as I measured the claims of the traditional theory against the growing body of evidence. I offered a tentative explanation of that evidence in 1970 and, a decade later, had both adequately weighed the main factors and, equally crucial, had summoned the will to override forebodings concerning attacks that might follow publication of my findings.

In fact, despite the press coverage,[2] traditional Qumranologists greeted the 1980 publication of my article on the scrolls in the *Proceedings of the American Philosophical Society* with studied silence. No one publicly came to the support of the theory, and no one overtly attacked it. I inferred that their hope was that if the silence was sufficiently persistent over time, the new theory might perhaps fade away of its own accord—a tactic in some ways preferable to direct rejoinder, and rather successfully used by old guard Qumranologists beforehand. A number of other scholars around the world did, however, send encouraging letters, and these helped to sustain a hope, over the next few years, of eventual debate on the subject.

The following year, however, things took a somewhat more intriguing turn. An illustrated version of the article that I had sent to the French journal *Archéologia* at their request was suppressed

by one or more of the journal's advisors—some of them colleagues at the Académie des Inscriptions et Belles Lettres of
Dupont-Sommer (who still maintained his distinguished presence
there). Both the text of the article and the many illustrations
accompanying it were mysteriously lost in Paris during the course
of the extensive posturing that followed, and no explanation
would ever be sent me by the editor of this journal regarding this
most unusual disappearance.

My strategy in response to such tactics was to set aside further
work on the scrolls while completing an expanded French version
of my study of the Jews of Rouen. This appeared early in the summer of 1985. Shortly thereafter, the monthly *L'Histoire* published
a résumé of my 1980 article on the scrolls, for the first time
bringing the basic elements of my argument for their Jerusalem
origin to a wide French audience, and unhesitatingly broaching
the problem of what the journal termed *pan-Essénisme*.[3] I followed with a new article in the *Annales*,[4] directed specifically
at the international community of historical researchers who
are its readers. It would finally break the long silence of the
Qumranologists.

In the weeks following publication of the *Annales* article, word
came from Paris that it had caused a stir at the Sorbonne and in
other academic circles. Students had apparently begun needling
their professors, with the disciples of de Vaux and Dupont-
Sommer naturally remaining true to their roots and entertaining
none of it. Early in 1987, they published the beautifully printed
Pléiade edition of the intertestamental writings, dividing all the
texts at their disposal into two categories: writings of the
Apocrypha and Pseudepigrapha as known in earlier editions of
the Christian Bible, and, by contrast, the writings of the "sect of
Qumran."[5] Since, however, some of the writings of the Apocrypha
and Pseudepigrapha had turned up fragmentarily among the
scrolls, these themselves, in the minds of the French editors,
became Essene writings, even though showing no affinities with
the Essene doctrines as described in classical sources. The
authors, of course, did not call the attention of their readers to the
theory of Jerusalem origin, nor as much as raise the possibility
that the claimed sectarians might have owned other books besides
their own heterodox writings. French readers were thus unwittingly induced to assimilate the Essene theory with no reflection
at all, in the form of an elegantly produced translation that took

on still greater authority by virtue of the editors' use of the expression "La Bible" at the head of the book's title. Lending comfortable support to the project, the prestigious Collège de France continued to offer its popular public lecture course, "The History of the Qumran Sectarian Community," taught by a member of the editorial group responsible for the Pléiade edition of the intertestamental writings.

In the new edition of his translation of the Qumran writings,[6] Geza Vermes undertook a similar treatment of the Qumran problem that same year. His introduction to this work continued to present the existence of a sectarian community at Qumran as a given fact, at the same time avoiding mention of most of the substantive problems with that notion long since brought into the open. Vermes refrained from including a translation of the *Copper Scroll* in his book. He did discuss it in a brief appendix, explaining that "it does not fall within the scope of the present book since it is a non-religious document":[7] an odd explanation, in that Vermes nowhere in his introduction had spoken of an intent to publish only the religious writings found at Qumran, while much of his introduction was in fact given over to historical rather than strictly religious questions. By offering a translation of this text, he would have allowed readers to judge its significance for themselves, but he apparently had no enthusiasm for such a project.

It is true that a few dissenting voices began to make themselves heard in Paris at that time. In the summer of 1987, Pierre Gibert, a Jesuit priest of independent spirit, called attention to my approach to the scrolls in a Parisian Catholic intellectual review, characterizing Dupont-Sommer's thesis, as had *L'Histoire*, in terms of "*pan-Essénisme*," and raising the question of the appropriateness of the Pléiade edition's categories.[8] In December, a review of the Pléiade work in *Le Monde* again raised, if only cautiously, the question of Dupont-Sommer's conception of the scrolls, putting the expression *pan-Essénisme* firmly into the French vocabulary and referring to my diametrically opposite treatment of the scrolls' origins in the *Annales* article.[9]

Paris was, at the same time, also the base for Ernest Marie Laperrousaz—another disciple of Dupont-Sommer, a professor at the Sorbonne who was one of the few surviving members of de Vaux's original archaeological team still active in research, and author, *inter alia*, of a compendious book on the archaeology of Qumran. It was Laperrousaz who, apparently somewhat enraged by the *Annales* article, finally forgot the rule of silence altogether, publishing a heated reply to the *Annales* article in defense of virtually all the main assertions of his predecessors:[10] The best site for Pliny's Essenes was Khirbet Qumran. The *Copper Scroll* was irrelevant to the question of origin of the other texts. The doctrinal contradictions between the various texts were due to the gradual development of Essenism. Josephus spoke of a second group of Essenes who took wives. The Roman conquest of Khirbet Qumran could only have happened in A.D. 68, not later. The Masada manuscript discoveries had no direct significance for the study of scroll origins. But to such claims, all in the nature of a defense of the old theory, Laperrousaz added two interrelated arguments representing a direct effort to contravene the theory of Jerusalem origin. First, since Josephus had reported the Roman discovery of great treasures *in* Jerusalem after its fall, a Jewish hiding of treasures or books in desert places was unlikely. Josephus's description implied that the Jews felt safer within the walls of the capital than anywhere else. Laperrousaz expressed his other argument as follows:

> Among the Scrolls . . . are numerous ones that express vigorous opposition to the groups in power in Jerusalem, i.e., the priests and doctors (of the Law). For what reasons, by virtue of what masochism, would these people in Jerusalem have taken such care to preserve texts of such a kind as they had in their possession?[11]

With some reflection, neither of these arguments could be considered convincing. On the one hand, Josephus expressly states that at the time of the arrival of John of Gischala and the Galilaean refugees at the gates of Jerusalem—i.e., over a year and a half before the siege—the elders of the city fully realized what fate was in store for them. They clearly had to make preparations for the siege, and could hardly have avoided the kinds of measures described in the *Copper Scroll*, even if they could not have hidden the entire wealth of Jerusalem this way. On the other hand, Laperrousaz's insistence that the scrolls would not have been worth hiding, since many of them express opposition to those in power in Jerusalem, revealed an unusually narrow understanding of the range of groups, both religious and social, living in the capital before and during the First Revolt. Perhaps the priests did not choose to hide works opposing their power, collected in their own library; but various *other* groups apparently did so, especially those groups opposing the priests. We must also remember that it was the Zealots who controlled the Temple mount and precincts during the revolt, and must surely ask what kind of books they would have chosen to hide away from the Romans. In any case, a number of scrolls found in the caves showed opposition, not to the priesthood *per se*, but to abuses of its privileges; while other texts showed only admiration for the priestly establishment. In light of the nature of Laperrousaz's arguments, I responded to him by underscoring their resemblance to various past efforts in different fields of research to shield favorite ideas in the process of dying.[12] (The fixation with a theorized all-pervasive Orphism—in Greek religion, a form of the cult of Bacchus or Dionysus having Orpheus as legendary founder—represents one such parallel phenomenon among many.)[13] I also expressed the hope that, "in the light of this discussion and its antecedents, the continuators of the work of Dupont-Sommer and de Vaux might willingly favor the diffusion of new ideas concerning the Scrolls—even if such ideas should oppose their own shared hypotheses in a fundamental way."[14] (The obloquy did not, however, lead to the recovery of the missing photographs from the French archaeological journal.)

In his *Annales* rejoinder, Laperrousaz did not respond to the problem posed by the nature of Khirbet Qumran itself, which had by 1987 become the focus of considerable attention. He addressed this problem two years later, in an article whose title is translatable as "The Qumran Establishment near the Dead Sea: Fortress or Convent?"[15] Here he affirmed that "for some time a hypothesis, itself already old, has been again taken up and propagated with a new dynamism, holding that . . . Qumran . . . was not a religious establishment but only a fort." Now taking refuge in the tactic of selective silence, Laperrousaz did not indicate (e.g., by a footnote or other means), who was responsible for this reprise, thus depriving readers of the opportunity to check his ensuing statements against those I had made in the *Annales* article and elsewhere relevant to the identification of Khirbet Qumran. The same selectivity regrettably invaded the body of his article, where he made no mention of various published descriptions of the evidence attesting to the fierce battle fought at the site during its supposed occupation by Essenes and to the military nature of the tower (see Chapter 1).

Instead, Laperrousaz repeated de Vaux's proposal that a settlement of Essenes at Qumran *interrupted* its use as a fortress before-hand and afterward, and attempted to show this was plausible by recourse to the well-known fact that not only fortresses, but also monasteries of the Byzantine period (i.e., from the fourth century A.D. onward) had watchtowers. Laperrousaz did not, however, show diagrams of these structures, which in terms of their dimensions never approached the massive, fortified tower of Qumran. The "protection of monasteries and even churches"[16] that Laperrousaz adduced is a known trait of such establishments, often made necessary by the fear of marauders; but "protection" of this kind was far more modest than the builders of Khirbet Qumran had in mind for their own site. No known desert monastery of Palestine and the surrounding region had such complex, well-designed facilities for the storage of water as Qumran (a fact not discussed by the author), none gave evidence of intense military activity in the past, and none was built at such a strategic location. What is more, beside the fact that no bona fide evidence showed that monks ever lived at Qumran, there was also no evidence in classical, pre-Byzantine sources that religious orders living in groups or separate communities (i.e., cenobites), to the extent they even existed then, were ever housed in fortresses. From yet a different perspective, no rational passerby could possibly have described the inhabitants of Khirbet Qumran during the days it stood intact as living there, to use Pliny's expression, "with only the palm trees for company."

The grim artificiality of Laperrousaz's explanation—that Qumran was first inhabited by warriors, then by Essenes, and then after A.D. 68 by warriors again—did not, alas, discourage other Qumranologists from opting for explanations along the same lines.[17] The military elements both in the site's architecture and in the archaeologists' findings were nevertheless prominent, and the belief that a sect either related to the Essenes or of the Essenes themselves actually lived there clashed with that clear-cut reality—and thus, in the mentality of the traditional Qumranologists, somehow had to be harmonized with it. However, the contradiction had not been fully expressed before my first several articles on the problem of Qumran origins appeared, and that is why the archaeological question, which had remained dormant for almost three decades, was again taken up only during the 1980s. In this respect, it is remarkable that in Jerusalem another explanation of the nature of Khirbet Qumran, yet more contradictory than the one supported by Laperrousaz and others, was soon to be pressed upon the public.

In the spring of 1987 I had published an article for the general scientific community in which, after a review of the archaeological evidence, I described Khirbet Qumran as a fortress, highlighting the inherent contradiction between this by now widely conceded archaeological conclusion and the basic premise of the Qumran-Essene hypothesis.[18] The article circulated widely in many countries, and afterward curator Broshi of the Shrine of the Book, somewhat more intrepid than his counterparts at the universities, addressed a reply to it.[19] Claiming that I had "documented only quasi problems and imaginary contradictions within the accepted theory," he went on to say, regarding the identification of Khirbet Qumran, that

> Mr. Golb is wrong. Anyone who has been to Qumran or studied photographs of the site can see that it was an undefended civilian complex. . . .

In my published reply I expressed astonishment at Broshi's bald assertion, pointing out that the archaeologists who excavated the site had described its military features in great detail. Broshi nevertheless soon launched a parallel attack, this time in the *Jerusalem Post*. There, again rejecting the identification of the site as a fortress, he stated that

> I am afraid Professor Golb has never seen a fortress or Kumran. Topographically, his building complex lies in a very poor position and most of its walls are flimsy. To think that this was meant to stand against an army is preposterous.[20]

By this time a Canadian newspaper chain had purchased the *Post*, and a retired army colonel, lacking all journalistic background, had become its president and publisher. This was accompanied by a sudden shift in the paper's editorial policy toward Israel's political right—a change that did not necessarily bode well for the *Post*'s policies in the realm of cultural controversy and interpretation. Nevertheless, I responded to Broshi's remarks by pointing out, in a letter mailed to the *Post* on 6 December, that they were "untrue in every particular [and] . . . not helpful to the public in their effort to grasp the fundamental issues. . . ." Reviewing the history of archaeological interpretation of the site, I urged that, if there were archaeologists or others who believed that Khirbet Qumran was, instead, a civilian site inhabited by pious sectarians who spent their time copying manuscripts there, they should defend their position by cogent written analysis or at least be willing to convene a conference in which the entire matter can be explored in depth.

When the *Post* failed to publish this response, I wrote again (26 December 1989), pointing out that Broshi in his letter had made several unfounded allegations, including the one that I had "never seen a fortress or Kumran." The *Post* again declined to publish my demurrer, thus suppressing from its pages, among other things, my call for a conference on the question of the site's nature.

Professor Jonas Greenfield, however, had sometime earlier agreed to take up with his colleagues the organization of a conference on the identification of the site. Taking time away from his responsibilities as editor of the *Israel Exploration Journal*, he now informed me (5 November 1989) that he had "begun getting the ball rolling" for a daylong conference on the archaeology of Qumran, perhaps to take place—as I had proposed to him—in Jerusalem around the time of the International Congress of Archaeology, in 1990. But when I wrote to Greenfield again to remind him of his earlier assurances, he eventually responded on 3 April 1990:

> I am very sorry that I cannot be a bearer of good tidings. . . . By the time that I returned from the States the program of the Archaeological Congress . . . had been set; those interested in reading papers had been in communication with the Congress for quite some time, and the various sections were full. The pre-congress session on the scrolls will be devoted to a report on publications, *with the audience limited*, and it will be quite technical. I have not been able to interest any other party in organizing a session dealing with the site of Qumran, and its problems. The Qumran group at the Institute for Advanced Studies [of the Hebrew University] is text-oriented and involved very much in work on unpublished material. (My italics.)

Thus, closed doors were still the rule for discussion of the Qumran texts as late as 1990. Meanwhile the *Post* continued to feature curator Broshi in its scrolls coverage, together with his view that the site was of a civilian nature. To this view he soon added the claim, first expressed by de Vaux and his colleagues, that it was something more—"the oldest known monastery," as he would later phrase it, "in the western world."[21] In a subsequent effort to refute my interpretation of Qumran origins, another traditional Qumranologist, J. A. Fitzmyer, would assert on the contrary that "such Christian terminology as 'monastery' and 'monks' should never have been applied in the first place to a Jewish site or the pre-Christian Jews who gathered there."[22]

Thus, in the attempt to eliminate opposition and bolster the fiction of a virtuous sect of Torah-expounding Essenes dwelling on the Qumran plateau, the site had become, in the hands of various parties, either a monastery or not a monastery, a sectarian fortress or not a sectarian fortress, and—to heed still other voices—either the home of Pliny's Essenes or else not the home of Pliny's Essenes but that of another, otherwise unknown, sect. No genuine consensus about the identification of Khirbet Qumran existed any longer by the late eighties. Each of the mutually contradictory positions was being pressed for the obvious purpose of defending the old theory—but their combined effect was to highlight the difficulty in which it found itself.* The various conflicting claims and the fact that the excavation of the site had never actually been completed rendered the resumption of digs there a matter of pressing necessity, but as late as April 1993 the curator of the Shrine of the Book would announce that the Antiquities Authority contemplated no impending return to the site for further excavation.[23]

Late in 1988, Philip Davies of Sheffield University added his voice to my own in questioning the Qumranologists' approach to the Khirbet Qumran site.[24] Davies frankly attributed the characterization of the site as a monastery to the fact that "de Vaux and Milik, as well as many other early commentators on Qumran, were Catholic priests." He emphasized that "the excavated structures were interpreted" with the "idea [of a monastery] in mind," and that the "well-fortified tower, inaccessible from ground level, and the evidence of military attack were downplayed."[25] Conclusions about the nature of the site, said Davies, had been improperly drawn by reliance on statements in the manuscripts found in the caves, and vice versa. This was due to the fact that at

---

*See Th. S. Kuhn, *The Structure of Scientific Revolutions* (Chicago, 2d ed., 1970), p. 71, to the effect that "proliferation of versions of a theory is a very usual symptom of crisis."

the heart of biblical archaeology lay "the goal of integrating literary and non-literary evidence"; it sought "to illuminate the biblical text through archaeology, [but] in the case of Qumran the
literature [was] . . . not the Bible but the scrolls found in the
caves. Once the ruins had come to be regarded as the place of origin of all the scrolls, integrating the results of the digging and the
contents of the scrolls became an almost inevitable temptation."[26]
The zeal of the archaeologists had, in this way, led them to push
for an impossibly early date of foundation of the settlement, so as
to harmonize that date with the period of events suggested in the
Habakkuk Commentary.

Pointing to the "new kind of chronology in the long term" that
the *Annales* school of historiography had been instrumental in
encouraging, Davies suggested that there were ways of pursuing
Qumran studies that did "not require exact chronology" or the
close, literal integration of archaeological and written data.[27]
Davies's paper, it may be remarked, had been solicited for publication by the editor of the *Biblical Archaeology Review*; however,
upon observing its criticisms of archaeological method employed
at Qumran, he refused to publish it on the grounds that it was too
controversial. This left the way open for its eventual appearance
in the *Biblical Archaeologist*. Ever ready to promote the romantic
myth of archaeological infallibility, the editor of the former
review, himself professionally trained as an attorney, then began
his own effort to cast doubt upon the identification of Khirbet
Qumran as a fortress.[28] Ironically, in running his increasingly
famous editorial campaign to free the scrolls, he had emerged, in
the eyes of the press and public, as a legitimate arbiter of judgment concerning the true and false of Qumranology.

In any event, more fissures had developed in the walls guarding
the Qumran-sectarian hypothesis by 1988. Six years earlier,
Maurice Baillet had published texts from Cave 4 that, sporadically, had come to be assigned to him.[29] These texts included not only
some prose fragments having affinities with the known apocryphal writings, and bits of a few versions of the *War Scroll*, but
also, most importantly, fifteen liturgical fragments. As they were
analyzed in ensuing years, it became apparent that the fragments
contained none of the characteristic vocabulary or ideas of the
Yahad texts or of any other heterodox trend observable in the previously published manuscripts.

Already in 1975, Moshe Weinfeld of the Hebrew University had argued compellingly that some of the religious poetry in the scrolls and in Ben Sira (Ecclesiasticus) was interrelated with certain liturgical pieces of the rabbinical tradition.[30] Quite some time before this, the five so-called noncanonical psalms published by J. A. Sanders had become the subject of a debate on the same topic, Sanders arguing that they showed no affinities with the ideas of the "sect of Qumran," M. Delcor and M. Philonenko of Paris—ever loyal to the teachings of their master Dupont-Sommer—that they reflected precisely those ideas.[31] The liturgical fragments published by Baillet in effect were a powerful reminder that the texts of the Qumran caves were anything but homogeneous. And this reminder, as we shall see below, was reinforced by publication in 1988 of fragments of the so-called *Psalms of Joshua*, whose editor, deeply trusting in the truth of the Qumran-Essene theory, nevertheless acknowledged the likelihood that the work came from elsewhere.

In the *American Scholar* of spring 1989, I considered new aspects of the controversy, offering a critique of both the evolution and stagnation in research and thinking in the period since 1980.[32] One of the main points I stressed was that, with every new piece of relevant information being uncovered, the old hypothesis was becoming increasingly unbelievable. A traditional Qumranologist, John Trever, thereupon published a reply, which I read with growing incredulity.[33]

An opening assertion that the basic idea I had presented ". . . was probably considered by most early scholars, but abandoned" was accompanied by the acknowledgment that "a few" of the manuscripts found at Masada may have come from Jerusalem—the first time I had heard such an admission from a traditional Qumranologist. Trever then hastily obscured its significance, however, by the utterly unfounded suggestion that when Jerusalem fell, the Essenes, in contrast to other Jews, had fled with Christians to the Roman cities of the Decapolis, in Transjordania. Trever also proposed that it was not Eliezer Sukenik who formulated the idea that the scrolls originated with the Essenes, but rather "Ibrahim Sowmy who started that idea among the Syrians." The drift of his arguments, unsubstantiated by any proof, was clear: The Essenes preferred the company of Christians over that of their fellow Jews, the Essene theory originated with a figure in East Jerusalem—and the Jerusalem theory also actually originated in the same circles, only to be discarded by them.

In the course of reiterating some of the stock platitudes of Qumranology, Trever hazarded fresh claims that were truly baffling: that three scrolls found in a single jar in the back of Cave 1 dated from "ca. 100, 75, and 25 B.C.E."; that each of these scrolls showed signs of "being a special scroll"; and that each pointed "to the founder of a special kind of community of Jews." This schema of three indeterminately "special" scrolls dated in a neat forward progression—each describing, according to Trever, the founder of a "special" religious community, and all found in a single jar within the very first Qumran cave discovered—appeared to be the outcome not of sober scholarly research, but of highly arbitrary speculation, tinged by the metaphysical. It constituted a representative example of the extremes to which traditional Qumran scholarship had been driven by the late 1980s in the effort to defend its dogmas.

Trever offered a yet more lurid example of these extremes by claiming to know exactly how certain damaged manuscript fragments found in Cave 1 were actually mutilated. He explained that the condition of this matted mass of fragments allowed him to draw only one conclusion: that they were being used at Qumran itself when it was attacked. "The evidence," he proposed, "was quite clear that three manuscripts had been torn and then trampled underfoot," the second Isaiah Scroll showing "clear signs of severe abuse, for it looked like it had been twisted with the intention of damaging it." This damage, Trever insisted, was caused by Romans at Qumran before the texts were hidden—all these claims constituting (as the reader was informed) one of the most serious arguments against the theory of Jerusalem origin.

Yet Trever had never published photographs showing either foot or hand imprints on the manuscripts, or evidence that it was at Qumran that they were actually used or damaged. Unless perhaps by laboratory procedures unique in the annals of science, one could not possibly have divined from their condition whether they were torn by beasts or men, and, if by the latter, whether by Jews, Romans, or others. Josephus describes at length the internecine strife among Jewish factions in Jerusalem in the months before the Roman siege, and the severe damage it caused to the Jerusalem archives and other buildings in the city.[34] If we choose to assume that the damage to these manuscripts was man-made, the cause is far more likely to have been this civil warfare. Trever's explanation, by contrast, required the reader to join him in believing that the Romans who vanquished Qumran damaged these particular scrolls, and then one or more defeated Essenes stealthily returned to the settlement while the Romans were there, discovered these damaged scrolls, spirited them out of the site along with jars, and successfully hid them to the north in a cave that was by this time well within the territory held by their ene-mies. All of this more nearly resembled a movie scenario than a genuine historical idea. Unflinchingly, Trever also claimed that the *Copper Scroll* "could have been deposited" in Cave 3 after Qumran's inhabitants had fled, thus resurrecting an argument dis-credited by recent investigations (see below, pages 321–322).

Having thus offered this contribution to intertestamental histo-ry, Trever then concluded his response with a comparison implic-itly drawing me into a circle of those who have "harassed the world of biblical scholarship."[35] Unfortunately, as we have by now observed, an appeal to such scholarship is not always appropriate in the context of Qumran studies. Several scholars of the Bible and biblical archaeologists *were* the first to study the scrolls; this does not necessarily mean, however, that they were the most qual-ified such scholars to engage in the work, and—as the long publi-cation delays and other developments have shown—it is in fact questionable whether biblical scholars should have been so domi-nantly put in charge of the edition of the nonbiblical scrolls to begin with. What this in effect accomplished was to give a clique, basically sharing the same values and goals, the unchallenged opportunity to promulgate ideas that, in the long run, few schol-ars trained primarily in history and philology could find reason-able. What hovered behind Trever's words was obvious unhappiness that those ideas were now being challenged. In feeling thus "harassed," he signalled nothing more than that he had not clear-ly thought through the problems inherent in his own conception of the meaning of the scrolls.

While Trever was occupying himself with his response at Claremont, two Qumranologists at the University of Groningen in the Netherlands, Professor A. S. van der Woude and Dr. F. Garcia Martinez, were planning what they apparently hoped would be a decisive rejoinder. I had met Garcia Martinez at the first Cracow conference in 1987. He had had no previous knowledge of the theory of Jerusalem origin, but we had discussed our mutually opposing views on the scrolls' origins in a cordial and open fashion. He had subsequently agreed to my coming to Groningen to discuss my views on the topic with his several students. The eventual course of action that he and his senior colleague pursued in handling the theory of Jerusalem origin, entirely out of keeping with the tenor of our earlier collegial discussions, forms one of the most telling episodes in the history of the struggle over the meaning of the scrolls.

As early as 1957, in a work on the messianic expectations of the "community of Qumran," van der Woude, eventually to become a member of the Royal Dutch Academy, had declared that this claimed group, the "exiles of the Judaean Wilderness," was either identical with or "near to Essenism," and that this view "was hardly any longer debated";[36] Garcia Martinez had subsequently expressed similar ideas. Later on they arrived jointly at a slightly altered form of the traditional theory, holding that the "sect of Qumran" was not a group of Essenes *per se*, but an offshoot of Essenism that, after breaking away from the main movement, settled at Qumran. *All* the scrolls, they claimed, were "part of a whole and form a unity that we can describe as a religious library . . . that reflects the interest of the group of Qumran. . . ."[37] The authors emphasized the harmonizing and synthetic nature of their theory.*

The so-called Groningen hypothesis was eventually put forward in two papers,[38] in the second of which the authors devoted approximately one half of their study to an attempted refutation of my views on Qumran origins. Trying to characterize Khirbet Qumran as a military site only in the periods before and after its supposed sectarian habitation, they claimed that the site's tower was not important to its inhabitants before its Roman capture;[39] but such a suggestion, as we have seen, clashes directly with the

---

*See the statement of the authors in *Revue de Qumran* **14**, no. 56 (April 1990), pp. 536–537, that their theory was "the combination in an integrated whole of the insights of A. S. van der Woude as to the application to more than one single Hasmonean ruler of the designation 'Wicked Priest' in the Habakkuk *pesher* . . . and the proposal of F. Garcia Martinez clearly to distinguish between the origins of the Qumran group and the origins of the parent group, the Essene movement, and to trace back to the Apocalyptic Tradition of the third century B.C. the ideological roots of the Essenes."

archaeological evidence as revealed by de Vaux and his colleagues. The Groningen scholars contended that the nearby cemetery could be only that of a sect[40]—but this was a mere gratuitous
assertion, not founded on any body of evidence, and as we have
observed, was contradicted by the closeness of the cemetery to the
site of habitation. Their interpretation of the absence of manuscripts at Khirbet Qumran itself—which to them, signaled that the
Romans merely had cleared it of all debris—neglected both (a)
that the site's conquerors cleaned only some of the areas, and (b)
that although the great amount of debris in the claimed "scriptorium" was *not* removed by the Romans, that area yielded no manuscript fragments whatever.

Pondering my criticisms, van der Woude and Garcia Martinez
similarly suggested that their presumed Qumran-sectarians did
have archives as well as a library, but that the archives were *totally lost*—this despite the fact that abundant *literary* manuscripts
were found in the caves. "Nobody can fathom the reasons," they
wrote, "why the men of Qumran decided to proceed in the way
they did and hid in different places their archives and their
library. . . ."[41]

Thus the two authors *imagined* an archive as having existed at
Qumran, to be subsequently hidden away; but no such act of
imagination could reasonably pass as an answer to the basic
objection I had raised to the traditional theory—that it was created without bona fide documentary sources, and that the absence
of sectarian documentary records put the existence of an Essene-
like "motherhouse" at Qumran into grave doubt. Insisting that the
hypothesized sect once had such records and that they then
entirely disappeared as if in a trace of smoke was tantamount to
offering no argument at all.

Carefully evading a discussion of what on-site evidence might
reasonably prove that Khirbet Qumran was the remains of a sectarian motherhouse, the two authors proceeded to remark that if I
demanded documents amidst sectarian literary texts, I must
observe the same rule for books of Jerusalem libraries. Since I
actually had often underscored the presence of the documentary
Copper Scroll among the literary scrolls of the caves, they appended the comment that this was a most "mysterious" document[42]—
one which must have belonged to the "sect of Qumran." For
according to the Groningen theory, all the scrolls in the caves had
to come from "the sect." The theory thus determined the nature of

the texts, and not vice versa. If the *Copper Scroll*, however, with its catalogue of great treasures, could indeed be made to belong to the claimed sect, then both "sect" and Groningen hypothesis emerged as far more enigmatic entities than the *Copper Scroll* could ever be. Here as elsewhere, the effort of Garcia Martinez and van der Woude was clearly to confute my arguments not because of genuine contradictory evidence, but simply so that their own theory might seem cogent.

The basic problem, however, was the two Groningen scholars' own vision of Qumran origins. They had apparently developed it in an attempt to modify their earlier conceptions, introducing new proposals along the way. Thus, one should "make a clear *distinction* between the origins of the Essene movement and those of the Qumran group," the latter having resulted from a split "within the Essene movement" (italics mine). This splinter group was the one that was supposedly "loyal to the Teacher of Righteousness" and which was "finally to establish itself at Qumran." The break "became complete" during the reign of John Hyrcanus, who "persecuted the Teacher of Righteousness in his desert retreat."[43]

On what grounds the authors felt free to assert that their proposed splinter group was the very group of Jews that settled at Khirbet Qumran is mystifying. As we have observed, the *Pesher Habakkuk* states only that the Wicked Priest pursued the Teacher of Righteousness to "the house of his exile," but there is no indication that this was at a communal or sectarian settlement in the Judaean Wilderness, rather than, let us say, Damascus or elsewhere. Wherever his house was, it surely could not have been at Khirbet Qumran, given the authors' own contention that—contrary to basic biblical laws of purity—the group living there was a sect possessing a cemetery located virtually adjacent to its site of habitation. Since Khirbet Qumran was the one fortress guarding the sea at the northwestern sector of the Dead Sea region and was closer to Machaerus than any of the region's other military sites, it is hardly likely on this basis alone that it was at the same time the home of a small and exotic sect.

Bent on elaborating their hypothesis, however, the Groningen team contended that their splinter group had its own special sectarian library—that is, all the scrolls whose remnants were found in the caves; they excluded the possibility that any of these were nonsectarian writings, or writings of other sects, because of the "exclusive character of the community and the repeated prohibition of contacts with non-members."[44] But with the striking variety of practices and beliefs manifest among the scrolls, the fact that certain individual texts expressed varieties of exclusivism merely showed them to be part of something much bigger, not the other way around. Even from such a unique text as the *Acts of Torah*, the only conclusion that our two scholars could draw was that Essenism followed "halakhic positions that now can best be described as Sadducaean."[45] They then added an additional proposition to the ones thus hazarded: that the Wicked Priest mentioned in the *Habakkuk Commentary* should be considered "a generic [priest] referring to different Hasmonaean High Priests in chronological order."[46] Judas Maccabaeus, Jonathan, Simon, John Hyrcanus, and Alexander Jannaeus, they explained, were all designated as "the Wicked Priest" by the claimed "sect of Qumran"[47]—even though there is not a single passage in the scrolls that uses this term in the plural, or that makes multiple connections of the sort the authors posit.

The undocumented combination of these various assertions serves as its own comment on the "Groningen hypothesis": The sect was Essenic yet not Essene, while laws of these quasi-Essenes were identical with Sadducaean ones; the "Wicked Priest" was many priests; the Hasmonaeans ceded a fortress to the very group that, according to the hypothesis, opposed them fiercely; exclusionist sects would not consult, and thus refused contact with, books containing the ideas of their opponents. Again: The *Copper Scroll* was an enigmatic writing not requiring consideration for the hypothesis, while the ancient notices of Hebrew manuscript discoveries near Jericho could be dismissed as irrelevant; archives of the "sect of Qumran" once existed but had simply never been found. The authors' disregard of the problem of the site's close proximity to the cemetery, and of the evidence of over five hundred scroll copyists, was a self-inflicted coup de grâce to their hypothesis.

The authors' insistence on the reality of "Essene works preserved at Qumran" and "Essene documents incorporated in later Qumran works"[48] was a mere variation of the Essenic fantasy elaborated earlier by Dupont-Sommer, and suggested that the real intent of their argument was a defense of van der Woude's original explanation of the origin of the scrolls. Their forced reasoning reflected no more than the need to sustain a deeply flawed argument. In this light, the consecration of half of their joint discus-

sion to an attempted refutation of the theory of Jerusalem origin
was a telling gesture.

All this came about in the wake of the authors' earlier failure to
notify me of their impending effort to refute the theory of
Jerusalem origin at the Groningen Congress on the scrolls they
had organized (20–23 August 1989). My proposal to debate the
fundamental issues with them at their conference, within the
same time frame they had allotted themselves, was made without
my knowing how they intended to use the occasion, and the proposal went altogether unanswered.[49] I would have been more than
willing to respond to their "refutation" in person, had I known it
was intended. The debate would undoubtedly have been an interesting one, and, what is of greater importance, readers of the
Revue de Qumran, edited by Garcia Martinez himself, in which the
conference proceedings were subsequently published, would have
had the benefit of studying not only the assertions of the two
authors but also my reply. Choosing to act as they did, however,
Garcia Martinez and van der Woude opted—most uncharacteristi-
cally for members of a Dutch university—to disregard the principles of free inquiry and open debate, merely for the goal of what
they hoped would be a convincing presentation of their views.

Soon after the Groningen scholars' piece appeared, Professor
Talmon of the Hebrew University took up the particular question
of the Masada texts. Talmon had been charged with the task of
editing those Masada fragments not earlier published by Yigael
Yadin, and made it his responsibility first of all to consider a fragment of approximately eight broken lines, described as coming
from a "pseudepigraphic scroll [related] to the Book of Joshua."[50]
Thanking the Fund for the Perpetuation of the Memory of Yigael
Yadin for permission to publish the fragment, Talmon explained
that it was discovered "in a room near the 'synagogue' in which
was found a concentration of written remnants, among them a
fragment which one must certainly relate to the Songs of the
Sabbath Sacrifice composition from among the Qumran finds—
without question a notable creation of an author who was one of
the members of the Yahad community."[51]

Professor Talmon is one of many Qumranologists who today
refrain from calling the supposed "sect of Qumran" the Essenes,
preferring the term Yahad, i.e., "Unity-group," after the designation appearing in the Manual of Discipline and elsewhere in the
scrolls. There can be little doubt that such texts were composed by

individuals belonging to one or more Unity-groups, but, to be convincing, the claim that the term was appropriated and used only by a single sect would require considerably more evidence than has so far been offered. It may well be that in first century B.C. Palestinian Jewish society, with its manifold parties, sects, and attendant political situations, the call for "oneness with the Lord" was taken up by more than a single sect. However, even on the assumption that all of the Qumran texts utilizing the word *yahad* stemmed from only one of them, it is a fact, as we have seen, that they still constitute a small fraction of the numerous texts found in the caves: approximately twenty out of the more than six hundred nonbiblical scrolls, plus some duplicates. Without arguments based on good internal evidence, it makes little sense to associate the hundreds of texts not bearing the *yahad* term with this proposed single group, simply because they were all found together in the Qumran caves. And as it happens, there is no mention of the *Yahad* in the *Songs of the Sabbath Sacrifice*, nor any other terminology leading logically to the conclusion that the work was written by an Essene, or a member of the *Yahad* group or groups. We will see that this would eventually be acknowledged, in a reversal of her earlier belief, by Professor Carol Newsom of Emory University, the editor of the text. But Talmon dealt with this problem simply by omitting any reference to her *volte-face*, which appeared in print well over a year before his own article.

Instead, building on the fact that the Joshua pseudepigraph was found in a room not far from the *Sabbath Sacrifice* locus, he proceeded to a description of the linguistic peculiarities of the Joshua text. He found that the spelling of two common words in the Masada text "reminds one of an outstanding scribal custom of the Qumran community."[52] He concluded that "just as other items discovered at Masada, particularly the fragment of *Songs of the Sabbath Sacrifice* and a fragment hypothesized to derive from a scroll of the Book of Jubilees, it is possible that the item under discussion as well testifies to the presence of the people of the *Yahad* of Qumran in the fortress of Masada on the eve of its fall." This conclusion was then repeated several times in the article, as a "possibility," "surmise," or "conjecture."

There was, however, no warrant for the conjecture. The Joshua pseudepigraph contains no perceptible idea characteristic of those found in the texts that, to Professor Talmon and others, express the ideas of the *Yahad*. Its several legible lines merely describe, in the style of the Book of Joshua, the Lord's trustworthiness in fighting on behalf of the Israelites up to the time of their arrival in the Promised Land, and in multiplying their numbers.*

The two spelling variants in this small fragment are among a great many occurring in the scrolls; they tell us nothing about sectarian ideas or affiliations. It is true that another Qumranologist, Emanuel Tov, had by 1986 already attempted to distinguish between what he calls "Qumran" and "non-Qumran" orthography.[53] The manuscripts containing the unusual "Qumran" spellings were, according to him, written by sectarians at Qumran, while the others—"many scrolls" according to his own assertion—were "brought from the outside."[54] Yet Professor Tov's system breaks down upon the slightest analysis: The scrolls, according to the very data he provided, have no consistent spelling patterns divisible into two categories. Instead, virtually each scroll exhibits its own pattern in varying degrees of "aberration" from the spelling that characterized what became the normative spelling forms of the Hebrew Bible. All that the variant spellings show, and can show, is that, as in other literate societies before the age of dictionaries and learned academies, no full standardization of spelling had taken place in Palestine by the first century A.D. It was, quite naturally, the books not deemed to have a sacred character that as a rule showed the greatest spelling permutations.

Tov's explanation had clearly been formulated to save the main kernel of the old hypothesis from extinction: If not all the scrolls could have been written at Qumran—as he acknowledged—then at least many of them, at all events those having the peculiar spellings and the more exotic ideas, could be claimed to have been written there, by the "sect of Qumran." Tov was in effect attempting a scholarly compromise between the constantly emerging contradictory evidence and the old view of Qumran origins. By 1993 he was suggesting that "the majority" of the scrolls were brought to Qumran from elsewhere.[55]

---

*The extant words may be translated approximately as follows: [. . .tha]t is beyond the Jor[dan] . . . [caused] them to fall befo[re. . .] day. . . and they were frightened . . . unto the Name of the Most High for they saw . . . fought for his people against their enemies . . . they did not . . . before them, for the Lord was with them; he blessed them and . . . that He had spoken to them came to pass unto them; not a thing . . . to the ground, . . . He multiplied unto them very much. The Lord . . .

In 1988 Carol Newsom of Emery University gave her support to Tov's idea with the publication of several Cave 4 fragments of a work conventionally (if inaccurately) called *The Psalms of Joshua*.[56] She offered "several reasons for thinking that the work was not composed by the Qumran community,"[57] suggesting the likelihood that it "was a text of somewhat earlier composition known and used in a broader stream of Second Temple Judaism." As more new texts from Cave 4 became known, the persistent problem challenging the traditional hypothesis raised its head again; and two years later, Professor Newsom expanded upon her earlier idea. "An appreciation of the diversity of the texts," she stated, "has led to a growing concern [on the part of Qumran scholars] to distinguish sectarian from nonsectarian texts."[58] It is here she acknowledged the lack of evidence for her own earlier claim that the *Songs of the Sabbath Sacrifice* was a sectarian text. Let us also note that she nonetheless accompanied this with the insistence that good reasons remained "for assuming that the documents . . . from the . . . caves . . . are indeed the remains of the library of the sect described in the Serekh ha-Yahad [= *Manual of Discipline*]."[59] This was, of course, another way of suggesting that the original Qumran-Essene formulation needed considerable modification: i.e., perhaps many of the scrolls were not originally written by members of a single sect, but they eventually all came to belong to a particular one, and it could still be held as an "assumption" that the sect that owned them was the very one whose ideas were described in the *Manual of Discipline*.

The grave weakness in Newsom's chain of assertions is that it rests upon no evidence, external or internal. There is no reference in the *Manual of Discipline* to the spiritual importance of possessing large libraries. The essential characteristic of the nonapocalyptic portions of this work is its emphasis on the *midrash*, or study of the deeper sense, of the Torah in group sessions one out of every three nights of the year under the guidance of Torah expounders (*Manual of Discipline*, column 6). Any ancient organized group among the Jews, indeed any individual of great wealth or zeal for knowledge, could have possessed libraries including part or even most of the works found at Qumran.

Newsom claimed that a sure sign certain scrolls belonged to the "Yahad of Qumran" was their being found in the caves in multiple copies. Yet only *some* of the works found in the caves in multiple copies have anything of a heterodox nature in them, and only a *part* of these can be linked up by their wording with the *Yahad* group. Other texts found in multiple copies showed no sectarianism at all, a fact that Newsom herself must have recognized insofar as she included them in a list that she published, naming all of the scrolls found in multiple copies.[60] The significance of the discovery of several fragmentary copies of various works in the caves is clearly not that they gave a sectarian color to themselves or the other works found there (which is what Dr. Newsom contended in her article). It is rather that they pointed to the relative popularity of certain works in segments of early first-century Palestinian society. Some of the works preserved in multiple copies, such as the calendars, biblical commentaries, *Manual of Discipline*, *Songs of the Sabbath Sacrifice*, the *Acts of Torah*, and others, may in addition have come from workshops of scribes either attached or unattached to libraries, whose contents were carried to the caves at the same time the scrolls of the libraries were.

There is nothing, at all events, in the existence of multiple copies of certain works to sustain the thesis that the various scrolls stored away all belonged to a single library in the hands of those who believed in the doctrines of the *Manual of Discipline*: We have seen, for example, that the *Acts of Torah*—found in six copies—reflects a sectarian mentality different in essence from that reflected in the *Manual*. Newsom's was only another way of defending the major element in the original hypothesis, which she did, in essence, by attempting to show that her particular construction of the evidence was not completely unbelievable. Like Tov's, her proposal of two scroll categories could only lead to further questioning of the original theory, despite the fact that both these disciples of the Harvard Qumranologists took care to fill their discussions with innumerable gratuitous references to the claimed scrolls produced "at Qumran" and the imagined special existence led there.

Now all of this was apparently sensed by Talmon, who attempted to combat its consequences, most surprisingly, by suggesting that even so innocuous a fragment as the Joshua pseudepigraph he had identified was brought to Masada from Qumran by members of the so-called *Yahad* group. This was, of course, a way of defending Yigael Yadin's own earlier explanation of the presence of so-called Qumran-like scroll fragments at Masada—i.e., that they were there because Essenes had carried them to the site after fleeing the Roman onslaught at Qumran. Talmon made no men-

tion, of course, of my criticism of Yadin's explanation, nor of my
view that the Masada texts must have derived from Jerusalem.
Nor did he mention my criticism of Newsom's original endorsement of Yadin's explanation, or the fact that since the criticism's
appearance, she had changed her mind: by acknowledging, let us
remember, that Yadin's idea had "something of the flavor of epicycles introduced to save the ptolemaic cosmology from erosion by
apparently contradictory observations"—stating instead that "the
presence of the Sabbath Songs at Masada requires one to reckon
with the possibility that the text was known and used in circles
quite distinct from the Qumran community."*

Newsom's new suggestion, given the fact that she was a student
of both Cross and Strugnell, was not without interest, especially
following Tov's suggestion of 1986 that many scrolls had been
brought to Qumran "from the outside." A new trend in thinking,
echoed as well by other Qumranologists, had obviously set in, and
Professor Talmon, still deeply committed to an older interpretation of the manuscripts' origins, apparently felt obliged to combat
it at all costs. Thus he developed explanations that, while consonant with Yadin's view of the origin of the Masada fragments, contained nothing that could even remotely be called cogent proof in
support of that view.

Talmon turned finally to the so-called *Psalms of Joshua* of Cave 4,
earlier consigned by Strugnell to Newsom, who was now convinced that there were several reasons to believe the work was not
composed by the "Qumran community." Foremost among those
reasons had been the fact that the Hebrew designations for the
Lord appearing in the fragments were not the same as those
favored by writers of certain other scrolls who Newsom believes
were indeed members of the claimed sectarian community of
Qumran. An additional reason: The idiom of the Joshua fragments
was in general very unlike that favored by the same imagined
group. Disregarding Newsom's arguments, Talmon urged upon his
readers the proposition that, since the Masada pseudepigraph and

---

*"Sectually Explicit Literature," p. 182. It is puzzling that Dr. Newsom
made her acknowledgment without reference to my criticism appearing in
the *American Scholar*. This is particularly so since—contrary to her reticence
regarding the theory of Jerusalem origin of the scrolls in her earlier endorsement of a sectarian identification for the *Songs*—she here sought to refute
the theory before acknowledging the difficulty of her own previous explanation of the Masada discovery.

the Qumran text were both imaginative expansions of the book of Joshua, and since one of these had been found at Qumran, it was reasonable to assume that the other *derived from the same place*. He then justified this assumption in the following way: "[The *Yahad* community] perceived themselves as standing in the same place and conditions as had the Israelites in the days of Joshua. But whereas those generations had conquered the land from the nations of Canaan among whom they dwelt, the sons of the *Yahad* were destined to conquer it from their [own] enemies, the Wicked Priest and his cohorts, in a war whose description occurs in the *War of the Sons of Light against the Sons of Darkness*."[61] Yet there is not a line of the *Manual of Discipline* or any of the other texts mentioning the *Yahad* in which the Book of Joshua is either quoted or even distantly referred to.

It need hardly be emphasized that Talmon's forced associative reasoning is far from being tantamount to a disciplined analysis of texts. There is no feature whatever of the pseudo-Joshua texts— not the idiom, nor the particular terminology, nor the ideas—that could warrant the objective association of these fragments with the score of *Yahad* writings.

Any doubt as to why Talmon resorted to such a method of dealing with these texts is dispelled by his final remark: "If this supposition should be verified, it will be sufficient to tip the balance in favor of the *Psalms of Joshua* and the *Joshua Pseudepigraph* from Masada being special writings of the Qumran community, and not writings of the general legacy of Israel that were brought to Qumran by those joining the sect."[62]

In brief, the primary purpose of the article was to preserve the old hypothesis of Qumran origins—substituting only the term *Yahad* for "Essenes"—after its revision had been perceived as essential by growing numbers of Qumranologists. Beyond that, it was to defend the late Yigael Yadin's explanation of a Qumran-Essene origin of the Masada fragments, now virtually abandoned by the editor of the text on which the explanation was based. The opening up of the texts and the accompanying recognition of the complexity of their contents had thus given rise, once again, to jejune explanations, always in order to protect sacrosanct ideas in the process of evaporating. It is difficult to believe that Yigael Yadin would have wished to have his memory perpetuated in this way.

*   *   *

On 6 September 1992, Professor Vermes, continuing his deep exploration of the fragments at Oxford, released information on yet another new text. The *Independent* newspaper then printed the photograph and translation of an Aramaic fragment (4Q246), emphasizing that it was publishing it "for the first time," and indicating that Vermes's full study of the text would appear the following month in a scholarly journal. The apocalyptic text spoke of a figure who will be proclaimed "son of God"—a phrase otherwise known only from the New Testament.[63] Other scholars had already suggested that the figure might represent a Jewish messiah, conceived of as being begotten of the Lord, still before the advent of the earliest Palestinian Christianity. As reported by the *Independent*, Dr. Vermes opposed this interpretation, asserting that the reference was to a usurper who was wicked. (The text is not complete, and the preserved lines are such that the choice of meanings will undoubtedly be debated at length by interpreters without necessarily ever producing full agreement.) Vermes then went on to assert that the "people of the saints of the Most High" referred to in the Book of Daniel (**7.**27) were those whom the author of the apocalyptic fragment had in mind in speaking of the "people of God" (a group also mentioned in the fragment) and that the latter were the "good Jews. *The Jews who lived at Qumran* near the caves where this fragment was found would have seen themselves as the people of the saints of the Most High." (My italics.)

In this way, although not discovering a single word or idea in the fragment that demonstrated a relationship with any of the *Yahad* texts, Professor Vermes once again attempted to protect the original Qumran-Essene hypothesis to which he had so deeply committed himself in earlier years.

We may now consider some additional aspects of Carol Newsom's 1990 conclusions that the contents of various texts found in the Qumran caves were not necessarily characteristic of the *Yahad* group but rather indicated use by those within a "broader stream" of intertestamental Judaism. Newsom, we will recall, had originally claimed that the scrolls could be divided into two categories: those belonging to "the sect" and those that were "pre-Qumranic," thus echoing a way of thinking most notably encouraged in America at her alma mater, Harvard University. In retracting her sectarian identification of the *Songs of the Sabbath Sacrifice*, she suggested that the work originated "outside of and *probably prior* to the emergence of the Qumran community."[64] Thus, although by 1990 she had freed herself of the idea that the *Songs* was sectarian, she still had difficulty acknowledging that this composition, and others equally nonsectarian in character, might well have been written *after* the claimed sect had come into existence.

Newsom offered no solid evidence for the view that such texts were "pre-Qumranic," but the source of her stance was unmistakable: the mesmeric conception, held by all traditional Qumranologists, of a fresh new movement sprouting within intertestamental Judaism and rejecting old habits of thinking and acting. Guided by the ever-charismatic Teacher of Righteousness and moving as pioneers to the serenely awesome desert of Judaea, the members of such a sect, in this conception, might have brought along some of their own writings stemming from the days their "sect" did not yet exist. That in the period of their communal life together they should have actively sought to secure books not reflecting the ideas of their purity-based movement would, by this mode of thinking, have been a preposterous notion. Since the leitmotif and most fundamental axiom of the Qumran-sectarian hypothesis was that the ideas of this sect were those expressed in the *Manual of Discipline*, such a conception would have constituted a disturbing element in the theory and directly clashed with the apparently exclusivist nature of the *Manual*. However, by defining these "outside" writings as earlier, "pre-Qumranic" works, one could ameliorate the difficulty. Newsom's formulation, in other words, represented another case of standing reason on its head by accommodating the findings to the old hypothesis at all costs, rather than changing the hypothesis in consonance with the findings as they were being progressively revealed.

It is in this light that her handling of the problem posed by the theory of the scrolls' Jerusalem origin needs to be considered. As a response to my discussion of the effect on the Qumran-Essene hypothesis of the order in which the discoveries were made, she relied on her erroneous belief that "it is not the order of discovery but the pattern of multiple copies that suggests that the scrolls do not simply represent a random collection of texts."[65] And although she conceded at the opening of her article that it seemed "worthwhile enough to consider the manuscripts without presuppositions as to their relationship with the ruins of Khirbet Qumran," in subsequent pages she still ended up invoking "the Qumran com-

munity" and the question of how texts were read "at Qumran." The
difficulty in actually casting aside such presuppositions, despite
the desire somehow to do so, was shown by her reference to "documents that are *demonstrably* of Qumran authorship" and her insistence that there were "good reasons for *assuming* that the
documents recovered from the . . . caves . . . are indeed the
remains of the library of the sect described in the Serek ha-
Yahad [= *Manual of Discipline*]."[66] Since (as Newsom hesitatingly
acknowledged) nothing whatever in the texts *did* in fact demonstrate that any of the scrolls originated at the Khirbet Qumran site,
the main burden of her observations, once again, took the form of
an effort to show that this premise of traditional Qumranology was
a *believable* one.

Thus, asking the question, "What does it mean to call a text
'sectarian'?," she proposed that it meant one of three things: that
the text "had been written by a member of the Qumran community"; that "it was the way a particular text was read . . . no matter
who had written it"; and that it could refer to "a way of describing
content or rhetorical stance" even though the latter category
"might well not include everything actually written by members of
the community."[67] Newsom then proceeded to show how various
Qumran texts could be made to fit into one or another of these
categories. For by the criteria she posited, many Qumran texts not
overtly heterodox in character could be defined as sectarian
enough, simply because the assumed "sectarians of Qumran"
might have found the ideas expressed in them to their liking, or
suitable to their own nonconformist ideas. Such an approach was,
in fact, in harmony with an important trend in modern literary
scholarship, exemplified in the work of Hans-Robert Jauss. "In a
very significant sense," stated Newsom, invoking the authority of
that figure, "a text is created through the reading process."[68]

Newsom certainly deserves credit for having attempted to
apply considerations in vogue in the field of modern literary criticism to Qumran studies—something not generally done in scrolls
research and, as such, worthy of attention. The considerations she
presented might indeed be persuasive when applied to ancient literary fragments of known and certain provenience. Once the
actual life situation of an original literary work has been demonstrated, unexpected deviations or incongruencies in it, as compared with other texts produced in the same known environment,
may then perhaps be explained by reference to the hypothetical

worldview of contemporary readers, rather than to the work's author. Such an effort, however, becomes folly when the particular surrounding environment of a text has not been established; in that case, the reader-response approach turns into nothing more than a guessing game, with favored theories of origin becoming springboards for the "discovery" within enigmatic texts of clues to the mentality of ancient readers. Par for the Qumranological course, Newsom did not deal in her discussion with most of the major problems in the old hypothesis—the *Copper Scroll*, the lack of literary autographs, and the other anomalies and pieces of evidence reviewed in these pages. Newsom's effort to bolster the hypothesis by arbitrarily appealing to a recent trend in literary hermeneutics thus transparently elided the very factors that made her appeal irrelevant.

Thus we see that by the early 1990s traditional Qumranologists, having emerged from silence, were increasingly seeking ways to refute the theory of Jerusalem origin, and in the process attempting to resolve or otherwise explain the burgeoning spectrum of problems that beset the traditional hypothesis. In the course of these efforts, they revealed a growing lack of agreement among themselves as to the nature and specifics of the theory they were defending. They could no longer claim a consensus on most of the major issues that informed the Qumran-sectarian hypothesis. Concomitantly, the era of suppression of ideas in Qumran studies appeared to be drawing to a close. Some scholars began to sense the need for increased dialogue with their nonconformist colleagues on the overriding issue of the origin and meaning of the manuscripts. Others, however, would express continuing resentment by further closed-door meetings combined with sporadic hints to the press about perpetrators of unacceptable ideas. Attempts would likewise be made to evade the import of my interpretation of scroll origins and of the nature of the Khirbet Qumran site—both by studious denial of its originality and the simultaneous dismantling of its components into disparate sections that were then presented without attribution or as original ideas of the presenters.

As this book went to press, the latest reported development was a meeting, late in May 1994, of a group of archaeologists and traditional scroll scholars to speculate further on Qumran. The *Jerusalem Post* reporter attending the meeting now described the site as "the mysterious community of Qumran." Various exegetical strategies to keep the old theory alive were hazarded at the meeting. One participant claimed that soldiers in antiquity "ate on particular kinds of dishes we don't find at Qumran." Emanuel Tov asked what evidence existed "that Qumran was a monastery housing an all-male community," to which Magen Broshi responded that the food services were all centered in one kitchen and one dining hall. In response to the suggestion that only a few score people had lived at Qumran at any one time, Shemaryahu Talmon was quoted as saying that "If only fifty persons lived there, where did all the graves come from?" He himself repeated his earlier proposal that Qumran was only a temporary retreat for members of "the Sect" who had come there for spiritual reasons from the regular "encampments" where they permanently resided. James VanderKam then stated that Talmon's explanations would make "the large number of graves even more inexplicable since they could not have lived out their lives there." Talmon responded that "longevity was not then what it is today" (*Jerusalem Post*, 27 May 1994). No one ventured to point out the increasingly obvious fact that the time had come to abandon a myth embraced for half a century.*

*For the events lying behind the meeting and which motivated the *Post* to publish a story about it, see below, pp. 359–360.

CHAPTER 11

The New York Conference
and Some Academic Intrigues

During 1990, I and my colleagues at the University of Chicago devoted considerable attention to planning the details of the international conference on the scrolls. We decided it should be concerned not only with the interpretation of the texts, but also with the archaeology of Khirbet Qumran and the application of scientific procedures to the study of the scrolls. In our formal proposal to the New York Academy of Sciences, we had indicated that Qumran scholars were becoming increasingly divided into two interpretive camps: "one, comprising the majority of Qumranologists, that supports the traditional view of the discoveries as emanating from a small sect . . . inhabiting Khirbet Qumran; and another, pressing new interpretations of the texts and of the nature of the Qumran site." The scholars, we pointed out, were further divided by the question of publication of the texts and of the related archaeological evidence, some, albeit a minority, favoring continuation of the system in which scrolls and materials were parceled out for exclusive study, others proposing "a more equitable procedure which might allow much wider scholarly access." As a result, one could speak "of a current crisis in Qumran studies as regards both method and interpretation . . . that shows no sign of abating, but on the contrary promises to become increasingly severe." We wished to hold the conference "to ponder these questions, and to propose solutions."

Without consideration of their individual positions on the main issues, we began making inquiries of colleagues around the world regarding their possible participation in the conference, and in the course of time received a surprisingly strong response. In June 1990 I increased my contacts with continental scholars through lectures at several German universities, and encouraged their participation in the conference. While Germany remained, on the whole, a bastion of traditional Qumranology, I was still able to engage in fair and open debate there on some of the fundamental issues. Scholars and students in Berlin and Göttingen even appeared to welcome the introduction of new perspectives in scrolls studies, and Professor Hartmut Stegemann of Göttingen eventually indicated his willingness to participate in the New York conference. On the other hand, Tübingen, with its strong and distinguished Pietist tradition, proved a more conventional font of learning, my critique of Qumranology meeting with much unsmiling opposition. No one from Tübingen, as it turned out, would attend the New York conference, but at least a debate had taken place there without overt acrimony. Soon after my presentation one participant in the discussion wrote to a German colleague that the "old hypothesis was beginning to crumble," but I entertained no real hope that it would do so in good speed at Tübingen.

In November 1991—during the very week of the official announcement apparently freeing the Dead Sea Scrolls for unrestricted use by all scholars—I found myself in Israel to deliver two public lectures in Hebrew on the texts. The audiences were large and my comments straightforward: Early scholars had committed a serious blunder in creating the sectarian hypothesis, Khirbet Qumran was the site of a pitched battle between Roman and Jewish forces during the First Revolt, the hiding of the scrolls was a product of the Roman siege on Jerusalem, and the custodians in charge of the scrolls and of the site were not serving the public properly by tenaciously maintaining the old explanations of the Qumran phenomenon in the public exhibitions under their control.

In general, my views were starting to receive increased notice in the Israeli, American, and European press, perhaps linked to a growing perception that the scrolls custodians had been engaging in a protracted act of suppression.[1] At the same time, scholars with relatively little at stake in the theoretical controversy were beginning to align themselves more closely with my position. The first was Dr. Philip Davies: Along with indicating in 1991 that the archaeology of Khirbet Qumran offered no support for its sectarian identification, he also pointed to the possibility of the scrolls' Jerusalem origin as best explaining the sectarian heterogeneity at work among them.[2] Almost simultaneously my theory was described in detail in *The Facts on File Scientific Yearbook*,[3] while L. Cansdale wrote that it was "basic to the whole question of the importance of the scrolls to both Judaic and particularly Christian scholarship," and, potentially, "to the way the study of the scrolls affects our knowledge of early Christianity."[4] In 1992, Dr. J. J. Price of Tel Aviv University, a historian of the Second Jewish Commonwealth, wrote that the theory "seems a more plausible explanation for the diversity in the nature, kinds and locations of the hundreds of manuscripts found in caves in the Judaean desert."[5] A similar reaction was expressed by Professor R. Pummer, a specialist on the Samaritans, and by the Augsburg New Testament scholar M. Klinghardt.[6] Several years before this support began to form, the English author of *Testament*, John Romer, expressed the view that the "theory of the Essene scriptorium makes a romantic tale, but, unfortunately, little sense. As texts from Jerusalem, the . . . Scrolls take on a much wider significance."[7]

In October 1992, the Austrian city of Graz—another center of traditional learning—was the site of a symposium on the basic issues in scrolls scholarship. I participated in this symposium, along with other scrolls scholars—among them Professors K. Schubert and F. Dexinger of the University of Vienna and S. Talmon of the Hebrew University—as well as with curator Broshi of the Shrine of the Book. Dexinger's position actually formed a bridge between my views and those of traditional Qumranologists: While not wishing to abandon altogether the notion of a particular sectarian group living at Khirbet Qumran, he still held that the problem of the scrolls' origins should be pursued by their internal analysis, without focusing on the identity of Khirbet Qumran. In his opinion, the latter procedure could only cloud the basic issue of the meaning of the texts. As to that meaning, Dexinger maintained that the scrolls did not merely serve as a repository of any particular sect's ideas, but were a mirror reflecting the doctrinal diversity of intertestamental Judaism: an important shift away from earlier Qumranological doctrine on the part of a highly respected continental scholar. The identical view was being expressed at approximately the same time by Klaus Berger of Heidelberg.*

---

*"By choosing a more careful approach than is common, we have freed the Qumran texts from artificial isolation, which treats them as if these were only the texts of a sect. We have the impression that people have made themselves excessively immune to these texts by classifying them as belonging to a sect, and that in this way they have become mummified. In truth, however, the heart of Judaism is beating in these exegeses and prayers. . . ." Cf. K. Berger, *Qumran und Jesus: Wahrheit unter Verschluss* (Stuttgart, 1993), p. 133. (My translation.)

In contrast, at the Graz meeting Schubert reiterated his assent
to the classical form of the hypothesis to which he had so deeply
committed himself since the 1950s. When I raised the problem
posed by the *Copper Scroll*, he responded enigmatically that the
text was "nonspecific," declining to elaborate further. Talmon
would also not comment on the *Copper Scroll*, except to claim that
it was an "anomalous" document, not relevant to his own view of
Qumran origins. This was rather different than the views he had
expressed in earlier essays: namely, that a Qumran sect, not identifiable with the Essenes, had collections of books reflecting not
only its own beliefs but those of other ancient movements in
Judaism—a view obviously touching in some respects on what I,
and now Dexinger, had been arguing. Klinghardt eventually summarized other elements in Talmon's explanation in the following
succinct way:

> He distinguishes between "Qumranic" scrolls . . . and others,
> although the criteria for this distinction did not really become
> clear. According to Talmon, the "Qumranic" scrolls reveal Khirbet
> Qumran as the center of the "Qumranites" in which members of the
> group spent only several years before they returned to their former
> places; it was on such occasions that the members brought their
> own scrolls to Qumran which are now part of the collection. Only
> during this part-time retreat to the desert did the members live in
> celibacy, the married ones leaving their families behind. The skele-
> tons of women and children at the Khirbet Qumran cemetery are of
> the part-time retreaters' families that had been shipped to the
> desert during their fathers' and husbands' stay at the center. The
> group is determined by its unique theology of covenant, consider-
> ing itself to be the people of the renewed covenant after the exile.
> This is meant to explain the intensification of the "Qumranites'"
> Halakhah (as opposed to the more liberal Halakhah of the
> Pharisees and early Christians), the concepts of purity and separa-
> tion, and the existence of the great amount of biblical manuscripts,
> for the group understands itself as the successor of biblical tradi-
> tion.[8]

Thus, while finally reaching out for a broader conception of the
importance of the scrolls themselves, Talmon, as of 1992, was still
unable to liberate himself from the old approach to Qumran origins. Acknowledging the disparity between the doctrines expressed
in the texts and those of the Essenes as described in the classical

sources, he still felt obliged to maintain the conception of a celibate sect living atop the Qumran plateau. The scenario of sectarians coming from their permanent homes to live there for sojourns of several years, and of the bodies of those wives and children who had meanwhile died being transported to Qumran for burial, was a painful artifice, unsupported by the wording of any of the manuscripts and demonstrating only that the old hypothesis had but a remote chance of being theoretically plausible.

The issues discussed at the Graz conference anticipated a number of controversies over the scrolls' meaning that were to follow in ensuing weeks. On 20 November, an open meeting was held on the campus of Stanford University at which I debated the issues with J. A. Fitzmyer (Catholic University) and Stephen Rix (Brigham Young University). An attendance of over six hundred at this conference showed the degree of public interest in the controversy. Like Schubert at Graz, Professor Fitzmyer took an uncompromising view on the basic questions, defending such traditionalist notions as Cross's palaeography of the texts, the claims relating to it that followed the radiocarbon tests, the identity of the Khirbet Qumran site as the home of Pliny's Essenes, and the connection of the cave manuscripts with that group. Like Talmon, Professor Rix moved toward a slightly more moderate position, claiming that the site was indeed that of sectarians, while the manuscripts might yet reflect multiform heterodoxy among the intertestamental Jews. The audience appeared to be particularly interested in the question of the scrolls' links with early Christianity. When a participant asked Fitzmyer how, in his view, my own interpretation of the manuscripts might illuminate this topic, he responded that he did not see why he had to address himself to that question.[9] (Apparently feeling obliged to address it nevertheless, Fitzmyer would later publish a response to an article of mine that had been directed mainly at Christian readers; his comments, as those of others earlier on, mainly involved defenses of the original sectarian interpretation of the scrolls, while not addressing the import of the totality of evidence available by the early 1990s for the problem of the scrolls' origins.)[10]

The conference on the Stanford campus immediately preceded the 1992 meeting in San Francisco of the Society of Biblical Literature, which included a few sessions on the scrolls (22 November 1992). I was particularly concerned to hear what changes, if any, might have taken place in the thinking of younger

scholars whom the official editorial committee had assigned previously unpublished scroll fragments to edit. Daniel Harrington,
of the Weston School of Theology, in reporting on a lengthy "sapiential," or "wisdom," text (classified as 4Q416–4Q419), observed
that the fragments "contained an extreme vocabulary with regard
to poverty," warnings against the abuse of one's wife, and other
features that showed it to belong to the genre of wisdom literature
exemplified by the apocryphal work Ecclesiasticus (Ben Sira). It
was "not Qumran/monastic, if you will," but may have been "pre-
Qumranic" in origin. Attempting to save the text for the "sect of
Qumran," D. Dimant of Haifa University responded that "we have
to enlarge our description of what is sectarian Qumran literature." In reporting on a fragmentary collection of prayers designated as 4Q443, E. Glickler Chazon of the Hebrew University
claimed that the text was written in so-called Qumran Hebrew
and was transcribed no later than the beginning of the first century B.C., but noted, once again, that it contained "no explicit sectarianism"; such texts as this, she suggested, had to be connected
with a "larger stream" of intertestamental Judaism. Sidnie A.
White of Albright College reported on fragments from Cave 4 designated as a "reworked Pentateuch" and having affinities with the
Temple Scroll, but "the nature of whose relationship with the
Temple Scroll was not clear." White too appeared to suggest that,
as in the case of the *Temple Scroll* itself, there was nothing to
prove these fragments originated with the "sect of Qumran," leading a member of the audience to urge that the variant readings in
the text, when compared with the *Temple Scroll*, showed a "struggle within the community as to how to handle the *Temple Scroll*
material": another effort on the part of traditional Qumranologists
to squeeze the new texts into the fold of Qumran sectarianism.
Such interplay dominated the sessions, leading the final speaker,
Joseph Baumgarten of Baltimore Hebrew University, to refrain
from characterizing the inhabitants of Khirbet Qumran as an
Essenic sect *per se* "in view of the sentiment prevailing at our
meeting."

By this time—precisely one year after the apparent changes in the
Antiquities Authority's scrolls policy were announced—the book
by Michael Wise and Robert Eisenman, *The Dead Sea Scrolls
Uncovered*, had appeared. The book combined Wise's painstaking
reconstructions and translations of fifty Qumran texts, many pre-

viously unpublished, with commentaries on these texts by Robert Eisenman. These commentaries reflected Eisenman's own thesis—not shared by Wise—that the scrolls represented an early stage of Jewish Christianity. The idea suffers from the same basic weaknesses found in the old Qumran-Essene hypothesis, extrapolating as it does a sweeping interpretation of scroll origins from material at work in relatively few of the texts. However that may be, the book caused a sensation at the Society of Biblical Literature meetings, more on account of Wise's transcriptions and translations than for any other reason.[11] The texts included a new edition and translation of the *Acts of Torah*. Many scholars were naturally eager to see what information the new texts might contain, while others—that is, those who had received official assignments from the Jerusalem committee—appeared furious upon realizing that their privileged status as text editors had been eclipsed.

Wise, my younger colleague at the University of Chicago, had worked on the texts for months with a group of our graduate students. A scholar of independent ideas, adept in classical and Semitic languages alike, and a brilliant reader and translator of the scrolls, he had succeeded in deciphering many interesting new texts, at least thirty for the first time in full. Other scholars had partially published or discussed some of these, and several had either appeared while Wise's own edition of them was being independently typeset, or had circulated as preliminary versions in the form of handouts or photocopies of transcriptions, but the majority were instructively fresh and new. During the course of Wise's work, we had met together in a seminar to study a few of the most important texts, including the *Acts of Torah*, but Wise and the four graduate students who assisted him accomplished virtually the entire process of transcription and translation.[12] The edition and translation of so many fragments in such a relatively short time span was a considerable achievement, particularly in view of the fact that the official group of almost sixty editors had not even come close to completing their own assignments—an average of approximately ten or twelve fragments per person—by November 1992. Intended for the general reader, and conceived of only as a preliminary edition and translation of a modest proportion of the unpublished texts—fifty out of approximately three hundred—the text studies were not accompanied by exhaustive references, but bibliographical sections titled

"Previous Discussions" were included after the edition of each text or group of texts.

A preliminary transcription by other scholars of the *Acts of Torah*,[13] as we have seen, had already circulated widely in *samizdat* photocopies. Several other texts had been the subject of reports at scholarly meetings; and some of them had been written about or partially published in preceding years by members of the monopoly. The subtitle of the book stated, correctly, that it contained "the first *complete translation and interpretation* of 50 key documents withheld for over 35 years" (italics mine). At the time of the book's publication, a group of Qumranologists comprised of "official" editors was spending a joint sabbatical year at the Annenberg Institute in Philadelphia. In the period between the close of the Society of Biblical Literature meeting of 1992 and the opening of the New York conference on the scrolls (14–17 December), they pondered what to do about the independent publication of Wise and Eisenman. The chemistry of their group interaction resulted in distribution of an accusatory letter to the media on the eve of the New York conference.[14]

In retrospect, this letter can be best understood as the opening salvo in a twofold strategy: (a) to discredit the authors of *The Dead Sea Scrolls Uncovered*, thus neutralizing the impact of the first independent edition of new Cave 4 scrolls produced (as were the Wacholder–Abegg transcriptions) in open defiance of the Antiquities Authority's monopoly; and (b) to counter the New York conference's general public impact and thus obscure the basic issues that might be raised there. Most of these issues would, of course, relate to the question of origin and significance of the scrolls; but others might revolve around the Antiquities Authority, thus involving serious questions of ethics and propriety.

Among such issues were the following:

- Assigning previously unpublished manuscripts to students as dissertation subjects;
- Giving responsibility for editing manuscripts to groups or committees (rather than to individual scholars having mastery of the necessary disciplines);
- A state agency's officially sanctioning a particular, problematic scientific dogma at the center of controversy and assigning important manuscripts to editors on the basis of their assent to that dogma;

- Claiming scientific verification of the dogma prior to publication of actual results of experiments;
- Awarding publication rights to scholars in consideration of financial grants by institutions affiliated with them.

Other questions might also be addressed: the nature and purpose of first editions of manuscripts; in new manuscript editions, the proper role for scholars other than the original editors; the proper relation between one's *discovery* of a manuscript and the claim of prior rights to its publication.

Thus, given their strong awareness of my public commitment to overturn their proprietorship over the scrolls, it was in a sense only natural for those linked to the official scroll committees to essay defensive measures in the face of the New York conference. It became obvious that various members had resolved to cancel the commitment to a policy of open access to these ancient texts—a commitment the "official" editors, in goodly measure, apparently felt had been forced upon them, and which they greatly resented. As a result of such concerns, and of the accusations being raised against the Eisenman–Wise book, I and the other organizers of the conference did decide in the end to schedule a discussion on the basic ethical issues.

Again only naturally, those participants linked to the Jerusalem editorial committee took up as much conference time as possible focusing—often in an unfortunately personal way—on problems at work in the Eisenman–Wise book that they claimed were grave.[15] It will become clear with a closer look at the nature of the accusatory letter that what in fact was the fundamental element of gravity was a continued concern with power at the expense of principle.

The letter entirely disregarded the wording of the subtitle of the book, instead asserting that "the volume claims to publish fifty previously unpublished texts."

This spurious assertion was followed by others. In the course of an exaggerated protest at the method the authors used to cite texts that had been previously published in part or full, the letter's writers threw in the unfounded assertion that "several unnamed publications" were behind the authors' work. Less trivially, they suggested that Eisenman and Wise were guilty of "often copying the original transcriptions with only minor modifications"; in fact, in each of the cases apparently being referred to, Wise had himself transcribed the texts painstakingly from the photographs. (In any case, contrary to what the letter's authors appeared to believe, introducing, through manuscript study, changes or improvements in the wording of previously transcribed and translated texts—a crucial aspect of the continuous process of editing ancient manuscripts—implies no illegitimate leaning on earlier work whatsoever, and requires no apologies.)

In the same vein, the letter asserted that, contrary to the editors' claim of originality, the transcription and translation of the *Acts of Torah* (4QMMT) found there was based on what the authors called the Strugnell–Qimron version. The only specific basis offered for this accusation was the presence of the same joins and transitions in both versions. While, as we shall see, along with the rest of the letter's contents the accusation in the end would be formally retracted by some of its signatories, it nevertheless would be renewed, on highly artificial grounds, in the course of Qimron's lawsuit against Hershel Shanks, James Robinson, and Robert Eisenman for inclusion of what Qimron claimed to be "his" text in the unauthorized facsimile edition of the Dead Sea Scrolls.

In this manner, the accusation, irresponsible in both its tone and tenor,* constituted a particularly nasty attack on independent investigation—one posing a potential threat to the very foundations of research on ancient manuscripts. To begin with, Michael Wise had reconstructed the text of the *Acts of Torah* from scratch, precisely as stated in the book's introduction. He used high-quality photographs of the original text fragments, newly liberated as a result of the collapse of the Antiquities Authority's unethical policies. He

---

*Here is the verbatim accusation (point 4 of the letter): "The claim of the editors not to have used the previously circulated edition of 4QMMT prepared by J. Strugnell and E. Qimron is laughable and manifestly dishonest. They write, 'We have gone through the entire corpus of pictures completely ourselves and depended on no one else's work to do this . . . *including the identification of overlaps and joins.*' [. . .] This claim is especially ludicrous. It must be a miracle that their edition made all the same joins and transitions between fragmentary manuscripts that Strugnell and Qimron had made after many years of research. . . . Again, we must emphasize that editors of ancient documents have a right to see their work published first under their own name, not under the name of others." The renewal of this accusation, in a trial in Jerusalem involving an entirely different book, was based on a claim that Shanks's "unauthorized" usage of the work set the stage for similar usage by others.

often worked in my presence and with my occasional advice. It is also the case that both Wise and myself—along with scholars all over the world who had been cut off from access to the *Acts of Torah* fragments—had eagerly perused the text's *samizdat* form upon receiving it in the mail in the late 1980s. Once read (and read, of course, with all the attention reserved for an important text unjustly kept until then out of circulation) such a manuscript can never be entirely "forgotten"—and unintentional echoes in later text editions emanating from earlier ones are, in fact, a commonly accepted phenomenon in manuscript investigation. Such contaminations can often be spotted as interpretive mistakes in earlier editions that are repeated in later ones. On several occasions I have discovered contaminations of this sort in my own work, and a few appeared in Wise's version of the *Acts* as well, as the unconscious repetition of mistakes that either Strugnell or Qimron made in the transcription whose photocopy had made its way all over the world by 1988. (In the lawsuit over the "unauthorized" scrolls edition, Qimron's lawyers would contrive to implicate *The Dead Sea Scrolls Uncovered* by citing the same contaminations as evidence for Wise's alleged malfeasance.)

By the same token, an inability tidily to forget the *samizdat* version may or may not have helped, to some small degree, increase the pace at which Wise went about reassembling the photograph fragments from scratch; it may or may not have been at work, at some indeterminate level of "echoing," in one or another decision regarding joins and transitions that he needed to make. But the insinuation that the identity of joins demonstrated deliberate recourse to the earlier version—something that would otherwise be a "miracle" (as the letter's authors put it), particularly in light of Strugnell's and Qimron's "many years of research," was absurd and, in effect, defamatory. The truth is that, as in the assembly of a puzzle, the interlinkage of joins and the flow of transitions in the *Acts of Torah* are virtually always clear and logical, representing a task that any competent manuscript scholar ought to be able to handle in a small fraction of the time it took the "official" editors. At its best, the expression of wonder at both the pace and nature of Wise's work revealed a sorry lack of understanding of palaeographic procedure; at its worst, it represented intentional calumny. Wise's procedure is common practice in manuscript research, entailing no breach of ethics whatsoever.

In any case, with the eventual decision by a perhaps sincere but nonetheless partial Israeli judge in favor of the baseless complaint of a fellow citizen, a passing episode of academic intrigue was transformed into a dangerous legal precedent. As of this writing, Michael Wise's work—and by implication, that of other independent scholars—proceeds under the threat of lawsuit by Qimron, based on the line of attack contained in the acccusatory letter. And what is here being challenged is not simply the career and reputation of a gifted and honest scholar, but also a basic facet of academic freedom: the ability of scholars of ancient manuscripts to proceed with their work without having to look over their shoulders in fear of being called to account for textual contaminations by a lay judge or jury forced to rule on technical questions of palaeographic method.

Those authors of the letter who attended the New York conference withdrew their charges on its final day. The withdrawal was the outcome of what appeared to be sincere and civil discussions, in the course of which—as is usual in such situations—both sides ceded as much as they thought was possible for the sake of compromise. Michael Wise—a young scholar with no desire whatever to find himself in a permanent state of war with the scrolls establishment and its politico-academic network—issued a statement acknowledging "deficiencies" in this market-oriented book's editing and production. It is true that, while the decision to substitute "previous discussion" sections for systematic reference notes was hardly extraordinary in the case of a book intended for a general readership, the book—produced with speed and only limited editorial control on Wise's part—could have been more fully documented with added time spent on its preparation. In addition, Eisenman and Wise had not included expressions of indebtedness to earlier Qumranologists in their introduction. In light of the fact that the world of traditional Qumranology had denied Eisenman and Wise, as well as many other independent scholars, access to the manuscripts they were concerned with most deeply, such restraint was not at all surprising. Nevertheless, confirming the ideals of protocol in scholarly interaction, Wise expressed the intent to rectify any possible deficiency in a future edition of the book.

For their part, those signatories of the letter present at the conference agreed, "in light of Professor Wise's statement and after obtaining additional information about the production of the book . . . to retract the statement [of protest] and all it implies." An important—potentially groundbreaking—conference on the scrolls was in the process of concluding; it seemed best to all parties to restore, if at all possible, the aura of civility that had marked the opening session and the efforts in subsequent sessions to deal with fundamental disagreements, both of method and of academic politics. Nevertheless, whether in retrospect Wise made the right decision in signing his statement remains to be seen: With only some of the accusatory letter's signatories putting their name to the retraction—i.e., those invited to the conference who did not cancel their appearances at the last moment—others apparently felt free, subsequently, to make use of Wise's concession any way they chose.[16] Moreover, were Qimron, in consultation with his Antiquities Authority allies, to decide to proceed with further legal action, he would of course try to benefit as much as he could from Wise's signed concession, linking it to whatever precedent was set in the earlier trial.

Useful or not as a strategic riposte, the attack on *The Dead Sea Scrolls Uncovered* revealed a great deal about the institutional controversy surrounding the scrolls. Throughout, the attack failed to distinguish between two widely different approaches to investigating ancient manuscripts: one based on open research in manuscript collections, with individuals working under dynamically *competitive* circumstances, the other consisting of group control of manuscript collections, with particular texts (often already worked on by others) assigned to selected editors in the hope of their expeditious publication. In the first case, a scholar may see in a manuscript what others have not, and legitimately lay claim to a new discovery. In the second case, as the scholarly work has not been achieved under competitive circumstances, it can hardly deserve that characterization.

Now a prior right of publication by the handpicked "official" scroll researchers was dubiously asserted on several occasions in the attack on *The Dead Sea Scrolls Uncovered*—thus conveying a continued hostility to the principle of competitive study of their contents. The assertion was made both in regard to the *Acts of Torah* and to other writings, misleadingly termed "discoveries." Wise and Eisenman, the letter indignantly claimed, were guilty of "making use of important discoveries by reputable scholars [and] presenting them as if they were their own original ideas." But the only such "discovery" mentioned, described as "major," was the fragment praising "Jonathan the King" (examined above in Chapter 9). In reality, Wise and Eisenman had referred to the lengthy and detailed description of the "discovery" that appeared in the magazine section of the *Jerusalem Post*. It appeared while they were engaged in completing their book and—as we will recall—*before* the scholarly account of the "discovery" was published in *Tarbiz*. As the *Post* piece furnishes the names of the editors, and as Wise was producing an independent version and translation of the text, the book's way of treating the not entirely edifying account of other researchers' efforts on the same text was perfectly in order.

The attack also put forward various distortions of basic palaeographic principles. Although the letter's signatories explained that their objections related to "ethics and integrity," they did not find it inappropriate, for example, to claim that the *Dead Sea Scrolls Uncovered* "abounds with errors and imprecisions in the transcription of the Hebrew and Aramaic documents and in translating and interpreting them." But as scholars of the Dead Sea Scrolls, they surely must have been aware that first editions containing large numbers of texts always have such errors: It is a truism of manuscript investigation that full understanding of ancient manuscripts is achieved, if ever, only after decades of study and restudy—and the Qumran scrolls are no exception to this rule. Inhering in this "criticism"—a nadir in the effort to sully Wise— was its reverse image: We may well doubt whether the letter's signatories could themselves have done as well as Wise in his work. He had dealt eruditely and efficiently with texts that often proved of great difficulty—without the aid of editorial committees or specially appointed palaeographers, such as have been put at the disposal of those "official" editors in need of aid in reading the manuscripts assigned them.

Despite the acrimonious sentiment engendered in the wake of the "official" scrolls scholars' efforts, the New York conference succeeded, for the first time in the history of Qumran studies, in bringing together scholars with radically opposing views to discuss the manuscripts and the Khirbet Qumran site. No participants were excluded or invited because of their political alignment vis-à-vis the traditional Qumranological community; papers on archaeology and radiocarbon dating intermingled with those on the texts themselves, giving the conference a unique character and helping to ensure scientific objectivity.[17]

Among the papers presented at the conference, the textual analysis of Dr. Matthias Klinghardt of the University of Augsburg, and the discussion by Pauline Donceel-Voûte (Catholic University of Louvain) of the archaeology of Qumran were particularly notable. Klinghardt subjected the *Manual of Discipline* to a new reading, showing that the ordinances in this text relating to such matters as initiation, membership fees, discipline at assemblies, communal meals, and penalties were "closely paralleled by similar, contemporary statutes of private associations [in] Hellenistic Egypt, Greece, and Rome." These analogies put the *Manual* into a wider context, showing that "the organizational and legal status of the *Yahad*, as well as the groups described in [certain] other scrolls . . . and early Christian congregations" were "basically identical, indicating that the *Yahad* was a synagogue community. . . ." Klinghardt concluded that many alleged peculiarities of the *Yahad* group, such as purity, priestly orientation, and self-definition as a particularistic unit "appear to be typical for such associations."

The relationship of the *Manual*'s ideas on social organization to those of Hellenistic societies had been anticipated by Professor Moshe Weinfeld in an important study,[18] but Klinghardt's independent analysis rejected a strictly sectarian conception of the *Manual*, focusing instead on its significance for an understanding of the way the very idea and establishment of the synagogue came about in ancient Judaea. His analysis represented a strong advance in applying the study of the scrolls to the general history of intertestamental Judaism.

Dr. Pauline Donceel-Voûte's lecture represented a new phase in the archaeological dimension of Qumran studies. Concentrating on the so-called scriptorium at Khirbet Qumran, she showed that the claimed "tables" of this room were in reality portions of benches that had been fastened to the walls. Drawing on all the available archaeological remnants, she concluded that the chances of the room in question actually having been a scriptorium were nil. Rather, it was a type of *triclinium* or *coenaculum*—that is, a private dining or banquet room.[19] In addition, pottery pieces and other artifacts, many of fine quality, found at Khirbet Qumran were *characteristic* of Roman Palestine, not anomalous; the elegance of many of the pieces found militated against the theory of an ascetic sect living there. These observations were particularly striking in light of the fact that the Ecole Biblique had asked Donceel-Voûte and her husband, Robert Donceel, to be the official continuators of de Vaux's work at Qumran. (As of 1994 they were preparing the final report on that excavation.) Their findings, of course, directly contradicted de Vaux's own ideas, underscoring the futility of the ongoing insistence on labeling the site the home of a sect and place of origin of the manuscripts found in the caves.

Concentrating on problems involved in identifying the Qumran cemetery, Dr. Z. J. Kapera of the Jagiellonian University in Cracow also offered an important presentation. Showing that de Vaux and his followers had disregarded much of the evidence relative to the cemetery, he distinguished between two current conceptions of the cemetery, one holding to its identification as a sectarian site in use for several generations, the other that it was a postbattle intrusion into the Qumran plateau. His lecture touched off a considerable debate, but the discussion made it clear that Kapera had succeeded in showing that the sectarian identification was in serious doubt.

Dr. Joseph Patrich of Haifa University and Dr. Jodi Magness of Tufts attempted to shore up the sectarian identification of Khirbet Qumran. Magness emphasized the relatively modest character of most of the pottery found at the site, stating that differences between it and that found at other Judaean sites "can be understood as reflecting differences in the character of their communities." This argument was in direct conflict with Donceel-Voûte's observation that a considerable amount of very fine pottery (of which she showed illustrations for the first time) had actually been found at the site—and that it was in fact *not* different from the pottery at other sites. Patrich, for his part, wished to show that "the caves were never used as permanent dwellings for the members of the . . . Sect, and that therefore, their dwelling places should be located within the boundaries of Khirbet Qumran. The size of the population should accordingly be reduced to about 50-70. The daily life at the site should be re-examined in accordance with these observations." This effort to preserve the sectarian conception of Khirbet Qumran did not address the vast water supply and other features of the site that tend to show it could hold far more than the fifty to seventy people Patrich spoke of. The fact that, as Magness observed, most of the pottery found at the site is plain and, as Donceel observed, some of it is of very high quality, remains most readily understandable by recourse to the site's identification as a fortress, whose garrison would have included a relatively large number of common troops and a considerably smaller number of privileged officers and their commandant.

Many new texts were analyzed at the conference, as well as some familiar ones. Three papers focused on the *Copper Scroll*, all emphasizing its authenticity. Dr. P. Kyle McCarter of Johns Hopkins University indicated that the text had been put away in an area in the rear of Cave 3, with the literary scrolls originally stacked high in front of it; and that it could thus not have been deposited after A.D. 70. There was little sense, he said, in the idea that later sequesterers would have hit upon that very cave and then tried to get behind the other scrolls in order to hide their text. Professor McCarter's own view of the *Copper Scroll* terminology was that it designated

> religious contributions made in support of the temple and its personnel . . . at least one important priestly family is mentioned by name, viz., . . . , "the House of Hakkoz," who at an earlier period had been entrusted with responsibility for the temple treasury. These clues point to an explanation of the relationship of the Copper Scroll hoard to the Jerusalem Temple.

With such observations, McCarter established a firm distance from his own mentor Frank Cross, who has always persisted in the view that the *Copper Scroll* was an imaginative product. McCarter was actually following in the footsteps of the late David Wilmot, who as a graduate student at the University of Chicago, during the last years of his life wrote his dissertation on this scroll; and by that of Professor Al Wolters (Redeemer College, Ancaster, Canada), who by the late eighties had himself arrived at the conclusion that it was an authentic document.[20] In Wolters's presentation at the conference, he stated that

> Milik's view that the [Copper Scroll] . . . was legendary . . . had an identifiable political background, and is contradicted both by the archaeological evidence and the judgment of most other scholars. Instead, the CS probably describes real treasure, is to be dated around 68 C.E., and has close connections with the Temple in Jerusalem. This conclusion is supported by the prominence of cultic terminology in the CS, and by Wilmot's proposal with respect to its genre.

Wolters nevertheless advocated a possible Zealot origin of the scroll, growing out of the notable role of this group in events in Jerusalem before and during the Roman siege.

Peter Muchowski of the Adam Mickiewicz University (Poznan) bolstered the view of the *Copper Scroll* as an authentic documentary artifact through a precise analysis of the Hebrew idiom of the text, demonstrating both its closeness to early rabbinic Hebrew and some divergences from it. Virtually all of the other papers represented similarly fresh groundwork for the investigation of the scrolls, as readers who peruse the conference's published proceedings may observe in detail.[21]

Some time after the New York conference took place, Z. J. Kapera would issue a report of his own on it,[22] in which he stated that

> What started in 1987 at Mogilany as a dispute about archaeological aspects of the Jerusalem hypothesis of Norman Golb and continued with the publication of an accusing article by Ph. R. Davies . . . on excavations in Khirbet Qumran ended in New York with the definitive collapse of the interpretation of the Qumran site as monastic center of the Essenes. We can possibly describe some of the ancient documents from the caves close to Qumran as sectarian, but in no way can we any more identify the site as a sectarian center with a big library. That has now ended once and for all and nobody is able to revive the official interpretation of Father de Vaux and his Scrollery team. Unanswered remain some questions: if they were not Essenes living in Qumran, who were the people living there, was Qumran really a fortress, who destroyed it and when exactly did it happen.[23]

The shift in thinking that was taking place in Qumran studies a year after the texts were released for open investigation was particularly emphasized by John Noble Wilford in his report on the conference in the *New York Times* science section.[24] George Brooke of Manchester University was quoted as saying that "We are still a long way from firm historical knowledge of the origin of the scrolls," Michael Wise that "Everything about the scrolls is being re-examined and rethought." L. Schiffman asserted that a single text, the *Acts of Torah*, showed "beyond question that either the sect was not Essene, but was Sadducean, or that the Essene movement must be totally redefined as having emerged out of

Sadducean beginnings" (we have, of course, examined the problems with this Sadducaean hypothesis in Chapter 7), while James VanderKam "insisted that the old consensus around the Essene hypothesis, though not as rock solid as before, was in no danger of crumbling." The article emphasized Dr. Donceel-Voûte's findings, and quite accurately pointed out that "adherents of the Essene hypothesis subjected her to tough questioning in accusatory tones." She was quoted as saying: "I am upset by the atmosphere of aggression throughout scrolls research. I went in with an open mind to look at the archaeology of the site. It shows that Qumran was part of the general society."

All told, one of the most important results of the conference was a greater public awareness of the controversy over the question of identification of the manuscripts and the Khirbet Qumran site—a development directly affecting plans for the American exhibition of the scrolls in 1993–94. A little over a month after the conference and Wilford's report, the *New York Times* announced that some of the least-viewed scrolls would be put on display, first in April 1993 at the Library of Congress, then at other American libraries.[25] Irene Burnham, director of interpretive programs at the Library of Congress, was quoted as saying that "the scroll enigma includes the basic uncertainty about what that community was. . . . [It] could be: a) a Roman fortress, b) a winter villa, c) home of the Essene sect, d) home of the Sadducees or e) none of the above. We're hoping to take all the stuff that has caused controversy and is the reason people are interested and put it out there and talk about it."

Clearly, the approach of the Library of Congress was one of principle at the outset: The Library did not wish to take sides or endorse particular positions in the growing controversy. At the New York Public Library, however, another view prevailed. In answer to the question "Is it difficult putting this together?" Dr. Leonard S. Gold, Dorot Chief Librarian of the Jewish Division at the New York Public Library, was quoted in the same *Times* article as stating: "It's difficult, yes. One has to approach organizing an exhibition with a point of view. *This exhibition is going to take the point of view there was a sect and that most of the scrolls were connected to the sect.* And we're going to try at the same time [to] mention the fact that there are scholars who hold other views and mention these other views. We're trying to express as many views as we can." (Italics mine.) I was quoted as saying, in response, that "The public will be led to believe they are all the writings of an ancient sect in Judaism, maybe the Essenes. But saying that these scores and scores of documents come from the pen of a single sect is no longer legitimate."

The *Times* article mentioned that I would be one of a group of scholars participating in a "scholarly symposium on the scrolls" also to be held at the Library of Congress. It explained that the "organizer of the symposium, Dr. Joseph Baumgarten, a professor of rabbinic literature at Baltimore Hebrew University, said the symposium would represent 'what you might say is the general consensus about the scrolls,' the traditional view." The article also informed readers that the "organizers and curators of the exhibit . . . declined to speculate on any connection between the proposal to mount the exhibit and the bitter fight by 'outside' scholars to have access to the texts that had been closely held among a small group of like-minded researchers." We shall see in the next chapter why such speculation was declined.

In the interval between the New York conference and the Library of Congress symposium, the long-awaited trial of the case brought by Elisha Qimron against the publisher and editors of the facsimile edition of the scrolls took place. The judge, Dalia Dorner of the Jerusalem district court, had the basic task of determining whether the transcriptions of manuscripts by scholars that included restorations of missing words and the joining together of disparate fragments of such texts to make larger wholes constituted original "creation" covered by copyright law. At a deposition in Philadelphia prior to the trial, John Strugnell, who had bestowed his transcription of the *Acts of Torah* on Qimron, was asked whether he thought this kind of work actually constituted such original "creation." He replied that what was involved in fact were acts of "reconstruction." When I appeared as an expert witness for the Eisenman defense during the trial, Qimron's attorneys asked me a similar question. I answered that any manuscript scholar who, in a lecture, defined his work of reconstruction as an act of creation would be laughed off the stage by his peers. The same question, however, elicited the opposite response from those testifying on Qimron's behalf—curator Broshi of the Shrine of the Book and Jacob Sussman of the Hebrew University, who as we have seen had collaborated with Qimron on the elucidation of the *Acts of Torah*.

Favoring the reply of the latter pair of witnesses, Judge Dorner ruled for Qimron on 30 March 1993. Citing Qimron's claims of mental and physical anguish as a result of Shanks's publication of the *Acts*, she awarded him a sum approximating $50,000, meant to include, as well, compensation for "actual damage not proved," and attorney's fees. Explicitly supporting Qimron's somewhat delirious assertion that the Teacher of Righteousness himself had composed the *Acts of Torah*, agreeing with Qimron's dubious formulation that he had been involved in "research and decipherment (of the manuscript) for eleven years," stating without proof, and without acknowledgment of my testimony, that Qimron had "discovered that the language [of the scroll] was earlier than that of the Mishnah"—and thereby issuing legal judgments about matters being debated by scholars of ancient texts—she also announced an injunction against further publication of "the composite text" of the *Acts of Torah*.[26]

The trial was preceded by the sending of letters to Eisenman and Wise by Qimron's attorneys, warning them not to proceed with any further publication of the manuscripts of *MMT*, and such letters were later sent to Wacholder and Abegg. Implicit in the letters was a claim by Qimron that, having worked on an *edition* of these fragments, he now held a copyright *on the manuscripts themselves*—and that subsequently no other scholar would have the right to work on a separate edition of the same manuscripts without his permission. Frankly revealing the retrenched position of the Jerusalem scroll committees and hinting at their intentions, Emanuel Tov hailed the judge's decision, stating: "This will serve as a precedent for the future. It justifies the work of our team, and I hope that other people planning to make improper use of of our group's material will now think twice."[27]

Taking due note of the potential danger for manuscript scholarship everywhere resulting from Dorner's decision, the attorney for Eisenman, Amos Hausner (son of the late Gideon Hausner, prosecutor in the Eichmann trial) filed an appeal to the Israel Supreme Court (to which Judge Dorner had in the meanwhile been appointed) at the end of April 1993. A separate appeal was filed shortly thereafter by the attorneys for Shanks. On 31 July Professors Wacholder and Abegg issued a request to the Federal District Court in Philadelphia for a declaratory judgment stipulating that Qimron could not copyright any portion of the Dead Sea Scrolls.

Reporting on reactions to this last legal move, the *Chicago Tribune* cited James Gardner, deputy director of the American Historical Association, as saying that the dispute "has implications that go far beyond biblical studies." Gardner noted that "scholars have traditionally been able to draw upon the work of their predecessors because of the legal doctrine of fair usage, which allows for limited borrowing from copyrighted material. But courts have been narrowing the definition of fair usage and expanding that of copyright. Historians and biographers, who depend upon such materials as published memoirs, already feel threatened, a trend that would accelerate if any one scholar could establish an exclusive claim to a major historical document like one of the Dead Sea Scrolls." Bill Ziobro, secretary-treasurer of the American Philological Association, was thereafter quoted as saying that "The vitality of the scholarly life depends upon a scholar's ability to freely state his agreements and disagreements with those who came before him. That's how the life of the mind and the human condition improves." (Ron Grossman in the *Chicago Tribune*, 2 August 1993.)

As of this writing both the Jerusalem appeal and the request to the American court are pending.

CHAPTER 12

The Importance
of the Dead Sea Scrolls

T he effort to unshackle the scrolls, and surrounding events, formed a significant episode in the sociology of knowledge. The attempt on the part of a group of scholars to control access to these ancient texts also necessarily meant an attempt to control ideas on their origin and significance—as was to be amply demonstrated by the 1993–94 American scroll exhibitions. The fundamental principle of fair play in scholarship did not in the end matter to those who gained entrance to the charmed circle. The press, for its part, both in news stories and editorials lived up to its calling in exposing what had been a repugnant state of affairs, as well as in bringing new interpretations of the scrolls to the attention of the public and encouraging access to them.

During the process of opening up the scrolls and the ensuing dialogue, those holding the monopoly still tried their utmost to maintain control, characterizing their opponents' actions and pronouncements as illegal or immoral. In this light, it was perhaps understandable—however devoid of propriety—that some of those benefiting from the monopoly would, as it broke up, either seek to suggest that the new texts were not really all that valuable, or else to raise questions about some of the principal figures involved in freeing them.

The most notable effort along these lines, however, involved a writer not directly implicated in the scandal as it unfolded. In a 1992 essay entitled "How Important are the Dead Sea Scrolls?"[1] Robert Alter of the University of California answered his titular query with unusually negative responses. As these came from a well-respected literary critic, and one whose opinions in this matter influenced the views of a public figure that would later be read by a mass audience, they require our careful attention. Particularly is this so if we are to be able to assess, free of prejudice, the value and importance of the scrolls, and their basic significance for our understanding of the development of Judaism and Christianity.

Alter asserted that the scrolls are of inferior literary and spiritual value, that they provide no significant link between biblical and early rabbinic thought, that the writers were physically isolated from the body politic of the Jews, and, in line with all of this, that the efforts of writers and scholars to free the texts were misguided. Our inquiry into his attack will reveal the powerful negative effect that the sectarian hypothesis has had upon representative members of the academy as well as others who sense a personal responsibility to ponder the meaning of the scroll discoveries. We may fairly ask whether Alter was justified in any of his strictures, which would, if well founded, have the effect of devaluing the scrolls and branding the effort to understand them a mere scholastic exercise.

Alter posited three central problems requiring resolution: "Who wrote these manuscripts, what they might have to say, and, above all, what is their intrinsic value as spiritual or literary productions"[2]—already thus revealing considerable bias of his own. A historian of the Jews would, by contrast, be concerned primarily with the value of the scrolls for understanding the nature of the history and culture of the Jews, as well as that of the earliest Palestinian Christians, during the period in which they were written. Alter did not appear concerned with what the scrolls might tell us about these basic matters, or even such questions as the emergent social and religious conflicts among those groups or the state of literacy and the culture of books in Jewish Palestine. Had he, nevertheless, in fact presented a fair and objective response based on the criteria he did posit, he would in a sense have suitably discharged his obligation. Instead, he passed in silence over the preponderance of evidence relating both to the scrolls and the Khirbet Qumran site, refrained from a discussion of most of the facts and circumstances surrounding the freeing of the scrolls, and altered my interpretation of their origin just enough to preserve his view that the authors of the scrolls were marginal and unimportant. This approach followed quite logically, to be sure, from a faith in the old hypothesis, which from the beginning so strongly emphasized the spiritual isolation of the "sect of Qumran."

"Challenges to the consensus are *vehement* but unconvincing," stated Alter, adding, after a brief dismissal of the views of Robert Eisenman on Qumran origins, that I had argued "in a less fanciful vein" that the scrolls "were not written at the Dead Sea and are *not sectarian productions.*"[3] (My italics.)

We will observe below how the same adjective recurs in the official catalogue of the American scrolls exhibitions that took place in 1993–94. It is puzzling that Alter should resort to this particular innuendo while in the same article referring to the editor of *Biblical Archaeology Review* as "leather-lunged," characterizing the efforts of newsmen and writers to make the public aware of scroll politics as "hullabaloo," and, as we shall see, bending ideas in the scrolls to his own purpose by speaking of them as "fulmination."

What is more, I never stated in my writings that the scrolls were "not sectarian productions," but, on the contrary, that they "represent various aspects of the actual state of Judaism at that time—with all its sectarian and heterodox complexities."[4]

Alter further attributed to me the suggestion that *"refugees* from the Roman onslaught against Jerusalem brought with them *a collection* of texts that covered *the whole spectrum* of literary productivity of *1st-century* Jewry" (my italics).[5] Rather, I proposed in all of my studies only what I have suggested in the present book: that the hiding was connected with the Roman siege on Jerusalem; that the task was quite likely accomplished by inhabitants (not uniquely "refugees") intent on preparing for the siege; that they hid away the contents of various libraries (not merely "a collection"); and that the hidden writings comprise fragments and pieces of the literature of the Jews written during the three intertestamental centuries (not "the whole spectrum of the literary productivity of 1st-century Jewry"). Thus, whereas Alter distorted my statements just enough to induce readers to believe that my interpretation of Qumran origins had a slightly bizarre allure, without his alterations the theory remains entirely consistent with the totality of facts now known about the scrolls.

Alter then compounded his distortion by attributing to me the view that the scrolls, once taken from Jerusalem, were hidden specifically at Qumran and nowhere else, and that people living at Qumran composed certain books: "[Golb's] contention is that refugees . . . brought with them a collection of texts. . . . While [he] *is surely right in saying there is no reason to assume that every Qumran text was actually composed at Qumran,* there are two lines of special pleading in his argument."⁶ Unfortunately, I never stated what Alter attributed to me in the italicized words; what I wrote was that there is no evidence that *any* manuscript found in the caves was written at Khirbet Qumran. Nor did I suggest a direct, single line leading solely from Jerusalem to Qumran, but rather that the discoveries were part of a much greater phenomenon: the hiding of Hebrew manuscripts in various caves and elsewhere in the Judean Wilderness during the war with Rome. The very fact that Alter did not as much as mention the *Copper Scroll* in his discussion revealed a bias against historical documents that is not pleasant to observe in the case of a serious literary critic.

Alter did mention a few archaeological findings that contribute to the theory of Jerusalem origin. But he offered no information about the discovery of scroll fragments at Masada, the earlier manuscript discoveries near Jericho, or other major pieces of evidence that vitiate the original sectarian hypothesis while showing that Jerusalem was the home of the manuscripts. He was silent concerning the lack of literary autographs among the cave manuscripts, the absence of any parchment at the Khirbet Qumran site itself, and the fact that several hundred scribes copied the texts.

Skipping over such bothersome details also facilitated Alter's claim of finding "two lines of special pleading" in my argument. One of these claimed lines was fictitious, and the other could be considered "special pleading" only by those intent upon preserving the original theory at the cost of common sense.

Alter explained that I "must insist upon striking ideological disparities among texts where the continuities of outlook and sensibility, *whatever the incidental discrepancies*, are impressive."⁷ (My italics.) Yet the question of the nature of the interrelationships among those Qumran texts that, by their contents, may be properly labeled as heterodox or sectarian were, at the very moment Alter was writing his article, being fiercely debated among scholars—including some of the most tenacious guardians of the old ideas about Qumran origins. The only relevant special pleading in evidence remains that of deeply traditional Qumranologists, who insist that, despite their inherent differences, all the texts have to be squeezed together into a single sectarian complex of ideas—an effort resulting, as we have seen, in utter confusion about the identification of the claimed "sect" among those Qumranologists themselves. Alter, championing the view of Prof. Sussman of the Hebrew University, stated that he found the Essene identification, in its modified form of Sadducaean subsect, to be the most plausible one. If, however, he were to attempt to back up this preference by recourse to all of the textual and archaeological evidence now at hand—not only some bits of it—he would be forced to engage in lines of argumentation that, today, most scholars would recognize as painfully illogical. The problems and contradictions in such identifications have not gone away despite the fact that Alter, following in Sussman's footsteps, chose not to discuss them in his article. Whatever "continuities in outlook and sensibility" exist among the scrolls may, on the other hand, be understood quite directly as reflecting the basic fact that all the scrolls were composed by Palestinian Jews of the intertestamental period.

Let us now consider the other case of what Alter termed my "special pleading." According to him, "from the absence of any *Pharisean* or early Christian documents in this supposedly eclectic collection of Jewish texts [Golb] is *compelled to conclude* that rabbinic Judaism and Christianity did not yet exist as movements, which is *surely allowing an initial premise to dictate a conclusion in the face of evidence that argues against it*" (my italics). This ostensible critique is in fact entirely hollow: By suggesting that the absence of Gospel or early rabbinic fragments among the Qumran finds might possibly indicate that neither rabbinic Judaism nor Christianity yet existed as movements before the destruction of the Second Jewish Commonwealth *circa* A.D. 70, I was raising a question that, in intelligent discourse, should obviously be posed about the Qumran finds. While Alter declared that I raised this possibility "in the face of evidence" against it, he did not hint at what this evidence is. We may guess that he meant traditions in the Gospels and in other parts of the New Testament about Jesus, his disciples, and early believers, or rabbinic dicta in the *Mishnah* and *Tosephta* describing charismatic intellects who lived before the destruction of the Second Temple, or rabbinic laws of the second century A.D. sometimes attributed to the Pharisees—in other words, traditions in literary and legal texts about an age of revelation, piety, or glory. If statements in these texts constitute what Alter meant by "evidence," then he was using the term far more loosely than would most professional students of the New Testament or the early rabbinic literature today.

The Qumran scrolls were deposited in the caves approximately in A.D. 70, and, being contemporary accounts, if they contain nothing of the Gospels or rabbinic dicta—which Alter's claimed Essenes would have had to study, if only to refute—this fact must be considered in weighing the question of the historical accuracy of early rabbinic and early Christian traditions. The letters of Paul, written several years before A.D. 70, do show the *preliminary* stages leading up to the early Christian movement, but the effect of the final destruction of the Second Jewish Commonwealth upon rabbinic hegemony and early Christianity's coalescence into a full-fledged movement still has to be assesed anew in light of the scroll findings.

Ironically, Alter offered his inaccurate and rather uninformed remarks about my theory of Qumran origins just as, in the wake of my articles, various traditional Qumranologists—even some on the official Jerusalem scroll committees whom Alter defended so generously—were slowly coming to admit, however grudgingly, that many if not most of the Qumran texts may well have come "from the outside." His approach surely reflected no inherent lack of acuity, but rather a satisfied comfort with the old attribution of the scrolls to a small fringe sect. In defending this notion, however, he delivered an attack on the scrolls' historical value that is cause for far greater concern than his treatment of my own views, and yet which follows from it axiomatically.

To fathom the nature and spirit of this attack, we must first recall that in my studies on the scrolls I had indicated that they represented not *all* of the writings of the Jews, but *"writings* of the Jewish people"—the most reasonable explanation, it would appear, of a cache of Hebrew manuscripts copied by at least five hundred scribes and containing such a great diversity of themes, ideas, and literary genres[8] (and we must remember that an incalculable number of other scrolls probably perished totally in the caves before remnants of some were discovered in our own century). In these texts we confront, in other words, a sizable body of literature, mostly unknown beforehand and from a period of Jewish history that had not previously been suspected of literary fecundity. Only the relatively few writings of the Apocrypha and Pseudepigrapha had been known, and many have precisely the qualities that Alter found so repugnant and, in his generalization of the facts, so common in the scrolls.

Much of the new body of literature clearly dates from the Hasmonaean age, a time when, in the words of the late Menachem Stern,

The persecution by Antiochus and the Maccabean revolt led to the spiritual and material independence of the Jewish nation both in Judea and outside. The Jewish monotheistic faith was saved, with momentous results for the world. In the second century [B.C.] . . . after centuries of subjection to imperial powers, an independent Jewish state had arisen under the leadership of the Hasmonaeans, and gradually expanding over the whole of Palestine, had achieved international recognition and status. Palestine became religiously and nationally "Greater Judaea," and this fact set its stamp on the religious, cultural, and ethnic character of the country for a long period. The existence of the Hasmonaean state was further accompanied by . . . vigorous religious development and by a strengthening of Judaism in the countries of the Diaspora.[9]

Many of the Qumran scrolls clearly reflect this development. The rest of the new literature, on the other hand, dates from the inception of Roman domination of Palestine in 63 B.C. until the destruction of the Second Jewish Commonwealth, when events of equally grave importance convulsed the Jewish people.

We may thus speak of a rich and unexpected source of new knowledge about these two periods, including texts referring to hitherto unknown events and personalities in Palestinian Judaism of those times. To study these texts for the purpose of a better understanding of the history and culture of the period in which they were written is as normal as it is essential. And yet, Alter's attitude toward that history appears to be singularly unenthusiastic. In one of the more remarkable passages of his essay, he declared that

the popular fascination with the Scrolls . . . sustained for over four decades and the inordinate hopes for a grand revelation from these scraps of parchment betoken one of the great modern illusions— that if only we could take within our grasp the material substance of the past, if only we could empty out the contents of its buried time capsules, we might touch an ultimate secret of origins, understand in a new and illuminating way how we came to be what we are.[10]

I suspect it would be difficult to find manuscript scholars (appearing in Alter's treatment to share their "modern illusions" with a world outside the ivory tower) who harbor the fantasy of revealing "an ultimate secret of origins." In articulating a sentiment akin to disdain for researchers who attempt to reconstruct aspects of the Jewish past from scraps of parchment, Alter would seem to have wished to align his own outlook with one he claimed, in several essays on the values at play in reading literature, to oppose unequivocally: namely, a form of vulgarized antirationalism accompanying the recent rise of "poststructuralist" discourse in American academic literary criticism. It is precisely a hallmark of this antirationalism to confuse the search for a larger, more accurate view of the world with the totalitarian effort to grasp "an ultimate secret of origins." In thus hazarding his argument, Alter regrettably deigned to embrace his opponents' intentional confusion. I am likewise obliged to note that Alter's ironic reference to understanding "in a new and illuminating way how we came to be who we are" appears to be a paraphrase of my description[11] of what is at stake in the scrolls debate. Alter was paraphrasing what many would consider to be the principal goal of all historical investigation, and the disdain he manifested for this "modern illusion" is unfortunate.

But Alter then proceeded to take on the role of historian, with altogether disastrous results. The authors of all these many manuscripts, he asserted, "withdrew from the teeming city to a rock-strewn desert"; the "air they breathed was an atmosphere of hypnotic words that insulated them from the changing winds of history"; the "sectarians . . . fled their Dead Sea dwelling in 68 C.E.," whereas by that time both "the early Christians (chiefly Paul) and the early rabbis had already taken decisive steps toward creating new systems of belief and religious practice out of the texts and ideas of the Hebrew Bible."[12]

With parchment clearly having been forsaken, where did Alter derive the "facts" that he divulges here so boldly? As we have observed, the archaeology of the Khirbet Qumran site yielded no proofs that it was inhabited by sectarians, or that the people who were living there either wrote books or fled the site in A.D. 68. Moreover, nothing has ever been found in the scrolls themselves proving that their authors were insulated from the dynamics of history; the idea that before A.D. 70 rabbinical figures or early Christians *as a group* took the decisive steps that he asserts they did, is a subject of great debate among scholars of both faiths. To suggest, in addition, that the ideas either of rabbinic Judaism or early Christianity developed directly from the books of the Hebrew Bible, untouched and uninfluenced by the intertestamental writings of the Jews, is in fact to leap across centuries in search of an ultimate truth of origins, and to do so while remaining untrammeled by the evidence of texts.

Scholars of the New Testament have demonstrated abundant parallels between ideas it contains and those found in the scrolls. Virtually all of rabbinic eschatology sprang from the ideas in the *intertestamental* literature, not from the Bible. It is absurd to suggest that Maccabees, Ben Sira, the Wisdom of Solomon and other Jewish writings of the intertestamental period had no influence upon the Jews of the first and second centuries A.D. The only prototypes of halakhic (that is, legal) discourse characteristic of the fundamental works of the early rabbis, the *Mishnah* and *Tosephta*, are those found—fragmentarily to be sure—among the Dead Sea Scrolls. The earliest pre-Midrashic commentaries on books deemed holy are those found in the Qumran caves. It is in fact altogether impossible to perceive any objective grounds for the startling conclusion to Alter's article.

Isolating the scrolls on the desert plateau of Qumran would, of course, help to diminish their significance, and with it that of all the intertestamental literature. Pliny the Elder, it is true, indicates that a group of celibate Essenes were living above En Gedi *after* the destruction of Second Temple Jerusalem, and Alter's predecessors claimed that this site was Qumran; but he himself accepted the notion that the supposed sectarian group fled their settlement in A.D. 68, *before* the destruction. As we have observed, scholars have tried as a result of this difficulty to change Pliny's text by simply omitting the reference to the destruction of Jerusalem, but without this convenient emendation, the entire identification falls apart.

In a similar fashion, Alter tried to harmonize uncooperative archaeological evidence with his story of isolated Qumran-Essene-Sadducaeans. He assured his readers that the twelve hundred graves adjacent to Khirbet Qumran were those of Essenes, who lived there about two hundred at a time—over a period of approximately five or six generations—but without explaining the resulting mysteries of the graves' regular alignment, why they showed no signs of stratification, and why they are so close to the site of habitation.[13] The claim about buried Essenes is ludicrous in the face of the archaeological evidence—and can only be understood as reflecting a deep desire to keep the scrolls in an isolated place. The same spirit of noninquiry was unfortunately manifest in Alter's refusal, after speaking of the "Sons of Light" as "few," to explain how this idea fit in with the gigantic ceremony of initiation envisioned in the *Manual of Discipline*, which called for the initiates to line up by "thousands, hundreds and tens."

Steadfastly maintaining the hypothesis that the scrolls were written and copied by a wilderness-dewlling sect at Khirbet Qumran, Alter had harsh words indeed for those he imagined living there. They represented "a dead end, not a nourishing source of either Judaism or Christianity." The "rocky ground" on which they lived "overlooked—spiritually as well as literally—a slate-gray sea of salt."[14] He sustained this rhetoric by emphasizing the strange imagery of the *War Scroll* and a few other texts, pointing by contrast to highlights of biblical literature, of which, he reminded his audience, he is a student. What he failed to note, but which any Bible student must, is that many of the books known collectively as the Bible were once individual writings that were part of a much greater mass of literary works circulating in that very intertestamental period that leaves him so cold.

The reticence is rather revealing, allowing us to make sense of Alter's rhetoric. Hovering as in a palimpsest behind his distaste for palaeography and his pronounced antihistoricism was an academic conflict far removed from that being played out in centers of Hebraic learning over the scrolls. A primary concern in his essay was to save the canonical understanding of literature—that is, an understanding based on study of the formal and thematic structures of commonly acknowledged great texts—from those latest inheritors of the poststructuralist agenda, the so-called New Historians, who are devoted to the ideal of demonstrating that literary works are, above all, reflections of the dominant ideologies at play in the societies and epochs from which they emerge. While it is reasonable to reject the extremism of the New Historians, diminishing as it does the worth of both individual creativity and the art it produces, it is unreasonable to deny the value of approaching literary works from a historical perspective. It is a worthy goal (for which Alter deserves credit) to honor the literary complexity and spiritual depth of what we have inherited as the Bible—but not, in critical scholarship, to treat it as primordially inscribed in a literary canon by a history-transcendent master hand.

The Jewish leadership of antiquity selected from a large mass of literature, over time, those writings that they felt to be sacred, but in the second century A.D., as we know from statements of the early rabbis, they were still debating whether certain books, e.g., the Song of Songs or Ecclesiastes, might be so considered.[15] The scrolls, by contrast, are discrete collections of texts. They include more dross—along with many outstanding lines of poetry and enticing prose that Alter refrains from quoting.

Inversely, while the Bible is a careful, deliberate selection, including many outstanding writings of ancient Hebrew culture, it also includes writings possessing somewhat less "intrinsic value" than Alter might allow. For instance: the long catalogues of animal sacrifices and incense burnings in the Pentateuch, and Chronicles with its seemingly endless lists of names. In between is a work such as Esther, containing a somewhat crudely entertaining story of Jewish vindication in Persia in which Esther, a Jewish woman, enters the harem of pagan(!) King Ahasuerus. Esther may be read as a poor, if perhaps politically necessary, substitute for the majestic but suppressed First Book of Maccabees (which has come down to us in Greek but was originally a Hebrew work), with its message of ultimate triumph over foreign domination through steadfast religious faith.

If we consider the Book of Esther apart from the mystique of its canonization, it becomes apparent that, academic politics aside, Alter's wish to diminish the scrolls' importance was ultimately based on a naïve confusion between poetic and moral value, on the one hand, and on the other, an apparent insensitivity to the value that literary texts may have for our understanding of history broadly considered. Even were the scrolls the largely inferior products Alter dismissed them as being, it would remain the case that weakly worded "derivative" writing may possess great value as an index to important currents of ideas and tastes. Many would consider the gnostic texts from Nag Hammadi and the Stoic manuscripts discovered in the private library of a villa in Herculanaeum to be in this category, and yet they are hardly the object of modern literary denunciation.

Indeed, the confusion was here so primary that its motives became almost obvious: Beyond the question of their "intrinsic value," Alter was manifestly discomfited by the scrolls' *implications*: by, among other things, the "brooding sense of sinfulness" he detected in several of the published texts. (I emphasize "several," because most of the scrolls contain no such outlook.) He preferred to banish this brooding sinfulness from the "teeming city" of Jerusalem to the "desert rock." Put the sinfulness and the brooding back in the city, and the interplay between intertestamental Judaism and various Hellenistic and eastern currents of thought, foreshadowed by some of the canonical writings, becomes all the more enticing a phenomenon. Intertestamental Judaism was not what we might today think of as "pure," and students of literature as well as of history should obviously avoid both myths of purity and those of origin.

Seemingly unable to accept this alternative, Alter was compelled to separate the authors of the Qumran texts from the wider body of Palestinian Jews. To these renegades, he then attached the stigma of "sustaining through literary pastiche and apocalyptic fulmination the illusion that they were still living at the heart of the biblical destiny . . . , *that they were continuing to write the Bible.*"[16] Despite this quite incredible accusation, not all apocalyptic is fulmination, and neither all nor most Qumran texts are afflicted by the pastiche that Alter attributed to them. Perhaps more to the point, the Jews of the first and second centuries B.C. would not even have known what the word "Bible" or its Hebrew equivalents meant. The "Bible" as such did not yet exist then, but was only in the (long) process of coming to be formed. Some of the late canonical writings—such as Daniel—read very much like certain works of the intertestamental period, and it is most difficult to perceive on what literary grounds critics might distinguish between them. By his standards of judgment, would Alter not be obliged to acknowledge that the Book of Daniel contains a good deal of "apocalyptic fulmination?"

Apparently not reflecting on this problem, Alter compounded his error in claiming that the Pharisees were at that very time "building a new edifice on the foundation of the Bible." Turning a blind eye to the intertestamental period in Jewish history altogether, he thus offered what is a mere gratuitous assumption, for which no proof exists in any pre-A.D. 70 source—neither in the intertestamental literature, nor Josephus or elsewhere. To bolster his view, however, he approvingly quoted the statement of Shemaryahu Talmon of the Hebrew University that in contrast to the writers of the Qumran texts, the earliest rabbinic figures "viewed the biblical era as a closed chapter and their own times as being profoundly different" from the earlier age.[17]

This proclaimed history, empty of all probative textual support, was then used by Alter to contrast an opinion he attributed to "Pharisees" with one supposedly held by the claimed desert sect whose existence he had set about championing. What he and Talmon both did was to compare ideas found in manuscripts written by Jews over a 300-year period before A.D. 70 with other ideas known only from texts of the post-Tannaitic period (i.e., the third and fourth centuries A.D.) in a way that made them seem contemporary with one another—hardly a sterling example of careful scholarship. It has never been determined whether any one group in the century and a half between the Hasmonaean revolt and the death of Herod the Great perpetually constituted what Talmon referred to as "the mainstream Jewish community," and the scrolls have only intensified the scholarly debate on this question.[18]

If any texts of those times exist that hint at the quest for a "new edifice" built on biblical foundations, they are precisely the ones from the Qumran caves that form the basis of the peculiar sectarian hypothesis that Alter chose to espouse. Foremost among them, the *Manual of Discipline* rejects money as spiritually defiling, favors commune-style purity groups, makes creative metaphorical use of biblical anthropomorphisms and sacrificial terminology, and, for the first time that we know, calls for organized, systematic group study of the Torah's "hidden" meanings. The *Damascus Covenant* expresses, among other ideas, the view that polygamy is immoral, something apparently never urged either by the Pharisees, Sadducees, or early rabbis: that is, precisely new edifices on biblical foundations. No records exist to show that the historical Pharisees sought such new edifices. If the spiritual and juridical leadership of the Jewish people fell to the Tannaim after the Temple was destroyed, it was in good measure because the priesthood had suddenly lost its power. The old traditional edifice crumbled and was destroyed in A.D. 70—not before—and it was only thereafter, as far as is known, that rabbinic leadership as such first emerged. The Tannaim did build a new and lasting edifice, but not until political circumstances obliged them to do so, and only long after other groups such as those reflected in the scrolls had begun their own search after the same goal.

On the other hand, if a certain number of the writers of the scrolls took refuge in apocalypticism, it was not because they

were "fulminators" as Alter suggests, but because they had sought
and in their opinion not found a more satisfactory answer to the
question so many people were asking: Why did the righteous continue to suffer and the wicked to prosper in a world governed by
the one true God? The Pharisees and Tannaim also did not produce a genuinely satisfactory answer to that question; something
good, they asserted, would be stored up for the righteous in a
world to come, and this in turn developed into the doctrine of the
physical resurrection of the dead. We need not choose sides in
such a debate. The question agitated both Jews and Christians for
centuries, and still does. One thing among many that we learn
from the scrolls is how Jewish authors of antiquity vied with one
another in producing imaginatively new answers to this and other
profoundly disturbing questions. The fact that this kind of literature is not to Alter's taste hardly diminishes its importance for the
history of Jewish thought and spirituality.

Alter's response to the events leading up to the freeing of the
scrolls was as remarkable as his historical speculation. After
describing anti-Jewish and anti-Zionist attitudes of certain members of the original non-Jewish editorial team, he could find nothing but kind words for the oversight committee formed by the
Israel Antiquities Authority, which, we will remember, included
two Hebrew University faculty members as well as curator Broshi
of Jerusalem's Shrine of the Book. Alter stated that Broshi "held
some forty half-day meetings with his advisory committee during
its first two years of operation. He also insisted that each scholar
assigned to edit a scroll be given an unambiguous deadline, with
1997 set as the date for submission of all materials and 2000 as
the date for the completion of publication." He described the
meetings as "energetic steps" that have been largely ignored "in
the recent outcry over the withholding of the Scrolls." Yet he said
nothing about the reasons underlying the general lack of enthusiasm for the so-called energetic steps.[19]

It was precisely the decisions of the oversight committee under
Broshi's chairmanship that caused the public outcry over the
withholding of the scrolls. The question of the number of meetings
held and the length of each meeting was not at all pertinent to
that fundamental issue. The oversight committee continued to
enforce the principle of exclusion practiced by the original editorial committee. In order to stifle the free and open exchange of

ideas, it decreed that only those researchers of whom it approved could examine the unpublished scrolls, and under this policy many researchers, myself and my students included, were prevented from studying these texts. The fact that Alter may not necessarily emphasize Qumran texts in his own teaching or have doctoral candidates in this field does not make the committee's effort less odious, and in glossing over what actually happened he showed obtuseness toward a basic value of learning.

Although the new committee obviously did not include anti-Semitic members, it did include those who fostered another goal inimical to the welfare of liberal and democratic societies. Instead of addressing this serious state of affairs, Alter allowed himself to champion both a discredited hypothesis and discredited committees, subtly suggesting that the Christian scholars who first held the monopoly were wicked and the Jewish scholars who took it over white knights. The record shows that, to the contrary, the particular religions of the parties did not in the end matter, and it remains quite remarkable that Alter did not perceive as much.

These various views of Alter would have merited far less extensive examination if not for a subsequent development. This was the appearance, in the official catalogue of the scrolls exhibitions that came to the United States in 1993, of a preface by the late president of the New York Public Library, Rev. Timothy S. Healy, consisting largely of the embrace of Alter's views on the scrolls.[20] The preface was in marked contrast to the same catalogue's foreword by Dr. James H. Billington, the Librarian of Congress, who pointedly refrained from adopting a position on the intensifying debate over the scrolls' origins and meaning.[21]

Dr. Healy, unlike the historian Billington, was primarily a literary scholar, indeed once a professor of English literature, and he undoubtedly had a professional sympathy for his fellow scholar of literature Dr. Alter. However, why, as the chief public official of one of the great institutions in America, he would step outside his appropriate role as its dispassionate administrator, attempting instead to influence the thinking of the general public on the merits of what was known to be a controversy among scholars, is a riddle painful even to mention in view of his sudden death on 30 December 1992, a few months before the catalogue was actually published. Echoing Alter, Healy even emphasized that the orientation of the writers of the scrolls encouraged "megalomaniacal self-

importance and a contempt for others as well as a kind of hallucinatory relation to present events."* The subsequent wide diffusion
of the catalogue with its endorsement, by a well-respected public
servant, of the Alter vision of an isolated and stultified sect cut off
from history, could not fail to convince many unsuspecting members of the general public to adopt this factually untenable idea.
By this action the basic rule of fair play in the public custodian-
ship of learning went unheeded, as it did in the New York Public
Library's subsequent display of the scrolls. And in that exhibition,
as in Alter's earlier devaluation of the manuscripts, what proved
to be most in evidence was the ultimately destructive consequence
of the Qumran-sectarian fixation.

The principles of open debate and institutional objectivity, deeply
ingrained in the Western democratic tradition, were championed
in Europe well over two centuries ago. The spirit of enlightenment that they betokened, ignited by the ideas of Voltaire,
Diderot, and other thinkers, was not long in reaching the American continent, and in 1780 found eloquent expression in the
American Philosophical Society's founding charter. The charter
emphasized that

*Here are other pertinent statements of Dr. Healy as they appear in the
catalogue (pp. 9–10): The scrolls "were written for and by a religious commune situated outside Jerusalem." The "Commune . . . appears to have lived
in total isolation, with heavy apocalyptic expectations. Alter says 'They withdrew from the teeming city to a rock-strewn desert, hearkening to the voice
of their master and awaiting the destruction of their enemies.'" Dr. Healy
went on to state: "The scrolls are clearly the works of a small sect, convinced
that it was continuing the great age of the composition of the Bible . . . and
essentially withdrawn from the vibrant, concomitant beginnings of both
Rabbinical Judaism and Christianity." Then came Healy's statement about
megalomaniacal self-importance and contempt for others, followed by his
assertion that "We would be hard put to find a more adequate general comment on the scholarly brawl that has erupted over the past three years."—It
is impossible to reconcile such statements with the view expressed earlier by
Healy in the same preface, to the effect that "In no sense did the New York
Public Library wish to involve itself or its people in the give-and-take of the
learned vendettas. . . . Any research library as inclusive as this one has a
catholicity of view that renders it immune to the ebb and flow of even the
most learned venom." Although Dr. Healy showed, by these utterances, a
baffling intolerance toward scholarly debate, he still was able to perceive
that it was not in keeping with the mission of the New York Public Library to
take part in the controversy.

the experience of ages shows that improvements of a public nature, are best carried on by societies of liberal and ingenious men, uniting their labours, without regard to nation, sect or party, in one grand pursuit, alike interesting to all, whereby natural prejudices are worn off, a humane and philosophical spirit is cherished, and youth are stimulated to a laudable diligence and emulation in the pursuit of wisdom.

It fell to a European thinker to enlarge on these principles in the following century. Writing in 1859, John Stuart Mill observed that even the concepts of the wisest members of society should, to merit approbation, "be submitted to by that miscellaneous collection . . . called the public"; he argued that man "is capable of rectifying his mistakes by discussion and experience. Not by experience alone. There must be discussion, to show how experience is to be interpreted. . . ."

As events leading up to the 1994 exhibition of the scrolls in America began to unfold, these words kept coming to mind with a freshness that belied their age. I had received an invitation to participate in the symposium at the Library of Congress scheduled for the April opening of the exhibition there, and, although the other nine scholars chosen for the panel were all, by design, traditional Qumranologists, I decided to participate. I fruitlessly urged the library to add other voices, so that the audience might have the opportunity to perceive the growing divergences of opinion on Qumran origins.[22] Concerned that, despite declarations to the contrary, a distorted presentation of the scrolls and related artifacts would also work its way into the exhibit itself, I wrote the appropriate parties at the library, urging that it not fall into the trap of endorsing any particular scholarly position on the fundamental issues.

The display in its preliminary form did indeed announce, on explanatory placards, the library's intention to present an objective exhibition. By contrast, however, the descriptions of the individual manuscripts—virtually all of them scroll fragments from Cave 4 that had never been displayed before—almost entirely reflected the views of traditional Qumranologists. I pointed out the discrepancy to one of the directors of the exhibit, who indicated it would be appropriate to add further descriptions of the individual manuscripts. The library thereafter limited itself, however, to publishing an explanatory brochure that, despite occasional lapses into the rhetoric of traditional Qumranology, sought to present an objective picture reflecting the exhibition's subtitle—"The Ancient Library of Qumran and Modern Scholarship."

Well over a year earlier, the library had locked itself into a difficult position. In December 1991, General Drori of the Antiquities Authority, apparently stung by the unfavorable publicity over the freeing of the scrolls, had come to the U.S. to propose a series of exhibitions. The agreement subsequently worked out between the Authority and the host institutions (the Library of Congress, the New York Public Library, and the M. H. de Young Memorial Museum of San Francisco)[23] called for the Authority to supply the written catalogue of the exhibitions—and the catalogue was written not under the supervision of the museums or of an objective academic body, but by the Antiquities Authority itself. The outcome was predictable: The catalogue, written and edited by Ayalah Sussman and Ruth Peled of the Antiquities Authority, with contributions by others, gave prominent expression to virtually all the basic ideas endorsed by the late Yigael Yadin, and either suppressed or barely mentioned all opposing ideas. This led the Israeli journalist Avi Katzman to ask if the State of Israel had embarked on a policy of official endorsement of the Qumran-Essene hypothesis.[24]

The Librarian of Congress, Dr. Billington, had expressly declared in his foreword to the catalogue that

> We . . . explore the various theories concerning the nature of the Qumran community, its identity, and its theology; and discuss the challenges facing modern researchers as they struggle to reconstruct the texts and contexts. . . ."[25]

No such explorations or discussions, however, were contained in the catalogue. Instead, the rote repetition of elements in the old hypothesis, to the exclusion of opposing ideas, was accompanied by a series of brazen misstatements apparently meant to reassure visitors to the exhibit that all was well in the world of Qumranology. Our review of these misstatements will serve to underscore, by contrast, many of the central observations about the scrolls that are found in this book.

Thus the catalogue solemnly informed readers that "not a stone has remained unturned in the desert" and that the "Qumran settlement has been exhaustively excavated."[26] In actuality, as of 1993 discoveries continued to be made in the Judaean Wilderness,[27] the cemetery of Khirbet Qumran remained mostly unexcavated, no final scientific report of de Vaux's excavation had been published,

and the site of habitation itself, given the controversy over its identification, still required far deeper probing than that achieved by the
latter's team in the 1950s. That is why several teams of archaeologists came to be deployed for intensive explorations ("Operation
Scroll") beginning late in 1993 at Qumran and at the sites of several clusters of caves in the Jericho area—a course of action that
shows only a prior reluctance to continue the explorations until
the urgency of the political situation forced the Authority to take that
course.[28] The catalogue went on to minimize the importance of the
adjacent cemetery of twelve hundred graves by obliquely stating that
"nearby" Khirbet Qumran "were remains of burials"—without further explanation.[29] Against the growing tide of scholarly opinion, it
offhandedly described the *Copper Scroll* as "containing a lengthy ros-
ter of real or imagined hidden treasures—a tantalizing enigma to
this day."[30] Faithfully echoing curator Broshi, the catalogue spe-
ciously claimed that the Khirbet Qumran structures "were neither
military nor private but rather communal in character."[31]

The catalogue also declared without warrant that "the destruction of the site . . . at the hands of the Roman legions" took place
"in 68 C.E."[32] It asserted that "scholarly opinion regarding the time
span and background of the . . . scrolls is anchored in historical,
paleographic, and linguistic evidence, corroborated firmly by carbon 14 datings"—a seemingly quite innocuous statement applicable to various theories of Qumran origins. It was accompanied,
however, by an assertion that "the bulk of the material, particularly the texts that reflected on a sectarian community, are originals
or copies from the first century B.C.E.," with an ensuing discussion
of "the Qumran sect's origins." The earlier remark about "historical, palaeographic and linguistic evidence" thus emerged as a
rhetorical device for legitimizing the widely rejected notion that
the ideas of only a single sectarian group were reflected in the
Qumran writings. As we have observed, many scroll scholars had
been forced considerably before 1993 to face up to the broad variety of religious ideas at work in the scrolls; and the radiocarbon
datings explicitly showed that copies of a good many of the so-
called sectarian Qumran texts could as well have been transcribed
in the opening decades of the first century A.D. As of 1993, no evidence whatever supported the catalogue's additional claim that
some of the texts may have been literary autographs.

The catalogue offered the statement that the accounts of Philo,
Josephus, and Pliny regarding the Essenes "are continuously

being borne out by the site excavations and study of the writings," but provided absolutely no indication of how this might be so. A similar obscurantism characterized the claim that, in contrast with Sadducees and Pharisees, "the Essenes were a separatist group, part of which formed an ascetic monastic community that retreated to the wilderness." "The retreat of the Jews into the desert," it was explained, "would enable them 'to separate themselves from the congregation of perverse men' (1Q Serekh [= *Manual of Discipline*] 5.2)."[33] In this way, the catalogue aligned itself with that group of Qumranologists who, basing themselves on an obvious misinterpretation of the *Manual*'s well-known "Wilderness" citation from Isaiah, naïvely claimed that the group described in the *Manual* literally migrated to the desert.

The catalogue repeated several familiar arguments for the credibility of the Qumran-Essene hypothesis—mostly extrapolated, however, from the wording of only a few texts found in the caves. Thus it declared that "customs described in ancient sources as Essene . . . are all echoed in the scrolls."[34] All the practices mentioned in the catalogue, however, appear in *a few* of the scrolls, and the fact that such ideas, as well as most of the practices and views attributed to the Essenes in the classical sources, do *not* occur in the great majority of the other Qumran texts, proved the very opposite of what the editors wished the public to believe.

When the catalogue claimed that "the persecution of the Essenes and their leader, the 'teacher of righteousness,' probably elicited the sect's apocalyptic visions,"[35] it stated as probabilities what was a mere series of unproven assumptions. The attempt to pin the apocalyptic scrolls precisely on that one small group, to the exclusion of other Jews, trivialized a significant genre of the Jewish literature from the intertestamental age.

Two of the three inkpots found at Khirbet Qumran, the catalogue explained, were located "in the vicinity of a large table, which suggested to the site's excavators scribal activity in a scriptorium. It is feasible," readers were told, "that many of the manuscripts were written or copied locally, although manuscripts of earlier date and other locations may well occur."[36] The catalogue thus implicitly adopted an old hypothesis of the early excavators without informing readers that those who continued de Vaux's work have concluded, after minute examination of the finds, that the table was not a table but a bench once infixed into the wall, and that the claimed "scriptorium" did not have the characteristics of such a workroom but, as we have seen, those of a dining parlor.

Surprisingly, in an appendix to the catalogue, A. Yardeni actually took up the theme of multiple scribal handwritings: "the variety of handwritings [in the scrolls]," she explained, "testifies to the activity of scores of scribes. It is reasonable, therefore, to believe that *a great many documents found in the caves of Qumran came from other places*."[37] While refraining, in connection with this idea, from mentioning Jerusalem or from indicating that there were not merely scores but at least five hundred different scribal handwritings attested in the scrolls, Yardeni at all events obviously made a most important admission. But by that token where was the proof of the belief so strongly supported in the catalogue that pious scribes sat at Khirbet Qumran transcribing manuscripts?

The Antiquities Authority's use of an exhibition catalogue to impose a bankrupt historical idea upon the lay public was obviously inappropriate. The Library of Congress should have exercised stronger leadership by repudiating any such imposition, particularly since the authors of the catalogue saw fit to devote only a single short paragraph to a cursory mention of other interpretations of Qumran origins. The catalogue, reappearing both at the New York Public Library exhibition in the autumn of 1993 and at the M. H. de Young Memorial Museum in San Francisco early the following year, was all the more troubling on account of what it augured for future "official" volumes in the Discoveries in the Judaean Desert series. In this series, facsimiles, transcriptions, and translations of the newly released scrolls are apparently to be accompanied, as the director of the Antiquities Authority has indicated, by "authoritative" (i.e., officially sanctioned) interpretations. For a glimpse at what these interpretations offer in the way of scientific integrity, we may briefly examine the way the authors of the catalogue, co-opting the services of "official" scroll editors, dealt with the individual texts featured in the exhibitions.

In describing the well-known *Songs of the Sabbath Sacrifice*, for example, the catalogue declared (p. 68) that the headings of the songs "reflect the solar calendar of the Qumran sect," that the "phraseology and terminology of the text are similar to those of other Qumran works," and that it "appears, therefore, that the Songs of the Sabbath Sacrifice is a sectarian work." There followed a transcription and translation of one of the fragments of this work by Carol Newsom, the original editor of the full text, who in 1991 *retracted* her earlier view that this work was the product of a sectarian author.[38] While Newsom's *original* text publication was cited in the catalogue, no reference appeared to her published retraction, and the editors of the catalogue abstained from as much as alluding to it. In a word, they failed to deal with the text in accordance with the norms of scholarly ethics.

A similar failure was obvious in the treatment of the song of praise honoring Alexander Jannaeus. We have seen earlier (Chapter 9) how the three editors of this text had dealt with the difficulty it posed: Finding no proof that this poem was "written by the authors of the community who inhabited Qumran" they had suggested that many of the scrolls were "the creative fruits of extensive Jewish groups in the Second Temple period," acknowledging that they were "not able to suggest a reason why a prayer for the peace of Alexander Jannaeus and his kingdom ended up at Qumran."

In the very act of expressing their allegiance to the traditional dogma, the three authors of the article had, by these last statements, inadvertently raised ponderous new questions about it. Nevertheless, they were asked to submit their text and translation for publication in the catalogue of the exhibitions. The introduction to their work by the authors of the catalogue, however, strikingly differed in its basic argument from that of the scholarly article. Instead of the emphasis on the "creative fruits of extensive Jewish groups" and the mystery of how the song of praise ended up at Qumran, the following remarkable change of wording appeared in the statement introducing this text:

> there is a high possibility, perhaps also alluded to in the *Nahum Commentary*, that Jonathan-Jannaeus, unlike the other Hasmonaean rulers, was favored by the Dead Sea sect, at least during certain periods (p. 40).

This "high possibility" had never been as much as alluded to in the authors' original article. What is more, readers of the catalogue were not told on what grounds it was now based. The earlier view of the scholars who had worked most on this fragment, as of Newsom regarding her own text, was thus altered in the catalogue just enough to promote the sectarian theory of Qumran origins being championed by the Antiquities Authority.*

---

*It is no less a mystery why the song of praise, as it appears in the catalogue, is neither edited nor translated in a way faithful to the original, as shown above, pp. 266–267.

A further instance of flagrant misrepresentation occurred in the case of the famous *Acts of Torah* (designated in the catalogue as *Some Torah Precepts*). The catalogue's introduction to these fragments (p. 64) explained that on the basis of "linguistic and theological considerations" that text "has been dated as one of the earliest works of the Qumran sect." This explanation omitted the facts that the Hebrew idiom of this writing was akin to early rabbinic Hebrew—hardly likely to date to any time before the early first century A.D.—and that both in its religious ideas and its ritual laws the text stood alone and apart from all of the other known scrolls. The catalogue thus claimed that the text was one of the earliest Qumran works not because of the linguistic and theological evidence but, once again, *despite* it.

Other statements concerning this text were similarly misleading. The catalogue claimed that the text was "addressed to 'the leader of Israel,'" but no such phrase is in the text. It stated that disagreements on ritual matters "caused the sect to secede from Israel," whereas the author of the epistle had stated only that his group "separated from the majority of the people"—a different concept altogether. The reader was informed that the commentary on Psalms from Cave 4 "relates that the 'teacher of righteousness' conveyed a letter to his opponent, the 'wicked priest'"—and that this "may well be a reference to this document [= the *Acts*]." It is, to be sure, somewhat ludicrous to connect a text written in proto-rabbinic Hebrew with events of the second century B.C.; it is much more so when this involves an event such as the sending of a specific letter. In any case, the very claim of the existence of such a letter was based only upon the *reconstruction* of a passage in the Psalms commentary, not upon the preserved words of the commentary themselves.*

The catalogue dealt with other texts in an equally unsatisfactory manner, ranging from misleading to confusing and incoherent. In discussing one of the *Manual of Discipline* fragments from Cave 4 (referred to in the catalogue as the "Community Rule"), the authors offered further remarks about the nature of "the sect": The

---

*See the edition of J. Allegro, *Qumran Cave IV, I (4Q158–4Q186)*, Discoveries in the Judaean Desert of Jordan V, (Oxford, 1968), p. 45. All that is left of the passage are some broken phrases translatable as follows: "The explanation (of Psalm **37**.32) concerns the wicked [pries]t who [. . . .] to slay him [. . . .] and the Torah because he sent to him. . . ." Who or what was sent, and by whom to whom, is not as much as hinted at in the passage.

Manual, they stated, contained regulations for "the members of the Yahad, the group within the Judaean Desert sect who chose to live communally" (p. 60). This seems connected to an earlier statement (p. 26) that part of the Essenes "formed an ascetic monastic community that retreated to the wilderness"; but the reader by this very token was bound to become confused as to whether the "Judaean Desert sect" was a part of a larger whole, viz. the Essenes, and that the "ascetic monastic community" was only a part within that part, or otherwise. If the Yahad group both lived in the desert and was celibate, it becomes quite bizarre that the score of writings attributable to that group, and the many other scrolls, say nothing whatever about the requirement of celibacy.

The difficulty in sustaining the desert-habitation theory as a whole actually formed the background to the subsequent translation by Qimron of a passage from the *Manual*. The translation was remarkably fluent compared with Qimron's translation of the *Acts of Torah* passage appearing in the catalogue. But the fluency began only after the first two sentences of the translation,* and was interrupted by a most enigmatic rendering of the "wilderness" passage from the *Manual* based on Isaiah **40**.3. The text presented was but a small fragment, representing part of column **9** of the relatively complete copy of the *Manual* found in Cave 1. The first reference to the "clearing of the way in the wilderness" had occurred in column **8** of the full text, where, as we have seen earlier, there could be no serious doubt as to the meaning: i.e., that the separation from "men of wickedness" alluded to in Isaiah's words *consisted* in the deep study (*midrash*) of the Torah (col. **8**, lines 13–15). Clearly aware of this fact, Qimron translated the second "wilderness" passage as "That is the *time for studying the Torah* (*lit.* clearing the way) *in* the wilderness."[39] (My italics.)

By this interpolated rendering, Qimron attempted to save what we have earlier shown to be a favorite notion of the traditional Qumranologists—that the authors of the *Manual* endorsed the idea of midrash of the Torah literally following upon self-exile in the wilderness, viz. at Khirbet Qumran. The text that Qimron

---

Catalogue, p. 61: "And according to his insight he shall admit him. In this way both his love and his hatred." This meaningless translation is unwarranted by the wording of the original Hebrew, where Qimron's sentences are merely phrases that form part of an actually much longer sentence unit yielding a quite satisfactory meaning.

translated, however, did not at all make a statement about studying the Torah in the wilderness, but rather clearly reiterated the idea (already expressed in column **8** of the full text) that the teaching "of wondrous and truthful secrets in the midst of the men of the Yahad" was in itself the ideal alluded to by the words of Isaiah concerning the "season of clearing a path in the wilderness." No command whatever occurs in the *Manual* about literal self-exile of the Yahad group to the desert. Qimron simply chose to create the impression of such a command by his translation.

Among the manuscripts catalogued was one (*Catalogue*, pp. 44–47) consisting of a portion of the Pentateuchal verses that went into the boxes of the phylacteries. The one depicted was found in Wadi Murabba'at, not at Qumran, but as we have seen earlier, a good many others were discovered in the Qumran caves themselves. The catalogue's authors, however, calmly avoided the necessity of discussing the problem posed by the variety of versions of the Qumran phylactery texts by not mentioning the contradictory details in those found at Qumran, details pointing directly to the multiform origin of the scrolls. Instead they merely displayed a later example (second century A.D.) from the Murabba'at caves. Having no organic connection with the Qumran finds, this fragment did not represent an embarrassment to the traditional theory and thus could be safely displayed.*

---

*As recently as 1992, David Rothstein of the University of California at Los Angeles stated that "it appears probable that [the circles responsible for the phylacteries] . . . constituted a broad spectrum of Palestinian (and diaspora) Jewry." See the text of his U.C.L.A. doctoral dissertation, *From Bible to Murabba'at: Studies in the Literary, Textual and Scribal Features of Phylacteries and Mezuzot in Ancient Israel and Early Judaism* (University Microfilms, 1993), p. 181. The author also recognized that "the scrolls attest to many methods of scribal correction" (ibid., p. 336) and "exhibit a wide array of practices reflecting the special status accorded the Tetragrammaton" (ibid., p. 343). Many features of the phylacteries were "perfectly consistent with the practices which prevailed in the early rabbinic period," and "the frequently encountered depiction of these exemplars as 'Essene' or 'sectarian' must be called into question" (ibid., p. 427). The author based his conclusions on a painstaking study of the individual texts and their comparison with pertinent statements in early rabbinic sources, but since the conclusions ran directly counter to the dogma being pressed by the Antiquities Authority personnel, no mention of the findings was made at the pertinent place in the exhibition catalogue.

The same cavalier approach spilled over into their descriptions of virtually each of the other texts presented. In the case of the Psalms scroll from Cave 11, the catalogue authors stated (p. 52) that it might be "of calfskin rather than sheepskin, *which was the common writing material at Qumran*." (My italics.) Yet no writing material has ever been found at Khirbet Qumran. What is more, the catalogue's description hid the fact that the very editor of the Psalms scroll in question had stated that this work—which contains several noncanonical psalms as well as some canonical ones—reflected ideas that are *anti*-Essenic.[40]

One of the most important texts, the *Damascus Covenant*, had been known and its identity had been debated before the Qumran discoveries. Declaring that despite many earlier identifications suggested for this text, "the discovery of similar material in the caves . . . confirmed a link between the Damascus Document and the literature of the Qumran community," the catalogue then explained that a fragment of the text—the one both displayed in the exhibit and published in the catalogue—included "the requirement of full disclosure in arranging marriage," and that according to Josephus "Essene men who married took every precaution to ascertain the good moral and physical characters of their wives": the clear message being that the *Damascus Covenant* was perforce an Essene text. From the contents of the *Covenant* and particularly its laws, however, this is not at all obvious; the relatively lengthy text, for example, says not a word in favor of celibacy.

In the *Covenant* fragment published in the catalogue, giving an unworthy woman in marriage to a man, or vice versa, is compared to violating the pentateuchal injunction against wearing garments of mixed cloth or plowing with an ox and ass together. We have observed (page 194) that the author of the *Acts of Torah* used these very same pentateuchal injunctions to argue against the marriage of priests with the daughters of nonpriestly fathers. In the *Damascus Covenant* there is no such marriage prohibition; the authors inveigh, instead, against polygamy and uncle–niece marriages. The catalogue (p. 29) spoke of the *Covenant*, the *Manual of Discipline*, and the *Acts of Torah* all together as "collections of rules and instructions *reflecting the practices of the commune*" (my italics)—whereas the contents of various passages in the Qumran texts reflect fundamental legal differences, pointing to a plurality of streams in intertestamental Judaism.

One must note that the catalogue failed to state both that the transcription of this fragment was actually made by J. T. Milik in the 1950s and eventually passed on to Dr. Baumgarten, whose edition and translation appear in the catalogue; and that other scholars published Milik's transcription of this and other fragments of the *Covenant* from Cave 4 in 1991.[41]

The consistent effort of the catalogue's editors to deflect public perception of the multiform nature of the scrolls was manifest in the arbitrary exegesis to which they subjected even the biblical scrolls. Thus, in presenting the scroll of Leviticus written in palaeo-Hebrew script, they stated (p. 48) that this feature of the text "seems to be just one manifestation of conservative traits that survived through generations and *surfaced in the Hasmonaean era*." (My italics.) This statement implied that palaeo-Hebrew—the original Hebrew script—was replaced by Aramaic square script (i.e., the script that came to be referred to as Hebrew) long before the Hasmonaean period, and that it then underwent a *resurgence* that brought it back into vogue in the second century B.C.: i.e., with the rise of the claimed "sect of Qumran."

There is no evidence of any sort, however, that such a process of surfacing ever occurred. What the presence of the palaeo-Hebrew Leviticus text, along with other biblical texts in the same script found in the caves, did show was that the tradition of copying pentateuchal scrolls in the original written form of Hebrew survived into the second century B.C. The custom of using the palaeo-Hebrew script would continue into the period of the Bar Kokhba revolt (A.D. 132–135). This tradition may indeed, by the first century B.C., have been carried on by relatively conservative groups, not necessarily by all the Jews of that period, but there is no way to relate such groups to the authors of the *Yahad* texts, who contented themselves with writing merely the Tetragrammaton in palaeo-Hebrew.

Some positive features did indeed characterize the catalogue. The color photographs were excellent, and transcriptions of the individual texts mostly accurate. The section on artifacts found during the excavations of Khirbet Qumran revealed interesting aspects of the material life of its inhabitants and, in the case of some of the items found in the caves, of the hiders of the scrolls. Yet even the impressive variety of jars and other artifacts, many of them similar to objects that have been discovered in Jerusalem itself, supported the view that the finds reflected the material culture of the Jews of Roman Judaea as a whole, and not that of an

isolated desert sect that considered wealth as something spiritually defiling.

Thus, despite the beauty of the catalogue and the intrinsic
interest of the manuscripts and artifacts, the editors' main
thrust—i.e., their treatment of the scholarly debate over Qumran
origins and the meaning of the scrolls—showed a blind partiality
to the old ideas, to the virtual exclusion of more recent interpretations. In so doing, they and those responsible for their work at
the Antiquities Authority not only misled the public but also damaged the reputation of Israeli scholarship and its many fine
achievements. And with posted descriptions of individual manuscripts based almost entirely on what the catalogue had to say
about them, the exhibit at the Library of Congress could not live
up to the standard of objective presentation that the Librarian
himself had promised. At the same time, by posting several placards at the exhibit alerting the public to the growing debate over
Qumran origins, issuing a modest disclaimer in the form of a
freely distributed brochure, and attempting to bring some semblance of balance into the symposium that it sponsored, the
library did make evident its eventual resistance, polite but
increasingly firm, to the Antiquities Authority's effort to maintain
total control of the interpretations and ideas concerning the
scrolls to be presented to the public.

The Authority would have a greater success in New York, where
the exhibit moved in the autumn of 1993, and eventually in San
Francisco. Dr. Leonard Gold, the chief librarian of the New York
Public Library's Jewish Division, had, as we have seen in the previous chapter, stated that the exhibition would "take the point of
view that there was a sect and that most of the scrolls were connected to the sect," and he fully lived up to his promise: Thus, just
after entering the exhibit—more detailed than the Library of
Congress version and as excellent in its physical presentation as
was the catalogue—the visitor came face-to-face with a large
explanatory placard posing the question: "Who were the people
who produced the scrolls?"—and responding, *inter alia*:

> Early scroll researchers identified as the Essenes the inhabitants of
> Qumran and the religious community reflected in some of the
> scrolls. . . . Because Pliny locates an Essene settlement near the
> western shore of the Dead Sea, north of En Gedi, his writing has

been an especially important part of the evidence in support of the Essene hypothesis.

Reflecting Gold's belief that the Essene theory had not "been refuted,"* such prose would appear to reflect a desire not so much to educate as to brainwash the public. This impression was only strengthened by the small signs referring to other theories scattered in odd corners of the exhibition hall next to individual books or articles, which contrasted notably with the large spaces devoted to the elucidation of the Qumran-Essene hypothesis. In the same manner, the curators borrowed their descriptions of individual manuscripts almost verbatim from the Antiquities Authority's catalogue: the same reticence about the significance of the phylacteries, the same downplaying of the *Copper Scroll*, the same misleading assertions about the *Acts of Torah*, and so forth. A substantial part of the exhibit (entitled "The Scrolls as Texts") was divided into three subsections, termed "The Hebrew Bible," "Apocrypha and Pseudepigrapha," and "Sectarian Writings"—with no mention of an obvious fourth literary category of scrolls, namely, intertestamental literature of the Jews that was neither biblical nor sectarian, and not included in the Apocrypha or Pseudepigrapha. With many Qumranologists, even some of the most traditional, recognizing by 1990 that much of the literature preserved in the caves was in this fourth category, the library's reticence indicated a zeal not only to parrot the interpretation in the official catalogue (p. 28), but entirely to foreclose other options despite the trend in scholarly interpretation.†

*Dr. Gold's view is thus expressed in a letter to me of 26 February 1993.

†A *New York Times* article of 8 October 1993 reviewing the exhibition suggests, in the spirit of the event, that "As many scholars have concluded, the scrolls were produced by the Essenes. . . . The ruins at Qumran are generally believed to be the remains of an Essene settlement. The writings of ancient historians . . . are cited in the exhibition *to support the Qumran-Essene connection*." (My italics.) The lopsided partiality of the exhibit was self-evident. And yet in response to my appeal to the library administration to remedy this situation (letter of 30 September 1993), the administrative vice-president wrote (13 October 1993) that he had "complete confidence that the exhibit's curator . . . *struck a balance between competing views* as professionally as possible within the confines of the space available to him." (My italics.) The same *Times* article stated that I had "written letters to the library complaining that [my] position was not represented in the exhibition." I expressed no such complaint, the correspondence focusing entirely on the Library's responsibility to present an impartial exhibition.

A very impressive model of the Khirbet Qumran site, not included in the Library of Congress exhibition, was on display at the New York showing, but proved to be only another tool for promoting the Essenic identification of the complex. The "elaborate water system," stated an accompanying placard, "with its cistern and pools, testifies to the group's preoccupation with ritual purity, and corroborates the evidence of the texts." Another placard did acknowledge that "scholars dissenting from the common view [*sic*] have suggested that Qumran was the site of a fortress or a villa," but, characteristically, the placard did not note the evidence supporting these other identifications.

The conflation of "education" with the Antiquities Authority's intentions was also sadly evident in the "Educator's Guide" and a "Student Guide" apparently intended for use at the junior and senior high school levels. Among the questions in the "Educator's Guide" to be posed to the unsuspecting students were the following:

> *Why do you think the people of the scrolls lived in Qumran?*
> *What was their relation to Jerusalem? . . .*
> *Why have these people chosen to separate themselves?*
> *Do you believe that the only way for these people to practice their faith is to isolate themselves?* ("Educator's Guide," p. 11)

The answers the students were encouraged to give to these and related questions posed by the educators included the following:

> The discovery [of pottery] *confirmed the connection* between the scrolls found in the caves and the artifacts found in the nearby [Khirbet Qumran] ruins. ("Student Guide," verso of third unnumbered leaf)

> *It is believed that the sect hid the scrolls in jars and placed them in the caves for safekeeping.* (Ibid., recto of fourth unnumbered leaf)

> The *Community Rule* [= *Manual of Discipline*] tells us about the sect *we believe* lived in the Qumran area, very likely the Essenes. (Ibid.)

> *. . . Some Torah Precepts* [= the *Acts of Torah*] *. . .* appears to have been written in the form of a letter by the leader of the Qumran community. (Ibid. All italics mine other than titles)

It goes without saying that institutions responsible for public culture and education must avoid even the semblance of impropriety. In the case of the New York Public Library, that semblance was gross—not only because of the extreme partisanship of the exhibition, its practice of censorship* and opposition to the free flow of ideas, and its attempt to indoctrinate young people who viewed it, but also because of the very particular circumstance that the library has benefited greatly from the laudable generosity of the Dorot Foundation of New York. The foundation, endowed by the late philanthropist D. Samuel Gottesman, made possible the restoration in 1984 of the D. Samuel and Jeane H. Gottesman Hall of the New York Public Library and established the Dorot Chief Librarianship of the library's Jewish division. Mr. Gottesman, however, had also contributed heavily to the purchase for Israel, through Yigael Yadin's personal mediation, of the four scrolls originally offered for sale by the Metropolitan of the Syrian Jacobite monastery of St. Mark. The heirs of the donor thereafter sponsored the construction of the Shrine of the Book in Jerusalem, where the seven original Dead Sea Scrolls continue to be housed. The Dorot Foundation has since contributed generously to archaeological expeditions in Israel, and that it enjoys a close and fruitful relationship with the Israel Antiquities Authority is a matter of public knowledge.

The library's exhibit was in notable harmony with the Antiquities Authority's well-documented intentions. The Authority itself managed to make crystal clear, despite its own earlier disavowals, that its effort to keep the scrolls from the eyes of independent scholars had not been merely for the sake of protecting rights of members of an "official" editorial team, but—more critically—was to discourage the spread of new ideas on the origin of the scrolls and the identification of their authors. Through its efforts, the Authority sought to protect the expressed beliefs of long-departed scholars whose memory was held to be sacred—a choice of conduct and action that remains inimical to the spirit of free inquiry. This holding operation necessarily meant turning away from an ethos of cogent historical understanding and religious openness that would have

*See the observation of M. Foucault to the effect that censorship takes three forms: affirming that something "is not permitted, preventing it from being said, [and] denying that it exists." Idem, *The History of Sexuality* 1: An Introduction (New York, 1978), p. 84.

made the American scroll exhibitions worthy of emulation.* By its extreme acquiescence in the Authority's exhibition plans, the New York Public Library made a mockery of the principle of custodial impartiality, laid waste to the ideal of open debate as an essential ingredient in the enlightenment of the public and the search for truth, and gave comfort to the Authority's repressive policies regarding the rights of independent scholars to investigate and publish the scrolls. The vast majority of the nonspecialized audience streaming into the exhibition halls, and particularly those who read the posted descriptions of the individual manuscripts, could only have come away with the idea that a small sect, living in a desert self-exile far from the vital core of Palestinian Judaism, somehow wrote the hundreds of texts discovered in the caves. What occurred was a remarkable failure of intellectual leadership in a situation where it was urgently required. It was as if those responsible for the exhibition had somehow forgotten, however temporarily, the principle enunciated in John Stuart Mill's incisive observation that

> it is not on the impassioned partisan, it is on the calmer and more disinterested bystander, that [the] . . . collision of opinions works its salutary effect. Not the violent conflict between parts of the truth, but the quiet suppression of half of it, is the formidable evil; there is

---

*The subsequent exhibition at the M. H. de Young Museum in San Francisco (26 February–29 May 1994) merely copied, on a smaller scale, basic elements of those that had preceded it, making no independent effort to give a balanced portrayal of scroll origins. This was shown not only in the way the individual scrolls were described, but also by (a) the museum's sponsorship of talks by lecturers who were well known as defenders of the traditional theory, (b) the apparent boycott of certain scholars who had taken part in the freeing of the scrolls, through exclusion of their publications from sale in the special bookshop adjacent to the exhibit, and (c) the use only of scholars sympathetic to the traditional theory as participants in the audio-guide program distributed to visitors. The audio-guide narrator was Robert Mac-Neil of public television, who went on record as expressing strong support for the Qumran-sectarian theory. The guide's claim that the Khirbet Qumran site and the scrolls found in the caves were organically interrelated was based on a series of overtly false archaeological assertions, discussed in my response to the exhibition that I sent to Harry S. Parker III, director of museums of the city of San Francisco, on 15 April 1994. See also my article, "The Dead Sea Scrolls and the Ethics of Museology," in the *Aspen Institute Quarterly*, no. 2 (Spring 1994), pp. 79–98.

always hope when people are forced to listen to both sides; it is when they attend only to one that errors harden into prejudices, and truth itself ceases to have the effect of truth, by being exaggerated into falsehood.[42]

While the display of scroll fragments was running its doctrinal course in New York and San Francisco, events in the Qumran region had begun to overtake the doctrine. The "Operation Scroll" search (see page 345 above) continued through the winter of 1994. As part of the search, the Authority's Yitzhak Magen and Amir Drori kept examining the Qumran site ever more closely. Under the headline "Recent revelations about Qumran promise to shake up Dead Sea Scroll scholarship," the *Jerusalem Post* (6 May 1994) announced that the two investigators had come to a startling conclusion: the site "was for more than half of its life a Hasmonean farmstead and military outpost." They were further quoted as stating that "We have to view Qumran as an integral part of the Hasmonean plan to settle and fortify the Jordan Valley."

Refraining from any reference to my earlier identification of the site as a Hasmonaean fort, the two Antiquities Authority figures proposed a compromise solution to the problem they were facing: Qumran was in the hands of the Hasmonaeans only for a hundred years, until—in 40 to 37 B.C.—"Herod wrested the throne from Antigonus, the last of the Hasmonean rulers." As Magen and Drori put it, the site was then "given by Herod to the Essenes with whom he had close ties." The adjacent cemetery, they explained, contained the graves of the mutually opposing troops of Herod and Antigonus who had fallen during a battle they had there.

There is, unfortunately, no evidence at all, either in the scrolls or in any other literature, that Herod the Great favored the Essenes—or that he would have placed a strategic fortress in their hands. Shrugging off the absurdity of imagining that a group of pious sectarians would ever settle adjacent to a cemetery, some Qumranologists were quick to seize upon the compromise proposal. "The problem is [that] we all bought de Vaux's version hook, line and sinker," asserted J. C. Greenfield. "The lateness of the Essene occupation strikes me as right. Neither Josephus nor the other historians tell us that they were there for a long time. . . . We are going to have to do a lot of rethinking."

According to Greenfield, part of the rethinking was that, if the

Essenes moved in so late, "many of the scrolls plainly had to have been written elsewhere." Likewise, the assumption of Qumranologists that the "place of exile" of the Teacher of Righteousness (*Pesher Habakkuk* **11**.6) was Khirbet Qumran "would no longer fit." The Jerusalem closed-door meeting that followed (see above, pages 303–304) was characterized by radical uncertainty over the nature of the Qumran site.

Thus by the spring of 1994 the revered paradigm was undergoing a decisive shift away from its deepest roots.

EPILOGUE

Judaism, Christianity, and the Scrolls

R eviewing the ancient writings discussed in the above chapters, we may perceive how they contribute to our understanding of a vital period in the history of the Jewish people. With virtually each new scroll fragment studied, our grasp of the prevailing mentality of intertestamental Judaism becomes less tenuous, encouraging new approaches as well as increased integration of areas of learning hitherto walled off from one another. And it becomes clear that the very manuscripts displayed in the American exhibitions will themselves lie at the heart of future investigation of the scrolls.

We may thus observe, as a notable example, how the *Paean to Alexander Jannaeus*—one of several Jewish historical personalities mentioned in the scrolls—emerges as the work of a Palestinian poet who took pride in that ruler's reign and had a conception of the overall unity of the Jewish nation, both in Palestine and in the widespread diaspora that already existed long before the destruction of the Second Temple. The hymn is one small fragment among many Hebrew poems found in the caves that have no apparent sectarian bias. From it, as from the others, we may note the lyrical richness of ancient Hebrew up to the very destruction of the Second Temple in A.D. 70; and we observe that virtually all of this poetry, as well as over three quarters of the prose texts, was composed in Hebrew, disproving the view that Aramaic had overtaken Hebrew as the main language of the Jews of Palestine in the first century A.D.

Other scrolls containing nonsectarian poetry are the *Psalms Scroll* from Cave 11, which includes extracanonical hymns occasionally reflecting Hellenistic ideas,[1] and the *Songs of the Sabbath Sacrifice*.[2] Cave 1 contained fragments of at least six such poetic compositions,[3] and Cave 4 many more poetic writings reflecting

361

various shades of religious expression,[4] one of the most important among them being the Pseudepigraphic Psalms collection.[5]

While the important eighteen-column *Hodayot* ("Thanksgiving Hymns") has been associated with the Essenes, this was primarily because it was found together with the *Manual of Discipline* in Cave 1, among the first seven discovered scrolls. Scholars have adduced certain similarities of expression with the *Manual*, but neither the ideas nor the Hebrew idiom of the *Hodayot* can on the whole be said to reflect the *Manual*'s particular environment; and again, the text contains no religious views attributed to the Essenes in the ancient sources. Its Hebrew idiom shows a continuity with that of the later biblical psalms; the ideas expressed in both these text-groups are largely drawn from one and the same spiritual fund, although in the *Hodayot* they are occasionally developed in idiosyncratic ways. Some of the hymns in this collection do indeed reflect the vicissitudes of an anonymous prophetic, or at least spiritually imbued, figure of intertestamental times. However, as we may now perceive from such writings as the *Acts of Torah* and other texts unknown in the early days of scroll discoveries, quite a few such personalities were active in Palestine during those times, and by ordinary standards of evidence we cannot legitimately connect the author of this work with any particular one of them.

The phylacteries of Qumran in their entirety, while only containing verses from the Pentateuch, comprise a valuable touch-stone pointing to the multiform origin of the scrolls as a whole. Similarly, the Leviticus scroll in palaeo-Hebrew script, together with other biblical and parabiblical scroll fragments in this script, constitute proof that there were Palestinian Jews who continued to use the original Hebrew script in Pentateuchal texts in the second century B.C.[6] These scrolls, along with the many other biblical texts and text fragments discovered in the caves, show that at the time the scrolls were hidden, there was not yet a single authoritative text of scriptural writings but rather different versions of the same texts that circulated widely among the Palestinian Jews. Some of these versions were closer to that of the (Greek) Septuagint version of the Bible, others to the Samaritan tradition, and still others to the traditional Massoretic text of the Hebrew scriptures that has survived among the rabbinic Jews until today. These various recensions indicate considerable diversity among the Palestinian Jews who used them. It is most difficult to imagine that any single sect would have refrained from making an important priority of definitively fixing its own version of holy writ. While the American scrolls exhibitions did not include biblical and parabiblical fragments in Greek, such texts as well form an important addition to the dossier of hard evidence relating to the nature of the Qumran cave finds as a whole.

K. H. Rengstorf has observed that "The collection of Biblical texts which has come so surprisingly to hand . . . proves that critical work on the texts went hand in hand with the transmission of the sacred texts in Judaism even in the pre-Christian era. Unfortunately, the importance of this fact is scarcely mentioned, let alone discussed, in connection with the Essene theory. Besides, it is not exactly well adapted to support . . . [it, for] the essence of religious sects or special religious groups [is] that they pay scrupulous attention to the exact text of their Holy Scriptures."*

The biblical *citations* used in the nonbiblical texts are also not uniform. The canonicity of the writings quoted is not certain in every case, and is a question that may have provoked debate among the parties and sects all through the intertestamental period. As mentioned earlier, the Jews did not settle upon the canonized "Holy Scriptures" with finality until the second century A.D.

The calendars also show a wide variety of practices among the intertestamental Jews. But where the one exhibited in America[7] shows the process of *intercalation*, i.e., of calendrically harmonizing the lunar and solar years, others appear to support the author of the Book of Jubilees in insisting on a strictly solar calendar. The investigation of the calendars continues intensively; much more study will be needed before we can venture to form hard, definitive conclusions as to whether it is appropriate to refer to any Qumran calendar as strictly "sectarian." What we have in most of them is a system of computation of the yearly cycles that was slightly more primitive than the particular lunisolar system eventually adopted by rabbinic Judaism.[8]

---

*See K. H. Rengstorf, *Hirbet Qumran and the Problem of the Library of the Dead Sea Caves*, pp. 11–12. Even so conservative a Qumranologist as Eugene Ulrich pointed out in his contribution to the Library of Congress symposium of 1993 that the variant readings in the biblical manuscripts found in the caves showed that they derived from different, not uniform, ancient "editions" (technically speaking, "recensions") of biblical texts. While Ulrich did not say as much, his own description clearly implied that the biblical texts had had a complex history, and could not possibly represent the biblical text-tradition of a single small sect.

Some of the writings—the ones most often cited when attributing the scrolls as a whole to Essenic sectarians—reflect the ideas of writers evidently sharing awareness of a common background of opposition to ruling powers in Jerusalem in the second century B.C. As we have seen, the *Manual of Discipline*[9] reflects one distinct radicalizing trend within this group of texts, emphasizing an apocalyptic mode of brotherhood initiation, strict spiritual dichotomies, heightened metaphorical interpretation of Torah-mysteries, and overriding purity-discipline. Let us recall that some other scrolls, such as the *Rules of the Congregation* (1QSa),[10] the *Benedictions* (1QSb),[11] and the group of blessings known as *4Q Berakhot*,[12] are perhaps allied with the brotherhood trend reflected in the *Manual*. Joseph Baumgarten has shown that texts from Cave 4 related to the *Manual of Discipline* of Cave 1 in fact reflect numerous differences with it in the specific area of punishments for infractions of the group's rules—a finding that, of course, raises still further questions about the nature and origin of these texts.[13]

The brotherhood theme is not as pronounced in the *Damascus Covenant*,[14] represented in the American exhibitions by an interesting Cave 4 fragment. The *Covenant*, showing fierce opposition to a group known as "the Builders of the Enclosure," recognizes both urban and nonurban modes of religious conduct characterized by observance of ritual laws; as we observed in Chapter 3, this text has been interpolated by a glossator, himself the follower of a separatist Torah-purity group originally formed by an "Expounder of the Torah" who led adherents of a "New Covenant" to Damascus. It may well be that the core of this work was written by the "Teacher of Righteousness" mentioned as its central figure.

Other texts are characterized by the midrashic interpretation of scriptural writings, both as concerns the authors' conceptions of the historical past and the future "end of days." The rhetoric of these and other *peshers* is characterized by hints and allusions in their historical and eschatological midrash elements. A few show particular concern for a "Teacher of Righteousness"—perhaps the same as the one connected with the migration to Damascus. The radicalizing tendencies of the *Manual of Discipline* are, however, once again absent from this group, which includes, in addition to the *pesher* on Hosea shown in America, those on Habakkuk,[15] Isaiah, Nahum, Zephaniah, Psalms, and possibly Micah, as well as some other prophetic writings.[16] The *War Scroll* belongs tangentially to this group of texts. Closely associated with them are the *Florilegium* and the *Testimonia* of Cave 4,[17] each of which, as the *pesharim* to Isaiah and Habakkuk, mentions a "Council of the Community."* These latter texts, however, speak of a single messiah from the stem of David rather than of two Messiahs, of Aaron and of David, belief in whom is endorsed by the authors of the *Manual of Discipline*. Most of the historical allusions in these texts, as in the *Damascus Covenant*, await, but may never achieve, definitive explanation. They hint at trends in ancient, pre-Tannaitic Judaism that tally only in part with Josephus's description of the "philosophies" or "heresies"—e.g., Sadducees, celibate and noncelibate Essenes, Pharisees, the related "fourth philosophy," and others such as the Zealots. We must also bear in mind that, beside these groups Josephus describes the ascetic and baptizing hermit Bannus, who "dwelt in the wilderness," as well as John the Baptist. The *Tosephta* (Yadaim **2**.20) mentions the "Dawn Bathers" who criticized the Pharisees for "invoking the Name (of the Lord) in the morning without having bathed," bringing to mind the "instructor who spoke to all the sons of the dawn" of one of the recently published scrolls. Other Jewish baptizing groups included the one implied in the Sybilline Oracles, the Hemerobaptists, Galilaeans, Masbuthaeans, and Nazaraeans.[18]

One of the most important writings of a doctrinally divergent nature found in the Qumran caves is the *Acts of Torah*. As we have seen (Chapter 7), the author uses Hebrew of a proto-Tannaitic character (similar to that in the *Copper Scroll*), thus showing authorship approximately in the early first century A.D. He emphasizes strict ritual purity in conjunction with sacrificial laws, upon which he expostulates at length. One or two ritual laws he champions reappear in later rabbinic texts as points of controversy between Sadducees and Pharisees. The polemical tone is highly

---

*In the Habakkuk *pesher* (**12**.3–4), however, the expression appears as a later interpolation: "The Lebanon is the council of the community and the beasts are the simple ones of Judah, doers of the Torah"—a passage directly interfering with the movement of thought. The sentence begins: "Its interpretation concerns the wicked priest who will be requited for what he did to (the) poor ones [then comes the interpolation as given above] in that the Lord will judge him for destruction just as he plotted to destroy (the) poor ones." The use of this explanatory gloss indicates adaptation of terminology of the *Yahad* movement to the *pesher* style of biblical interpretation.

subdued, in contrast to that of the *Damascus Covenant* and of the *pesher*-texts. No mystical apocalypticism whatever is expressed in the work, which appears to represent a sectarian trend reminiscent of aspects of Josephus's description of the Pharisees.

The *Temple Scroll*[19] reflects an independent trend of its own. It shares a few of the views espoused by the author of the *Damascus Covenant*—e.g., prohibition of polygamy and uncle–niece marriages, and of an Israelite's presence in the Holy City in a state of sexual impurity. However, its author, himself clearly a charismatic figure who must have claimed prophetic gifts, stands largely outside the literary and doctrinal traditions of those responsible for other works. His particular method of Torah augmentation, reduction, and emendation in the cause of sustaining a polemical trend is otherwise unknown in the Qumran texts.

The scrolls include many rhetorical paraphrases of Biblical writings, giving the appearance of a large number of authors vying with one another to enrich and embellish the holy writings and, especially, to make them more palatable and acceptable to the Palestinian Jews, who by that time had been subjected, willingly or not, to an intense process of Hellenization. These texts are among the many works discovered in the Qumran caves that show no separatist tendencies, but appear to be fragments of Palestinian Jewish literature popular in the first century B.C. and in the decades prior to the First Revolt. The Aramaic *Book of Enoch*, of which a fragment was included in the American exhibitions, very considerably influenced the idiom of the New Testament and patristic literature, more so in fact than any other writing of the Apocrypha and Pseudepigrapha.[20]

The scroll fragments include other such writings of an apocryphal and pseudepigraphic nature, such as Jubilees, Testament of Levi,[21] and some previously unknown. Among the latter is the Aramaic *Genesis Apocryphon*, containing an embellished description of events in the lives of Noah and Abraham. The language of this text, it may be observed, is closely similar to that of the *Targum to Job* of Cave 11, which, as the *Genesis Apocryphon*, shows no sectarian affinities. Apocryphal and apocalyptic texts have been found, in relative abundance, in Caves 1, 2, 3, 4, and 6.[22] Essenism is noticeable in virtually none of these texts, which at the same time reflect the religious views of many individual writers of the second and first centuries B.C. Other such texts that cannot be attributed to any particular sect include a writing that interprets the significance for the future of the sounds of thunder (i.e., a *brontologion*), those that relate aspects of the physical self to mental and moral characteristics (physiognomic texts), still other magical and/or divination texts, visionary and pseudo-prophetic writings, and even "beatitudes" of the kind known from the New Testament. Many scroll fragments in these latter groupings have, since the unlocking of the scrolls in 1991, been transcribed and translated by Michael Wise and the University of Chicago team, and others are being studied in various centers of Qumran research both here and abroad.[23]

We see, then, that the scrolls reveal a great variety of themes and genres, often conflicting contents, and, to a very large extent, absence of identifiable sectarianism or heterodoxy. That is precisely why scholars to varying degrees and in increasing numbers have begun in recent years to speak not merely of the ideas of the "sect of Qumran," but of the currents in ancient Judaism that the manuscripts reflect. Others, not necessarily addressing the contents of the texts but only, at times, such characteristics as the multiplicity of handwritings and large variety of spelling patterns, now assert that "some," "many," "a great many," or even a "majority" of the scrolls were not actually written at Khirbet Qumran. What is left for traditional Qumranologists who have begun moving away from the old ideas are the concepts of a sect living at Qumran, of manuscripts stored away in nearby caves, and of a not quite definable relationship between the two entities. In the thinking of most of these writers, the idea of a scriptorium at Qumran is no longer really tenable and thus, for them, no longer important.

Instead, the concept of a *library* at Qumran—rather than the scriptorium—takes on greater urgency, for with this other regulative principle to aid the understanding, one might still lay claim to the idea of a sect having lived there; one, that is, whose members did not necessarily write or even copy books, but at least gathered various writings together, "from the outside," for their putative desert retreat. Many years ago the idea grew up that this claimed library was actually located within Cave 4. However, as the implication has sunk in that this proposal would mean the claimed sectarians were putting scrolls for study and consultation in a cave instead of within one of the fine stone buildings of Khirbet Qumran itself, enthusiasm for the idea has slackened and the search begun for a room within the central complex that might be conceived of as serving this end. And even though no solid evidence has emerged of such a room, simply imagining one has become a new basis for clinging to the idea of a sect living there in antiquity.

As the full force, however, of the actual archaeological evidence relative to the site begins to sink in—evidence that only began to be debated openly in the late eighties—there can be little doubt that this idea too will gradually be abandoned. The site itself has already become basically irrelevant for the question of identification of most of the manuscripts, and as scholars come to perceive and to acknowledge more openly that even the *Yahad* sectarian movement can be fully understood without that crutch and stands in no scientific need of it, discourse on Qumran origins will gradually flow away from the mystique of archaeological revelation that nourished the old theory, and toward more sober interpretations of the individual texts within their Palestinian Jewish context. In the course of this process, the question of the bearing of these texts on the nascent rabbinic Judaism and earliest Christianity of the first and second centuries A.D. will necessarily take on increasing relevance.

Relying on the old consensus that the texts derived from a small, desert-based extremist sect, scholars of rabbinic Judaism have for the most part found no reason to search out connections of earlier forms of Judaism with that of the rabbis, and they have neglected the scrolls in both their research and teaching. Once the sectarian paradigm no longer informs the intellectual mentality of those pursuing the history and beliefs of the Tannaitic masters, they will be obliged to confront the fact that, however fragmentary, the scrolls too are the product of Palestinian Judaism. The contents of these manuscripts will then have to be compared and contrasted with the early rabbinic practices and beliefs that emerged dominantly in the same land during the century following the disaster of A.D. 70.

There can be no doubt that a radical shift in both Jewish hegemony and religious and social thinking occurred during the decades following the destruction of the Second Temple. The message of the priests had been that the Jews could count on the Lord to save them if only, in accordance with the biblical precepts, the animal sacrifices were faithfully performed; and when this failed to happen in A.D. 70, the priests suffered a disastrous loss of credibility. Afterward, their actual responsibilities would be limited to the performance or observance of several religious rituals, such as offering the priestly blessing (Num. **6.**24) in the synagogues, "redeeming" first-born male children (Ex. **13.**13),[24] not frequenting places of ritual impurity (e.g., cemeteries), and not marrying divorcees. In an agreement apparently worked out with the Roman government several decades after the fall of Jerusalem, the Jewish leadership was, instead, vested in a new governing figure, the Palestinian Patriarch, who granted not only religious but also both legislative and judicial authority to the heirs of the Pharisees—i.e., the rabbis or, more specifically, the Tannaim.

Centering its values on the ideals of learning and piety, this new power elite developed a system of legislation that became authoritative not only in Palestine but throughout the Jewish diaspora. It instituted schools for the teaching of the Law according to its evolving rabbinical interpretation, and for the exposition and defense of the beliefs of Judaism as incorporated in the canonized books.[25] These schools became the fundamental centers in which Jewish thought evolved and were declared by the rabbinic law to be of even greater holiness than synagogues. Among the Tannaitic masters were those who came to deem the study of the Law superior to all other acts of piety and worship combined.

Yet until 1948, nothing in the literature of the Jews before the time of the first rabbinical texts (second century A.D.) seemed to provide any indication of how systematic schooling in the Law and Jewish belief began. Only the publication of the *Manual of Discipline* shed light on this question. For the *Manual* revealed a program in group instruction in the Law for the pious purity-brethren of the *Yahad*: "There should not be lacking, wherever ten men (of the *Yahad*) be found, an expounder of the Torah day and night . . . the *rabbim* shall be diligent in unity a third of all the nights of the year by reading in the book, expounding judgment, and offering blessings in unity . . ." (column **6**, lines 7–8). Group instruction in the law apparently first began in this and similarly pious circles. This gradually led to institutionalized study and expounding of the Torah in communal buildings that Greek-speaking people called synagogues (*synagogé*, literally assembly)*

---

*This term represented the effort to seek an equivalent to Hebrew *bet hakenesset*, literally "house of the congregation, or assemblage, (of Israel)."

and thereafter to the formal institution of houses of study in the Tannaitic period, after the rabbinical class had achieved its commanding role in Palestinian Jewish society.

Systematic arrangement of the laws of the Jews also began during the intertestamental period, but the *Damascus Covenant* and the *Acts of Torah* show that it was at first a limited exercise, its results applicable only to adherents of individual groups and parties. The early code contained in the *Covenant* allows for no differences of legal opinion, and we gain the impression that the members of the group portrayed in the *Acts of Torah* were likewise of a single mind in the realm of ritual practices. A more flexible *modus vivendi* came into operation, however, with the rise of the Tannaim: Building on the modest achievements of their predecessors, they enlarged them greatly and, what is more significant, made room for the expression of differences of opinion concerning legal and ritual practices within the corpus they developed. Thus, the Tannaim discovered that the kind of divisions that had torn intertestamental Judaism into a number of opposing groups could be integrated into a *common system*—a phenomenon that led to the development of a new mode of pluralism whose significance has been largely ignored.

The dynamic interchange of varying and sometimes diametrically opposing legal and social ideas within the pages of the *Mishnah* and *Tosephta* represents the embodiment of this process. Its elaboration enabled the Tannaim to discourage the growth of sectarian rivalries and ideological extremism, which, by the time of the defeat of the Second Revolt (A.D. 132–135), the Jewish body politic could no longer afford to cope with.[26] The scroll evidence makes clear, at all events, that the process the Jews developed so remarkably in the second century A.D.—one that the Roman government did not, over time, prevent or oppose—had its beginnings in far earlier jurisprudential activity. At the same time, with the discovery of the *Songs of the Sabbath Sacrifice* it has become clear that the mystical *Hekhalot* literature of rabbinical Judaism also had antecedents in Second Temple Jewish thought.[27] We may expect that interest in the affinities of rabbinical Judaism with its predecessors will grow as the scrolls continue to be explored and published and as neglected pages of the old rabbinic literature come to be turned in the quest for new knowledge.

*   *   *

While scholars have tended to neglect the question of the scrolls' relationship to rabbinic Judaism, their liaisons with earliest Christianity have often occupied the very center of their interest. The great majority of writers on this subject have found striking links between ideas and practices described in the manuscripts and those attributed to the earliest Christians in the New Testament and other sources.[28]

Similarities to early Christian practices and ceremonies were among the first features of the scrolls to gain wide attention. One of the most important of these is the sacral meal.[29] Passages from two of the most important scrolls describe communal meals in detail, the first of these being in the *Manual of Discipline* (**6**.2–8). We will recall that, according to this passage, whenever ten men of the Council of the *Yahad* were to come together for a meal, they would all take their seats in their appointed rank. The priest officiating over the group was to pronounce blessings over bread and wine before anyone might eat. A similar passage appears in the so-called *Messianic Rule*, whose apocalyptic tenor is more pronounced. Here, the Messiah of Israel himself is depicted as being present at the meal; it is still, however, the priest who says the blessing over the bread and wine. In the New Testament a similar scene appears. According to passages in the three Synoptic Gospels and one in the writings of Paul (1 Cor. **11**.23–26), Jesus took bread and wine at the Passover meal before his crucifixion and said a blessing, then distributed these items to his disciples with the command that they should "do this as often as you come together, in remembrance of me."[30] In the scrolls, it is the priest who presides over a communal meal (but not the Passover ceremony) and pronounces the blessings, while in the Gospels, it is Jesus (treated in Heb. **5–7** as a priestly figure) who presides at a Passover meal.

While the similarities between the meals are worthy of attention, the differences are of course also important. The two Hebrew passages envision a well-ordered meal where a strict hierarchy is observed, whereas the New Testament passages have no such order in mind. The two scrolls present none of the symbolism of bread for flesh, or of wine for blood, that appears in the New Testament passages. On the other hand, one may only speculate about the degree of similarity of the meals of the Tannaitic purity-brethren, the *haberim* or friends, to the one described in the *Manual of Discipline*; there are, unfortunately, no rabbinical texts that actually divulge how these latter ceremonies were conducted.

In the New Testament, baptism is a sign of entrance into the faith, perhaps even a prerequisite, and seems in some passages to be almost mandatory for salvation.[31] There is a passage in the *Manual of Discipline* that may refer to baptism (**5**.13), stating that the unrepentant would be denied entrance into the waters. Most scholars who have discussed baptismal practices of the *Yahad* group have depended on Josephus's description of the Essenes, as well as the presence of water cisterns at the Khirbet Qumran site, to buttress their accounts—arguments that the reader may perhaps by now recognize as unwarranted.[32] Baptismal rituals were widespread in early rabbinic and early Christian times, and their antecedents in first-century B.C. and first-century A.D. Palestine can hardly be narrowed down to the practices of a single group.

One of the new texts translated by Wise (4Q414) may well be a liturgy for a baptismal ceremony, giving possible support to the idea that baptism was an important rite of the *Yahad* group.[33] Yet both the *Manual of Discipline* and this newly published text might be referring to nothing more than the ritual washings that became a common feature of early rabbinic Judaism and, in attenuated form, continue to be practiced to this very day by observant Jews. Thus, it is impossible to determine much about the place of baptism in the life of the *Yahad* group from these passages. All we can say is that both the early Christians and the *Yahad* group practiced ritualistic lustration—a not very striking similarity, considering how widely attested the practice is. The *Manual*'s descriptions of practices concerning food and drink "purities" of the *rabbim*, and restrictions applying to them, strikingly resemble the practices carried on by the "friendship" groups of early rabbinic times. We may also observe, however, that ritual eating is mentioned in the Letter to the Colossians, while in Paul's Letter to the Galatians (**1–2**) he discusses whether Jewish and gentile Christians might eat together, i.e., in purity.

According to the Book of Acts, the early Christians dwelt together, "and had all things in common. They were selling their property and possessions, and were sharing them with all, as anyone might have need" (Acts **2**.44–45). Likewise, the *Manual* prescribed that those entering the community were to have their wealth placed in a common fund for the use of all of the community members.[34] Such an unusual practice might seem too unique to appear by chance in two different groups in ancient Judaism. In fact, however, communal sharing of property not only existed among several different groups of Jews, but was also evidently held up as an ideal in many parts of the ancient Hellenistic world, as we learn from the fellowship associations that recent scholarship has linked with the practices and concepts of the *Manual of Discipline*. Thus Philo, addressing himself to a non-Jewish audience that must have appreciated the virtues he described, praised the Jewish Therapeutae of Egypt because they sold their possessions and distributed their bounty among any who had need; and he seemed to regard the communalism of the Essenes as their most laudable characteristic.[35]

In sum, relatively little is known of analogous practices of early Christianity and the *Yahad* group that cannot be attributed to the common cultural milieu that the two movements shared with others. This fact discourages the notion of a direct, organic connection between the two groups—but this is not to say that the scrolls as a whole tell us nothing about early Christianity. Several of them illuminate the teachings attributed to Jesus in the Gospels or the ideas of the New Testament in important ways. A considerable number of the scrolls were, after all, produced only several decades before the New Testament began to form. These and the early Christian texts tend to share the same cultural and historical setting and to express many of the same concerns. However, Christianity differed significantly in its ideas about how the spiritual crises of the times should be resolved.

The use of cognate theological ideas and terminology in the scrolls and the New Testament illustrates the common milieu. The epithet "*the* Holy Spirit" (however elusive its precise meaning) is used as a titular designation only in the scrolls and the New Testament.[36] Likewise, the phrase, "Sons of Light," designating the righteous people of God, is found both in some of the scrolls and in one of the Gospels (Luke **16**.8); however, the corresponding term in the scrolls, "Sons of Darkness," is never found in the New Testament. Along with the specific title "Sons of Light," the general dualism of "light and darkness" appears both in several of the scrolls and in some of the New Testament books, especially the "Johannine" literature (i.e., the Gospel and Epistles of John).[37] (This imagery is also found extensively in the biblical Book of Isaiah, and was widely employed in antiquity.) The term "mystery," appearing in some of the scrolls as a designation of hidden eschatological truth or inexplicable deviations from perfect divine goodness, is used by Paul to describe the manifestation of God's salvation through Jesus, a belief that could only be comprehended by some.[38] The same term, however, was used throughout the Hellenistic world in reference to religious cults that had secret rites of passage.

Common features of the scrolls and the New Testament, on the other hand, have often illuminated the latter in important ways, particularly in the area of biblical interpretation.[39] While nothing like the scriptural commentaries, i.e., the *pesharim*, appears in the New Testament, the same general understanding of the nature of the Jewish scriptures and use of its prophecies is found both there and in the scrolls. The way that New Testament texts—especially the Gospels—use those scriptures had for a long time been a puzzle to scholars. The New Testament frequently quotes passages out of context and applies them to Jesus and other figures as if they were prophecies about them, even though a check of their biblical contexts reveals that the passages originally had no import at all relative to Christian history. A famous example is Matthew **2**.18, where, in connection with the birth of Jesus and the flight to Egypt, Herod's "slaughter of the innocents" is said to fulfill Jeremiah **31**.15, "A voice was heard in Ramah . . . Rachel weeping for her children; she refused to be comforted, because they are no more." In the context of Jeremiah, the prophecy refers uniquely to the Babylonian Exile.

This practice has led more than one reader of the Gospels to accuse the evangelists of misappropriation or even deliberate deception. In the scrolls, however, we find that the same procedure was followed by the biblical interpreters who authored the *pesharim*. The authors of these texts drew passages from the prophets out of their contexts and applied them to events in the immediate past or future—events that they believed had eschatological significance. Thus, the New Testament authors were using a method of argumentation and interpretation that would have been quite familiar to at least a portion of their Jewish audience. The early midrashists* of rabbinic Judaism would themselves build

---

*Rabbinic masters of the second through fourth centuries A.D. who expounded what they considered to be the deeper meaning of scripture. See Glossary.

upon this method, which must have been popular not only among members of the *Yahad* movement but also among many Jewish authors in intertestamental times except for the Sadducees.[40]

In both the majority of the scrolls and the New Testament we find a belief in a God who is intimately involved in human affairs, punishing or rewarding His people as He sees fit. (By contrast, the Sadducees, according to Josephus, believed that God stood aloof from world events, but no texts found in the Qumran caves express this belief.) Between God and humanity, however, a myriad of angels acted as intermediaries. Angels appear in many of the scrolls, assisting humans in battle in the *War Scroll* (columns **7**, **11**), guiding their actions in the second part of the *Manual*, and worshipping God in the *Songs of the Sabbath Sacrifice*. In the New Testament, too, angels have such functions. In the Gospel of Luke (chapters **1** and **2**), angels announce the coming of Jesus and instruct his parents and others on the proper course of action. In the Book of Revelation, angels worship God in the heavenly temple (chapters **4–5**) and carry out the punishments of God against the unrighteous (chapters **8–10**).

The scrolls have helped to illuminate some particularly puzzling questions about angels in the New Testament. In a passage in his First Epistle to the Corinthians, Paul adjures that when women worship, they are to have their heads covered, "because of the angels" (I Cor. **11**.10). What he had in mind—whether the angels, for example, were paragons of modesty or were watching from heaven—is not certain, and the scrolls may suggest an answer. The *Messianic Rule* stipulates:

> No man who is struck with any kind of human uncleanness shall enter into the assembly of God, nor will any man smitten with it be confirmed for office in the midst of the congregation: no man smitten in his flesh, or crippled in his feet or hands; none lame, blind, deaf, or mute; none smitten with a visible blemish in his flesh; nor an old man who stumbles and cannot keep still in the midst of the congregation. None of these shall enter to hold office in the midst of the congregation of the men of the Name, *for the Angels of Holiness are with their congregation*. (IQSa **2**.4–9)

The passage states that angels are present whenever the council assembles for deliberation, and implies that these angels are offended by any display of physical impairments. While as far as we know the Christians never disbarred the lame or blind from their assemblies, the practice of women going without a hair-covering veil was, according to Paul, unacceptable to the angels. The practice was perhaps regarded as daring; while humans may have tolerated it, the angels were apparently deemed to be more sensitive to such matters.[41]

There is also some similarity between the doctrine of "Two Spirits" found in the *Manual* (column **3**) and certain New Testament passages. According to the *Manual*, human souls are guided by two spiritual beings or angels: The Spirit of Light attempts to lead humanity in ways of righteousness, and is the ruler over all righteous individuals, while the Spirit of Darkness tempts people to act wickedly, and rules completely over the wicked. In the New Testament, Satan frequently appears as a spirit who tempts people to do evil, even attempting to sway Jesus himself to wickedness (Matt. **4**.1–11). The First Epistle of John speaks of the Spirit of Antichrist that is opposed to the people of God, and attempts to lead them astray. This Spirit is the opposite of the Spirit of Truth, or Spirit of God (**4**.1–6).[42]

According to the early Christians, the vast majority of people were following the ways of wickedness, rather than the ways of truth—an idea earlier expressed by the authors of the *Damascus Covenant*.[43] Undoubtedly this shared conclusion did not reflect any doctrinal interdependence, but rather emerged from kindred observations about the corruption of their society. Such corruption was rampant at the highest levels of the priesthood and the aristocracy. In both the *Damascus Covenant* and the New Testament we find strong condemnations of the religious establishment, especially the Temple hierarchy.[44]

It is important to observe, however, that nowhere in the scrolls is there found an overt condemnation of the sacrificial cult *per se* but rather of the corruption of its then leadership. Priests are central figures in the *Damascus Covenant* and the *Manual of Discipline*, although in the *Manual* they do not perform sacrifices. The authors of other scrolls, such as the *Temple Scroll* and the *Songs of the Sabbath Sacrifice*, clearly regarded the sacrifices as indispensable. None of the scrolls, and thus none of the groups they represent, appear to advocate the abolition of the Temple or the cult. Yet, this seems to be precisely what the New Testament advocates in such passages as Acts **7**.48–50. In fact, according to Gospel tradition, it was Jesus's opposition to the Temple that caused the priests to seek his death.[45] Even in the eschatological Jerusalem, according to Revelation **21**.22, there would be no Temple, for "the Lord Almighty and the Lamb" (Jesus) are its Temple. Rabbinical Judaism, by contrast, envisioned the eventual or ultimate reinstitution of the Temple in a restored Jerusalem; with that end in mind, the Tannaim elaborately incorporated the ritual laws of Temple sacrifice into the rabbinical legislation.

Nonetheless, both early Christianity and the authors of certain of the scrolls looked for alternatives to a sacrificial system in order to deal with the problem of human sinfulness. One answer of early Christians was the vicarious suffering and death of Jesus.[46] The Letter to the Hebrews saw the death of Jesus as the sacrifice *par excellence* that made all other sacrifices obsolete. An idea of this kind is not present in any of the scrolls that have survived. But the idea that a righteous individual could take away the sins of another by his own suffering is found in the *Manual of Discipline* (**8**.3–4), which states that the Council of the *Yahad* would atone for iniquity by "the practice of justice and suffering the sorrows of affliction." The *Manual* and the New Testament have both drawn from the Book of Isaiah's image of the "Suffering Servant" (chapters **52–53**). He suffers affliction and grief for the sins of his people. While the *Manual* interpreted this passage as implying a collective atonement by some for the sins of others, some early Christians conceived of it as a reference to the Messiah. The pietism of the early rabbinic masters appears to have developed as a viable alternative response to the fundamental problem.

It has been suggested that one of the scrolls might also refer to a Messiah who is put to death.[47] Having discussed this text in Chapter 8, we need not go over the issues in detail again, except to observe that if there is indeed a reference to an executed messianic figure in this text, it is the first such reference to be found in a pre-Christian text. In later pseudepigrapha and rabbinic literature, the concept of a dying messiah is already well entrenched, so it is not impossible to suppose that its roots are pre-Christian.*

---

*See 4 Ezra **7**.28–29. In the rabbinic literature, the Messiah, son of Joseph, travels to Jerusalem, where he is slain in battle. He is followed by the Messiah, son of David, who puts to death the kings of the nations and restores Judah to glory. See, for example, *Babylonian Talmud*, Sukkah 52a, and Targum Pseudo-Jonathan to Exodus **40**.11.

A better attested intertestamental messianic figure is undoubtedly that of an avenging warlord who would deliver the people of
God from the oppression of the ungodly. In scrolls where a messianic figure acts as a deliverer, he often appears to be identified
as the "Prince of the Congregation."[48] His main role is to lead the
troops of Israel into battle against the nations and restore its
national glory. A somewhat similar role is assigned to Jesus in the
New Testament, but with the nationalistic implications stripped
away. At his second coming, Jesus comes with the hosts of heaven
to execute vengeance against the enemies of the people of God.
This idea of the office of Jesus may be found in Matthew **24**,
which tells how the "Son of Man" would come in power and great
glory at the end of the world to judge all the peoples, and even
more graphically in the Book of Revelation (chapter **19**), where
Jesus is pictured returning as a warrior on a white horse who
destroys the "great beast" (Rome) and the kings of the earth. As
one might expect, Jesus is not depicted as exalting Israel to world
hegemony, but instead as establishing the reign of the saints of
God over the nations.

An important difference between the New Testament conception
and that of the *War Scroll*, the *Pesher Isaiah*, the *Pesher on Psalms*,
and other scrolls, is that in the New Testament the people of God
have no part in the final battle. Rather, the vengeance of God is left
to Him and His angels.[49] This may indeed be one of the most striking differences between ideas in the New Testament and those
found intermittently among the scrolls: In consonance with the
spirit expressed in the Book of Proverbs, "When your enemy falls,
rejoice not," (**24**.17) and "If your enemy be hungry give him bread
to eat" (**35**.21), the New Testament repeatedly urges its readers not
only to love and care for one another, but to love and do good to
their enemies as well (see especially Matt. **5**.43–47). This same
conception is taken up repeatedly in the rabbinic literature as
well.* But in those scrolls where the Teacher's enemies, the foreign
nations, or the ungodly are spoken of, they are shown no mercy.
The *Manual of Discipline* orders "eternal hatred in a spirit of
secrecy for the men of perdition" (**9**.21–22), and "to hate all the

*Cf., e.g., *Babylonian Talmud*, Sanhedrin 39b, "The very works of My own
hands [i.e., the Egyptians] are drowning in the [Red] Sea, and you [Israelites]
would [dare] sing songs?" See further the numerous passages cited in the
Jewish Encyclopaedia **5** (New York and London, 1904) p. 159.

sons of darkness, each according to his guilt in the vengeance of God" (1.10–11). And yet the intertestamental Ben Sira (Ecclesiasticus), fragments of which were recovered at Masada, counseled "Forgive your neighbor the hurt he has done you . . ." (28.2).[50] But there can be little doubt that despite the advice of the expounders of proverbs, the vicissitudes of the Hasmonaean state in the end encouraged some xenophobia among its inhabitants.

Other New Testament messianic ideas might have precursors in the scrolls. In one important text (4Q246) written in Aramaic, a figure called "the Son of God, Son of the Most High" appears. Although the first column of the text is broken, making an identification uncertain, it has been plausibly suggested that this figure is none other than the Messiah.[51] This apocalyptic fragment may thus provide an important precursor to the New Testament's designation of Jesus as the "Son of God." Prior to its publication, the idea of the Messiah as God's son had not been attested in pre-Christian Jewish texts. It was often suggested that the idea derived not from Judaism, but from the Greco-Roman royal ideology, where kings were believed to have been adopted by the gods. (We may observe the appearance of similar themes also in ancient Near Eastern texts.) This scroll may thus provide a Jewish antecedent to an idea once thought to be a Hellenistic-Christian innovation.

In addition, we now have a text (4Q521) that speaks in its first line of a messiah who commands "heaven and earth"—a far more exalted picture of a Messiah than is usually found in Jewish texts of this period.[52] This image is quite reminiscent of a New Testament passage in which Jesus orders a storm to cease. His amazed disciples ask, "What manner of man is this, that even the wind and sea obey him?" (Mark 4.35–41). The Qumran text appears also to be speaking, toward its end, of a Messiah who raises the dead on behalf of the Lord. The passage may be rendered as follows:

> [. . . The hea]vens and the earth will hearken to His Messiah,
> [The sea and all th]at is in them. He will not turn aside from the commandment of Holy Ones.
> Take courage, all you who seek the Lord, in His work.
> Will you not thus find the Lord, all you who bear hope in your hearts?
> Surely the Lord will seek out the pious, and will call the righteous by name.

Over the poor will His spirit hover; faithful ones will He restore by
His might.

He will honor pious ones on the throne of the eternal kingdom,

Release the captives, make the blind to see, raise up th[ose bent
low].

For[ev]er will I cling [to Him aga]inst the [po]werful, and [trust] in
His lovingkindness,

A[nd His] go[odness (will be) forever. His] holy [Messiah] will not
be slow [in coming.]

As for the wonders that have not (henceforth) been, the Lord will
do (them), when he (i.e., the Messiah) [come]s;

Then will he heal the sick and resurrect the dead; to the oppressed
will he announce glad tidings,

. . . he will lead the [ho]ly ones, he will shepherd [th]em. . . .[53]

The messianic actions described, then, imply the kind of supernat-
ural powers that Jesus exercised according to the Gospel of John,
where he revives his dead friend Lazarus, explaining, "I am the resurrection and the life. Whoever believes in me, even though he may
die, he will live again; he who lives and believes in me will never die"
(11.25–26). On the other hand, the theme of a physical resurrection
of the dead in a messianic age to come, without radical apocalyptic
overtones such as one encounters in some of the scrolls, was
apparently a Pharisaic innovation among the intertestamental
Jews. Thereafter, this theme took on increased vigor among the rabbinic Jews as well. It was one of the strong points in common
between rabbinic Judaism and early Christianity, and remained so
for centuries, some would say even until today. The view
expressed in the scroll fragment in question can, at all events, not
legitimately be classified as a "sectarian" doctrine.

Another interesting scroll may provide background against
which to understand an enigmatic passage in the New Testament
Epistle to the Hebrews. The Epistle (5–7) compares the high
priesthood of Jesus to that of Melchizedek, the priest-king of the
city of Salem who was honored by Abraham (Gen. 14). The author
says that he has much to say about Melchizedek that would be difficult to explain, since his readers are "dull of hearing" (Heb.
5.11). He does, however, explain that Melchizedek was a priest of a
lineage superior to that of the Levitical priests, since even
Abraham paid him homage (7.1–6). Furthermore, Melchizedek
continues to serve as a priest forever, in some sense as if he were

the Son of God himself (**7**.3). Now a similar image of this hoary figure appears in a scroll fragment from Qumran Cave 11, the so-called Melchizedek text of Cave 11.[54] According to this scroll fragment, Melchizedek is a heavenly spirit responsible for the judgment of the angels, apparently serving a role similar to that of the archangel Michael.* It is he who exacts vengeance for the people of God, battling against Satan and the spirits under his command. This picture of Melchizedek is in many ways different from that in the Book of Hebrews, which emphasizes that Melchizedek was a priest. Both, however, share a reverence for this ancient figure, as well as some conception of his exaltation to a superior position in heaven. The scroll demonstrates that speculation about Melchizedek was not confined to early Christian circles, but was the product of a wider Palestinian Jewish environment.

The above examples suffice to suggest both the extent and the limits of intertestamental Judaism's contribution to the birth and growth of Christianity.[55] The scrolls cannot as a whole or in part, however, legitimately be called "Christian" or "Judaeo-Christian" documents. To do so is tantamount to arbitrarily Christianizing Hebrew and Aramaic manuscripts whose authorship and eventual concealment by numerous Jewish groups is demonstrated by the totality of evidence.

In a judicious summary of differences and similarities between the scrolls and early Christian writings, Klaus Berger of Heidelberg has emphasized several salient features of both bodies of literature. What he finds missing in the Qumran texts is a "notion of the kingdom of God . . . comparable to that expressed by Jesus . . . but only a present one in heaven, or one in which those who offer hymns or Israelites alone have a part." He finds in the scrolls no pronounced orientation toward charismatic figures, no reports about martyrs, and virtually no names of religious personalities or of the localities where they performed their missions. The performance of wonders or exorcisms is seen only in the case of the patriarch Abraham laying hands on Pharaoh's head to heal him, as related in the *Genesis Apocryphon*; and the concept of a general

---

*The archangel Michael appears prominently in Enoch, the Septuagint translation of Deuteronomy, the Testaments of the Twelve Patriarchs, the Book of Revelation, and elsewhere. He serves variously as Israel's angelic patron, lawgiver, and mediator, and as one of the seven archangels who at the Final Judgment will execute the Lord's commands.

resurrection of the dead at one point in future time is never stated with clarity in the scrolls. These features contrast, of course, with their New Testament counterparts. On the other hand, important similarities include the cataloguing of virtues and vices (paranesis), admonitions, visionary descriptions, the already noted style of noncontextual biblical interpretation, descriptions of a heavenly Jerusalem, and apocalypses. Berger sees the effort toward spiritual change within Israel, so characteristic of some of the movements reflected in the scrolls, as an important feature of early Christian texts as well.[56]

The letters of Paul were certainly circulating before A.D. 70, but may not have made their way to Palestine until later. Other Christian documents were perhaps taken from Jerusalem by early believers before the siege began in A.D. 70. Eusebius (*Church History* III.**5**.3) tells us that Christians abandoned Jerusalem before the siege began and fled to the city of Pella. If true, this may possibly explain why no writings demonstrably attributable to Christians are found among the scrolls, unless it be the case that the newly forming group in Palestine did not yet have any literature of their own at the time the scrolls were consigned to the caves.* The parallels between the scrolls and the New Testament do serve to make an important point, however: They unequivocally testify to the fact that various Christian traditions recorded in the New Testament were at home in the world of ancient Judaism. Yet considerably before the end of the first century A.D., the developing faith had moved beyond its Palestinian cradle and into the Greco-Roman world. By the end of the second century A.D., the church would be more gentile than Jewish, and its theology and practice increasingly reflect the non-Jewish environment.

Taken from Jerusalem libraries and personal collections at a crucial hour and hidden away in many places in the wilderness, the

---

*A Greek fragment from Cave 7 (7Q5) has been claimed by several writers to be from the Gospel of Mark, but it has so few words, and of such little significance (e.g., Greek *kai*= "and") that most New Testament scholars would now appear to firmly reject this identification on the grounds that the fragment could as well be from the *Iliad* or other works of ancient Greek literature. See most recently B. Mayer (ed.), *Christen und Christliches in Qumran?*, Eichstätter Studien, N.F. 32 (Regensburg, 1992), and the review by L. Stuckenbruck in *The Qumran Chronicle* **2**, no. 3 (June 1993), pp. 195–197.

Dead Sea Scrolls are the remnants, miraculously recovered, of a hoard of spiritual treasures of the Jewish people of Second Commonwealth times. They are the heritage of the Palestinian Jews of that time as a whole, according to various parties, sects, and divisions that served as the creative source—so an increasing number of scholars have come to perceive—of a multitude of spiritual and social ideas. Before the discovery of the scrolls, we could not draw so emphatic a conclusion about the Jews of intertestamental times. Much is still lacking of their literature, and there is little chance that we will ever be able to grasp the full magnitude of the creative power of this people in the days of the Hasmonaeans and their successors. One may only wonder how many works of the ancient literature of the Jews perished totally in the caves near Khirbet Qumran and elsewhere in the Judaean Wilderness, and whether others remain there awaiting discovery. But those scrolls that were saved, relatively few though they may be, invite us toward gradually more sophisticated historical reflection.

We may see today that coming to terms with the individual concepts and practices at work in the scrolls does not require their being forced into a narrow sectarian bed, either of Essenism or any other single group, but rather calls for the careful extrapolation of their individual ideas through content analysis, and a gradual shaping of those ideas into the various spiritual currents that characterized Palestinian Judaism of the intertestamental era. The recognition of the variety of spiritual streams in prerabbinic Judaism was, to be sure, already anticipated sixty years ago.[57] The discovery of the scrolls and creation of the Qumran-Essene hypothesis had the paradoxical effect of placing this view in obscurity, and increasingly so as pan-Qumranism became rampant. The scrolls in effect now give us valuable details of the broader picture that, long before they were discovered, had already begun to be sensed by serious students of Josephus, the intertestamental writings, and the rabbinic literature.

At the turn of that era, a great many Hebrew authors had become deeply concerned with eschatological and messianic themes. The scrolls were written a century and more before the age of the early rabbinic masters who molded Judaism in the wake of the destruction of the Second Temple and the Bar Kokhba revolt, and thus reflect aspects of religious and social thinking often not characteristic of rabbinic Judaism. This thinking also found its echo in some of the writings later gathered together as the Apocrypha and Pseudepigrapha—writings themselves created by intertestamental Judaism during the two centuries before the war with Rome. But with the publication of more and more scrolls, the Judaism of that period has emerged as a far more complex, richly textured, and subtle phenomenon than it was ever believed to have been before. The scrolls are imbued with the rich literary heritage of the Jewish people in an age of crisis leading up to and marking the early beginnings of Christianity.

Seen in this light, the scrolls offer a portrait of underlying spiritual factors that generated events leading up to the First Revolt. We observe the tortured evolution of Jewish thinking from its early basis in Mosaic religion toward new religious and social values. That evolution was accomplished by struggle, among themselves, of various groups and individuals. The dynamics of a vigorous and often anguished interchange of ideas created a climate of fervor and zeal in intertestamental Jewish Palestine, eventually leading to militant opposition to Roman rule. The anguish undoubtedly reigned throughout those regions of Palestine where the Jews were heavily settled. It was, however, in Jerusalem, the religious and political capital, that it expressed itself most intensely.

The Romans knew that Jerusalem would be their chief prize. This was not only because it represented the polity of the Jews. They perceived that by its stubborn will to exist, the city continued to carry the message to the pagan world that a final time would arrive when Rome's own swords, which had conquered so much of that world, might be beaten into plowshares and all mankind come streaming up to the Temple of the Lord in Jerusalem (Isaiah **2**.2–4; Micah **4**.1–4).

The Jews, for their part, deeply feared that the Romans intended to destroy the Temple, the physical embodiment of the Jewish ideals. They hoped that by saving their collections of scrolls and thereby the words that expressed their beliefs and aspirations of centuries—by literally hiding those words, that is, until the terror had passed—the time would yet come when the message of the Jews and of Judaism to the nations of the world might be heard again.

The hiding away of the writings of the Jews at the time of the First Revolt thus emerges as an historic act of desperation. Through such efforts, the Hebrew scriptures and many other writings of the Palestinian Jews were given the chance of survival.

In reflecting on this secret confined within the Qumran caves for so many centuries, may we not ask, if only as travelers contemplating a far-off horizon: When the Temple burned and blood flowed through the streets of Jerusalem, what witness to that sight could have imagined that a daughter religion, spawned in relative obscurity in the Jews' midst, would adopt those scriptures and then go on to flourish and profoundly influence the thinking of the Western world? Who could have believed that the Jews themselves, defeated at the hands of the Romans throughout Palestine, would emerge again, in renewed creativity of spirit, as bearers of a rational and messianic culture?

Figure 14
Cliff and escarpment west of Khirbet Qumran, with some of the
manuscript-bearing caves.

Glossary

Aaronites, Aaronic priests Those males descended from Aaron, the brother of Moses. According to the Pentateuch, only descendants of Aaron were imbued with the status of *kehunah*, i.e., Jewish ritual priesthood.

apocalyptic A type of literature and its associated beliefs, purporting to reveal the future, particularly the "End of Days," through symbolic visions or dreams and interpretations, often given by an angel. Apocalypticism often designates, in addition, a worldview that foresees a cataclysmic change between the current world order and the new order that the Lord is to initiate personally. See also *eschatology*.

Apocrypha Writings of Jewish authors, composed approximately between 150 B.C. and A.D. 100, that are included in manuscripts of the *Septuagint* (q.v.), but which were never recognized as canonical by the rabbinical Jews. See *Pseudepigrapha*.

Aramaic A northwest Semitic language widely used in the Near East from before the tenth century B.C. until after the rise of Islam (and still used today in certain pockets of the Near East). It was one of the languages most widely used by the Jews in the centuries when the scrolls were written, the others being Hebrew and Greek. See *Syriac*.

autograph A text written by its original author in his own handwriting, as opposed to one that has been copied by someone else.

Babylonian Captivity The period of destruction of the First Temple and exile of the Judaeans to Babylonia, which occurred between 597 B.C. (the fall of King Jehoiachin) and 538 B.C.

Bar Kokhba A Jewish leader, regarded by his followers as the Messiah, who led an unsuccessful revolt against the Romans in A.D. 132–135. In contemporary manuscripts his name appears as Simeon ben Kozibah.

Belial The spirit of evil in intertestamental literature, as a rule equivalent to Satan.

Boethusians A term used in rabbinic literature for a Jewish sect that opposed the Pharisees. They have been sometimes identified as a group of Sadducees, and may have shared some of the beliefs of the latter. A recent view holds that the Hebrew terms *bytwsyn*, *bytysyn*, traditionally rendered as "Boethusians," in reality were slightly altered forms of *byt 'ysin*, "House [= 'school' or 'community'] of Essenes."

Cairo Genizah manuscripts The written contents of the storage area of the Palestinian synagogue of the Jews of mediaeval Fustat (Old Cairo, Egypt), including letters, legal documents, and literary texts, many of which contain actual dates and datable historical references. See also *genizah*.

canon, canonization Canon, with respect to Jewish belief, refers to those biblical books that were accepted by the Jews as divinely inspired and authoritative (i.e., as part of the Hebrew Bible). Canonization refers to the process whereby certain books came to be regarded as authoritatively holy while others were excluded.

codex (pl. **codices**) A group of manuscript pages stitched together on one side to form a book. The codex came into wide use in early Christian times, largely replacing the *scroll* (q.v.).

coenobite A monk who, emulating the practice of *St. Pachomius* (q.v.), lives in a monastery or closed religious community, as opposed to Antonian or Stylitic solitude, such as is practiced by the followers of Saint Anthony of Egypt (third century A.D.) and of Saint Simeon Stylites (fifth century A.D.).

colophon An inscription, usually at the end of a manuscript, giving the name of the work, its author, date and place of composition, and sometimes other information.

Elephantine Island in upper Egypt, near Aswan, where a Judaean military colony was located in the fifth century B.C. Approximately forty Aramaic letters, written to and by the inhabitants of the colony, were discovered there.

Enoch According to Genesis 5:21–23, an antediluvian hero who, because of his piety, was taken to heaven without dying. He much later became the subject of many legends, and is the main character in the Book of Enoch, in which he reports on what he learned during his visits to heaven.

eschatology That branch of religious literature and belief having to do with aspects of the afterlife, as the Final Judgement, bodily resurrection, eternity of the soul, etc.

Essenes A Jewish religious subgroup described by Josephus, Philo, and Pliny the Elder, noted for their communal way of life, their asceticism, and their ideas about fate and immortality.

First Revolt The Jewish rebellion against Roman rule that began in A.D. 66 and reached its climax with the destruction of Jerusalem and the Jewish Temple in A.D. 70. The final action of the war, the capture of the Jewish fortress of Masada by the Romans, occurred by A.D. 74.

First Temple Period Ca. 950 B.C. to 586 B.C.; the period in Israelite history from the construction of Solomon's temple until its destruction by invading Babylonians.

genizah (Hebrew: "storage room") A designated place, often located in synagogues, for the storage of texts that have become worn out from use, but cannot be destroyed because of their holiness. The most famous medieval genizah was discovered in a synagogue in Fustat, or Old Cairo; see *Cairo Genizah manuscripts*.

gloss A marginal or interlinear passage introduced into a text, usually by a glossator, i.e., someone other than the original author. During ancient and mediaeval times, the glosses were, in later copies or editions of such texts, often blended into the sentences or paragraphs on which they commented, and are sometimes retrievable only by textual analysis (e.g., by examining the logic and flow of the ideas being expressed).

gnosticism A form of religious thinking widespread in the Roman Empire, and adopted in various forms by Jewish and Christian heretics. Taking its name from the Greek word for "knowledge," it taught that its adherents could receive secret knowledge from the deity. Its most characteristic belief was a strict "dualism," emphasizing that the world and matter were evil, while only spirit could be good. This belief led some Gnostics to extreme asceticism and others to moral license.

Great Revolt See *First Revolt.*

haber, *Haburah* The *haber* (Hebrew, "friend") was a full-fledged member of a *Haburah* (Hebrew, "friendship society"), the *purity-brethren* (q.v.) of the Tannaitic period.

halakha (adj. **halakhic**) Terms designating Jewish ritual and civil laws (e.g., Sabbath observance, tithing, contracts, etc.), as well as texts concerned with them (as opposed to *haggadic* texts, which are concerned with theological or devotional matters).

Hasmonaean A title designating the Jewish dynasty that began to assume power in Judaea beginning with the Maccabean Revolt (ca. 167 B.C.) and continued to rule until the Roman conquest of Judaea (67 B.C.). The Hasmonaeans are also called (inaccurately) "Maccabees" (q.v.). The Hasmonaean dynasty included Judas Maccabaeus, Jonathan, Simon, John Hyrcanus, Aristobolus I, Alexander Jannaeus, Alexandra Salome, Hyrcanus II, and Aristobolus II.

Hasidim, Assidaeans "Pietists"; a sect of Jews that opposed the adoption of aspects of Greek culture by other Jews before the outbreak of the persecution by Antiochus Epiphanes (167 B.C.), and continued to exist into the time of the Hasmonaean dynasty.

Hekhalot Mystical Jewish writings apparently composed during the first few centuries after the destruction of the Second Temple, and characterized by descriptions of the "palaces" or "halls" (Hebrew, *hekhalot*) to be encountered by those (mystics) worthy of beholding the "Divine Chariot" (*merkabah*) of the Lord described in the Book of Ezekiel.

Hellenistic A term that refers to the mixture of Greek and Near Eastern cultures that began to develop after Alexander the Great's conquests ca. 332 B.C.

heresiographers Religious scholars who specialized in the study of heresies, particularly in order to be able to refute them. They often collected the works, and wrote detailed descriptions of the beliefs, of sectarians.

heterodoxy Departure from what is widely thought to be the generally accepted normative belief of a religion. With respect to intertestamental Judaism, "orthodoxy" (i.e., the normative beliefs) is difficult to define because of the state of fluctuation of Judaism at that time.

Idumaeans The name for the inhabitants of Idumaea (Edom in the Bible), who during intertestamental times continued to inhabit a large area of land to the east and south of the Dead Sea.

intercalation The addition of a month to the lunar year, in order to make it match more closely the length of the solar year. The lunar year is equal to 354 days, 11 days shorter than the solar year. Thus, twice every seven years, the rabbis would intercalate a month at the end of the year, so that the various holidays would continue to fall in their proper seasons.

intertestamental The period roughly falling between the end of the time described in the latest books of the Hebrew Bible and the birth of the New Testament.

Iron Age II Archaeological term applying particularly to Palestine, for the period from the beginning of the United Monarchy, ca. 1000 B.C., until the Babylonian Exile, 586 B.C., roughly corresponding to the *First Temple Period* (q.v.).

Josephus Flavius Jewish historian, born of a priestly family ca. A.D. 37, died after A.D. 95. He served as general in charge of the defense of Galilee during the First Revolt, and was taken prisoner after his surrender to Vespasian. He was released from prison after accurately predicting that Vespasian would become emperor, and was given a house and pension in Rome, where he wrote histories of the Jews for his curious Greco-Roman audience, based on his own experiences and the writings of his predecessors.

Judaean Wilderness The low-lying steppeland of Judaea west of the Dead Sea and east of the central hill country.

Karaism A branch of Judaism that arose ca. A.D. 800 as a reaction against some aspects of *rabbinic Judaism* (q.v.) and reached its height in numbers and influence in the early Middle Ages. The Karaites rejected the teachings of the rabbis and elements of contemporary Judaism that they considered mystical or magical, preferring what they regarded as a more conservative practice and belief based directly on the Bible.

Khirbeh (Arabic) A ruin or destroyed place; thus Khirbet Qumran = "ruin of Qumran."

laura A monastery consisting of separate rooms or huts for early Christian monks who would come together for meals and worship.

Levites Members of the Israelite tribe of Levi (one of the ancient Twelve Tribes of Israel) or their descendants. The Levites were responsible for the maintenance of the Temple and sacrificial system, and it was to this tribe that the Aaronic priests belonged.

Maccabaeans/Maccabees A name often used for the *Hasmonaeans* (q.v.), the Jewish dynasty that reigned in Judaea ca. 164 B.C. to 67 B.C. The term comes from the surname of Judas Maccabeus, early leader of the revolt against Antiochus Epiphanes.

Madaba map A sixth-century A.D. map of Palestine, forming the mosaic floor of a Byzantine church located in the ancient town of Madaba (Medeba), modern al-'Asimah, in what is now west-central Jordan. It preserves many important details of the geography of Roman and Byzantine Palestine.

Masada Important Jewish fortress situated just west of the Dead Sea and south of En Gedi. This site was the location of the final battle of the First Revolt, which ended in the mass suicide of Masada's 960 Jewish inhabitants.

Massoretic Pertaining to the Massorah, or "tradition." The term as a rule refers to collections of early mediaeval textual traditions about the proper reading of the Hebrew Bible and to versions of it based on these traditions. The *Tiberian* Massoretic text is the one most widely used today.

midrash (pl. **midrashim**; Hebrew, "expounding") A method of rabbinic biblical interpretation in which a passage of Scripture is quoted, and then a meaning or various meanings are drawn from the text. *Midrashists* employed a variety of techniques, including allegories, word plays, and *gematria* (assigning numerical values to words) in order to determine the meaning of a text. Midrashim are divided into two categories: *halakhic* midrashim, which comment primarily on biblical laws, and *haggadic* midrashim, which expound mainly on theological or devotional aspects of the biblical text.

Mishnah The central legal text of early rabbinic (= *Tannaitic* [q.v.]) Judaism. The *Mishnah*, compiled early in the third century A.D., contains ordinances on such matters as marriage, Sabbath observance, sacrifices, ritual purifications, civil law, etc. See also *Tosephta*.

nahal (Hebrew) A seasonal brook or river together with its riverbed; see *wadi*.

Origen One of the early Christian theologians, lived ca. A.D. 185–235, notable for his extensive scholarly writings and biblical commentaries.

orthography A term referring to the way that words are spelled in a manuscript or printed text.

ostraca Pieces of ancient broken pottery inscribed with names or messages.

Pachomianism A form of desert monasticism in which monks live (i.e., as *coenobites* [q.v.]) together in monasteries or settlements located in the wilderness. Named for St. Pachomius (ca. A.D. 292–348), founder of the movement.

palaeo-Hebrew script A form of alphabet used in ancient Israel. Some of the oldest of the Dead Sea Scrolls were written in this script, and in other scrolls the *Tetragrammaton* (q.v.) was written in palaeo-Hebrew script as a sign of reverence. It was gradually replaced by the so-called Aramaic square script that remains the script of Hebrew texts today.

Pentateuch The Five Books of Moses (Genesis, Exodus, Leviticus, Numbers, Deuteronomy); see *Torah*.

pesher (Hebrew, "interpretation") In the scrolls, "pesher" particularly refers to a method of interpreting prophetic texts that relates their verses to events in their authors' recent past or near future.

Pharisees One of the major Jewish groups described by Josephus and other ancient sources. By Josephus's time, they were the largest of the groups and had the popular support of the people. They were characterized by their "free" interpretation of the Bible, adherence to oral traditions, and belief in angels and other spiritual beings, in divine providence cooperating with free will, and in the resurrection of the dead.

Philo of Alexandria Jewish philosopher, biblical exegete, and historian, born ca. 20 B.C., died after A.D. 40; a native of Alexandria, Egypt. His writings are an important source of information on the life and thought of upper-class Jews, particularly in the Roman Diaspora.

phylacteries (from the Greek; Hebrew, *tefillin*) Capsules containing verses of the Pentateuch and worn by observant Jews in literal fulfillment of the precept to "bind these words that I command you this day upon your hand, and they shall be for frontlets between your eyes" (Deut. **6**.8).

Pliny the Elder Roman naturalist, historian, and statesman, ca. A.D. 23–79; wrote about ancient Palestine and described a settlement of Essenes by the Dead Sea above En Gedi.

Poimandres The first treatise in the corpus of Hermetic writings; it is a proto-Gnostic document written perhaps in the second century A.D. In it, a semidivine being named Poimandres ("shepherd of men") reveals the creation of the world, the union of spirit and matter after the Fall, and the method of redemption.

priests See *Aaronites*.

Pseudepigrapha Texts characteristically written under a false name. The term usually refers to those early Jewish and Christian works written in the name of ancient biblical figures, often giving imaginative retellings of biblical stories or professing to tell the future, that were included among the apocryphal writings (see *Apocrypha*) in the Septuagint.

purity, "the purity" Items of clothing, food, and drink that are ritually pure (see *ritual purity*); in the case of the *Manual of Discipline*, usually believed to refer to the consecrated food eaten in the ritual meals of the *Yahad* group. See *Yahad*.

purity-brethren Groups found throughout the Greco-Roman world who separated themselves from greater society and vowed to live according to strict rules of *ritual purity* (q.v.). The Dead Sea Scrolls *Yahad* group was such an association.

Qumran Northern Dead Sea desert plain where Khirbet Qumran and Wadi Qumran are located.

rabbinic Judaism The form of Judaism that became most widely accepted from the second century A.D. on. It espoused various teachings of the rabbis ("masters" or "great ones") or *hakhamim* ("sages") as binding for Jewish thought and practice. Rabbinic Judaism harks back to the earlier Pharisaic Judaism; like the Pharisees, the rabbinic Jews accepted the validity of oral tradition, beliefs in angels and spirits, and the resurrection of the dead.

ritual purity In the case of the Jews, the special state of cleanness required of those who would observe the laws of the Pentateuch relating to the pure and impure and take part in various religious ceremonies. Ritual purity involved both the avoidance of certain people (e.g., lepers), items (e.g., a corpse), or animals (e.g., mice) considered as defiling, and the performance of certain kinds of washings and other rituals in order to purify oneself after coming into contact with things considered defiling.

sacerdotal Referring to the Temple or priesthood.

Sadducees One of the chief Jewish sects of antiquity, according to Josephus and other early sources. The most characteristic views of the sect were the "literal" interpretation of the Bible, and the rejection of oral traditions, belief in angels, spirits, divine providence, or the resurrection of the dead. The Sadducees were closely linked to the Jewish aristocracy and the Temple establishment, and were reduced to an increasingly minor sect soon after the destruction of the Second Temple in A.D. 70.

Samaritans Inhabitants of the region of Samaria in Palestine who were not exiled with the Judaeans to Babylonia. They maintained belief in the holiness of the Pentateuch to the exclusion of other writings deemed holy by the Jews and included in the Hebrew Bible. Their center was Neapolis (Nablus), and they offered sacrifices not on the Temple Mount but on Mt. Gerizim; a few hundred still survive today.

scriptorium A room in which texts are copied, especially in mediaeval monasteries.

scroll A roll of parchment, papyrus, or other material containing written texts, with the sheets being sewn or otherwise fastened together one next to the other so as to facilitate the rolling up of the joined text. In biblical times, the Hebrew term *sefer* designated not a *codex* (q.v.) but a scroll, which preceded the codex throughout the Mediterranean world.

Second Jewish Commonwealth Narrowly speaking, the Jewish state at the time of the kingdom of the Hasmonaeans (q.v.), who ruled in Judaea from ca. 160 B.C. to 67 B.C.; more broadly, the same state until the destruction of the Second Temple and Jerusalem by the Romans in A.D. 70.

Second Temple Period Ca. 520 B.C. to A.D. 70; the period from the rebuilding of the Jewish Temple at Jerusalem until the victory of the Romans over the Jews during the First Revolt.

sectarian Having the characteristics of a sect; i.e., a dissenting religious group adhering to a distinctive body of beliefs and practices.

Septuagint The ancient Greek translation of the Jewish scriptures, but including also the writings known as the Apocrypha and Pseudepigrapha, that was in use among the Jews of Alexandria.

Shrine of the Book A building of the Israel Museum in Jerusalem, in which are located some of the Dead Sea Scrolls.

sicarii The "daggermen" or "assassins" led by Menahem b. Jair, Eliezer b. Jair, and Simeon bar Giora, who took the leading role in the First Revolt against Roman rule. Whether or not they are identifiable with the Zealots remains a matter of debate.

Simon the Maccabee Younger brother of Judas and Jonathan who took over the revolt after Jonathan's death (142–135 B.C.). During his reign, Judaea was granted self-government and freedom from tribute by the Seleucid Empire.

stratigraphy The method used by archaeologists to date artifacts found in a site on the basis of the formation of layers of soil, rock, etc.

Synoptic Gospels The first three Gospels—i.e., Matthew, Mark and Luke—so called because of the similarity in their contents, statements, and order.

Syriac A dialect of Aramaic (q.v.) that became widely used in Syria and Mesopotamia from late pre-Christian antiquity until it was largely displaced by Arabic. It continues in use in some Eastern Christian churches until today.

Talmud (Babylonian; Palestinian) The authoritative legal corpus of *rabbinic Judaism* (q.v.), consisting of the Hebrew *Mishnah* (q.v.) and Aramaic Gemara or commentary. The Babylonian Talmud, eventually considered to be the more authoritative of the two Talmuds, consists of the *Mishnah* and commentary by rabbinic teachers mainly of Babylonia; the Palestinian (or Jerusalem) Talmud consists of the *Mishnah* and commentary mainly by Palestinian rabbinic teachers.

Tannaitic Referring to the Tannaim (Tannaites), or early generations of rabbinic teachers. The actual Tannaitic period of rabbinic Judaism is generally held to span the period from A.D. 70 to about A.D. 220, the traditional time of compilation of the *Mishnah* (q.v.).

targum (Hebrew, "translation") Any of numerous Aramaic translations of portions of the Hebrew Bible. "The Targum" usually refers to the so-called *Targum Onqelos* to the Pentateuch.

tefillin See *phylacteries*.

terminus a quo (*ante quem*) The earliest possible date for a manuscript, event, etc.

terminus ad quem (*post quem*) The date after which an event, etc., could not have occurred.

Tetragrammaton The Hebrew equivalent of the four letters YHWH, which represent the name of the Lord in many parts of the Bible. The name was regarded as too holy to be pronounced, and so was vocalized in mediaeval manuscripts of the Hebrew Bible with the vowels of the Hebrew word *adonai*, an epithet signifying "God."

Titus Roman general, son of *Vespasian* (q.v.), who was responsible for the siege of Jerusalem during the First Revolt. He later succeeded his father as Emperor (A.D. 79–81).

Torah Hebrew ("the Law" or "the Teaching") particularly designates the first five books of the Bible, otherwise known as the *Pentateuch* (q.v.) or Five Books of Moses (to whom they are traditionally attributed). Among the rabbis, the term became used more generally for Jewish law, both oral and written.

Tosephta Literally, "The Addition," i.e., to the *Mishnah*. A large collection of laws and legal and ritual opinion of early rabbinic Judaism (early third century A.D.), very similar to the *Mishnah* (q.v.) in style and contents. The legal rulings of the *Tosephta* were not granted the same authority by the rabbis as those in the *Mishnah*, although historically they are of equal importance and derived from the same original corpus of early rabbinic legal and social views.

unicum A unique thing; esp., a text that exists only in a single manuscript, without necessarily being the author's own autograph.

Vespasian Roman general who was sent to Palestine to put down the First Revolt. He succeeded in conquering Galilee and much of Judaea, but when forced to return to Rome to assume the role of Emperor (A.D. 69–79), he left the capture of Jerusalem to his son Titus.

wadi (Arabic) A seasonal river or stream; Hebrew, *nahal* (q.v.).

"wings" An intermediate status of purity practiced by neophytes intent upon entering a Tannaitic friendship society (*haburah* [q.v.]).

Yahad (Hebrew, "Unity," "Oneness") A term appearing in several of the Dead Sea Scrolls that designates a particular pious group of purity-loving brethren who composed some of the scrolls.

Zadokite A descendant of Zadok, from whose lineage the High Priests of Judah had been selected since the time of King Solomon. The Zadokites were deposed by Antiochus Epiphanes in exchange for a bribe. The Hasmonaeans, who later assumed the High Priesthood, were not of the Zadokite line, and therefore (in the opinion of some) unqualified to assume the office.

Zealots A militant Jewish religious group described by Josephus, who were prime instigators of the First Revolt. Josephus seems to regard the Zealots as a well-defined group that came into existence during the revolt; however, there is evidence that the term (which primarily means "one zealous for the Law of the Lord") may have been widely used before and even after the Revolt for any who violently opposed Roman rule. See *sicarii*.

Zoroaster Persian religious leader (also called Zarathustra), lived ca. 600 B.C. (?); founded Zoroastrianism, a religion whose central belief is the eternal struggle between Good and Evil, or Truth and Falsehood.

Endnotes

Chapter 1. The Qumran Plateau

1. G. Dalman, in *Palästina Jahrbuch des Deutschen evangelischen Instituts für Altertumswissenschaft des heiligen Landes* **10** (1914), pp. 9–10 (my translation); and M. Avi-Yonah, *Map of Roman Palestine*, 2nd ed. (Jerusalem, 1940), map section.
2. Cf. Flavius Josephus, *Jewish Antiquities*, **18**.20, ed. Ralph Marcus, Loeb Classical Library (Cambridge, Mass., 1961); Philo Judaeus, *Every Good Man Is Free*, **12**.75, ed. and trans. F. H. Colson, Philo, vol. 9 (Cambridge, Mass., 1941).
3. Described in detail by Flavius Josephus, *The Jewish War*, **2**.122–161, ed. and trans. H. St. J. Thackeray, Loeb Classical Library, vol. 2 (London, 1927), pp. 368–385; Philo Judaeus, *Every Good Man Is Free*, **12–13**; idem, *Hypothetica*, **11**.1–18, ed. and trans. F. H. Colson, Loeb Classical Library, vol. 9 (Cambridge, Mass., 1941), pp. 436–443.
4. Josephus, *Antiquities*, **18**.19, ed. Ralph Marcus, Loeb Classical Library; Philo, *Hypothetica*, **11**.8.
5. Philo Judaeus, *Every Good Man Is Free*, **77–78**, pp. 54–55.
6. Philo, *Every Good Man is Free*, **79**, pp. 56–57; Josephus, *Antiquities*, **18**.21.
7. *Antiquities*, **18**.18–22.
8. *War*, **2**.154–155.
9. Ibid., **2**.121.
10. *Hypothetica*, **11**.14.
11. *War*, **2**.161–162.
12. *Antiquities*, **18**.19.
13. *Every Good Man Is Free*, **75**, pp. 54–55.
14. *War*, **2**.128, 148.
15. G. Lankester Harding, in *Palestine Exploration Quarterly* **84** (1952), p. 104.
16. Ibid., p. 105.
17. R. de Vaux, *L'archéologie et les manuscrits de la mer Morte* (London, 1961), p. 28 f. (All translations from this edition given here and below are mine.)
18. Ibid., p. 28.
19. F. M. Cross, *The Ancient Library of Qumran and Modern Biblical Studies* (London, 1958), p. 45.
20. Ibid., p. 6.

21. See S. Ilan and D. Amit, "The Water System of Qumran" (Hebrew), *Teba' wa'ares* **24** (1982), pp. 118–122. B. G. Wood, "To Dip or to Sprinkle? The Qumran Cisterns in Perspective," *Bulletin of the American Schools of Oriental Research* **256** (1984), pp. 45–60.
22. De Vaux, *L'archéologie*, pp. 4–5; cf. his earlier descriptions in *Revue biblique* **60** (1953), pp. 83–106 (first season); ibid., **61** (1954), pp. 208 ff. (second season); and ibid., **63** (1956), pp. 533–577 (third, fourth, and fifth campaigns).
23. *Dictionnaire archéologique de la Bible* (Jerusalem and Paris, 1970), p. 170 (article of A. Negev).
24. De Vaux, *L'archéologie*, p. 33.
25. See N. C. Debevoise, *A Political History of Parthia* (Chicago, 1938), pp. 109 ff.
26. Ibid., pp. 15 ff.
27. Ibid., p. 20.
28. On the siege of Jerusalem, see particularly Jonathan Price, *Jerusalem Under Siege* (Leiden, 1992).
29. Josephus, *The Jewish War*, **4**.464, ed. and trans. H. St. J. Thackeray, Loeb Classical Library, vol. 2 (London, 1927), pp. 370–371.
30. De Vaux, *L'archéologie*, pp. 29–33.
31. De Vaux, ibid., p. 15 (my translation).
32. Josephus, *War*, **5**.50–277; cf. Price, *Jerusalem Under Siege*, pp. 127–144.
33. Josephus, *War*, **5**.69.
34. De Vaux, *L'archéologie*, pp. 33 ff.
35. Cross, *Ancient Library*, p. 47.
36. De Vaux in *Revue biblique* **61** (1954), p. 234. On the *sicarii* and their activities in the First Revolt, see Josephus, *War*, **4**.400–405, 410–419, and *passim*.
37. Philo Judaeus, *Every Good Man Is Free*, op. cit., **12**, p. 54; trans. J. Moffatt in *Encyclopaedia of Religion and Ethics*, **5** (New York, 1912), p. 396.
38. Josephus, *War*, **2**.125, op. cit., pp. 370–371.
39. Cf. Pliny the Elder, *Natural History*, book 5, **15**.73; trans. H. Rackham, Loeb Classical Library, vol. 2 (London, 1942), p. 277.
40. See Ch. S. Clermont-Ganneau, *Archaeological Researches in Palestine during the Years 1873-1874*, vol. 2 (London, 1896), pp. 14–16.
41. See de Vaux, *L'archéologie*, pp. 37 f., 45 f., 69, 81, 96 f.
42. De Vaux, *L'archéologie*, pp. 96–97; idem, *Archaeology and the Dead Sea Scrolls* (Oxford, 1972), p. 128 f.
43. Josephus, *War*, **8**.160–161.
44. Pliny the Elder, *Natural History*, p. 277 (italics mine).
45. Josephus, *War*, **5**.145, pp. 242–243.
46. De Vaux, *L'archéologie*, p. 103; idem, *Archaeology and the Dead Sea Scrolls*, p. 133.
47. Pliny the Elder, *Natural History*, book 5, **14**.69 and **15**.72, pp. 272–275.
48. Ibid., pp. 98–99.
49. See Josephus, *War*, **1**.267, ed. Thackeray, pp. 124–125.
50. I am once again obliged to Prof. Eph'al for this calculation. See the article on Herodium by Ehud Netzer in *Biblical Archaeology Review*

(July/Aug. 1988), pp. 18–33, where the dimensions of the two large cisterns are given. Netzer states that the third cistern (not fully excavated) "seems to have been much smaller."

51. Netzer, ibid., p. 23.
52. Cf. de Vaux, *L'archéologie*, pp. 40 ff., 51 f., 79; and ibid., plates xv, xxii, xxix.
53. De Vaux, *L'archéologie*, pp. 8–9.
54. Ibid., p. 8.
55. See the plan in de Vaux, ibid., plate 39, locus no. 4; and compare the plans of the Masada synagogue in Y. Yadin, *Masada, Herod's Fortress and the Zealots' Last Stand* (London, 1966), pp. 181, 185.
56. See de Vaux, *L'archéologie*, p. 8.
57. De Vaux, *Archaeology*, pp. 23, 81.
58. Cf., e.g., F. M. Cross, *Ancient Library*, p. 49 (speaking of the room's function as "clear and significant"); G. Vermes, *Discovery in the Judean Desert* (New York, Paris, Rome, 1956), p. 14 ("A *scriptorium* [was] found on the upper floor"); C. Fritsch, *Qumran Community*, p. 5 ("There is little doubt that this was the scriptorium where manuscripts were copied by scribes of the community").
59. Dupont-Sommer, *Essene Writings* (1961), p. 63.
60. Cf. particularly B. M. Metzger, "The Furniture of the Scriptorium at Qumran," *Revue de Qumran* **1** (1959), pp. 509–515; idem, "When did the Scribes Begin to Use Writing Desks?," *Akten des XI internationalen Byzantinisten-Kongress 1958* (1960), pp. 355–362; and, in defense of his own hypothesis, de Vaux, op. cit., pp. 30 f.
61. J. C. Greenfield in *Journal of Near Eastern Studies* **35** (1976), p. 288; he reiterated and further developed this view during his lecture at the Eleventh World Congress of Jewish Studies, 29 June 1993.
62. See A. K. Bowman et al., *Vindolanda: The Latin Writing Tablets* (London, 1984).
63. See de Vaux, *L'archéologie*, p. 80; *Archaeology and the Dead Sea Scrolls*, p. 103.
64. De Vaux, *L'archéologie*, p. 80 (my italics).
65. For illustrations of the ostraca of Qumran and Masada, cf., e.g., de Vaux, *L'archéologie*, plate XV, b; Y. Yadin, *The Excavation of Masada, 1963–64: Preliminary Report* (Jerusalem, 1965), plate 19, c and d.
66. See de Vaux, *L'archéologie*, pp. 12 ff.
67. See G. Vermes, *The Dead Sea Scrolls: Qumran in Perspective* (London, 1981), p. 12.
68. De Vaux, *L'archéologie*, p. 12 ff.
69. Cf. K. Preisendanz, *Papyrusfunde und Papyrusforschung* (Leipzig, 1933), p. 113.
70. See P. Benoit, J. T. Milik, R. de Vaux, et al., *Les grottes de Murabba'at. Texte* (Discoveries in the Judaean Desert II, Oxford, 1961), p. 31 and note 4. For the En Ghuweir pottery, cf. the photographs in *Eretz-Israel* **10** (1971), plates 49–50.
71. De Vaux, *Archaeology and the Dead Sea Scrolls*, p. 33; cf. ibid., pp. 54–55, note 1. For the Jericho pottery, see J. L. Kelso and D. C. Baramki,

Excavations at New Testament Jericho and Khirbet en-Nitla, Annual of the American Schools of Archaeology 29–30 (1955), p. 26 and Plate 23, no. A115; and for that of Quailba, see *Annual of the Department of Antiquities of Jordan*, vols. 4 and 5 (1960), p. 116: "The most interesting finds were that of an inkwell and a cylindrical jar which are closely paralleled by similar objects discovered at Qumran." (Statement of Farah S. Ma'ayeh).

72. De Vaux, *L'archéologie*, p. 102.

73. De Vaux, *Archaeology and the Dead Sea Scrolls*, p. 135, note 3.

74. De Vaux, *Archaeology and the Dead Sea Scrolls*, pp. 89–90.

75. See P. Bar-Adon in *Hadashot Arkheologiot* (Jerusalem), April 1968, pp. 24–28; April 1969, pp. 29–30; idem, "Another Settlement of the Judaean Desert Sect at En Ghuweir on the Dead Sea," *Eretz Israel* **10** (1971), 72–89.

76. De Vaux, *Archaeology and the Dead Sea Scrolls*, p. 89.

77. See M. Broshi in M. Broshi et al. (eds.), *Megillot midbar yehudah— arba'im shenot mehqar* (Jerusalem, 1992), p. 62 (my translation).

78. See the plan of the cemetery by S. Tsemel in *Revue de Qumran* **75**, Dec. 1969; and by A. Strobel, in *Zeitschrift des deutschen Palästina-Vereins* **88** (1972), p. 79, fig. 4.

79. See N. Haas and H. Nathan, "Anthropological Survey of Human Skeletal Remains from Qumran," *Revue de Qumran* **6** (1968), pp. 345–352. On Z. J. Kapera's report, see Chapter 11, p. 320.

80. C. Roth, *The Historical Background of the Dead Sea Scrolls* (Oxford, 1958); G. R. Driver, *The Judaean Scrolls: The Problem and a Solution* (Oxford, 1965).

81. This project, based upon de Vaux's notes and records, is now being undertaken by Profs. Robert Donceel and Pauline Donceel-Voûte of Louvain and Dr. J.-B. Humbert of the Ecole Biblique in Jerusalem. As I show in Chapter 11, their views on the identification of the site have come to differ considerably from de Vaux's own.

82. Josephus, *Antiquities*, **13**.180–183, ed. Marcus, Loeb Classical Library (Cambridge, Mass., 1961), pp. 315–316.

83. Josephus, *Antiquities*, **8**.397, pp. 426–427. Cf. *Jewish Encyclopaedia*, article "Machaerus," **8** (New York and London, 1904), p. 245. Within the confines of the present Hashemite Kingdom of Jordan, Machaerus is being excavated in stages by an Italian team.

84. Josephus, *War*, **7**.163–209, pp. 552–565.

85. See L. duPuy de Podio, *Die Brieftaube in der Kriegskunst* (Leipzig, 1872).

86. See the pertinent section of the Madaba map as depicted, e.g., in Ze'ev Vilnai, *Eretz Yisrael bitemunot uv'mapot 'atiqot* (Jerusalem, 1961), p. 68.

87. See particularly Prof. Menashe Harel, "The Route of Salt, Sugar and Balsam Caravans in the Judean Desert," *GeoJournal* **2**.6 (1978), pp. 549–556.

88. Harel, ibid., p. 550 (my italics).

89. Ibid., pp. 554–556; cf. Josephus, *War*, **4**.479–480. Harel assumes that Sodom was at the southern tip of the Dead Sea and that the sea itself was approximately the same size and shape as it is now. J. Rugerson, *Atlas of the Bible* (New York, 1985), on the contrary, states (p. 194): "Two-thirds

of the way down the Dead Sea, a piece of land juts into it from the eastern side. This is known as el-Lisan (the tongue), and it is a significant fact that to its north the depth of the Dead Sea is about 400m (1312 feet) while to its south the depth is only 6m (19.7 ft) or so." Rugerson assumes that "in biblical times the area to the south of the tongue was dry, and that the cities of the plain, including Sodom, were located in the eastern part of this dry area." There is apparently no decisive proof as yet for either view of this southernmost portion of the sea.

Chapter 2. The Manuscripts of the Jews

1. J. Mann, *The Jews in Egypt and Palestine under the Fatimid Caliphs*, 2 vols. (Oxford, 1920, 1922); E. Ashtor (Strauss), *History of the Jews in Egypt and Syria Under the Rule of the Mamlukes* (Hebrew), vols. 1–2 (Jerusalem, 1944–51), vol. 3 (Jerusalem, 1970); S. D. Goitein, *A Mediterranean Society* (5 vols., Berkeley and Los Angeles, 1967–87).
2. See my studies in "New Light on the Persecution of French Jews at the Time of the First Crusade," *Proceedings of the American Academy for Jewish Research* **24** (1966), pp. 1–63; "Le toponyme hébraique MNYW et son identification avec Monieux (Vaucluse), *Revue internationale d'onomastique* **20** (1968), pp. 241–54; and "Monieux," *Proceedings of the American Philosophical Society* **63** (Feb. 1969) pp. 67–94.
3. André Dupont-Sommer, *The Essene Writings from Qumran* (Oxford, 1961; Cleveland and New York, 1962).
4. Dupont-Sommer, *The Essene Writings from Qumran* (1962 ed.), p. 15.
5. Ibid., p. 67.
6. Ibid., p. 66.
7. P. Benoit, J. T. Milik, R. de Vaux, et al., *Les Grottes de Murabba'at*, Texte (Discoveries in the Judaean Desert **2**, Oxford, 1961) and Plates (Discoveries in the Judaean Desert **2**, Oxford, 1961).
8. See particularly Y. Yadin, *Bar-Kokhba* (London and Jerusalem, 1971); and N. Lewis, Y. Yadin, and J. C. Greenfield (eds.), *The Documents from the Bar Kokhba Period in the Cave of the Letters* (Jerusalem, 1989).
9. *Archaeology and the Dead Sea Scrolls*, p. 104; my italics.
10. *Bulletin of the American Schools of Oriental Research* 135 (Oct. 1954), p. 29.
11. See *Manual of Discipline*, **6**.20–22.
12. F. M. Cross, *The Ancient Library of Qumran and Modern Biblical Studies* (New York, 1958), p. 90.
13. Y. Yadin, *The Message of the Scrolls* (New York, 1962), p. 161.
14. Philo Judaeus, *Every Good Man Is Free*, **12**.75; Josephus, *Antiquities*, **18**.21.
15. Dupont-Sommer, *Essene Writings*, p. 15.
16. *Ancient Library*, p. 147.
17. See, e.g., J. Deiss, *Herculaneum* (Malibu, n.d.); W. Jashemski, *The Gardens of Pompeii* (New Rochelle, N.Y., 1979).
18. See J. W. B. Barns et al., *Nag Hammadi Codices: Greek and Coptic Papyri*

from the Cartonnage of the Covers, Nag Hammadi Studies, vol. 16 (Leiden, 1981), pp. 2–11; and Chapter 4 of this book.

19. See Bezalel Porten, *The Archives of Elephantine* (Berkeley and Los Angeles, 1968). On the scribes of the Elephantine papyri, see pp. 97–98 of this book.

20. See Edmund Wilson, *The Scrolls from the Dead Sea* (New York, 1955), p. 46; idem, *The Dead Sea Scrolls* (New York, 1969), p. 47.

21. See C. T. Fritsch, *The Qumran Community: Its History and its Scrolls* (New York, 1956), p. 4.

22. J. A. Sanders, *The Psalms Scroll from Qumran Cave 11*, Discoveries in the Judaean Desert of Jordan **4** (Oxford, 1965), p. 63 (italics are Sanders's).

23. Cf., e.g., E. Wilson, op. cit., p. 45: "[The Essenes'] monastery, built crudely of gray blocks of stone, still stands, as was noted by Pliny, some distance away from the shore. . . ."

Chapter 3. 1947: The First Scroll Discoveries

1. Basic publications and translations of the scrolls discussed in this chapter are the following: **Manual of Discipline:** M. Burrows (ed.), *The Dead Sea Scrolls of St. Mark's Monastery* II (New Haven, 1951); English translations: W. H. Brownlee, *The Dead Sea Manual of Discipline, Translation and Notes* (B.A.S.O.R., Supplementary Studies, nos. 10–12, 1951); P. Wernberg-Møller, *The Manual of Discipline, Translated and Annotated with an Introduction* (Leiden, 1957). **Genesis Apocryphon:** J. A. Fitzmyer, *The Genesis Apocryphon of Qumran Cave 1* (Rome, 1971). **The War Scroll:** Y. Yadin, *The Scroll of the War of the Sons of Light against the Sons of Darkness* (Oxford, 1962); E. Lohse (ed. and trans.), *Die Texte aus Qumran* (Munich, 1964), pp. 180 ff. **The Damascus Covenant:** Solomon Schechter, *Fragments of a Zadokite Work—Documents of Jewish Sectaries* I (Cambridge, 1910); Ch. Rabin, *The Zadokite Documents* (Oxford, 1954; 2nd ed., Oxford, 1958). **Pesher Habakkuk:** M. Burrows (ed.), *The Dead Sea Scrolls of St. Mark's Monastery* I (New Haven, 1950). **Rule of the Community,** or **The Messianic Rule:** D. Barthélemy and J. Milik, *Qumran Cave 1*. Discoveries in the Judaean Desert **1** (Oxford, 1955), pp. 108–111. On the relation of the **Hodayot** to the poetry of the intertestamental Jews as revealed by the Qumran texts, see Epilogue, pp. 361–362.

2. Sukenik's acquisitions: see Y. Yadin, *The Message of the Scrolls* (New York, 1952), pp. 15–52; his statement on the Essenes: see E. Sukenik, *Megillot Genuzot* (Jerusalem, 1948), p. 16 (my translation).

3. Dupont-Sommer's statement: *The Essene Writings from Qumran* (Oxford, 1961), pp. 66, 93. Yadin's: *The Message of the Scrolls* (New York, 1962), p. 174. Cross's: *The Ancient Library of Qumran and the Essenes* (New York, 1958), pp. 71 f. Cf., e.g., Dupont-Sommer, *Essene Writings*, p. 65; and G. Vermes, *The Dead Sea Scrolls—Qumran in Perspective* (Cleveland, 1978), pp. 96–97.

4. J. M. Allegro, *Qumran Cave 4, I (4Q158–4Q186)*, Discoveries in the Judaean Desert **5** (Oxford, 1968), pp. 11–30.

5. See particularly L. Ginzberg, *Eine unbekannte jüdische Sekte* (New York, 1922). English translation: *An Unknown Jewish Sect* (New York, 1976).
6. R. de Vaux, *Archaeology and the Dead Sea Scrolls* (London, 1973), pp. 112–113; A. Jaubert, "Le pays de Damas," *Revue Biblique* **65** (1958), pp. 214–248; R. North, "The Damascus of Qumran Geography," *Palestine Exploration Quarterly* **87** (1955), pp. 34–48; F. M. Cross, *Ancient Library*, pp. 59 f.; M. Burrows, *More Light on the Dead Sea Scrolls* (New York, 1958), p. 227. C. Fritsch had earlier suggested that the migration took place from Qumran itself to Damascus during the reign of Herod (*The Qumran Community: Its History and its Scrolls* [New York, 1956]), but as R. de Vaux then pointed out (*Archaeology*, op. cit., p. 112), such a theory did violence to the "internal evidence and . . . palaeography."
7. F. M. Cross, "The Early History of the Qumran Community," in *New Directions in Biblical Archaeology*, David Noel Freedman and Jonas C. Greenfield, eds. (Garden City, N.Y., 1971), p. 77. (Italics mine.)

Chapter 4. The Qumran-Essene Theory: A Paradigm Reconsidered

1. See D. Barthélemy, O. P. and J. T. Milik, *Qumran Cave 1*. Discoveries in the Judaean Descrt **1** (Oxford, 1955). On the poetry preserved in the scrolls, see below, Epilogue, pp. 361–362.
2. Ibid., p. 45: ". . . la bibliothèque de la Communauté Essénienne."
3. Ibid., pp. 102–107.
4. Milik, *Qumran Cave 1*, p. 103, note 2 (my translation from the French).
5. See M. Wise, "Accidents and Accidence: A Scribal View of Linguistic Dating of the Aramaic Scrolls from Qumran," in *'Abr-Nahrain Supplement* **3** (1992), p. 143. On the Elephantine manuscripts, see above, p. 59. For the number of scribes who wrote the extant Elephantine papyri, see the survey in B. Porten, *Archives from Elephantine* (Berkeley, 1968), pp. 192–194.
6. M. Baillet et al., *Les 'Petites Grottes' de Qumrân*. Textes. Discoveries in the Judaean Desert **3** (Oxford, 1962), p. 85 (statement of Baillet).
7. Cf. ibid., p. 100, termed by the editors "Un texte de la secte."
8. See the eventual descriptions of the texts in J. T. Milik, *Dix ans de découvertes dans le désert de Juda* (Paris, 1957), pp. 23–39; F. M. Cross, *The Ancient Library of Qumran and Modern Biblical Studies* (London, 1958), pp. 9–38, 52–145; revised ed. (New York, 1961), pp. 30–47, 70–106.
9. On *mezuzot* in general, see *Jewish Encyclopaedia*, **8** (New York and London, 1904), pp. 531–532, and **10** (New York and London, 1905), pp. 21–28.
10. Cf. "Letter of Aristeas," verse 159, in R. H. Charles (ed.), *The Apocrypha and Pseudepigrapha of the Old Testament*, **2** (Oxford, 1913), p. 109.
11. Cf. Josephus, *Antiquities*, 4.213, ed. Thackeray, vol. **4** (Cambridge, Mass., 1967), pp. 578–579.
12. See D. Barthélemy, in *Qumran Cave I*. Discoveries in the Judaean Desert **1** (Oxford, 1955), pp. 72–76, Plate 14, fig. 10 (1Q13); K. G. Kuhn, "Phylakterien aus Höhle 4 von Qumran," *Abhandlungen der Heidelberger*

Akademie der Wissenschaften (*Philosophische-Historische Klasse* 1; Heidelberg, 1957) (4Qa–d); M. Baillet, in Discoveries in the Judaean Desert **3** (Oxford, 1962), pp. 149 ff., Plates 32–33; figs. 8–11 (Groups 1–4; 8Q3); Y. Yadin, *Tefillin from Qumran—XQ Phyl 1–4* (Jerusalem, 1969); J. T. Milik, in R. de Vaux and J. T. Milik, *Qumran Grotte 4, II.i. Archéologie . . . et ii. Tefillin, Mezuzot et Targums*, DJD **6**; (Oxford, 1977), pp. 33–85 and plates 4–27 (21 phylacteries, 7 *mezuzot*).

13. Cf. J. T. Milik, in R. de Vaux and J. T. Milik, *Qumran Grotte 4, II.i. Archéologie. . . et ii. Tefillin, Mezuzot et Targums*, DJD **6** (Oxford, 1977), pp. 34 ff.
14. Cf. Milik, ibid., p. 39. The passages of these latter phylacteries include only Ex. **13**.1–10 and 11–16, and Deut. **6**.4–9 and **11**.13–21.
15. Milik, ibid., p. 39.
16. Milik, ibid., p. 47 (my translation).
17. See Paul Kahle, *The Cairo Genizah*, 2nd ed., p. 242; and E. Sukenik, *Megillot genuzot* (1948), p. 15.
18. Kahle, ibid., p. 241, notes 2 and 3, and p. 242.
19. See de Vaux in *Revue Biblique* **56** (1949), p. 236.
20. See H. H. Rowley, *The Zadokite Fragments and the Dead Sea Scrolls* (1952), p. 49, note 6.
21. O. Eissfeldt, *Theologische Literaturzeitung* **74** (1949), cols. 597–600, *apud* O. Braun, in *Oriens Christianus* 1 (1901), pp.138–152; see particularly p. 304 f.; translated by G. R. Driver, *The Hebrew Scrolls from the Neighborhood of Jericho and the Dead Sea* (Oxford, 1951), pp. 25–26.
22. See above note.
23. See the summary of these efforts in H. H. Rowley, *The Zadokite Fragments and the DSS*, p. 22, note 4.
24. See Y. Yadin, *The Message of the Scrolls* (New York, 1962), pp.76 ff (my italics).
25. Thomas Kuhn, *The Structure of Scientific Revolutions* (Chicago: 1st ed., 1962; 2nd ed., 1970); Alexander Kohn, *False Prophets* (New York, 1986).
26. See James R. Robinson, *The Facsimile Edition of the Nag Hammadi Codices: Introduction* (separate insert in Facsimile Edition, Codex VI: Leiden, 1972), p. 4, and references to publications by Jean Doresse and others given there, note 13; J. W. B. Barns, in Martin Krause (ed.), *Essays on the Nag Hammadi Codices in Honour of Pahor Labib* (Leiden, 1975), p. 17; J. W. B. Barns, G. M. Browne, and J. C. Shelton, *Nag Hammadi Codices: Greek and Coptic Papyri from the Cartonnage of the Covers* (Leiden, 1981), p. 5 (by Shelton).
27. Cf. Barns in *Essays on the Nag Hammadi Codices in Honour of Pahor Labib*, p. 17.
28. Barns, ibid., p. 13 (my italics). On St. Pachomius and his monasteries, see Glossary s.v. "coenobite."
29. R. de Vaux, *Archaeology*, p. 104 (my italics). See also Shelton in *Nag Hammadi Codices . . . Cartonnage*, p. 2.
30. Shelton, ibid., pp. 2, 5, and 11.
31. Jean Doresse, *The Secret Books of the Egyptian Gnostics* (New York, 1960), pp. xi–xii, 250, 249, and 251.

32. See T. Säve-Söderberg, "Gnostic and Canonical Gospel Traditions," in U. Bianchi (ed.), *The Origins of Gnosticism: Colloquium of Messina 13–18 April 1966* (Leiden, 1970), pp. 552–562; cf. ibid., pp. 552–553.
33. Ibid., p. 553; the translation is that appearing in Doresse's *Secret Books*, p. 143.
34. See Säve-Söderberg, op. cit., p. 553; and cf. J. Barns, in M. Krause (ed.), *Essays on the Nag Hammadi Papyri*, p. 16.

Chapter 5. The *Copper Scroll*, the Masada Manuscripts, and the Siege of Jerusalem

1. K. G. Kuhn in *Revue Biblique* **61** (1954), pp. 193–205.
2. Quotations from letters written to and by Allegro at this period may be found in M. Baigent and R. Leigh, *The Dead Sea Scrolls Deception* (London, 1991), pp. 45 ff.
3. See particularly Baigent and Leigh, ibid., pp. 45–63. Allegro's notoriously anti-Semitic book, *The Chosen People* (Garden City, N.Y., 1972), is not mentioned by the authors.
4. All quotes are from J. M. Allegro, *The Dead Sea Scrolls* (Penguin Books, 1956), pp. 183–184.
5. See A. Dupont-Sommer, *Essene Writings from Qumran*, p. 383.
6. Dupont-Sommer, *Essene Writings*, p. 381 f., 385.
7. See, for example, *The Times* of London (1 June 1956), p. 12.
8. Baigent and Leigh, op. cit., pp. 54 ff.
9. See Chaim Rabin in *The Jewish Chronicle* (June, 1956); and K. G. Kuhn in *Theologische Literaturzeitung* **81** (1956), cols. 541–546.
10. See Baigent and Leigh, op. cit., pp. 54 ff.
11. F. M. Cross, *Ancient Library of Qumran and the Essenes*, p. 18, note 29.
12. A. Dupont-Sommer, *Essene Writings*, pp. 392 ff. (English translation of *Les Ecrits Esséniens* [1959]; my italics.)
13. Dupont-Sommer, *Essene Writings*, pp. 379 ff.
14. See Milik in *Revue Biblique* **66** (1959), pp. 321-357; Dupont-Sommer, *Essene Writings*, pp. 389 ff.
15. *Essene Writings*, p. 393 f.
16. *Essene Writings*, p. 386; Josephus, *War*, **6**.387–391; ed. Thackeray, vol. **3**, pp. 486–489.
17. *War*, **6**.432, ed. Thackeray, vol. **3**, pp. 500–501.
18. R. de Vaux, *Archaeology and the Dead Sea Scrolls*, pp. 108–109.
19. J. Allegro, *The Treasure of the Copper Scroll* (London, 1960); J. T. Milik, "Le Rouleau de Cuivre provenant de la grotte 3Q (3Q15)," in M. Baillet et al., *Les 'Petites Grottes' de Qumrân: Textes*, Discoveries in the Judaean Desert of Jordan **3** (Oxford, 1962), pp. 211–302, 314–317; and *Planches* (Oxford, 1962), plates xliii–lxxi. A Hebrew volume on the scroll, based primarily on Allegro's transcription, appeared subsequently: B.-Z. Lurie, *Megillat hanehoshet* (Jerusalem, 1963).
20. See particularly Al Wolters, "Apocalyptic and the Copper Scroll," *Journal of Near Eastern Studies* **49** (1990), pp. 145–154, and numerous sources there cited.

21. See R. de Vaux in *Revue Biblique* (1961), pp. 146–147; and Milik, "Rouleau de Cuivre," p. 299 (my translation).

22. See the survey by Al Wolters in "Apocalyptic and the Copper Scroll," op. cit.; idem, "History and the Copper Scroll," in M. Wise et al. (eds.), *Methods of Investigation of the Dead Sea Scrolls and the Khirbet Qumran Site*, Annals of the New York Academy of Sciences, vol. 722 (New York,1994), pp. 285–298.

23. Ed. Milik, p. 298.

24. *Copper Scroll*, col. **8**, line 3. The Hebrew term *sefer* (pl., *sefarim* or *sefarin*) at first designated a scroll, but when the *codex* (i.e., leaves bound together to form a book in the more modern sense) came into use, the same Hebrew term was applied to it.

25. See *Copper Scroll*, cols. **5**.7; **11**.1, 4, 11, 15. Allegro read the pertinent expression as a meaningless *btkn 'sln* (a mistake repeated by Milik), and it was G. Sarfati who finally offered the correct decipherment *ktbn 'sln*, "the [or their] writings are next to them" (i.e., to the treasures described beforehand).

26. See M. Avi-Yonah, N. Avigad, et al., "The Archaeological Survey and Excavation of Masada, 1955–1956," *Israel Exploration Journal* **8** (1957), pp. 1–60.

27. See G. Adam Smith, *The Historical Geography of the Holy Land* (London, 1894), pp. 512–513.

28. Josephus, *War*, **4**.399–405, 516.

29. Siege and capture of Herodium: Josephus, *War*, **7**.163; of Machaerus, ibid., **7**.164–209; of forest of Jardes, ibid., **7**.210–215.

30. See Josephus, *War*, **7**.270–406, ed. Thackeray, Loeb Classical Library, vol. 3 (1967), pp. 576–619; and cf. the valuable historical summary by M. Avi-Yonah et al. in *Israel Exploration Journal* **7** (1957), pp. 1–8.

31. G. A. Smith, *Historical Geography*, p. 514.

32. J. Strugnell, "The Angelic Liturgy at Qumran," in *Vetus Testamentum Supplementae* **7** (1960), pp. 318 ff.

33. See A. Jaubert, *The Date of the Last Supper* (Staten Island, 1965); S. Talmon, "The Calendar of the Covenanters of the Judean Desert," in C. Rabin and Y. Yadin (eds.), *Aspects of the Dead Sea Scrolls* (*Scripta Hierosolymitana* 4, Jerusalem, 1958), pp. 162–199.

34. Josephus, *War*, **2**.567 (in **3**.11, John participates in the expedition against Ashkelon).

35. Y. Yadin, *The Excavation of Masada, 1963–64* (1965), pp. 107–108.

36. Yadin, *Masada*, p. 174.

37. Yadin, *Masada*, p. 173 f.

38. Cf. Josephus, *War*, **4**.398 ff., ed. and trans. Thackeray, Loeb Classical Library, vol. **3**, pp. 116 ff. For the approximate time of its capture, see *War*, **2**.408, ed. Thackeray, vol. 2, pp. 482–483.

39. See Cecil Roth, "Qumran and Masada: A Final Clarification Regarding the Dead Sea Sect," *Revue de Qumran* **5** (1964–66), pp. 81–87.

40. E. Wilson, *The Dead Sea Scrolls: 1947–1969* (New York, 1969), p. 210 f.

41. C. Newsom and Y. Yadin, "The Masada Fragment of the Qumran Songs of the Sabbath Sacrifice," *Israel Exploration Journal* **34** (1984), p. 77. On Essene suffering under the Romans, see Josephus, *War*, **2**.152–153.

42. C. Newsom, *Songs of the Sabbath Sacrifice: A Critical Edition* (Atlanta, 1985).
43. Masada fragment 1, ed. Newsom, pp. 168–169.
44. Masada fragment 2 and overlapping 4Q fragment, ed. Newsom, p. 172.
45. *Songs*, 4Q405, ed. Newsom, p. 303 (my translations).
46. C. Newsom, *Songs*, p. 74, note 11.
47. See *American Scholar* **58** (Spring 1989), pp. 201–202.
48. See *Biblica* **69** (1988), pp. 138–146; and my remarks in the *American Scholar* (Spring 1989), pp. 201–202.
49. C. Newsom, "'Sectually Explicit' Literature from Qumran," in W. Propp et al. (eds.), *The Hebrew Bible and its Interpreters* (Winona Lake, Ind., 1990), pp. 180, 182.
50. Yadin, *Excavation of Masada*, pp. 103–110.
51. Yadin, ibid., p. 107.
52. Wilson, *The Dead Sea Scrolls*, p. 210.
53. See Siegfried Wagner, *Die Essener in der wissenschaftlichen Diskussion, vom Ausgang des 18. bis zum Beginn des 20. Jahrhunderts. Eine wissenschaftliche Studie* (Berlin, 1960; = Beihefte zur Zeitschrift für die alttestamentliche Wissenschaft 79), esp. Chap. 1; G. Vermes and M. D. Goodman, *The Essenes According to the Classical Sources*, Bibliography, "Pre-Qumran Literature" (Sheffield, 1989), p. 101; *Encyclopaedia of Religion and Ethics*, **5** (New York, 1920), p. 401, bibliographical note.
54. Josephus, *War*, **4**.120; ed. Thackeray, Loeb Classical Library, vol. 3 (1968), pp. 36–37.
55. Josephus, *War*, **4**.121–128; ed. Thackeray, vol. 3, pp. 36–39.
56. Trans. Thackeray, vol. 3, p. 567.
57. Cf. *War*, **5**.347, and also **5**.331 ff.
58. Trans. Thackeray, vol. 3, p. 355 (my italics).
59. Josephus, *War*, **2**.427; ed. Thackeray, Loeb Classical Library, vol. 2 (1967), pp. 490–491.
60. In the ensuing years the following publications of Masada texts, ostraca, and coins have taken place: Y. Yadin, *The Ben Sira Scroll from Masada* (Jerusalem, 1965); C. Newsom and Y. Yadin, "The Masada Fragment of the Qumran 'Songs of the Sabbath Sacrifice,'" *Israel Exploration Journal* **34** (1984), pp. 77–78; Sh. Talmon, "Fragments of the Hebrew Texts from Masada" (Hebrew), *Yadin Memorial Volume = Eretz Israel* **10** (Jerusalem, 1990), pp. 278–286; Sh. Talmon, "A Fragment from Masada of an Apocryphon to the Book of Joshua" (Hebrew), *Chaim Rabin Festschrift*, ed. M. Goshen Gottstein et al. (Jerusalem, 1992), pp. 147–157; J. Aviram, G. Foerster, and E. Netzer (eds.), *Masada I—The Yigael Yadin Excavations 1963–1965: Final Reports*; Y. Yadin and J. Naveh, "The Aramaic and Hebrew Ostraca and Jar Inscriptions"; Y. Meshorer, "The Coins of Masada" (Jerusalem, 1989); H. M. Cotton and J. Geiger, with a contribution by J. D. Thomas, "The Latin and Greek Documents" (Jerusalem, 1989).

Chapter 6. Scroll Origins: Rengstorf's
Theory and Edmund Wilson's Response

1. See J. Allegro, with the collaboration of A. A. Anderson, *Qumran Cave 4, I (4Q158–4Q186)*, Discoveries in the Judaean Desert of Jordan, 5 (Oxford, 1968). For the Cave 11 publication of 1965, see above, p. 400, note 22.
2. K. H. Rengstorf, *Hirbet Qumran und die Bibliothek vom Toten Meer*, Studia Delitszchiana 5 (1960); idem, *Hirbet Qumran and the Problem of the Dead Sea Caves* (Leiden, 1963).
3. Rengstorf, *Hirbet Qumran* (1963), p. 22.
4. See H. Bardtke, in *Theologische Literaturzeitung* 87 (1962), pp. 820–823; *Theologische Rundschau* 33 (1968), pp. 101–105; K. H. Rengstorf, in S. Wagner (ed.), *Bibel und Qumran. Beziehungen zwischen Bibel- und Qumranwissenschaft. Hans Bardtke zum 22.9.1966*, (Berlin, 1968), pp. 156–176.
5. De Vaux, *Archaeology*, p. 106.
6. Cf. R. H. Charles, *The Apocrypha and Pseudepigrapha of the Old Testament* I (Oxford, 1913), p. 134.
7. See *Babylonian Talmud*, Ketubbot 106a. For Nahum the Scribe (Hebrew, *lablar*), see *Mishnah*, Peah 2.6.
8. Josephus, *Antiquities*, 5.61, comp. 3.38 and 4.303.
9. Rengstorf, *Hirbet Qumran and the Problem*, pp. 19–21.
10. Letter of K. H. Rengstorf to M. Klinghardt dated 14 March 1992.
11. E. Wilson, *The Dead Sea Scrolls: 1947–1969* (New York, 1969), p. 171.
12. Ibid., p. 171.
13. Ibid., p. 173.
14. On the so-called intertestamental writings, see further *Interpreter's Dictionary of the Bible*, s.v. "Apocrypha," vol. 1, pp. 161–166.
15. On the special books of the Essenes, see Josephus, *War* 2.142: "[The Essene] swears, moreover . . . carefully to preserve the books of the sect and the names of the angels."
16. E. Wilson, *Upstate: Records and Recollections of Northern New York* (New York, 1971).
17. E. Wilson, *The Fifties* (New York, 1986), p. 253.
18. Cf. N. Golb, *Toledoth hayehudim be'ir rouen bimé habenayim* (Tel Aviv, 1976).
19. Ibid., p. 231.
20. Paris-Normandie, 2 September 1976. For the reports that followed, see N. Golb in *Proceedings of the American Academy for Jewish Research* 48 (1981), p. 100, note 1.
21. This and all other pertinent documentation relative to the negotiations arc contained in a special file located in the archives of the Direction d'Architecture at the Palais Royale in Paris.
22. See B. Blumenkranz, "Un ensemble synagogal à Rouen: 1096–1116," in *Académie des Inscriptions et Belles-Lettres—Comptes rendus* (Nov./Dec. 1976), pp. 663–687; idem, *Art et archéologie des Juifs en France médiévale* (Toulouse, 1980), pp. 276–303; and my response in *Les Juifs de Rouen au Moyen Age* (Rouen, 1985), pp. 21–30, and in earlier discussions there cited.

Chapter 7. The *Temple Scroll*, the *Acts of Torah*, and the Qumranologists' Dilemma

1. See *New York Times* (23 October 1967).
2. See Y. Yadin, in *Biblical Archaeology Review* (Sept./Oct. 1984), p. 36.
3. Y. Yadin, *Megillat hamiqdash*, 3 vols. (Jerusalem, 1977); English translation: Y. Yadin, *The Temple Scroll*, **1** and **2** (Jerusalem, 1983) and **3** (Jerusalem, 1977). Popular version: Y. Yadin, *Megillat hamiqdash* (Tel Aviv, 1990).
4. See B. A. Levine, "A Further Look at the Mo'adim of the Temple Scroll," in L. Schiffman (ed.), *Archaeology and History in the Dead Sea Scrolls* (Sheffield, 1990), p. 65. See further B. A. Levine, "The Temple Scroll: Aspects of its Historical Provenance and Literary Character," *Bulletin of the American Schools of Oriental Research* **232** (1978), pp. 3–24.
5. Y. Yadin, *Megillat hamiqdash*, **3**, p. 304 (my translation).
6. See above, p. 63.
7. See N. Golb, "The Problem of Origin and Identification of the Dead Sea Scrolls," Proceedings of the American Philosophical Society **124** (February 1980), pp. 1–24.
8. See particularly Z. Kapera's article in *The Qumran Chronicle*, **3**, nos 1–3 (Dec. 1993), pp. 19–23.
9. See below, notes 11 and 12.
10. *Biblical Archaeologist* **19** (1956), p. 92.
11. J. T. Milik, in Discoveries 3, p. 222 (my translation).
12. J. T. Milik, *Dix ans de découverte*, p. 36.
13. F. M. Cross, "The Development of the Jewish Scripts," in G. E. Wright (ed.), *The Bible and the Ancient Near East. Essays in Honor of William Foxwell Albright* (Garden City, N.Y., 1961), pp. 133–202.
14. J. M. Baumgarten in *Journal of Jewish Studies* **31** (1980), pp. 162–163.
15. E. Qimron and J. Strugnell, "An Unpublished Halakhic Letter from Qumran," in Janet Amitai (ed.), *Biblical Archaeology Today* (Jerusalem, 1985), pp. 400–407; see the similar but abbreviated article by the same authors in *Israel Museum Journal* **4** (1985), pp. 9–12.
16. Qimron and Strugnell, ibid., p. 400 (my italics).
17. Qimron and Strugnell, ibid., p. 406.
18. See Joel Kraemer in Arthur Hyman (ed.), *Maimonidean Studies* (New York, 1991), p. 81.
19. See Qimron and Strugnell, op. cit., p. 400.
20. See E. Qimron, *The Hebrew of the Dead Sea Scrolls* (Atlanta, 1986), pp. 9, 24, 26, 31, 48, 58, 59, and *passim*.
21. See *Biblical Archaeologist* **48** (June 1985), pp. 68–82; *The Sciences* **27** (May/June 1987), pp. 294–312; *The American Scholar* **58** (Spring 1989), pp. 177–207.
22. *American Scholar*, ibid., pp. 203–206.
23. See Z. J. Kapera in *Qumran Cave Four and MMT—Special Report* (Cracow, 1991), pp. 61–62.
24. L. Schiffman in G. Brooke (ed.), *Temple Scroll Studies* (Sheffield, 1989), p. 245.
25. Ibid., p. 244. Earlier publications of Schiffman: *The Halakhah at Qumran*

(Leiden, 1975); *Sectarian Law in the Dead Sea Scrolls: Courts, Testimony and the Penal Code* (Chico, Calif., 1983).

26. Qimron and Strugnell, "Unpublished Halakhic Letter," p. 402.
27. Schiffman, ibid., p. 239.
28. Ibid., p. 245.
29. Schiffman, ibid., p. 245.
30. Dots within brackets = holes in the manuscript.
31. See, for example, *Jewish Encyclopaedia*, **9** (New York and London, 1905), pp. 661 ff.
32. The plural pronoun is here used, in contrast to all the following passages where the addressee is designated in the singular.
33. A blend of passages from Deuteronomy **30** and **31**.
34. See the photographs of the text as published in Eisenman and Robinson, *A Facsimile Edition of the Dead Sea Scrolls*, **2** (Washington, 1991), plates 1045, 1426, 1427, 1439, 1440, 1441, 1442, and 1471.
35. *War*, **2**.165–166.
36. See L. Ginzberg, *The Legends of the Jews*, **4** (Philadelphia, 1954), pp. 81–121, and **6** (Philadelphia, 1959), pp. 245–276; and sources there cited.
37. Josephus, *Antiquities*, **18**.14–15, ed. Marcus, pp. 12–13.
38. Josephus, *War*, **2**.162–164; a lengthier description appears in *Antiquities* **18**.12–15.
39. *War*, **2**.165–166; cf. *Antiquities* **18**.
40. See Mark **12**.18–27; Matthew **22**.23; Luke **20**.27; Acts **23**.8.
41. *War*, **2**.154–155.
42. See *Jewish Encyclopaedia*, **5** (New York & London, 1903) pp. 209–218; **10** (1905), pp. 382–385.
43. *Tosephta*, Kelim I, **1**.8.
44. *Tosephta*, Kelim I, **1**.12; *Sifre*, Naso.
45. *Mishnah*, Berakhot **1**.1.
46. See *Mishnah*, Parah **3**.7; *Tosephta*, Parah **5**.4; Maimonides, *Mishneh Torah*, Parah **1**.13–14.
47. See Schiffman, op. cit., p. 251; Sussman in *Tarbiz* **59** (1989–90), p. 28.
48. Schiffman, op. cit., p. 251.
49. See Sussman, "Research on the History of Halakhah and the Scrolls of the Judaean Wilderness" (Hebrew), *Tarbiz* **59** (1989–90), pp. 20, 21, 24, and *passim* (my translations).
50. Josephus, *Antiquities*, **18**.23–24.
51. Josephus, *Antiquities*, **13**.297.
52. J. Sussman, op. cit., pp. 48–57.
53. L. Schiffman, "The New Halakhic Letter (4QMMT) and the Origins of the Dead Sea Sect," *Biblical Archaeologist* **53** (June 1990), pp. 64–73.
54. Schiffman, ibid., p. 71, note 1.
55. Ibid., p. 64 (my italics).
56. H. Stegemann, "The Literary Composition of the Temple Scroll and its Status at Qumran," in G. Brooke, *Temple Scroll Studies*, p. 131.
57. Schiffman, "New Halakhic Letter," p. 65.
58. Ibid., p. 66.
59. Ibid., p. 66.

60. Ibid., p. 67.
61. Ibid., p. 68, col. 1, with which compare p. 67, cols. 2 and 3.
62. Ibid., p. 68.
63. *Damascus Covenant*, folio 1, lines 9–11.
64. See Schiffman, op. cit., pp. 69–71.
65. Schiffman, "The Significance of the Scrolls," *Bible Review* **6**, no. 5 (Oct. 1990), pp. 18–27, 52.
66. Ibid., p. 23.
67. Ibid., p. 22.
68. Ibid., p. 23.
69. Ibid., p. 23.
70. See N. Golb in *Proceedings of the American Philosophical Society* **124** (1980), pp. 10–11: "The cogent inference to be drawn from the presence of Hebrew manuscripts at Masada is that Jewish *sicarii* inhabiting the site possessed scrolls which they had brought there after taking the fortress in A.D. 66, while other Jews, of Jerusalem, took scrolls with them in addition to basic possessions needed for survival, in withdrawing to that site. . . ." The Qumran and Masada manuscripts stemmed from first-century Palestinian Jews and were remnants of a literature showing a "wide variety of practices, beliefs and opinions." Determination of the nature of the concepts and practices described in the scrolls might be best achieved "not by pressing them into the single sectarian bed of Essenism, but by separating them out from one another, through internal analysis, into various spiritual currents which appear to have characterized Palestinian Judaism of the intertestamental period."
71. Schiffman, "Significance of the Scrolls," p. 24.
72. See *Biblical Archaeologist* **48** (June 1985), pp. 81–82.
73. Schiffman, "Significance," p. 25 (my italics).
74. Golb, in *Proceedings of the American Philosophical Society* **124** (1980), p. 11.
75. See Schiffman, "Significance," pp. 25–26; republished in H. Shanks (ed.), *Understanding the Dead Sea Scrolls* (New York, 1992), pp. 45–46. The misrepresentation took the form of various assertions, each remarkably inaccurate, concerning either my views on Qumran origins, the nature of the Khirbet Qumran site, or my methods of investigation. Some examples: Schiffman claimed that (1) I had put forth a theory that the scrolls "are the library of the Jerusalem Temple"—as we have seen, the view of K. H. Rengstorf, not mine; (2) I had failed to support my theory "by a study of, or citations to, the texts themselves"—where my first published presentation of the theory was accompanied by numerous quotations taken directly from the sources (cf. *Proceedings of the American Philosophical Society* **124** [1980], pp. 6, 7, 15, 18, 20, 21, 22, 23); (3) I had "ignored the evidence" he had adduced from the *Acts of Torah*—where I had found his arguments based on that writing, like Strugnell's and Qimron's, merely to be without merit (cf. *American Scholar* [Spring 1989], pp. 203–205); (4) I had "ignored the clear sectarian emphasis of the collection as a whole"— a direct obliteration of Schiffman's own secondhand insight into the scrolls' importance as "the primary source for the study of Judaism in all

its varieties," that also passed over my own earlier focus on different forms of heterodoxy in the scrolls. (Cf. my remarks in *Proceedings* [1980], pp. 2–3, 14–15; *Journal of Near Eastern Studies* **49** [1990], pp. 110–113.)

76. Schiffman, "Significance," p. 23.
77. See J. Strugnell, "4Q MMT and Its Contributions to Qumran Studies: The State of the Questions," in E. Ulrich and J. VanderKam (eds.), *The Community of the Renewed Covenant—The Notre Dame Symposium on the Dead Sea Scrolls* (South Bend, Ind., forthcoming 1994).

Chapter 8. Power Politics and the Collapse of the Scrolls Monopoly

1. See G. Vermes, *The Dead Sea Scrolls in English*, 3rd ed. (London and New York, 1987), p. xii.
2. See particularly the article by J. N. Wilford in the *New York Times*, 21 Nov. 1989, "Science Times" section.
3. See Ph. Alexander and G. Vermes in *The Qumran Chronicle*, **2**, no. 3 (1993), pp. 153–154.
4. See the article of Ron Grossman in the *Chicago Tribune* (11 Nov. 1991): In Grossman's interview with the chief American editor, Dr. Ulrich, the latter acknowledged "that Oxford Center funds are being provided to some American biblical scholars, but he refused to disclose their names."
5. See statement of Alexander and Vermes in *The Qumran Chronicle* (1993), p. 155.
6. See *Chicago Tribune*, ibid.
7. See *The Qumran Chronicle* **2**, no. 1 (Dec. 1992), pp. 14–15.
8. See P. Alexander and G. Vermes, in *The Qumran Chronicle* **2.**, no. 3, p. 155.
9. See *Biblical Archaeology Review* (Nov./Dec. 1989), p. 56.
10. See *Allgemeiner Journal* (20 Sept. 1991).
11. See *New York Times* (5 Sept. 1991), and B. Z. Wacholder and M. G. Abegg, *A Preliminary Edition of the Unpublished Dead Sea Scrolls*, vol. 1 (Washington, D.C., 1991).
12. *New York Times* (22 Sept. 1991).
13. For the letter of Ulrich, see the reproduction in the publisher's foreword to R. H. Eisenman and J. M. Robinson, *A Facsimile Edition of the Dead Sea Scrolls*, **1** (Washington, D.C., 1991), p. xlii. For the causes behind Moffett's decision, see *Chicago Tribune* (22 Sept. 1991); *Pasadena Star-News* (25 Sept. 1991). Cf. Moffett's statement relative to the matter as made at the 1991 meeting of the Society of Biblical Literature and as contained in the (unpublished) transcript of the session on the freeing of the scrolls, p. 11.
14. See *New York Times* (23 Sept. 1991).
15. See above, note 13; *New York Times* (20 Nov. 1991).
16. See, e.g., *New York Times* (27 Nov. 1991).
17. See *New York Times* (27 Nov. 1991); *Los Angeles Times* (28 Nov. 1991); *Chicago Tribune* (29 Nov. 1991).
18. *New York Times*, ibid.; *Chicago Tribune* (29 Nov. 1991).

19. See *The Comprehensive Aramaic Lexicon Newsletter*, no. 9 (Feb., 1992), pp. 1 and 5. Kaufman is incorrect in attributing the decision of the Huntington to free the texts to the influence of the editor of the *Biblical Archaeology Review*. The circumstances under which the decision was made have been described above, p. 229.

20. See G. Vermes in *Journal of Jewish Studies* (Spring 1992), p. 84. (Dr. Vermes himself is editor of this journal.)

21. In *The Higher* (*The Times Higher Education Supplement*) (8 Nov. 1991).

22. See N. Golb in *The Qumran Chronicle* **2**, no. 1 (Dec. 1992), pp. 3–25; and Ph. Alexander and G. Vermes, ibid. **2**, no. 3 (June 1993), p. 156.

23. See *Chicago Tribune* (10 July 1992).

24. George Bonani, Magen Broshi, Israel Carmi, Susan Ivy, John Strugnell, and Willy Wölfli, "Radiocarbon Dating of the Dead Sea Scrolls," *'Atiqot* **20** (July 1991), pp. 27–31.

25. *'Atiqot* **20** (July 1991), pp. 27–32. The quoted statement is contained at the top of the first page of the article, in the form in which it was sent out by facsimile to various parties in Europe and America.

26. See *Journal of Jewish Studies* (Spring 1982), pp. 101–136.

27. Letter of E. Tov to me dated 9 Dec. 1992.

28. *Religious Studies News* **7**, no. 1 (Jan. 1992), p. 4. (This periodical journal is published by the American Academy of Religion and the Society of Biblical Literature for their members; it has a circulation of approximately 14,000 copies per issue.)

29. Transcript of SBL meeting, pp. 3–4.

30. Ibid., p. 2.

31. Ibid., p. 6.

32. Ibid., p. 6.

33. Ibid., pp. 8–9.

34. Ibid., p. 11.

Chapter 9. Myth and Science in the World of Qumranology

1. See F. M. Cross, "The Development of the Jewish Scripts," in G. E. Wright (ed.), *The Bible and the Ancient Near East. Essays in Honor of William Foxwell Albright* (Garden City, N.Y., 1961), pp. 133–202.

2. See N. Avigad, "The Palaeography of the Dead Sea Scrolls and Related Documents," in C. Rabin and Y. Yadin (eds.), *Aspects of the Dead Sea Scrolls* (= *Scripta Hierosolymitana IV*: Jerusalem, 1958), pp. 56–87.

3. See W. Wölfli et al., "Radiocarbon Dating of the Dead Sea Scrolls," *'Atiqot* **20** (July 1991), pp. 27–31.

4. Associated Press release of 1 April 1991.

5. *Journal of Jewish Studies* (Spring 1992), pp. 101–136.

6. See Josephus, *War* **1**.97; *Ant.* **13**.380–381.

7. See Esther and Hanan Eshel and Ada Yardeni, "A Scroll from Qumran which Includes Part of Psalm 154 and a Prayer for King Jonathan and his Kingdom" (Hebrew), *Tarbiz* **60** (1991), pp. 296–327 (my translations here and following).

8. Ibid., pp. 316–317.
9. Ibid., p. 317 (my italics).
10. Ibid., p. 317.
11. See *Proceedings of the American Philosophical Society* **124**, no. 1 (1980), p. 11.
12. See *Journal of Jewish Studies* (Spring 1992), pp. 114, 123, 125.
13. See the interview with me by Avi Katzman in *Haaretz* (6 Dec. 1991).
14. *Tarbiz*, ibid., p. 317.
15. *Tarbiz*, ibid., p. 324.
16. *Tarbiz*, ibid., p. 324 (in the Hebrew text, *mismakh*).
17. *Tarbiz*, ibid., pp. 295–296.
18. *Tarbiz*, ibid., pp. 297, 318 ff. For the first use of the technique of tabular representation of the entire consonantal repertory of a Hebrew manuscript, cf. N. Golb and O. Pritsak, *Khazarian Hebrew Documents of the Tenth Century* (Ithaca and New York, 1982), pp. 16–19.
19. *Tarbiz*, ibid., p. 310 bottom.
20. *Tarbiz*, ibid., pp. 305, 311, 313.
21. *Tarbiz*, ibid., p. 297, col. b, line 1. The verb in question is *'ur*, "arise."
22. *Tarbiz*, ibid., pp. 322–323.
23. Cf. the Hebrew edition in *Tarbiz*, ibid., p. 297, col. 3.
24. *Tarbiz*, ibid., p. 307.
25. Herbert Chayyim Youtie, *The Textual Criticism of Documentary Papyri—Prolegomena* (University of London, 1958), pp. 66–67.

Chapter 10. The Deepening Scrolls Controversy

1. H. E. Del Medico, *L'Enigme des manuscrits de la mer Morte* (Paris, 1957); see further his *Le Mythe des Esséniens* (Paris, 1958).
2. See *New York Times* (29 April 1980); *International Herald Tribune* (7 May 1980); *Scientific American* (June 1980), p. 85.
3. See Claude Aziza, "Les manuscrits de la mer Morte: une hypothèse non-conformiste," in *L'Histoire*, no. 79 (June 1985), pp. 81–83. (For "pan-Qumranism," see *Proc. of the American Philosophical Society*, 1980, p. 9.)
4. N. Golb, "Les Manuscrits de la mer Morte — une nouvelle approche du problème de leur origine," in *Annales—Economies, Sociétés, Civilisations*, no. 5 (1985), pp. 61–88.
5. *La Bible. Ecrits intertestamentaires* (Paris, 1987), "edited by A. Dupont-Sommer and M. Philonenko, with numerous collaborators, a general introduction by M. Philonenko and A. Caquot, a general bibliography and an index" (my translation). (Dupont-Sommer was already deceased when the work was published.)
6. G. Vermes, *The Dead Sea Scrolls in English Translation* (London and New York, 1987).
7. G. Vermes, op. cit., p. 308.
8. See *Etudes* **367**, nos. 1–2 (July/Aug. 1987), pp. 122–124.
9. Cf. *Le Monde* (25 Dec. 1987), "Le Monde des Livres," p. 13 (article by Jean-Louis Schlegel).

10. See *Annales* **42**, no. 6 (Nov./Dec. 1987), pp. 1305–1312, and my response, ibid., pp. 1313–1319. A list of Laperrousaz's writings on Qumran subjects is conveniently appended by him to his response, ibid., p. 1312.

11. Cf. Laperrousaz, ibid., p. 1306 (my translation).

12. See above, note 10.

13. See particularly the criticism of E. R. Dodds, *The Greeks and the Irrational* (Berkeley, 1951), pp. 147 ff.

14. *Annales*, ibid., p. 1319.

15. Ernest-Marie Laperrousaz, "L'établissement de Qoumran près de la mer Morte: Forteresse ou Couvent?," in *Eretz-Israel* **20** (1989), pp. 118–123. The translations from the French are mine.

16. Laperrousaz, ibid., p. 120.

17. Cf., e.g., F. Garcia Martinez and A. S. van der Woude in *Revue de Qumran* **56** (April 1990), p. 528: "Although the Khirbeh was constructed as a stronghold in the VIII century B.C. and was adapted by the Romans as a military post after the destruction, the site *during the two centuries of sectarian occupation* cannot be described as a military fortress" (my italics).

18. See *The Sciences* **27**, no. 3 (May/June 1987), pp. 40–49.

19. Ibid., **28**, no. 1 (Jan./Feb. 1988), pp. 14–15; cf. my reply, ibid., pp. 15–16.

20. See my letter in the *Jerusalem Post* (1 Nov. 1989), and Broshi's reply, ibid. (25 Nov. 1989).

21. Statement of M. Broshi delivered during his lecture at the Graz symposium on the scrolls, 18 Oct. 1992.

22. See *Christian Century* **110**, no. 10 (24–31 March 1993), p. 328.

23. Announcement made by M. Broshi during his lecture at the Library of Congress Symposium on the Scrolls, Washington, D.C., 22 April 1993.

24. See Ph. Davies, "How Not to Do Archaeology. The Story of Qumran," in *Biblical Archaeologist* (Dec. 1988), pp. 203–207.

25. Davies, ibid., p. 205.

26. Davies, ibid., p. 204.

27. Davies, ibid., p. 207.

28. See, e.g., H. Shanks in *Biblical Archaeology Review* (March/April 1993), p. 67.

29. See Maurice Baillet, *Qumran Grotte 4, III (4Q482–4Q520)*. Discoveries in the Judaean Desert 7 (Oxford, 1982).

30. M. Weinfeld, "Traces of the Qedusha Yoser and the Pesuqé de-Zimra in the Qumran Scrolls and Ben Sira," *Tarbiz* **45** (1975–76), pp. 15–26.

31. Cf. M. Delcor, "Cinq nouveaux psaumes esséniennes?," *Revue de Qumran* **1**, no. 1 (1958), pp. 85–102; idem, *Les hymnes de Qumran (Hodayot)* (Paris, 1962), pp. 302–312; M. Philonenko, "L'origine essénienne des cinq psaumes syriaques de David," *Semitica* **9** (1959), pp. 35–48; J. A. Sanders, "Two Non-Canonical Psalms in 11QPs^a," *Zeitschrift für die alttestamentliche Wissenschaft* **76** (1964), pp. 64–76; idem, *The Dead Sea Psalms Scroll* (Ithaca, 1967), pp. 108–109.

32. See N. Golb, "The Dead Sea Scrolls—A New Perspective," *American Scholar* **58**, no. 2 (Spring 1989), pp. 177–207.

33. See letter of J. Trever in *American Scholar* **58**, no. 4 (Autumn 1989), pp. 626–627.

34. See Josephus, *War*, **2**.254–458; **5**.1–**6**.435.
35. See letter of J. Trever, op. cit., p. 627, and my reply, ibid., pp. 628–632.
36. See A. S. van der Woude, *Die messianischen Vorstellungen der Gemeinde von Qumran* (Assen, 1957), p. 217 (my translation).
37. F. Garcia Martinez and A. S. van der Woude, "A 'Groningen' Hypothesis of Qumran Origins," *Revue de Qumran* **14**, no. 56 (April 1990), pp. 521–541.
38. See F. Garcia Martinez, "Qumran Origins and Early History: A Groningen Hypothesis," in *Folia Orientalia* **25** (1988), pp. 113–136; F. Garcia Martinez and A. S. van der Woude, "A 'Groningen' Hypothesis of Qumran Origins and Early History," in *Revue de Qumran* **14**, no. 56 (April 1990), pp. 521–541.
39. Ibid., p. 528.
40. Ibid., p. 528–529.
41. Ibid., p. 530.
42. Ibid., p. 533.
43. Ibid., p. 539.
44. Ibid., p. 524.
45. Ibid., p. 538.
46. Ibid., p. 537.
47. Ibid., p. 539.
48. Ibid., p. 537.
49. Letter to Garcia Martinez, 29 Nov. 1988.
50. S. Talmon, "A Fragment from a Pseudepigraphic Scroll to the Book of Joshua from Masada" (Hebrew), *Shai lehayyim rabin* (Jerusalem, 1991), pp. 147–157. All translations from this article that follow here are mine.
51. Talmon, ibid., p. 147.
52. Talmon, ibid., p. 150.
53. See E. Tov, "The Orthography and Language of the Hebrew Scrolls Found at Qumran and the Origins of These Scrolls," *Textus* **13** (1986), pp. 31–57.
54. Tov, ibid., p. 47.
55. Letter to the author from Prof. Tov dated 17 Jan. 1993.
56. Carol Newsom, "The 'Psalms of Joshua' from Qumran Cave 4," *Journal of Jewish Studies* **39** (1988), pp. 56–73.
57. Newsom, ibid., p. 59.
58. Newsom, "'Sectually Explicit' Literature from Qumran," in W. Propp et al. (eds.), *The Hebrew Bible and its Interpreters* (Winona Lake, Ind., 1990), pp. 167–187; cf. ibid., p. 172.
59. Newsom, ibid., pp. 179 ff. Compare pp. 136–138 above.
60. Newsom, ibid., p. 170.
61. Talmon, "Fragment," pp. 156–157.
62. Talmon, ibid., p. 157.
63. See, e.g., J. Fitzmyer, *A Wandering Aramaean* (Missoula, Mont., 1979), pp. 90–93.
64. See Newsom, "'Sectually Explicit' Literature," p. 184.
65. Newsom, ibid., p. 171.
66. Newsom, ibid., pp. 177 and 185 (my italics).
67. Newsom, ibid., pp. 172 f.

68. Newsom, ibid., p. 174, referring to H. Jauss, *Toward an Aesthetic of Reception*. Theory and History of Literature **2** (Minneapolis, 1982).

Chapter 11. The New York Conference and Some Academic Intrigues

1. See, e.g., the detailed articles by Avi Katzman in *Haaretz* (6 Dec. 1991 and 29 Jan. 1993); by Frank Eskenasi in *Libération* (28 Nov. 1991); by Vera Kornicker in *Le Figaro* (22 Feb. 1993); by Michael d'Antonio in the *Los Angeles Times* (2 Oct. 1991); and by Katharine Whittemore in *Lingua Franca* (Dec. 1991), pp. 27 ff.
2. See P. R. Davies, "Sadducees in the Dead Sea Scrolls?," Z. J. Kapera (ed.), *Qumran Cave Four—Special Report* (Cracow, 1991), pp. 85–94.
3. See M. de Canio (ed.), *The Facts on File Scientific Yearbook 1991* (New York and Oxford, 1992), pp. 83–84.
4. See Lena Cansdale, "The Qumran Scrolls: A 2,000 Year Old Apple of Discord," *Ancient History: Resources for Teachers* **21**, no. 2 (Macquarie University, 1991), pp. 98–99.
5. Cf. Jonathan J. Price, *Jerusalem under Siege: The Collapse of the Jewish State 66–70 C.E.* (Leiden, 1992), p. 198.
6. Cf. Reinhard Pummer in Ferdinand Dexinger and Reinhard Pummer (eds.), *Die Samaritaner* (Darmstadt, 1992), p. 44; and Matthias Klinghardt in *Die Welt*, "Kulturwelt," no. 36 (12 Feb. 1992)
7. See John Romer, *Testament. The Bible and History* (London, 1988), p. 144, and related observations, ibid., pp. 138ff.
8. See M. Klinghardt, "Qumran Nowhere? A Symposium on the Origin of the Dead Sea Scrolls and the Khirbet Qumran Site (Graz, Austria, 17–18 Oct. 1992)," *The Qumran Chronicle* **2**, no. 1 (Dec. 1992), pp. 31–37; for the citation, see ibid., p. 35. Talmon's explanation for the female skeletons was expressed at the Graz conference, but does not appear in the printed form of the proceedings that followed. J. B. Bauer, J. Fink, and H. D. Alter (eds.), *Qumran—ein Symposion*: Grazer Theologische Studien 15 (Graz, 1993), pp. 117–171.
9. No publication ensued from the Stanford meeting, but the entire proceedings were videotaped (*Unraveling the Mysteries of the Dead Sea Scrolls*; Provo, Utah: Foundation for Ancient Research and Mormon Studies, 1992). Cf. the report in the *San Francisco Chronicle* (26 Nov. 1992).
10. See N. Golb, "The Qumran-Essene Hypothesis: a Fiction of Scholarship" in *Christian Century* 109, no. 36 (9 Dec. 1992), pp. 1138–1143; J. A. Fitzmyer, ibid. (24 March 1993), pp. 326–329; and my response to Fitzmyer, ibid., pp. 329–332.
11. Robert Eisenman and Michael Wise, *The Dead Sea Scrolls Uncovered* (Shaftesbury, U.K., and Rockport, Mass., 1992).
12. These included David Clemens, Michael Douglas, Deborah Friedrich, and Anthony Tomasino (who served as associate director of the project).
13. Eisenman and Wise, op. cit., pp. 182–200; the title given by the authors is "First and Second Letters on Works Reckoned as Righteousness."

14. The letter was reported on in the *New York Times* of 13 Dec. and 18 Dec. 1992; see *Biblical Archaeology Review* (March/April 1993), pp. 66–67.

15. Participants in this discussion included Profs. Eric Meyers, Lawrence Schiffman, James VanderKam, and myself, with a contribution (by proxy) by Prof. James Robinson.

16. A particularly regrettable instance of this effort appears in the truculent review by Jonas Greenfield—a member of the scrolls oversight committee —of the Wise and Eisenman book, in the *Jerusalem Post* (19 Feb. 1993).

17. The thirty papers delivered during the sessions, published together with the full debate on each one, appear in the *Annals of the New York Academy of Sciences*, vol. 722 (1994).

18. Cf. M. Weinfeld, *The Organizational Pattern and the Penal Code of the Qumran Sect* (Fribourg and Göttingen, 1986).

19. See Pauline H. E. Donceel-Voûte, "'Coenaculum'—La salle à l'étage du Locus 30 à Khirbet Qumran sur la mer Morte," in *Banquets de l'Orient* (*Res Orientales* **4**, 1992), pp. 61–84.

20. Cf., e.g., A. Wolters, "Apocalyptic and the Copper Scroll," *Journal of Near Eastern Studies* **49** (April 1990), pp. 145–154.

21. Beside those already mentioned, speakers participating in the conference included Profs. Moshe Bernstein (New York), George Brooke (Manchester, U.K.), James Charlesworth (Princeton), John Collins (Chicago), Ferdinand Dexinger (Vienna), Robert Eisenman (Long Beach, Calif.), Joseph Fitzmyer, S.J. (Washington, D.C.), Peter W. Flint (Notre Dame, Ind.), Norman Golb (Chicago), Samuel Iwry (Baltimore), Michael Knibb (London), Dr. Robert Johnson (Rochester, N.Y.), Lawrence Schiffman (New York), Eileen Schuller (Halifax, N.S.), Morris Shamos (New York) (on behalf of Dr. Willi Wölfli, Zurich, Switzerland), Yacov Shavit (Tel Aviv), Hartmut Stegemann (Göttingen, Germany), James VanderKam (Notre Dame, Ind.), Sidnie White (Reading, Penn.), Michael Wise (Chicago), Dr. Philip Callaway (Jonesboro, Ga.), and Mr. Torlief Elgvin (Jerusalem). Session chairmen included Profs. James Charlesworth, Joseph Fitzmyer, Norman Golb, Eric Meyers (Durham, N.C.), and Dennis Pardee (Chicago); and Drs. Ephraim Isaac (Princeton) and Z. J. Kapera. (The communication of Dr. U. Glessmer of Hamburg is also included in the published proceedings.)

22. See Z. J. Kapera, "Khirbet Qumran No More a Monastic Settlement," *The Qumran Chronicle*, vol. 2, no. 2 (February 1993), pp. 73–84.

23. Ibid., p. 74.

24. See *New York Times*, "Science Times" (22 Dec. 1992).

25. See *New York Times* (27 Jan. 1993) (article by Felicity Barringer).

26. See the law report by A. F. Landau in the *Jerusalem Post* of 9 April 1993. On the trial and the judgment see further the reports in the *Jerusalem Post* (2, 3, and 5 Feb. 1993); the *New York Times* (7 Feb. and 31 March 1993); and particularly B. W. W. Dombrowski, "A Miscarriage of Justice in Jerusalem," *The Qumran Chronicle* 2, no. 3 (June, 1993), pp. 139–140. The attorneys for the plaintiff were Advocates Yitzhak Molcho, Ya'acov Meltzer, and Yael Langer, and for the defendants, Advocates Dov Frimer

and Yosef Gelman (appearing for Shanks, Robinson, and the Biblical Archaeology Society) and Amos Hausner (appearing for Eisenman).
27. See *New York Times* (31 March 1993).

Chapter 12. The Importance of the Dead Sea Scrolls

1. Robert Alter, "How Important are the Dead Sea Scrolls?" *Commentary* (February 1992), pp. 34–41.
2. Ibid., p. 34.
3. Ibid., p. 38.
4. *American Scholar* **58**, no. 2 (Spring 1989), p. 200.
5. *Commentary*, (February 1992) p. 38 (my italics).
6. Ibid., (my italics).
7. Ibid. (my italics).
8. Cf. *American Scholar*, p. 184.
9. M. Stern in S. Safrai and M. Stern (eds.), *The Jewish People in the First Century*, I (Assen, 1974), p. 216.
10. *Commentary* (February 1992), p. 41.
11. *American Scholar*, ibid., p. 207.
12. *Commentary* (February 1992), p. 41.
13. Ibid., p. 39.
14. Ibid., pp. 39, 40.
15. See, e.g., *Mishnah* Yadaim **3**.5; Eduyoth **5**.3.
16. *Commentary* (February 1992), p. 39 (my italics).
17. S. Talmon, *The World of Qumran from Within* (Jerusalem and Leiden, 1989), p. 25.
18. See particularly E. P. Sanders, *Paul, the Law, and the Jewish People* (Philadelphia, 1983); idem, *Jesus and Judaism* (Philadelphia, 1985).
19. *Commentary* (February 1992), p. 35.
20. Cf. *Scrolls from the Dead Sea: an exhibition of scrolls and archaeological artifacts from the collections of the Israel Antiquities Authority* (hereinafter, *Catalogue*), [edited by] Ayala Sussman and Ruth Peled (Washington, 1993), pp. 9–11.
21. Ibid., pp. 6–7.
22. See the detailed criticism of the eventual makeup of the panel expressed by Ron Grossman in the *Chicago Tribune*, 28 April 1993. The dates of the Library of Congress Exhibition were 29 April–1 Aug. 1993.
23. The exhibition was shown at the New York Public Library from 2 Oct. 1993 to 8 Jan. 1994 and at the M. H. de Young Memorial Museum, San Francisco, from 26 Feb. to 29 May 1994.
24. See *Haaretz* (30 Apr. 1993).
25. See *Catalogue*, p. 6.
26. Ibid., p. 23.
27. See the reports on the manuscript fragments found in a cave near Jericho in 1986, in *Biblical Archaeology Review*, Sept./Oct. 1989, pp. 48–53; on the juglet of oil found in 1989, in a cave approximately 4 kms. north of

Khirbet Qumran (*Biblical Archaeology Review*, Sept./Oct. 1989, pp. 34–35); and on the possibilities for further excavations of the Bar Kohkba caves inland from En Gedi, ibid., Jan./Feb. 1993, pp. 50–57.

28. See, e.g., the articles in the *Jerusalem Post*, 15 Nov. and 26 Nov. 1993; and the *New York Times*, 19 Nov. 1993.
29. Cf. *Catalogue*, p. 25.
30. Ibid., p. 24.
31. Ibid., p. 25.
32. Ibid., p. 26.
33. Ibid., p. 26.
34. Ibid., p. 27.
35. Ibid., p. 26.
36. Ibid., p. 95.
37. Ibid., p. 131 (my italics).
38. C. Newsom, "Sectually Explicit Literature," p. 184.
39. *Catalogue*, p. 61.
40. J. A. Sanders, *The Psalms Scroll of Qumran Cave 11 (11QPsª)* (Oxford, 1965), p. 63 (quoted above, p. 63).
41. See B. Z. Wacholder and M. G. Abegg, *A Preliminary Edition of the Unpublished Dead Sea Scrolls* (Washington, 1991), pp. 1–59.
42. This and the quotation earlier in the chapter are taken from J. S. Mill's *On Liberty*.
43. See *Jerusalem Post*, 6 May 1994, Magazine, pp. 6, 8, and 10; 27 May 1994, p. B8.

Epilogue: Judaism, Christianity, and the Scrolls

1. J. A. Sanders (ed. and trans.), *The Psalms Scroll of Qumran Cave 11*. Discoveries in the Judaean Desert of Jordan **4** (Oxford, 1965).
2. Cf. C. Newsom, *Songs of the Sabbath Sacrifice: A Critical Edition* (Atlanta, 1985).
3. D. Barthélemy and J. T. Milik (eds.), *Qumran Cave 1*. Discoveries in the Judaean Desert **1** (Oxford, 1955), pp. 130–134, 136–143.
4. These include the psalm group designated as 4QPsª, 4QPsᶠ, 4Q510, and 4Q511. See further the texts published by Allegro, Discoveries . . . **5**, pp. 67–77, and by Baillet, Discoveries . . . **7**, pp. 73–286 (approximately fifteen compositions). Liturgical and hymnic texts found in the "lesser caves" include one in Cave 3 (Baillet, Milik, and de Vaux, Discoveries . . . **3**, p. 98) and two in Cave 6 (ibid., pp. 131, 133–135).
5. E. M. Schuller (ed. and trans.), *Non-Canonical Psalms from Qumran—A Pseudepigraphical Collection* (Atlanta, 1986); these texts are classified as 4Q380 and 4Q381.
6. See Patrick W. Skehan et al., *Qumran Cave IV. Palaeo-Hebrew and Greek Biblical Manuscripts*. Discoveries in the Judaean Desert **9** (Oxford, 1992). For other Greek fragments found in Qumran Cave 7, see above, p. 100.
7. *Catalogue*, pp. 72–75. The text published is an excerpt from a longer one that was previously published in full with an English translation by M.

Wise in Eisenman and Wise, *The Dead Sea Scrolls Uncovered*, pp. 109–112, while the text itself was published by Wacholder and Abegg in *A Preliminary Edition of the Dead Sea Scrolls*, vol. I, pp. 68–69.

8. See particularly the discussion by Michael Wise, *Thunder in Gemini* (Sheffield, 1994), pp. 186–239 (chapter on an annalistic calendar from Cave 4).

9. M. Burrows (ed.), *The Dead Sea Scrolls of St. Mark's Monastery*, 2 (New Haven, Conn., 1951).

10. Barthélemy and Milik, *Qumran Cave I*, pp. 107–118.

11. Ibid., pp. 118–130.

12. J. T. Milik, "Milki-sedeq et Milki-resa' dans les anciens écrits juifs et chrétiens," *JJS* 23 (1972), p. 136.

13. Cf. J. Baumgarten in *Journal of Jewish Studies* **43** (1992), pp. 268–276.

14. S. Schechter (ed. and trans.), *Fragments of a Zadokite Work: Documents of Jewish Sectaries*, Vol. 1 (Cambridge, 1910); Ch. Rabin (ed. and trans.), *The Zadokite Documents* (Oxford, 1954; 2nd ed., 1958).

15. M. Burrows, *The Dead Sea Scrolls of St. Mark's Monastery*, **1**, pp. 55–61.

16. J. M. Allegro (with the collaboration of A. A. Anderson), *DJD V: Qumran Cave 4: I (4Q158–4Q186)*(Oxford, 1968), pp. 11–30; 31–36; 37–42; 42–50; 51–53; 53–57; 57–60.

17. Ibid., pp. 53–57 and 57–60.

18. The most systematic attempt to treat the historical allusions in the texts remains that of J. Amousin, "The Reflection of Historical Events of the First Century B.C. in Qumran Commentaries (4Q161; 4Q169; 4Q166)," *Hebrew Union College Annual* **48** (1977), pp. 123–152. On the various baptizing groups, see Josephus, *Vitae* **11**, ed. and trans. Thackeray (Cambridge and London, 1976), pp. 6–7 (Bannus); idem, *Antiquities* **18**.116–119, ed. and trans. Feldman (Cambridge, 1969), pp. 80–85 (John the Baptist); and, for a general overview, Joseph Thomas, *Le Mouvement baptiste en Palestine et Syrie (150 av. J.–C.–300 ap. J. C.)* (Gembloux, 1935). The "sons of the dawn" text is 4Q298, published by Eisenman and Wise, *The Dead Sea Scrolls Uncovered*, p. 164.

19. Y. Yadin, *Megillat hamiqdash*, vols. **1–3** (Jerusalem, 1977); *The Temple Scroll: The Hidden Law of the Dead Sea Sect* (London, 1985); Michael O. Wise, *A Critical Study of the Temple Scroll from Cave 11* (Chicago, 1990).

20. See "Enoch, (Ethiopic) Book of," in J. Hastings (ed.), *Dictionary of the Bible*, **1** (Edinburgh, 1898), pp. 705–708 (art. of R. H. Charles); J. T. Milik, *The Books of Enoch. Aramaic Fragments of Qumran Cave 4* (Oxford, 1976).

21. Barthélemy and Milik, *Qumran Cave I*, pp. 82–107, 152.

22. See N. Avigad and Y. Yadin (eds.), *The Genesis Apocryphon* (Jerusalem, 1956); J. A. Fitzmyer, *The Genesis Apocryphon of Qumran Cave 1* (Rome, 1971); J. P. M. van der Ploeg, A. S. van der Woude, and B. Jongeling (eds.), *Le Targum de Job de la Grotte 11 de Qumran* (Leiden, 1971); M. Baillet, J. T. Milik, and R. de Vaux, O.P., *Les 'Petites Grottes' de Qumrân. Discoveries in the Judaean Desert of Jordan* **3** (Oxford, 1962), pp. 77–89, 96–98, 99, 116–28.

23. See Eisenman and Wise, *The Dead Sea Scrolls Uncovered*, where fifty texts

are fully published. (As contrasted with the transcriptions and translations, the interpretations of these texts preceding each item are, as noted
earlier, primarily the work of Dr. Eisenman.) For the beatitudes, see also
Benedict V. Viviano, "Beatitudes Found among Dead Sea Scrolls,"
Biblical Archaeology Review, Nov./Dec. 1992, pp. 53 ff.

24. See also Ex. **34**.20; Num. **18**.15–17.
25. See *Tosephta*, Yadaim **2**.16 (ed. Zuckermandel, p. 683): "Master Yosi the
son of the Damascus woman stated: I was with the first elders when they
came (= transferred their academy) from Jamnia to Lydda. One day I
found Master Eliezer sitting in the shop of some bakers in Lydda. He
said, 'What new thing did you deal with today in the house of study?' I
said to him, 'But we are *your* students, and it is from your waters that we
drink!' He said to me, 'Nevertheless, what new thing?' I thereupon
informed him *of the laws, and of the responses against the sectarians*, (that
we had studied). . . ." (The passage is by some, however, construed as
meaning ". . . and the responses according to the counting of opinions,"
reading *minin*, "heretics," as *minyan*, "counting.")
26. On the Jews of Palestine after A.D. 135, see particularly M. Avi-Yonah, *The
Jews Under Roman and Byzantine Rule* (Jerusalem, 1984), p. 61.
27. On the *Hekhalot* literature, see *Jewish Encyclopaedia* **6** (New York, 1906),
pp. 332–333.
28. Among the many volumes on this topic are: K. Stendahl (ed.), *The Scrolls
and the New Testament* (New York, 1957); J. Carmignac, *Christ and the
Teacher of Righteousness* (Baltimore, 1962); M. Black, *The Scrolls and
Christian Origins* (New York, 1961); N. S. Fujita, *A Crack in the Jar: What
Ancient Jewish Documents Tell us about the New Testament* (New York,
1986); James Charlesworth (ed.), *Jesus and the Dead Sea Scrolls* (Garden
City, N.Y., 1992). This last volume includes a handy overview written by
Charlesworth of comparisons and contrasts between teachings in the
scrolls and those in the New Testament, entitled "The Dead Sea Scrolls and
the Historical Jesus," pp. 1–74. The reader should be aware, however, that
Charlesworth views the Qumran corpus as originating from a rather insu-
lar group of Essenes, and thus sees parallels between the bodies of literature as evidence of links between the Essenes and early Christianity.
29. See K. G. Kuhn, "The Lord's Supper and the Communal Meal at
Qumran," in K. Stendahl, *The Scrolls and the New Testament*, op. cit., pp.
65–93; M. Black, "Qumran Baptismal Rites and the Sacred Meal," in *The
Scrolls and Christian Origins*, op. cit., pp. 91–117.
30. Cf. Matt. **26**.26–29, Mark **14**.22–25, and Luke **21**.4–23.
31. See Acts **2**.38, **8**.36–37, **10**.47–48.
32. See, e.g., M. Black, "Qumran Baptismal Rites," op. cit.
33. R. Eisenman and M. Wise, *The Dead Sea Scrolls Uncovered*, pp. 230 ff.
34. For an early discussion of this similarity, see Sherman Johnson, "The
Dead Sea Manual of Discipline and the Jerusalem Church of Acts," in K.
Stendhal, *The Scrolls and the New Testament*, op. cit., pp. 129–142.
35. On the Therapeutae, see Philo, *The Contemplative Life* 2, and on the
Essenes, *Every Good Man Is Free*, pp. 85–87; see further above, p. 395,
notes 2–14.

36. In the Hebrew Bible, the term is often used in a genitive relationship, e.g., "thy holy Spirit," "his holy Spirit," but never in the absolute state as a title.

37. For a collection of studies on parallels between Johannine literature and the scrolls, see J. Charlesworth (ed.), *John and the Dead Sea Scrolls* (New York, 1990).

38. The term *raz*, "mystery," appears in several of the scrolls, including the *Manual*, the *Hodayot* (Thanksgiving Scroll), the *Pesher Habakkuk*, and the *War Scroll*. For the frequent use of the term *mysterion*, "mystery," in the New Testament and Greek texts in general, see, e.g., J. Hastings (ed.), *A Dictionary of the Bible*, **3** (Edinburgh, 1927), pp. 465–469 (article of A. Stewart).

39. For an easily accessible discussion of biblical interpretation in the Qumran texts—a subject that has been treated extensively—see F. F. Bruce, *Biblical Exegesis in the Qumran Texts* (Grand Rapids, Mich., 1959).

40. For Josephus's description of the rigidity of scriptural interpretation among the Sadducees, see above, pp. 205–206.

41. For a further discussion, see J. Fitzmyer, "A Feature of Qumran Angelology and the Angels of I Cor. 11.10," *New Testament Studies* **4** (1957–58), pp. 48–58.

42. See further the excellent treatment of K. G. Kuhn, "New Light on Temptation, Sin, and Flesh in the New Testament," in K. Stendahl (ed.), *The Scrolls and the New Testament*, pp. 94–113.

43. For New Testament references to this idea, see especially Matt. **7**.13–14; Rom. **1**.28–32, **3**.10–18. Cf. *Damascus Covenant*, especially cols. **1–8**.

44. Cf. particularly *Damascus Covenant*, **5**.6–7, **6**.11–19. In the New Testament, see Matt. **21**.1–2, 23–27; Acts **7**.48–50.

45. See Matt. **26**.61, Mark **14**.57–58.

46. See Luke **22**.19–20, Eph. **1**.7–8, Col. **1**.19–20, Heb. **2**.17–18, and many other passages.

47. 4Q285, popularly called the "Pierced Messiah" text, is published in preliminary form in Eisenman and Wise, *The Dead Sea Scrolls Uncovered*, pp. 24 ff, and by G. Vermes in the 1993 catalogue of the American exhibition of the scrolls, p. 82.

48. The title "Prince of the Congregation" is used in the *War Scroll* and the *Messianic Rule*, as well as in the *Damascus Covenant* (**7**.20), the *pesher* on Isaiah (4Q161 A.2) and the recently published war-scroll-type text, 4Q285 (Eisenman and Wise, *The Dead Sea Scrolls Uncovered*, p. 29).

49. This idea is stated explicitly in several passages of the New Testament. See, e.g., 1 Pet. **4**.12–19; Rom. **12**.17–21; Matt. **5**.39–47.

50. The Masada text begins only with chapter 39 (small fragments) and thus does not include the passage in question.

51. See Eisenman and Wise, *The Dead Sea Scrolls Uncovered*, pp. 68–69. See also John Collins, "A Pre-Christian 'Son of God' Among the Dead Sea Scrolls," *Bible Review* (June 1993), pp. 34–39; and Emile Puech, "Fragment d'une apocalypse en Araméen (4Q246 = pseudo-Dan[b]) et le 'Royaume de Dieu,'" *Revue Biblique* **99** (1992), pp. 98–131.

52. See Eisenman and Wise, *The Dead Sea Scrolls Uncovered*, pp. 19–23. The messianic image seems more akin to that of apocalyptic texts like 1 Enoch than to that of the War Scroll or the *pesharim*.

53. See Michael O. Wise and James D. Tabor, "The Messiah at Qumran," *Biblical Archaeology Review*, Nov./Dec. 1992, pp. 60–63. (My translation is based on Wise's edition of the text, but differs somewhat from that of Wise and Tabor, ibid., p. 62)

54. For the text, see A. S. van der Woude, "Melchizedek als himmlische Erlösergestalt in den neugefunden eschatologischen Midraschim aus Qumran-Höhle XI," in *Oudtestamentische Studien* 15, ed. P. A. H. de Boer (Leiden, 1965), pp. 345–373. See also M. de Jonge and A. S. van der Woude, "11Q Melchizedek and the New Testament," *New Testament Studies* 12 (1966), pp. 301–326; J. T. Milik, "*Milki-sedek* et *Milki-resa'* dans les anciens écrits juifs et chrétiens," *Journal of Jewish Studies* 23 (1972), pp. 95–144.

55. See above, p. 420, note 28.

56. See K. Berger, *Qumran und Jesus. Wahrheit unter Verschluss?* (Stuttgart, 1993), pp. 129–133.

57. See Julius Guttman, *Die Philosophie des Judentums* (Munich, 1939), p. 39.

Selected Bibliography

I. General Studies on the Dead Sea Scrolls
and Related Subjects

Allegro, John Marco *The Dead Sea Scrolls*. Hammondsworth, U.K.: 1956.

———. *The Dead Sea Scrolls and the Christian Myth*. Newton Abbot, U.K.: 1979.

Baigent, Michael, and Richard Leigh. *The Dead Sea Scrolls Deception*. New York: 1991.

Berger, Klaus. *Qumran und Jesus. Wahrheit unter Verschluss?* Stuttgart: 1993.

Black, Matthew. *The Scrolls and Christian Origins*. London: 1961.

Bruce, F. F. *Second Thoughts on the Dead Sea Scrolls*. London: 1956.

Burrows, Millar. *The Dead Sea Scrolls*. New York: 1955.

———. *More Light on the Dead Sea Scrolls*. New York: 1958.

Cross, Frank Moore. *The Ancient Library of Qumran and Modern Biblical Studies*. 2nd ed. Grand Rapids, Mich.: 1980.

Del Medico, H. E. *L'Enigme des manuscrits de la mer Morte*. Paris: 1957.

———. *Le Mythe des Esséniens*. Paris: 1958.

Driver, Godfrey Rolles. *The Judaean Scrolls*. Oxford: 1965.

Dupont-Sommer, André. *The Essene Writings from Qumran*. Oxford: 1961.

Dupont-Sommer, André, and M. Philonenko (eds). *La Bible. Ecrits intertestamentaires*. Paris: 1987.

Eisenman, Robert H., and Michael O. Wise. *The Dead Sea Scrolls Uncovered*. Shaftesbury, U.K. and Rockport, Mass.: 1992.

Fritsch, C. T. *The Qumran Community: Its History and its Scrolls*. New York: 1956.

Fujita, N. S. *A Crack in the Jar: What Ancient Jewish Documents Tell Us about the New Testament*. New York: 1986.

Gaster, Theodore H. *The Dead Sea Scriptures in English Translation*. Garden City, N.Y.: 1956.

Ginzberg, Louis. *An Unknown Jewish Sect*. New York: 1976.

Knibb, Michael A. *The Qumran Community*. Cambridge: 1987.

Milik, Josef T. *Ten Years of Discovery in the Wilderness of Judaea*. London: 1959.

Rabin, Chaim. *The Zadokite Documents*. Oxford: 1954. 2nd ed. Oxford: 1958.

Rengstorf, Karl-Heinrich. *Hirbet Qumran und die Bibliothek vom Toten Meer*. Studia Delitzschiana **5** Stuttgart: 1960.

————. *Hirbet Qumran and the Problem of the Dead Sea Caves*. Leiden, Netherlands: 1963.

Roth, Cecil. *The Historical Background of the Dead Sea Scrolls*. New York: 1959.

Sanders, E. P. *Paul, the Law and the Jewish People*. Philadelphia: 1983.

————. *Jesus and Judaism*. Philadelphia: 1985.

Shanks, Hershel (ed.). *Understanding the Dead Sea Scrolls*. Washington, D.C.: 1992.

Sussman, Ayala, and Ruth Peled (eds.). *Scrolls from the Dead Sea: An Exhibition of Scrolls and Archaeological Artifacts from the Collections of the Israel Antiquities Authority*. Washington, D.C.: 1993.

Talmon, Shemaryahu. *The World of Qumran from Within*. Jerusalem and Leiden: 1989.

Vermes, Geza. *Discovery in the Desert*. New York, 1956.

————. *The Dead Sea Scrolls: Qumran in Perspective*. London: 1977.

————. *The Dead Sea Scrolls in English*. 3rd ed. Sheffield: 1987.

———— and M. D. Goodman. *The Essenes According to the Classical Sources*. Sheffield, U.K.: 1989.

Wacholder, Ben Zion. *The Dawn of Qumran: The Sectarian Torah and the Teacher of Righteousness*. Cincinnati: 1983.

Yadin, Yigael. *The Message of the Scrolls*. London: 1957.

II. Archaeology of Khirbet Qumran and the Judaean Wilderness

Allegro, John Marco. *Search in the Desert*. Garden City, N.Y.: 1964.

Avi-Yonah, Michael, N. Avigad, et al. "The Archaeological Survey and Excavation of Masada, 1955–1956." *Israel Exploration Journal* **7** (1957), pp. 1–60.

Bar-Adon, Pesah. "Another Settlement of the Judaean Desert Sect at Ein Ghuweir on the Dead Sea." *Eretz Israel* **10** (1971), pp. 72–89.

Clermont-Ganneau, Charles S. *Archaeological Researches in Palestine during the Years 1873–1874*. **2**. London: 1896.

Davies, Philip R. "How Not to Do Archaeology. The Story of Qumran." *Biblical Archaeologist* (Dec. 1988), pp. 203–207.

————. *Qumran*. Guildford: 1982.

Donceel-Voûte, Pauline H. E. "'Coenaculum'—La salle à l'étage du Locus 30 à Khirbet Qumran sur la mer Morte." *Banquets de l'Orient* (*Res Orientales* **4**, 1992), pp. 61–84.

Haas, N., and H. Nathan. "Anthropological Survey of Human Skeletal Remains from Qumran." *Revue de Qumran* **6** (1968), pp. 345–353.

Harding, G. Lankester. "Khirbet Qumran and Wady Murabba'at." *Palestine Exploration Quarterly* **84** (1952), pp. 104–109.

Ilan, S., and D. Amit. "The Water System of Qumran" (Hebrew). *Teba' wa'ares* **24** (1982), pp. 118–122.

Kapera, Z. J. "Khirbet Qumran No More a Monastic Settlement." *The Qumran Chronicle* **2**, no. 2 (February 1993), pp. 73–84.

Klinghardt, Matthias. "Qumran Nowhere? A Symposium on the Origin of the Dead Sea Scrolls and the Khirbet Qumran Site (Graz, Austria, 17–18 Oct. 1992)." *The Qumran Chronicle* **2**, no. 1 (Dec. 1992), pp. 31–37.

Laperrousaz, Ernest-Marie. "L'établissement de Qoumran près de la mer Morte: Forteresse ou Couvent?" *Eretz-Israel* **20** (1989) (= Y. Yadin Memorial Volume), pp. 118–123.

——. *Qoumran, l'établissement essénien des bords de la mer Morte: histoire et archéologie du site.* Paris: 1976.

Metzger, B. M. "The Furniture of the Scriptorium at Qumran." *Revue de Qumran* **1** (1959), pp. 509–515.

Vaux, Roland de. *L'archéologie et les manuscrits de la mer Morte.* London: 1961.

——. *Archaeology and the Dead Sea Scrolls.* London: 1973.

Wood, B. G. "To Dip or to Sprinkle? The Qumran Cisterns in Perspective." *Bulletin of the American Schools of Oriental Research* **256** (1984), pp. 45–60.

III. Specialized Studies and Textual Editions

(*DJD* = *Discoveries in the Judaean Desert*)

Allegro, John Marco. *Qumran Cave 4, I (4Q158–4Q186). DJD* **5**. Oxford: 1968.

——. *The Treasure of the Copper Scroll.* London: 1960.

Amousin, J. "The Reflection of Historical Events of the First Century B.C. in Qumran Commentaries (4Q161; 4Q169; 4Q166)." *Hebrew Union College Annual* **48** (1977), pp. 123–152.

Avigad, Nahum. "The Palaeography of the Dead Sea Scrolls and Related Documents." In Ch. Rabin and Y. Yadin, eds. *Aspects of the Dead Sea Scrolls* (= *Scripta Hierosolymitana IV*). Jerusalem: 1958, pp. 56–87.

—— and Y. Yadin, eds. *The Genesis Apocryphon.* Jerusalem: 1956.

Aziza, Claude. "Les manuscrits de la mer Morte: une hypothèse non-conformiste." *L'Histoire* **79** (June 1985), pp. 81–83.

Baillet, M., J. T. Milik, and Roland de Vaux. *Les 'Petites Grottes' de Qumrân. DJD* **3**. Oxford: 1962.

——. *Qumran Grotte 4, III (4Q482–4Q520). DJD* **7**. Oxford: 1982.

—— and J. T. Milik. *Qumran Cave 1. DJD* **1**. Oxford: 1955.

Benoit, P., J. T. Milik, R. de Vaux, et al. *Les Grottes de Murabba'at. 1. Texte* and *2. Planches. DJD* **2**. Oxford: 1961.

Brooke, George (ed.). *Temple Scroll Studies.* Sheffield, U.K.: 1989.

Brownlee, W. H. *The Dead Sea Manual of Discipline, Translation and Notes. Bulletin of the American Schools of Oriental Research*, Supplementary Studies, nos. 10–12, 1951.

Bruce, F. F. *Biblical Exegesis in the Qumran Texts.* Grand Rapids, Mich.: 1959.

Burrows, Millar (ed.). *The Dead Sea Scrolls of St. Mark's Monastery.* 2 fascicles. New Haven, Conn.: 1951.

Cansdale, Lena. "The Qumran Scrolls: A 2,000 Year Old Apple of Discord."

In *Ancient History: Resources for Teachers*. **21**, no. 2. Macquarie University: 1991, pp. 98–99.

Carmignac, J. *Christ and the Teacher of Righteousness*. Baltimore: 1962.

Charlesworth, James, (ed.). *Jesus and the Dead Sea Scrolls*. Garden City, N.Y.: 1992.

———. "The Dead Sea Scrolls and the Historical Jesus." In J. Charlesworth, (ed.). *Jesus and the Dead Sea Scrolls*. Garden City, N.Y.: 1992, pp. 1–74.

———, (ed.). *John and the Dead Sea Scrolls*. New York: 1990.

Collins, John J. "A Pre-Christian 'Son of God' Among the Dead Sea Scrolls." *Bible Review* (June 1993), pp. 34–39.

Cross, Frank Moore. "The Development of the Jewish Scripts." In G. E. Wright, (ed.). *The Bible and the Ancient Near East. Essays in Honor of William Foxwell Albright*. Garden City, N.Y.: 1961, pp. 133–202.

Davies, Philip R. "Sadducees in the Dead Sea Scrolls?" In Z. J. Kapera, (ed.). *Qumran Cave Four—Special Report*. Cracow: 1991, pp. 85–94.

Delcor, M. "Cinq nouveaux psaumes esséniennes?" *Revue de Qumran* **1**, no. 1 (1958), pp. 85–102.

———. *Les hymnes de Qumran (Hodayot)*. Paris: 1962.

de Jonge, M., and A. S. van der Woude. "11Q Melchizedek and the New Testament." *New Testament Studies* **12** (1966), pp. 301–326.

Eisenman, Robert H., and J. M. Robinson. *A Facsimile Edition of the Dead Sea Scrolls*. 2 vols. Washington, D.C.: 1991.

Eshel, Esther, Hanan Eshel, and Ada Yardeni. "A Scroll from Qumran which Includes Part of Psalm 154 and a Prayer for King Jonathan and his Kingdom" (Hebrew). *Tarbiz* **60** (1991), pp. 296–327.

Fitzmyer, J. A. *The Genesis Apocryphon of Qumran Cave 1*. Rome: 1971.

———. "A Feature of Qumran Angelology and the Angels of I Cor. 11.10." *New Testament Studies* **4** (1957–58), pp. 48–58.

———. "Scroll Origins: An Exchange on the Qumran Hypothesis." *Christian Century* **110**, (24 March 1993), pp. 326–332.

Garcia Martinez, F. "Qumran Origins and Early History: A Groningen Hypothesis." *Folia Orientalia* **25** (1988), pp. 113–136.

——— and A. S. van der Woude. "A 'Groningen' Hypothesis of Qumran Origins and Early History." *Revue de Qumran* **14**, no. 56 (April 1960), pp. 521–541.

Golb, Norman. "The Problem of Origin and Identification of the Dead Sea Scrolls." *Proceedings of the American Philosophical Society* **124** (February 1980), pp. 1–24.

———. "Les Manuscrits de la mer Morte—une nouvelle approche du problème de leur origine." *Annales—Economies, Sociétés, Civilisations* **40**, no. 5 (1985), pp. 1133–1149.

———. "Who Hid the Dead Sea Scrolls?" *Biblical Archaeologist* **48** (1985), pp. 68–82.

———. "Who Wrote the Dead Sea Scrolls?" *The Sciences*, **27**, no. 3 (1987), pp. 40–49.

———. "Réponse à la 'Note' de E.-M. Laperrousaz," *Annales ESC* **42**, no. 6 (1987), pp. 1313–1320.

———. "The Dead Sea Scrolls—A New Perspective." *The American Scholar* **58**, no. 2 (Spring 1989), pp. 177–207.

———. "The Dead Sea Scrolls: An Exchange (Response to John Trever)." *The American Scholar* **58**, no. 4 (Autumn 1989), pp. 628–632.

———. "Khirbet Qumran and the Manuscripts of the Judaean Wilderness: Observations on the Logic of their Investigation," *Journal of Near Eastern Studies*, **49** (1990), pp. 103–114.

———. "The Qumran-Essene Hypothesis: a Fiction of Scholarship." *Christian Century* **109**, no. 36 (9 Dec. 1992), pp. 1138–1143.

———. "The Dead Sea Scrolls and the Ethics of Museology." *Aspen Institute Quarterly* **6**, no. 2 (Spring 1994), pp. 79–98.

Johnson, Sherman. "The Dead Sea Manual of Discipline and the Jerusalem Church of Acts." In Krister Stendahl. (ed.). *The Scrolls and the New Testament*. New York: 1957, pp. 129–142.

Kuhn, K. G. "Phylakterien aus Höhle 4 von Qumran." In *Abhandlungen der Heidelberger Akademie der Wissenschaften*. Philosophische-Historische Klasse 1. Heidelberg: 1957.

———. "New Light on Temptation, Sin, and Flesh in the New Testament." In Krister Stendahl (ed.). *The Scrolls and the New Testament*. New York: 1957, pp. 94–113.

———. "The Lord's Supper and the Communal Meal at Qumran." In Krister Stendahl (ed.). *The Scrolls and the New Testament*. New York: 1957, pp. 65–93.

Laperrousaz, Ernest-Marie. "Note sur l'origine des manuscrits de la mer Morte." *Annales ESC* **42**, no. 6 (1987), pp. 1305–1312.

Levine, Baruch A. "The Temple Scroll: Aspects of its Historical Provenance and Literary Character." *Bulletin of the American Schools of Oriental Research* **232** (1978), pp. 3–24.

———. "A Further Look at the *Mo'adim* of the *Temple Scroll*." In Lawrence H. Schiffman, (ed.), *Archaeology and History in the Dead Sea Scrolls. The New York University Conference in Memory of Yigael Yadin*. Sheffield, U.K.: 1990, pp. 53–66.

Lohse, Edward. *Die Texte aus Qumran*. Munich: 1964.

Milik, J. T. "Le Rouleau de Cuivre provenant de la grotte 3Q (3Q15). Commentaire et texte." In M. Baillet et al. *Les 'Petites Grottes' de Qumran. Textes et Planches. DJD* **3**. Oxford: 1962, pp. 211–317 (*Textes*) and plates xliii–lxxi (*Planches*).

———. *The Books of Enoch. Aramaic Fragments of Qumran Cave 4*. Oxford: 1976.

———. "Milki-sedeq et Milki-resa' dans les anciens écrits juifs et chrétiens." *Journal of Jewish Studies* **23** (1972), pp. 95–144.

Newsom, Carol E. *Songs of the Sabbath Sacrifice: A Critical Edition*. Atlanta: 1985.

———. "The 'Psalms of Joshua' from Qumran Cave 4." *Journal of Jewish Studies* **39** (1988), pp. 56–73.

———. "'Sectually Explicit' Literature from Qumran." In W. Propp, B. Halpern, and D. N. Freedman (eds.), *The Hebrew Bible and its Interpreters*. Winona Lake, Ind.: 1990, pp. 167–187.

—— and Y. Yadin. "The Masada Fragment of the Qumran 'Songs of the Sabbath Sacrifice.'" *Israel Exploration Journal* **34** (1984), pp. 77–78.

Philonenko, M. "L'origine essénienne des cinq psaumes syriaques de David." *Semitica* **9** (1959), pp. 35–48.

Puech, Emile. "Fragment d'une apocalypse en Araméen (4Q246 = pseudo-Dan^b) et le 'Royaume de Dieu.'" *Revue Biblique* **99** (1992), pp. 98–131.

Qimron, Elisha. *The Hebrew of the Dead Sea Scrolls*. Atlanta: 1986.

—— and J. Strugnell. "An Unpublished Halakhic Letter from Qumran." In Janet Amitai (ed.).. *Biblical Archaeology Today*. Proceedings of the International Congress on Biblical Archaeology. Jerusalem: 1985, pp. 400–407.

Roth, Cecil. "Qumran and Masada: A Final Clarification Regarding the Dead Sea Sect." *Revue de Qumran* **5** (1964–66), pp. 81–87.

Rothstein, David. *From Bible to Murabba'at. Studies in the Literary, Textual and Scribal Features of Phylacteries and Mezuzot in Ancient Israel and Early Judaism* (UCLA Doctoral Dissertation, 1992). University Microfilms, Ann Arbor, Mich.: 1993.

Sanders, J. A. *The Psalms Scroll from Qumran Cave 11 (11QPs^a)*. DJD **4**. Oxford: 1965.

——. "Two Non-Canonical Psalms in 11QPs^a." *Zeitschrift für die alttestamentliche Wissenschaft* **76** (1964), pp. 64–76.

——. *The Dead Sea Psalms Scroll*. Ithaca, N.Y.: 1967.

Schechter, Solomon. *Fragments of a Zadokite Work—Documents of Jewish Sectaries* **1**. Cambridge: 1910.

Schiffman, Lawrence. "The Temple Scroll and the Systems of Jewish Law in the Second Temple Period." In G. Brooke. (ed.), *Temple Scroll Studies*. Sheffield, U.K.: 1989, pp. 239–255.

——. "The New Halakhic Letter (4QMMT) and the Origins of the Dead Sea Sect." *Biblical Archaeologist* **53** (June 1990), pp. 64–73.

——. *Law, Custom and Messianism in the Dead Sea Sect* (Hebrew). Jerusalem: 1993.

Schuller, Eileen M. *Non-Canonical Psalms from Qumran—A Pseudepigraphical Collection*. Atlanta: 1986.

Skehan, Patrick W., Eugene Ulrich, and Judith E. Sanderson. *Qumran Cave 4: IV. Palaeo-Hebrew and Greek Biblical Manuscripts*. DJD **9**. Oxford: 1992.

Stegemann, Hartmut. "Some Aspects of Eschatology in Texts from the Qumran Community and in the Teachings of Jesus." In Janet Amitai (ed).*Biblical Archaeology Today*. Proceedings of the International Congress on Biblical Archaeology. Jerusalem: 1985.

Stendahl, K. (ed.), *The Scrolls and the New Testament*. New York: 1957.

Strugnell, John. "The Angelic Liturgy at Qumran." *Vetus Testamentum Supplementae* **7**. Leiden, Netherlands: 1960, pp. 318–345.

Talmon, Shemaryahu. "The Calendar of the Covenanters of the Judean Desert." In C. Rabin and Y. Yadin. (eds.), *Aspects of the Dead Sea Scrolls* (*Scripta Hierosolymitana* **4**). Jerusalem: 1958, pp. 162–199.

——. "A Fragment from a Pseudepigraphic Scroll to the Book of Joshua from Masada" (Hebrew). In M. Goshen-Gottstein, Sh. Morag, and S. Kogut (eds.). *Shai lehayyim rabin*. Jerusalem: 1991, pp. 147–157.

Tov, Emanuel. "The Orthography and Language of the Hebrew Scrolls Found at Qumran and the Origins of These Scrolls." *Textus* **13** (1986), pp. 31–57.

———. *Textual Criticism of the Hebrew Bible*. Minneapolis, Minn. and Assen, Netherlands: 1992.

———. *The Greek Minor Prophets Scroll from Nahal Hever (8HevXIIgr)*. *DJD* **8**. Oxford: 1990.

Vaux, Roland de and J. T. Milik. *Qumran Grotte 4*, II. *DJD* **6**. Oxford: 1977.

Viviano, Benedict V. "Beatitudes Found among Dead Sea Scrolls." *Biblical Archaeology Review* **18**, no. 6 (Nov./Dec. 1992), pp. 53–55, 66.

Wacholder, Ben Zion, and M. G. Abegg. *A Preliminary Edition of the Unpublished Dead Sea Scrolls*. Vol. 1, Washington, D.C.: 1991. Vol. 2, Washington, D.C.: 1993.

Weinfeld, Moshe. *The Organizational Pattern and the Penal Code of the Qumran Sect*. Fribourg and Göttingen: 1986.

———. "Traces of the Qedusha Yoser and the Pesuqé de-Zimra in the Qumran Scrolls and Ben Sira (Hebrew). *Tarbiz* **45** (1975–76), pp. 15–26.

Wernberg-Møller, P. *The Manual of Discipline, Translated and Annotated with an Introduction*. Leiden, Netherlands: 1957.

Wise, Michael O. *A Critical Study of the Temple Scroll from Cave 11*. Chicago: 1990.

———. *Thunder in Gemini and Other Essays on the History, Language and Literature of Second Temple Palestine*. Sheffield: 1994.

——— and James D. Tabor. "The Messiah at Qumran." *Biblical Archaeology Review* (Nov./Dec. 1992), pp. 60–63.

——— and Norman Golb, John Collins, and Dennis Pardee (eds.), *Methods of Investigation of the Dead Sea Scrolls and the Khirbet Qumran Site*. Annals of the New York Academy of Sciences, **722**. New York: 1994.

Wolters, Al. "Apocalyptic and the Copper Scroll." *Journal of Near Eastern Studies* **49** (April 1990), pp. 145–154.

Woude, A. S van der. *Die messianischen Vorstellungen der Gemeinde von Qumran*. Assen, Netherlands: 1957.

———. "Melchizedek als himmlische Erlösergestalt in den neugefunden eschatologischen Midraschim aus Qumran-Höhle XI." In P. A. de Boer (ed). *Oudtestamentische Studien* **15**. Leiden: 1965, pp. 345–373.

Yadin, Yigael. *The Ben Sira Scroll from Masada*. Jerusalem: 1965.

———. *The Scroll of the War of the Sons of Light against the Sons of Darkness*. Oxford: 1962.

———. *Tefillin from Qumran—XQ Phyl 1-4*. Jerusalem: 1969.

———. *The Temple Scroll*, Vols. 1 and 2, Jerusalem: 1983. Vol. 3, Jerusalem: 1977.

———. *The Temple Scroll: The Hidden Law of the Dead Sea Sect*. London: 1985.

IV. Other Manuscript and Textual Studies, Editions, and Translations

Ashtor (Strauss), Eli. *History of the Jews in Egypt and Syria Under the Rule of the Mamlukes*. Vols. 1 and 2, Jerusalem: 1944–51. Vol. 3, Jerusalem: 1970.

Blass, Friedrich. *Palaeographie, Buchwesen, und Handschriftenkunde*. Munich: 1892.

Charles, R. H.(ed.). *The Apocrypha and Pseudepigrapha of the Old Testament*. 2 vols. Oxford: 1913.

Charlesworth, James. *The Old Testament Pseudepigrapha*. **1**. Garden City, N.Y.: 1983. **2**. Garden City, N.Y.: 1985.

Colson, F. H., G. H. Whitaker, and R. Marcus (eds. and trans.). *Philo*. 12 vols. Loeb Classical Library. Cambridge, Mass.

Cowley, Arthur (ed. and trans.). *Aramaic Papyri of the Fifth Century B.C.* Oxford: 1923.

Deiss, Joseph. *Herculaneum: Italy's Buried Treasure*. New York: 1966.

Doresse, Jean. *The Secret Books of the Egyptian Gnostics*. New York: 1960.

Gigante, Marcello. *La bibliothèque de Philodème et l'épicurisme Romaine*. Paris: 1987.

Goitein, S. D. *A Mediterranean Society*. 5 vols. Berkeley and Los Angeles: 1967–87.

Golb, Norman. *Les Juifs de Rouen au Moyen Age. Portrait d'une culture oubliée*. Rouen: 1985.

———. "New Light on the Persecution of French Jews at the Time of the First Crusade." *Proceedings of the American Academy for Jewish Research* **24** (1966), pp. 1–63.

——— and O. Pritsak. *Khazarian Hebrew Documents of the Tenth Century*. Ithaca and London: 1982.

Grant, Michael. *Cities of Vesuvius: Pompeii and Herculaneum*. New York: 1976.

Kahle, Paul. *The Cairo Genizah*. 1st ed., London: 1947; 2nd ed., Oxford: 1959.

Lewis, Naphtali, Yigael Yadin, and Jonas C. Greenfield (eds.). *The Documents from the Bar Kokhba Period in the Cave of Letters*. Jerusalem: 1989.

Mann, Jacob. *The Jews in Egypt and Palestine under the Fatimid Caliphs*. 2 vols. Oxford: 1920, 1922.

Pagels, Elaine. *The Gnostic Gospels*. New York: 1979.

Parsons, P. J., and J. R. Rea (eds.). *The Oxyrhynchus Papyri*. 79 vols. London: 1898–1991.

Porten, Bezalel. *The Archives from Elephantine*. Berkeley and Los Angeles: 1968.

——— and Ada Yardeni. *Select Aramaic Papyri from Ancient Egypt*. Rolling Hills Estates, Calif.: 1986.

Rackham, H., W. H. S. Jones, and D. E. Eichholz (eds. and trans.). *Pliny: Natural History*. 10 vols. Loeb Classical Library. Cambridge, Mass.

Robinson, James M. (ed.). *The Nag Hammadi Library in English*. San Francisco: 1977.

——— (ed.). *The Coptic Gnostic Library*. J. Robinson, Martin Krause, and

Frederik Wisse, series eds., *Nag Hammadi Studies*. Leiden, Netherlands: 1975–91.

Thackeray, Henry St. John, Ralph Marcus, Allen Wikgren, and Louis H. Feldman (eds. and trans.). *Josephus*. 9 vols. Loeb Classical Library. Cambridge, Mass.: 1926–65.

Youtie, Herbert Chayyim. *The Textual Criticism of Documentary Papyri— Prolegomena*. London: 1958.

Zilliachus, Henrik, et al. *Fifty Oxyrhynchus Papyri*. Helsinki: 1979.

V. History, Geography, and Scientific Methodology

Avi-Yonah, Michael. *Map of Roman Palestine*. 2nd ed. Jerusalem: 1940.

———. *The Jews Under Roman and Byzantine Rule*. Jerusalem: 1984.

Bickerman, Elias. *The Jews in the Greek Age*. Cambridge, Mass.: 1988.

Cohen, Shaye J. D. *Josephus in Galilee and Rome—His Vita and Development as a Historian*. Leiden, Netherlands: 1979.

———. *From the Maccabees to the Mishnah*. Philadelphia: 1987.

Davies, W. D., and L. Finkelstein (eds.). *Cambridge History of Judaism*. Vol. 2: *The Hellenistic Age*. Cambridge: 1989.

Dexinger, Ferdinand, and Reinhard Pummer (eds.). *Die Samaritaner*. Darm– stadt, Germany: 1992.

Hengel, Martin. *Judaism and Hellenism*. 2 vols. Philadelphia: 1974.

Kohn, Alexander. *False Prophets*. Oxford and New York: 1986.

Kuhn, Thomas S. *The Structure of Scientific Revolution*. 2nd. ed. Chicago: 1970.

Price, Jonathan J. *Jerusalem under Siege: The Collapse of the Jewish State, 66–70 C.E.* Leiden, Netherlands: 1992.

Rugerson, J. *Atlas of the Bible*. New York: 1985.

Safrai, S., and M. Stern (eds.). *The Jewish People in the First Century*. 2 vols. Assen, Netherlands: 1974.

Samaran, Ch. (ed.). *L'Histoire et ses méthodes*. Paris: 1961.

Sanders, E. P. *Paul, the Law, and the Jewish People*. Philadelphia: 1983.

Schürer, Emile. *A History of the Jewish People in the Age of Jesus Christ*. Revised and updated by Fergus Millar and Geza Vermes. 4 vols. Edinburgh: 1973–87.

Smith, G. Adam. *The Historical Geography of the Holy Land*. London: 1894.

Yadin, Yigael. *Masada, Herod's Fortress and the Zealots' Last Stand*. London: 1966.

———. *Bar-Kokhba*. London and Jerusalem: 1971.

Index

ABBREVIATIONS

H   Book of the Hebrew Bible
N   Book of the New Testament
A   Book of the Apocrypha or Pseudepigrapha

Page numbers in italics refer to illustrations.

433